The Acts
of the Apostles

VOLUME I
(Chapters 1—7)

$6.95

by

Oliver B. Greene

The Gospel Hour, Inc., Oliver B. Greene, Director
Box 2024, Greenville, South Carolina 29602

FOREWORD

I have entered into this study under the leadership—yea, the *urging*—of the Holy Spirit. In these days when apostasy has claimed much of that which bears the name of Christianity, I believe there is urgent need for true believers to catch a renewed vision of the early Church, the true New Testament Church which is the body of Christ. We need to realize the power of the Holy Spirit *in* that Church, for it is through Him that the Lord Jesus Christ carries on His work on earth today.

The book of Acts is one of the most important books in the Bible, and is one of the most *influential* books of all time, and in the pages that follow I have humbly and faithfully sought the leadership of the Holy Spirit in rightly dividing the Word of Truth. Therefore as we enter into this study my sincere prayer is that we may be led into deeper consecration, influenced to more complete dedication, and inspired to greater service to the glory of Him who said, "Go ye therefore, and teach all nations, baptizing them in the name of the Father, and of the Son, and of the Holy Ghost: Teaching them to observe all things whatsoever I have commanded you: and, lo, I am with you alway, even unto the end of the world!"

The Author

CONTENTS

THE ACTS OF THE APOSTLES

THE ACTS OF THE APOSTLES

INTRODUCTION

Although the book we are to study is called *The Acts of the Apostles,* there is no evidence that this title was given by divine authority—nor even by Luke, through whom God gave the book. However, with little variation, that name has been given to this part of God's Word throughout the Church dispensation. I think a better title would be *The Acts of the Risen, Glorified Christ Jesus the Lord.*

The book of Acts records the doings of the apostles as they were moved by the Holy Spirit, and contains chiefly the record of the works of two men—Peter and Paul. Others are, of course, mentioned from time to time, but Peter and Paul were the two apostles most prominent in the founding and organizing of the New Testament Church, and the book of Acts records their labors.

Peter was commissioned by Christ to use the keys of the kingdom to open the door—first to the Jew, and then to Gentiles. On the Day of Pentecost he preached primarily to the nation of Israel and called on them to repent. Later, he preached to the household of Cornelius, where the Gospel of the grace of God was first received by the Gentiles.

In the Gospel that bears his name, Luke by inspiration records the life of Christ *in the flesh.* In Acts he records (also by inspiration) the life of Christ *in the Spirit.* There are some who question Luke's authorship of Acts, but I personally believe God gave this book through the inspired pen of that beloved physician. Both books open in much the same way, both are addressed to the same person:

In Luke 1:3 we read, "It seemed good to me also, having had perfect understanding of all things from the very first, to write unto thee in order, *most excellent Theophilus.*"

Similarly, in Acts 1:1 we read, *"The former treatise have I made, O Theophilus,* of all that Jesus began both to do and teach."

It would seem that the book of Acts is a continuation of the Gospel of Luke, for it takes up the history of the ministry of Christ at the exact spot where it was discontinued in Luke, and mentions the "former treatise" which covered "all that Jesus began both to do and teach, until the day in which He was taken up, after that He through the Holy Ghost had given commandments unto the apostles whom He had chosen" (Acts 1:1,2).

We do not know exactly *when* Acts was written, but most Bible authorities agree that it was written between A. D. 65 and A. D. 70. The key verse is found in the first chapter, verse 8: "But ye shall receive power, after that the Holy Ghost is come upon you: and ye shall be witnesses unto me both in Jerusalem, and in all Judaea, and in Samaria, and unto the uttermost part of the earth."

It has been suggested that the book of Acts was probably written in Rome, since in chapter 28, verse 16, Luke refers to his arrival in Rome with Paul, and no mention is made of his *departure* from that city.

It is in the book of Acts that we find the inspired record of the fulfilled promise of the coming of the Holy Spirit, and of His work. In John 14:16—18 Jesus promised the disciples that He would send another Comforter who would be with them and would dwell in them. In John 16:7—11 He explained that it was expedient for them that He return to the Father's house, else the Comforter would not come; but when He departed, He would send the third Person of the Trinity, the Holy Spirit. In John

15:26,27 Jesus said to them, "When the Comforter is come, whom I will send unto you from the Father, even the Spirit of truth, which proceedeth from the Father, *He shall testify of me: and YE ALSO SHALL BEAR WITNESS, because ye have been with me from the beginning.*"

He then instructed the apostles to tarry in the city of Jerusalem until this promised coming of the Spirit should be fulfilled, until they were endued with power from on high (Luke 24:49).

The four Gospels—Matthew, Mark, Luke, and John—record the life, ministry, miracles, and teachings, death burial, and resurrection of the Lord Jesus Christ; but it is clear that Jesus contemplated the most glorious victories of His Gospel as taking place after He returned to the Father and the Holy Spirit should exert His influence and power. This is what Jesus meant when He said to His disciples in John 14:12, "Verily, verily, I say unto you, He that believeth on me, the works that I do shall he do also; *and greater works than these shall he do;* because I go unto my Father."

In the *Old Testament* we find prophesied and pointed out the purpose of the heavenly Father in regard to the plan of redemption.

The Gospels give the record of what the Lord Jesus Christ *did* in accomplishing redemption, the record of His finished work which made salvation possible for poor, lost sinners.

Then in *Acts* we find the record of the work of the third Person of the Trinity, the Holy Spirit, in bringing sinners under conviction and drawing them to Christ. Without the record given in Acts we could not fully understand the way in which the Holy Spirit operates in convicting and drawing men to Christ, the way He operates in the new birth and occupies the heart of the believer *after* the new birth.

The book of Acts records the account of the most remarkable display of divine power, mercy, and grace this world has ever known—*Pentecost,* the birthday of the New Testament Church.

In Acts we also find the inspired record of *the power of the Gospel,* the effect of the Gospel on the minds and hearts of mankind when it is preached in its purity and simplicity. The Gospel message in Acts was preached to *every class* of people and not *to the Jew only* as it was preached in the Gospels, but to "whosoever will"— beggars, kings, Jews, Gentiles, rich, poor, bond, free, slave, and master.

In Acts we find the record of the organization of the New Testament Church, founded in obedience to the words of Christ. The apostles tarried in Jerusalem as He had instructed them, until the Day of Pentecost was fully come. What Jesus had promised *happened as promised:* the Church was born *through obedience to the Word* and is founded on the simple message of the death, burial, and resurrection of Jesus Christ.

The book of Acts contains many model sermons— direct, simple, and powerful. Any young minister who wishes to learn the Bible way to preach powerful sermons that produce results will find pure instruction there.

Not only do we find model *sermons* in Acts, we also find the model *Church.* In character, the early New Testament Church was very simple—no pomp or splendor, no magnificent ceremonies, no costly, elaborate buildings. But the men and women who made up its membership had yielded their hearts to Jesus and were wholly surrendered to the Holy Spirit. In this first Church, the believers were unselfish, they denied themselves, they were benevolent. They were all evangelists, and they went everywhere preaching the Gospel. They were faithful to the Truth—the Word of God—and thus the Church grew and spread.

The book of Acts is the connecting link between the four Gospels, the Epistles, and the rest of the New Testament. It sheds important light on other New Testament books, especially the Epistles of Paul.

It also furnishes evidence that Christianity is the way of salvation, the one true way purchased by Jesus with His blood. Within thirty years, believers in the early Church preached the Gospel to every part of the civilized world and went into many parts of the *heathen* world. They carried the message to the largest cities, the smallest villages, and out into the highways and byways. As Paul testified in chapter 26, verse 26, what these early Christians did was not "done in a corner." They did not try to hide their faith. On the contrary, they put their faith on display by preaching the pure Gospel of the grace of God, *expecting great things OF God*—and He did not disappoint them! Within a few years churches were established in Jerusalem, Antioch, Corinth, Ephesus, Philippi, and Rome. The Gospel of the grace of God had gone into Arabia, Asia Minor, Greece, Macedonia, Italy, and the dark continent of Africa.

These first believers were not wealthy, not many of them were educated people, and only a *very* few—such men as Paul—were influential before their conversion. *But they knew CHRIST, they were FILLED with the Spirit, they were armed with the power of God,* and they claimed victory in Jesus' name. The world *recognized* them wherever they went! They were, indeed, a "peculiar people." God Almighty was with them, He honored their faith and gave them victory that the world was forced to acknowledge. We might call them "dare-saints" for Jesus Christ.

The city of Jerusalem is in the foreground in Acts, for the message was to begin there—"to the Jew first." The Jew *had* the message first, but rejected it. Then the good news of salvation was carried to the Gentiles.

We need to study the book of Acts very carefully and prayerfully. It is drastically needed today, for its message takes us back to the *beginning* of the Church and shows us the path the Lord Jesus marked out for His Church here on earth during this Dispensation of Grace. I trust and pray that our lives will be enriched as we study each and every verse in the twenty-eight chapters of this most important portion of God's Word.

THE ACTS OF THE APOSTLES

CHAPTER I

1. The former treatise have I made, O Theophilus, of all that Jesus began both to do and teach,

2. Until the day in which he was taken up, after that he through the Holy Ghost had given commandments unto the apostles whom he had chosen:

3. To whom also he shewed himself alive after his passion by many infallible proofs, being seen of them forty days, and speaking of the things pertaining to the kingdom of God:

4. And, being assembled together with them, commanded them that they should not depart from Jerusalem, but wait for the promise of the Father, which, saith he, ye have heard of me.

5. For John truly baptized with water; but ye shall be baptized with the Holy Ghost not many days hence.

6. When they therefore were come together, they asked of him, saying, Lord, wilt thou at this time restore again the kingdom to Israel?

7. And he said unto them, It is not for you to know the times or the seasons, which the Father hath put in his own power.

8. But ye shall receive power, after that the Holy Ghost is come upon you: and ye shall be witnesses unto me both in Jerusalem, and in all Judaea, and in Samaria, and unto the uttermost part of the earth.

9. And when he had spoken these things, while they beheld, he was taken up; and a cloud received him out of their sight.

10. And while they looked stedfastly toward heaven as he went up, behold, two men stood by them in white apparel;

11. Which also said, Ye men of Galilee, why stand ye gazing up into heaven? this same Jesus, which is taken up from you into heaven, shall so come in like manner as ye have seen him go into heaven.

12. Then returned they unto Jerusalem from the mount called Olivet, which is from Jerusalem a sabbath day's journey.

13. And when they were come in, they went up into an upper room, where abode both Peter, and James, and John, and Andrew, Philip, and Thomas, Bartholomew, and Matthew, James the son of Alphaeus, and Simon Zelotes, and Judas the brother of James.

14. These all continued with one accord in prayer and supplication, with the women, and Mary the mother of Jesus, and with his brethren.

15. And in those days Peter stood up in the midst of the disciples, and said, (the number of names together were about an hundred and twenty,)

16. Men and brethren, this scripture must needs have been fulfilled, which the Holy Ghost by the mouth of David spake before concerning Judas, which was guide to them that took Jesus.

17. For he was numbered with us, and had obtained part of this ministry.

18. Now this man purchased a field with the reward of iniquity; and falling headlong, he burst asunder in the midst, and all his bowels gushed out.

19. And it was known unto all the dwellers at Jerusalem; insomuch as that field is called in their proper tongue, Aceldama, that is to say, The field of blood.

20. For it is written in the book of Psalms, Let his habitation be desolate, and let no man dwell therein: and his bishoprick let another take.

21. Wherefore of these men which have companied with us all the time that the Lord Jesus went in and out among us,

22. Beginning from the baptism of John, unto that same day that he was taken up from us, must one be ordained to be a witness with us of his resurrection.

23. And they appointed two, Joseph called Barsabas, who was surnamed Justus, and Matthias.

24. And they prayed, and said, Thou, Lord, which knowest the hearts of all men, shew whether of these two thou hast chosen,

25. That he may take part of this ministry and apostleship, from which Judas by transgression fell, that he might go to his own place.

26. And they gave forth their lots; and the lot fell upon Matthias; and he was numbered with the eleven apostles.

Introduction

Verses 1 and 2: *"The former treatise have I made, O Theophilus, of all that Jesus began both to do and teach, until the day in which He was taken up, after that He through the Holy Ghost had given commandments unto the apostles whom He had chosen."*

"The former treatise have I made, O Theophilus...."

Theophilus, (meaning "friend of God") is mentioned in the very beginning of Acts in almost the same manner as he is spoken of in the opening verses of the Gospel of Luke, where we read, "It seemed good to me also, having had perfect understanding of all things from the very first, to write unto thee in order, *most excellent Theophilus,* that thou mightest know the certainty of those things, wherein thou hast been instructed" (Luke 1:3,4). This bears out the belief that Luke the beloved physician, writer of The Gospel of Luke, was the one chosen of God as the human instrument to record the book of Acts.

Both Luke's Gospel and the book of Acts are addressed to *Theophilus,* but this does not mean that the message recorded in these books is to Theophilus alone. Luke's message is to *all believers* in the New Testament Church.

We know very little about Theophilus, but there are indications that he was a very prominent and influential man. Bible antiquity tells of a man by that name who lived in the city of Antioch. He owned a beautiful palace called *the Basilica,* which palace he dedicated to the preaching of the Gospel. Luke and others are said to have delivered Gospel messages there—in fact, it is not impossible that Luke *also* lived in Antioch, although this is not recorded in Scripture. We know history is not *inspired,* but there were historians in those days just as there have been historians down through the ages even unto this present day—and events recorded in the annals of history are generally accepted as reliable.

The Gospel of Luke records *the beginning* of what the Lord Jesus Christ did and what He taught on earth as the Man Christ Jesus. Acts *continues* that record—but the scene changes as He continues His work from heaven. The Gospels do not give the full account of all that Jesus did and said; they give only the account of *the foundations* which He laid, foundations on which the Church should afterward be built as He promised in Matthew 16:18. Notice that Jesus said in that Scripture,

"Upon this rock *I WILL BUILD my Church.*" The time
was yet future.

In Luke 24:19 the disciples on the road to Emmaus
spoke of Jesus as "a Prophet mighty in deed and word
before God and all the people." His *life* spoke first,
and then He spoke with words; but His works prove
that He was more than just a prophet: *He was God the
Son, God in flesh.*

Also, here in the first chapter of Acts we find a much
fuller account of the *ascension* of Jesus than Luke gave
in the closing of his Gospel, and this furnishes a definite
connection between the Gospel of Luke and the book of
Acts.

Notice in verse 2, Jesus was taken up *"after that He
through the Holy Ghost had given commandments unto
the apostles whom He had chosen."* That the New Testament Church might be divinely ordered and wholly
divine, the Spirit of the Lord was upon the anointed Son
of God. In this as in His other works and words, Jesus
worked and *spoke* as the Spirit ordered or directed:

"And (Jesus) came to Nazareth, where He had been
brought up: and, as His custom was, He went into the
synagogue on the sabbath day, and stood up for to read.
And there was delivered unto Him the book of the prophet Esaias. And when He had opened the book, He found
the place where it was written, *The Spirit of the Lord
is upon me, because He hath anointed me to preach the
Gospel to the poor; He hath sent me to heal the broken-
hearted, to preach deliverance to the captives, and re-
covering of sight to the blind, to set at liberty them that
are bruised, to preach the acceptable year of the Lord.*

"And He closed the book, and He gave it again to
the minister, and sat down. And the eyes of all them
that were in the synagogue were fastened on Him. And
He began to say unto them, *This day is this Scripture
fulfilled in your ears.* And all bare Him witness, and
wondered at the gracious words which proceeded out of

His mouth. . ." (Luke 4:16—22).

The Resurrection Ministry of Christ

Verse 3:   *"To whom also He shewed Himself alive after His passion by many infallible proofs, being seen of them forty days, and speaking of the things pertaining to the kingdom of God."*

We see proof of inspiration in the way the Lord Jesus is brought to mind in these opening verses of Acts.   In these first three verses we see His earthly life, works, and teachings.   We learn that He was truly taken up into heaven *after* He had given commandments to His disciples through the Holy Spirit. We also learn in these first three verses that *"by many infallible proofs"* He showed Himself alive after His crucifixion, that He was seen of His disciples for forty days after His resurrection, and that He taught them *"of the things pertaining to the kingdom of God."*

The opening verses of the book of Acts clearly state the foundation upon which the Gospel and the Church of the living God rest—namely, *the BODILY resurrection of the Lord Jesus Christ*; in *fact*, His bodily resurrection is the paramount truth declared here.   As the Apostle Paul declared, "If Christ be not risen, then is our preaching vain, and your faith is also vain.   Yea, and we are found false witnesses of God; because we have testified of God that He raised up Christ: whom He raised not up, if so be that the dead rise not.   For if the dead rise not, then is not Christ raised: and if Christ be not raised, your faith is vain; ye are yet in your sins.   Then they also which are fallen asleep in Christ are perished.   *If in this life only we have hope in Christ, we are of all men most miserable"* (I Cor. 15:14—19).

Jesus presented Himself alive *"by many infallible proofs"*—proofs that were beyond controversy and could not be denied.   He was seen by the disciples over a period of forty days, and Paul tells us in I Corinthians 15:6 that on one occasion He was seen by more than five hundred brethren at one time. *Only here* are we told *the number of days* Jesus manifested Himself to His disciples between His resurrection and His ascension. *Only here* do we find the statement that He showed Himself alive *by many infallible proofs.*

At evening on the first day of the week—the same day Jesus rose from the dead—the disciples were in an upper room and all the doors were closed "for fear of the Jews." Then suddenly Jesus stood in their midst and said to them, *"Peace be unto you!"* He showed them the nail-prints in His hands and the wound in His side, and "then were the disciples glad, when they saw the Lord" (John 20:19,20).

Thomas was not present when Jesus appeared that first time, but eight days later He appeared again when Thomas was with them. Again the doors were shut when Jesus appeared in their midst, and again He greeted them with *"Peace be unto you."* He then turned to Thomas and said, "Reach hither thy finger, and behold my hands; and reach hither thy hand, and thrust it into my side: and be not faithless, but believing." Thomas answered, "My Lord and my God!" Then Jesus said to him, "Thomas, because thou hast seen me, thou hast believed: blessed are they that have not seen, and yet have believed" (John 20:27—29).

In the Gospel of Luke we are told that when Jesus first appeared to the disciples and said, "Peace be unto you," they were terrified, supposing that they were seeing a spirit. But Jesus said to them, "Why are ye troubled? and why do thoughts arise in your hearts? Behold my hands and my feet, that it is I myself: handle me, and see; for a spirit hath not flesh and bones, as ye see me have.

"And when He had thus spoken, He shewed them His hands and His feet. And while they yet believed not for joy, and wondered, He said unto them, Have ye here any meat? And they gave Him a piece of a broiled fish, and of an honeycomb. And He took it, and did eat before them. And He said unto them, These are the words which I spake unto you, while I was yet with you, that all things must be fulfilled, which were written in the law of Moses, and in the prophets, and in the psalms, concerning me. *Then opened He their understanding, that they might understand the Scriptures"* (Luke 24: 36—45). Thus Jesus presented Himself to them, the *living* Christ.

During the forty-day period between His resurrection and His ascension, Jesus spoke to the disciples *"of the things pertaining to the kingdom of God"*—but the words He gave them on these occasions, the instructions they received, are not given to us here, except that they tarry in Jerusalem until the Day of Pentecost. (Read John 21:25.)

There is much misunderstanding and confusion among church people concerning the *kingdom of heaven* and the *kingdom of GOD* spoken of here. The "kingdom of heaven" in the Greek reads "kingdom of the *heavens"* and is a statement peculiar to the Gospel of Matthew. It speaks of the Millennium, the one thousand year reign of Christ here on earth when He reigns as the Son of David. Luke 1:32,33 declares, "He shall be great, and shall be called the Son of the Highest: *and the Lord God shall give unto Him the throne of His father David: and He shall reign over the house of Jacob for ever; and of His kingdom there shall be no end."*

This kingdom is called "the kingdom of the heavens" because it is the rule of the heavens right here on earth. This is the period described in Isaiah chapter 11, verses 1—9, when "the earth shall be full of the knowledge of the Lord, as the waters cover the sea." In that day there will be peace on earth, good will among men. Swords will be beaten into plowshares and spears into pruning hooks when the kingdom of heaven is here upon this earth and King Jesus, Son of David, sits on the *throne* of David in Jerusalem (Isa. 2:4).

In Daniel 2:34, 35 we read, "Thou sawest till that a stone was cut out without hands, which smote the image upon his feet that were of iron and clay, and brake them to pieces. Then was the iron, the clay, the brass, the silver, and the gold, broken to pieces together, and became like the chaff of the summer threshingfloors; and the wind carried them away, that no place was found for them: and the stone that smote the image became a great mountain, and filled the whole earth."

Then in Daniel 7:23—27 we read, "Thus he said, The fourth beast shall be the fourth kingdom upon earth, which shall be diverse from all kingdoms, and shall devour the whole earth, and shall tread it down, and break it in pieces. And the ten horns out of this kingdom are ten kings that shall arise: and another shall rise after them; and he shall be diverse from the first, and he shall subdue three kings. And he shall speak great words against the most High, and shall wear out the saints of the most High, and think to change times and laws: and they shall be given into his hand until a time and times and the dividing of time. But the judgment shall sit, and they shall take away his dominion, to consume and to destroy it unto the end. And the kingdom and dominion, and the greatness of the kingdom under the whole heaven, shall be given to the people of the saints of the most High, whose kingdom is an everlasting kingdom, and all dominions shall serve and obey Him."

In both of these passages from Daniel, the *kingdom of heaven* is in view. The "stone cut out without hands" is the Lord Jesus Christ, the "chief corner stone" of whom Peter speaks in I Peter 2:6: "Wherefore also it is contained in the Scripture, Behold, I lay in Sion a chief corner stone, elect, precious: and he that believeth on Him shall not be confounded."

This Stone will destroy the Gentile world systems.
The government of righteousness will then be set up here
on earth.   The kingdom of heaven is covenanted to David's seed (II Sam. 7:8–10).   We also read of this kingdom in Zechariah 12:8.

John the Baptist came on the scene preaching, *"Repent
ye: for the KINGDOM OF HEAVEN is at hand"* (Matt.
3:2); but Israel rejected their King and therefore the kingdom was postponed until a future time.   The King *will*
come; He will come as King of kings and Lord of lords,
He will sit on the throne of David, and He will reign
on this earth for one thousand glorious years.   Yes, *the
kingdom of heaven* will be here on earth after the return
of King Jesus in glory.   (Study Matthew 24:29 through
25:46; Luke 19:12–19; and Acts 15:14–17.)

In Matthew 6:9–13 we find the prayer which Jesus
taught His disciples to pray.   Matthew's Gospel is primarily to Israel and has to do with the kingdom.   Therefore Jesus taught His disciples to pray, "Our Father
which art in heaven, Hallowed be thy name. *Thy kingdom come. Thy will be done in earth, as it is in heaven.*
Give us this day our daily bread.   And forgive us our
debts, as we forgive our debtors.   And lead us not into
temptation, but deliver us from evil: For thine is the
kingdom, and the power, and the glory, for ever. Amen."

At the time Jesus gave His disciples this model prayer,
the Church was yet future.   The prayer, therefore, applied
to the kingdom of heaven, not to the New Testament
Church.   The kingdom of heaven will be here on earth,
a *visible* kingdom, and is to be distinguished from *the
kingdom of GOD*.   They are not one and the same although they have many things in common. The kingdom
of God can be entered only through the miracle of the
new birth:

Jesus said to Nicodemus, "Except a man be born
again, he cannot see the kingdom of God. . . Except a
man be born of water and of the Spirit, he cannot enter

into the kingdom of God" (John 3:3,5). The kingdom of *heaven* is the earthly sphere of the reign of righteousness here on earth.

It is true that some of the parables in Matthew speak of the kingdom of heaven, and the same parable in Mark and Luke speaks of the kingdom of *God;* but this does not change the divine fact that the two kingdoms are not identical. For instance, the parable of the wheat and tares given in Matthew 13:24—30 and the parable of the net given in Matthew 13:47—50 have to do with the kingdom of heaven, not the kingdom of God; for *in the kingdom of GOD* there are neither tares nor bad fish.

The kingdom of heaven will come with outward show; Israel will see and recognize their King:

"And I will pour upon the house of David, and upon the inhabitants of Jerusalem, the spirit of grace and of supplications: and they shall look upon me whom they have pierced, and they shall mourn for Him, as one mourneth for his only son, and shall be in bitterness for Him, as one that is in bitterness for his firstborn. . . And one shall say unto Him, What are these wounds in thine hands? Then He shall answer, Those with which I was wounded in the house of my friends" (Zech. 12:10; 13:6). At that time, Jesus will stand on the Mount of Olives (Zech. 14:4).

The kingdom of GOD does *not* come with outward show. Jesus said to the Pharisees, *"The kingdom of God cometh not with observation:* neither shall they say, Lo here! or, lo there! for, behold, *the kingdom of God is WITHIN YOU"* (Luke 17:20,21). The kingdom of God is within—a spiritual kingdom in the inner man: "For the kingdom of God is not meat and drink; but righteousness, and peace, and joy in the Holy Ghost" (Rom. 14:17).

The kingdom of heaven will be manifested in majestic glory here on earth. At that time the curse will be lifted and there will be world peace. (Again I refer you to the eleventh chapter of Isaiah.) The kingdom of *heaven* will

ultimately merge into the kingdom of *God* when Jesus
has reigned until He has put all enemies under His feet.
He will then deliver up the kingdom to God, even the
Father:

"Then cometh the end, when He shall have delivered
up the kingdom to God, even the Father; when He shall
have put down all rule and all authority and power. For
He must reign, till He hath put all enemies under His
feet. The last enemy that shall be destroyed is death.
For He hath put all things under His feet. But when
He saith all things are put under Him, it is manifest
that He is excepted, which did put all things under Him.
And when all things shall be subdued unto Him, then
shall the Son also Himself be subject unto Him that put
all things under Him, that God may be all in all" (I Cor.
15:24—28).

In the book of Acts the Gospel is offered *first to the
Jew.* Peter preached to the Jews on the Day of Pentecost, and the apostles *witnessed* to the people of Israel
through Acts chapter 7. *Stephen* delivered a message to
the Jews, a message which angered them to a point where
they rushed upon him "with one accord, and cast him
out of the city, and stoned him." He died with a prayer
on his lips that God would forgive his executioners: "And
he kneeled down, and cried with a loud voice, *Lord, lay
not this sin to their charge.* And when he had said this,
he fell asleep" (Acts 7:54—60).

After the death of Stephen the disciples and other
Christians were scattered and "went every where preaching the Word" (Acts 8:4). It was shortly after the death
of Stephen that God saved Saul of Tarsus and anointed
him as the apostle to the Gentiles (Rom. 11:13), thus
giving the message of saving grace to those who until
that time had been excluded, "without Christ, being
aliens from the commonwealth of Israel, and strangers
from the covenants of promise, having no hope, and without God in the world" (Eph. 2:12).

Verse 4: *"And, being assembled together with them, commanded them that they should not depart from Jerusalem, but wait for the promise of the Father, which, saith He, ye have heard of me."*

This "assembling together" took place ten days before Pentecost. The disciples were commanded to tarry in Jerusalem and *"wait for the promise"* of God the Father which they had heard from the lips of Jesus the Son:

"I will pray the Father, and He shall give you another Comforter, that He may abide with you for ever; even the Spirit of truth; whom the world cannot receive, because it seeth Him not, neither knoweth Him; but ye know Him; for He dwelleth with you, and shall be in you" (John 14:16,17).

We notice that Jesus *"COMMANDED them that they should not depart from Jerusalem . . . ."* (This same command is given in verse 49 of the last chapter of the Gospel of Luke.) Jesus did not *suggest* that these people tarry in Jerusalem if it did not conflict with other plans or if they found it convenient. His instructions constituted a *command,* not a suggestion.

Verse 5: *"For John truly baptized with water; but ye shall be baptized with the Holy Ghost not many days hence."*

In Matthew 3:11 John the Baptist said, "I indeed baptize you with water unto repentance: but *He that cometh after me* is mightier than I, whose shoes I am not worthy to bear: *He shall baptize you with the Holy Ghost, and with FIRE."*

In our present verse in Acts, Jesus did not mention the baptism of *fire* because this has nothing to do with Pentecost. *The baptism of fire* refers to the time when He will "gather His wheat into the garner" and will "burn up the chaff with unquenchable fire" (Matt. 3:12). This will take place when Jesus returns to this earth the second time.

"Ye SHALL BE baptized with the Holy Ghost not many days hence." This baptism was just as sure to happen as Jesus is the Son of God and His Word is truth! The disciples were to remain in Jerusalem *with the assurance that they WOULD BE BAPTIZED with the Holy Ghost* "not many days hence." Pentecost was just as sure to happen as *Calvary* was sure to happen.

Christians today are NOT commanded to wait for this promise from the Father because God's promise concerning the coming of the Holy Ghost was fulfilled at Pentecost. Today we do not tarry *ten* days, *one* day, or one *minute.* If we hear and obey the Word of God, we will not be misled through tradition and man-made doctrines concerning the Holy Spirit: "If ye then, being evil, know how to give good gifts unto your children: *how much more shall your heavenly Father give the Holy Spirit to them that ask Him?"* (Luke 11:13).

The heavenly Father *will* give the Holy Spirit to those who ask Him. Any person hungering and thirsting for salvation can *receive* salvation by simply asking the Lord Jesus to come into his heart; and when *Jesus* comes into a heart, the *Holy Spirit* comes in, too. All born again believers are possessors of the Holy Spirit. (Study Romans 8:9—16; I Corinthians 6:19; Galatians 4:6; I John 2:20,27.) We will discuss this more fully later in our study.

It is definitely unscriptural and out of order for any person in this Dispensation of Grace to tarry, beg, and agonize for the coming of the Holy Spirit. God the Father *kept* His promise; the Holy Ghost *came* at Pentecost, He is in the world *today,* and all who receive Jesus *immediately become recipients* of the Holy Ghost!

Verse 6: *"When they therefore were come together, they asked of Him, saying, Lord, wilt thou at this time restore again the kingdom to Israel?"*

Jesus knew the thoughts and anxieties of the disciples

concerning the kingdom. He knew they did not yet fully
understand that the kingdom (the kingdom of God within
the heart, the Church Age, the Dispensation of Grace)
would come *before* He would reign from Jerusalem from
the throne of David. So as on former occasions He spoke
with sympathy and understanding. These men were Jews,
and as Jews they were thinking only of an earthly kingdom as their hope, an earthly king to deliver them from
slavery and bondage. They had been looking for their
King whose coming John the Baptist had announced, and
up to this moment they could not understand why the
expected kingdom had not been set up. Therefore they
asked, *"Lord, wilt thou at this time restore again the
kingdom to Israel?"*

Verse 7: *"And He said unto them, It is not for you
to know the times or the seasons, which the Father hath
put in His own power."*

Notice, Jesus did not rebuke these men, He did not
accuse them of ignorance nor did He tell them that they
were altogether mistaken. He answered their question—
but not directly. The kingdom *would be* restored, indeed
it would; but *the time of the restoration* was not to be
revealed to them. The *Father* knew when that time
would be, and He had put these things *"in His own
power."* Therefore they were not to ask questions concerning the kingdom; this was not for them to know at
that point. A *better* hope was theirs—a heavenly, glorious, spiritual hope; and they should be concerned about
"that blessed hope, and the glorious appearing of the
great God and our Saviour Jesus Christ" (Tit. 2:13)—coming first *for* His saints, then coming *with* His saints to
reign over the millennial earth. They were to be concerned with the kingdom of God within themselves, not
with the kingdom of heaven, the kingdom which would
one day be restored to Israel.

These men were about to become part of the body of

Christ, the New Testament Church which would be born ten days later on the Day of Pentecost; and theirs was a much more glorious hope than the earthly hope of Israel: "For the Lord Himself shall descend from heaven with a shout, with the voice of the archangel, and with the trump of God: and the dead in Christ shall rise first: then we which are alive and remain shall be caught up together with them in the clouds, to meet the Lord in the air: and so shall we ever be with the Lord. Wherefore comfort one another with these words" (I Thess. 4:16—18).

In Titus 2:11—14 we read, "For the grace of God that bringeth salvation hath appeared to all men, teaching us that, denying ungodliness and worldly lusts, we should live soberly, righteously, and godly, in this present world; looking for that blessed hope, and the glorious appearing of the great God and our Saviour Jesus Christ; who gave Himself for us, that He might redeem us from all iniquity, and purify unto Himself a peculiar people, zealous of good works."

Then in Acts 15:13—18 we read, "After they had held their peace, James answered, saying, Men and brethren, hearken unto me: Simeon hath declared how God at the first did visit the Gentiles, to take out of them a people for His name. And to this agree the words of the prophets; as it is written, After this I will return, and will build again the tabernacle of David, which is fallen down; and I will build again the ruins thereof, and I will set it up: that the residue of men might seek after the Lord, and all the Gentiles, upon whom my name is called, saith the Lord, who doeth all these things. Known unto God are all His works from the beginning of the world."

Ten days hence, these men would become the first members of the New Testament Church; therefore Jesus directed their attention away from the earthly hope of Israel concerning the kingdom of heaven on earth. In the

end of this Day of Grace, after the Rapture, there will
be a faithful remnant of the Jews called, and *they* will
know the times and the seasons *"which the Father hath
put in His own power."* They will see their Messiah,
their King, and they will recognize Him by the prints of
the nails in His hands. (In connection with this, study
Romans chapter 11.)

The Greek word translated *"power"* in this verse is
not the same word used in verse 8. The meaning here
is *"absolute disposal"* and could have been rendered
authority. The question asked by the disciples here concerning the kingdom was irrelevant to their present calling, business, and future ministry.

The Key to the Book of Acts

Verse 8:   *"But ye shall receive power, after that the
Holy Ghost is come upon you: and ye shall be witnesses
unto me both in Jerusalem, and in all Judaea, and in
Samaria, and unto the uttermost part of the earth."*

In this verse, Jesus again declares the apostolic commission—but before that commission could be carried out,
the disciples must be endued with power from on high,
and they were to receive that power by the coming of
the Comforter, the Holy Spirit, as promised in John 14.
They *received* that power on the Day of Pentecost, as
we will learn in chapter 2.

Jesus did not promise His disciples that they would
receive power if they met certain conditions, or if they
could meet the requirements in prayer and meditation.
He plainly declared, *"Ye SHALL receive power, after
that the Holy Ghost is come upon you."* They would
receive power for witnessing just as surely as He had
died on the cross! He had declared, "As Moses lifted up
the serpent in the wilderness, *even so MUST the Son of
man be lifted up"* (John 3:14). The "lifting up" of Jesus
was a divine *must;* and now if God's commission was to

be carried out, it was a divine imperative that these disciples receive power from above. They did not possess this power within themselves; it must come from God—and *it would come* when the Holy Ghost came as promised, fifty days after the resurrection of Jesus. He had already called and appointed them, and now He would empower them and send them to be witnesses.

They were to begin *at home*—in Jerusalem, the place where He had been arrested, condemned, and crucified; the place where He conquered death and rose again. They were to deliver this message first in Jerusalem, then in Judaea, then in Samaria, and from thence *"unto the uttermost part of the earth."* WHY? Because *"God so loved THE WORLD,* that He gave His only begotten Son, that *whosoever* believeth in Him should not perish, but have everlasting life"* (John 3:16). The message of salvation is for the whole world.

The apostles' ministry was confined to the area of Jerusalem and Judaea until the death of Stephen, after which they were "scattered abroad" (Acts 8:4). Then Philip went to Samaria, the first to minister with authority in that area. After he had been there preaching, and the Samaritans had received the Word of God, Peter and John went into Samaria and taught the Samaritans further concerning the Holy Spirit (Acts 8:5—25). Then the disciples moved on to the uttermost part of the known world at that time. Paul, Barnabas, Silas, Mark, and Timothy were among those who became "foreign missionaries."

God never sends *any* of His children—ministers, evangelists, or missionaries—on an errand for Him without first preparing them for the mission laid out for them. This was true in the case of the disciples. Jesus knew they were weak from the standpoint of the flesh and they could not face what lay ahead of them unless they were given power from above.

This receiving of power was something altogether different from what the disciples had just asked of Jesus.

He would not give them an earthly kingdom at this time, but He would give them something much better. During the Jewish economy, temporal blessings as a reward for obedience were poured out upon the chosen people Israel (Deut. 28:1—14); but this is the Dispensation of Grace. The ascended Lord is now seated at the right hand of the Father to make intercession for His believing children, and He is now blessing His people with *spiritual* blessings. In Luke 21:15 He said to His disciples, *"I will give you a mouth and wisdom, which all your adversaries shall not be able to gainsay nor resist!"* He would give them wisdom, words, *and power* that their enemies would be forced to recognize as coming from Almighty God. Thus would these weak disciples be enabled to become effective witnesses for the Lord Jesus Christ.

In Luke 24:45—53 we read that Jesus opened the disciples' understanding, *"that they might understand the Scriptures,* and said unto them, Thus it is written, and thus it behoved Christ to suffer, and to rise from the dead the third day: and that repentance and remission of sins should be preached in His name among all nations, beginning at Jerusalem. And ye are witnesses of these things. And, behold, I send the promise of my Father upon you: but tarry ye in the city of Jerusalem, until ye be endued with power from on high.

"And He led them out as far as to Bethany, and He lifted up His hands, and blessed them. And it came to pass, while He blessed them, He was parted from them, and carried up into heaven. And they worshipped Him, and returned to Jerusalem with great joy: and were continually in the temple, praising and blessing God. Amen."

The Holy Ghost was promised to the disciples to give them power to become effective witnesses unto Christ, not that they might live a "holier than thou" life among other people—and certainly not that they might boast of their experience on the Day of Pentecost! The only reason God blesses His children *today* is that we might be effective witnesses, living epistles read of men, good soldiers in the army of the Lord, doing all things to God's glory! You may rest assured that when a minister or layman testifies boastingly of his own power, declaring that others need "HIS EXPERIENCE," that minister or layman is not filled with the Spirit of God; he is filled with *pride*.

In Ephesians 5:18−21 we read of the evidence of a Spirit-filled life: "Be not drunk with wine, wherein is excess; but be filled with the Spirit; speaking to yourselves in psalms and hymns and spiritual songs, singing and making melody in your heart to the Lord; giving thanks always for all things unto God and the Father in the name of our Lord Jesus Christ; submitting yourselves one to another in the fear of God."

According to the Scriptures, one who is filled with the Spirit, possessed, controlled, and led by the Spirit, will not be boasting of his own accomplishments. He will be singing and praising God, giving thanks to the heavenly Father in the name of the Lord Jesus Christ. Such a person is sure to create a hunger and thirst for Jesus in the hearts of the unsaved. Pride and the Holy Spirit do not abide in the same heart.

Verse 9: *"And when He had spoken these things, while they beheld, He was taken up; and a cloud received Him out of their sight."*

Jesus had told His disciples on many occasions that He would return to the Father, and we have here the *record* of His return. He was taken up even as the disciples were looking at Him, *"and a cloud received Him out of their sight."* What a moment that must have been in the lives of the disciples!

As Jesus was taken up from them, they followed Him with eager eyes, gazing in rapt amazement. They were witnessing the ascension of the One in whom they had believed, the One in whose company they had traveled

for more than three years. They had listened to His
wonderful words of life, they had witnessed His marvelous miracles. Not only had they been with Him in
His body of humiliation, they had also been with Him
for the past forty days as He had appeared to them on
many occasions in His resurrection body. Now He was
being taken up into glory to sit at the right hand of the
Majesty on high.

I like to believe that Jesus ascended gradually, slowly,
affording the disciples plenty of time to witness His ascension and give a clear, understandable report of what
they saw. I like to believe that He was lifted higher and
higher as they stood gazing after Him, beholding Him in
human form, in a body—and then a cloud received Him,
shutting Him from view. (Greek authorities tell us that
the Greek word translated "received" literally means
"to take in." Therefore in the Greek this verse would
read, "And then a cloud *took Him in* out of their sight.")

I do not believe the "cloud" here was just an ordinary
vapor cloud like those we see in the sky today. I believe it was the same cloud which overshadowed Jesus
on the Mount of Transfiguration when Peter suggested
that three tabernacles be built—one for Jesus, one for
Elijah, and one for Moses. Elijah and Moses were great
men of God; but when Peter put them on the same level
with God's only begotten Son, God overshadowed the
mountain with a cloud of shekinah glory, "and behold a
voice out of the cloud, which said, This is my beloved
Son, in whom I am well pleased; hear ye Him. And
when the disciples heard it, they fell on their face, and
were sore afraid. And Jesus came and touched them, and
said, Arise, and be not afraid. And when they had lifted
up their eyes, they saw no man, save Jesus only" (Matt.
17:1—8 in part).

I believe the cloud that received Jesus in His ascension
was the same cloud that filled Solomon's temple: "And
it came to pass, when the priests were come out of the

holy place, that the cloud filled the house of the Lord, so that the priests could not stand to minister because of the cloud: *for the glory of the Lord had filled the house of the Lord"* (I Kings 8:10,11). This was the same cloud which appeared so often in the history of Israel—a "glory cloud."

For the disciples, the vision climaxed at this point. The shekinah glory that engulfed Jesus and took Him out of their sight put an end to their walking by *sight.* From that moment forward, *they walked by FAITH.*

Not only was this a glorious experience for the *disciples,* but it must also have been a glorious moment in *heaven* when the Lord Jesus Christ ascended to the right hand of God the Father and took His seat on the throne. What a glorious scene that must have been! Surely all the angels, cherubim, seraphim, and spirits of saints witnessed the seating of Jesus in the highest seat of heaven. He had been gone from His place in heaven for the many years since the Holy Ghost overshadowed Mary. Now He had returned to the Father's house, and upon the merit of His finished work He is now seated at the right hand of the Majesty—our Advocate, our great High Priest, to appear there for you and for me.

"Seeing then that we have a great High Priest, that is passed into the heavens, Jesus the Son of God, let us hold fast our profession. For we have not an High Priest which cannot be touched with the feeling of our infirmities; but was in all points tempted like as we are, yet without sin. Let us therefore come boldly unto the throne of grace, that we may obtain mercy, and find grace to help in time of need" (Heb. 4:14—16).

"My little children, these things write I unto you, that ye sin not. And if any man sin, we have an Advocate with the Father, Jesus Christ the righteous: and He is the propitiation for our sins: and not for our's only, but also for the sins of the whole world" (I John 2:1,2).

"For there is one God, and one Mediator between God

and men, THE MAN CHRIST JESUS" (I Tim. 2:5).

There Is A Man in Heaven

The Lord Jesus Christ lived here on earth in a body of humiliation. In that body He died on the cross, was buried, and rose again. This same Jesus passed through the heavens in a human (but glorified) body *of flesh and bones.* The life of the flesh is in the blood—and Jesus gave His life that we might have life. Therefore His glorified body was bloodless; He presented His blood to the Father for the remission of sins. Nevertheless, in His resurrection body He was a *man.* He invited His disciples to touch Him, handle Him, and prove to themselves that He was not a spirit. It is extremely important that we recognize the fact that the Lord Jesus Christ passed through the heavens with a *real, glorified, body of flesh and bones, and IN that body He went to a literal place*—the Father's house—where He was given a seat "on the right hand" of the throne of God the Eternal Father in heaven. And now *there is a MAN in heaven*—the Man Christ Jesus. To deny this fact is to deny the very foundation of the Gospel, the foundation of salvation; for if Jesus did not ascend into the heavens as recorded here, then *we have no hope,* because He is the Mediator, He is our great High Priest. *He is the propitiation for our sins!*

This verse of Scripture is tremendously important because it sets forth proof that the Lord Jesus was taken up *bodily* in the presence of His disciples. Bodily He returned to the Father. It pleased God to give us this record as Luke wrote, inspired of the Holy Ghost, that we might believe this tremendous truth and divine doctrine of the ascension of Jesus; and His *Person,* His ascension bodily into the presence of God's glory, should be just as real to our hearts today as it was to the disciples who were eyewitnesses of His ascension. Those who *deny* the *bodily resurrection and bodily ascension* of Jesus are ministers of Satan! Oh, yes—just as surely as *God* has ordained ministers, so does *the devil* have ordained ministers:

"For such are false apostles, deceitful workers, transforming themselves into the apostles of Christ. And no marvel; for Satan himself is transformed into an angel of light. *Therefore it is no great thing if his ministers also be transformed as the ministers of righteousness; whose end shall be according to their works"* (II Cor. 11:13—15).

This Same Jesus Will Return Bodily to This Earth

Verses 10 and 11: *"And while they looked stedfastly toward heaven as He went up, behold, two men stood by them in white apparel; which also said, Ye men of Galilee, why stand ye gazing up into heaven? This same Jesus, which is taken up from you into heaven, shall so come in like manner as ye have seen Him go into heaven."*

The cloud of shekinah glory had shut the Saviour from view, but the disciples could not stop gazing at the spot where they had last seen Him. No doubt they could still see the cloud as it ascended, moving gradually and slowly out of sight; and as long as they could see the cloud they kept on gazing into the heavens.

As the disciples stood gazing at the brightness where they had last seen Jesus, *"Two men stood by them in white apparel, which also said . . . Why stand ye gazing up into heaven?"* Jesus had clearly *told* His disciples that He would return to the heavenly Father, and He had also told them what they were to do after He left them and while they awaited His promised return to them. They were to go into Jerusalem and wait there until the Day of Pentecost should come, and they had fully understood His instructions. Now He had actually left them and returned to the Father as He had said He would do, and there was no point in their standing gazing up into the sky.

"*This same Jesus, which is taken up from you into heaven, shall so come in like manner as ye have seen Him go into heaven.*" Here again is the promise of the second coming of Christ, given in clear, understandable words.   In John 14:2,3 He had assured the disciples, "I go to prepare a place for you.   And if I go and prepare a place for you, *I WILL COME AGAIN, and receive you unto myself; that where I am, there ye may be also.*" And now in our present verse we are clearly told *how* He will return—"*in like manner as ye have seen Him go.*"   He will return *BODILY, in a cloud of glory,* and we will be caught up to meet Him in the clouds in the air—"and so shall we ever be with the Lord."

Could it be made any clearer?   How could anyone misunderstand the words of the two heavenly visitors here?   Under the law, the testimony of two witnesses declared a testimony to be true. Therefore God sent *two* witnesses, and the two gave the same testimony.   How could anyone fail to grasp the simple fact of the second coming of Jesus Christ?   He will come personally, visibly, in glory, *exactly as the disciples witnessed His ascension!*

We must not confound this event with "the blessed hope," the Rapture of the Church.   When Jesus comes *in visible form* as He was taken up, He will come to Israel to establish the kingdom of heaven upon earth. The coming of the Lord in His visible aspect is described in the prophetic books of the Old Testament.   For example, it is spoken of in Daniel 7:13,14:

"I saw in the night visions, and, behold, One like the Son of man came with the clouds of heaven, and came to the Ancient of days, and they brought Him near before Him.   And there was given Him dominion, and glory, and a kingdom, that all people, nations, and languages, should serve Him: His dominion is an everlasting dominion, which shall not pass away, and His kingdom that which shall not be destroyed."

It is of this visible kingdom that we read in Revelation 1:7: "Behold, He cometh with clouds; and every eye shall see Him, and they also which pierced Him: and all kindreds of the earth shall wail because of Him. Even so, Amen."

When Jesus comes *"in like manner"* as the disciples witnessed His ascension, the saints will come with Him:

"When Christ, who is our life, shall appear, *then shall ye also appear with Him in glory"* (Col. 3:4).

"To you who are troubled rest with us, when the Lord Jesus shall be revealed from heaven with His mighty angels, in flaming fire taking vengeance on them that know not God, and that obey not the Gospel of our Lord Jesus Christ: Who shall be punished with everlasting destruction from the presence of the Lord, and from the glory of His power; *when He shall come to be glorified in His saints,* and to be admired in all them that believe (because our testimony among you was believed) in that day" (II Thess. 1:7−10).

We must not confuse the two stages of the second coming: *First,* Jesus will come in the Rapture to *receive* His saints, and all believers will be caught up in the clouds to meet Him in the air. *Then,* He will come *WITH His saints* to reign here on earth for one thousand years. *The hope of the Church is the RAPTURE*−the time when we will be caught up to meet Jesus. His return "in like manner" as He ascended will be His coming to the nation Israel, in that glorious day when He will stand on the Mount of Olives just outside Jerusalem:

"And His feet shall stand in that day upon the mount of Olives, which is before Jerusalem on the east, and the mount of Olives shall cleave in the midst thereof toward the east and toward the west, and there shall be a very great valley; and half of the mountain shall remove toward the north, and half of it toward the south" (Zech. 14:4).

The Rapture of the Church (before Jesus comes visibly and in glorious manifestation to Israel) is revealed in I Thessalonians 4:13—18. Paul wrote to the believers in Thessalonica, "I would not have you to be ignorant, brethren, concerning them which are asleep, that ye sorrow not, even as others which have no hope. For if we believe that Jesus died and rose again, even so *them also which sleep in Jesus will God bring with Him.* For this we say unto you by the word of the Lord, that we which are alive and remain unto the coming of the Lord shall not prevent them which are asleep. For the Lord Himself shall descend from heaven with a shout, with the voice of the archangel, and with the trump of God: and *the dead in Christ shall rise first: Then we which are alive and remain shall be caught up together with them in the clouds, to meet the Lord in the air: and so shall we ever be with the Lord.* Wherefore comfort one another with these words."

To confuse the Rapture of the Church with the time when Jesus will be revealed to Israel would be disastrous, to say the least. (Please read again Zechariah 12:10; 13:6; and 14:4.) There are many other Scriptures which describe the glorious kingdom of heaven on earth, the time when Jesus will reign from the throne of David and the Church will reign with Him. (As previously suggested, a study of the eleventh chapter of Isaiah will prove helpful in connection with this millennial reign of Christ.)

The Disciples Wait for Pentecost

Verse 12: *"Then returned they unto Jerusalem from the mount called Olivet, which is from Jerusalem a sabbath day's journey."*

Luke 24:52 tells us that the disciples *worshipped* Jesus before they returned to the city of Jerusalem: "And they worshipped Him, *and returned to Jerusalem with great joy!"*

"Then returned they unto Jerusalem from the mount called Olivet." The Lord Jesus ascended from the eastern side of the Mount of Olives ("the mount called Olivet") near the little city of Bethany: "And He led them out *as far as to Bethany,* and He lifted up His hands, and blessed them. And it came to pass, while He blessed them, He was parted from them, and carried up into heaven" (Luke 24:50,51).

This place was *"a sabbath day's journey"* from Jerusalem. The Jewish law demanded that a person travel *only two thousand paces* (seven and one-half furlongs) on the Sabbath. This is not quite one mile as we measure distance. This was not fixed by Mosaic Law, but the *Jewish teachers* declared it unlawful to travel more than two thousand paces on the Sabbath. They arrived at this distance through tradition, because as the Israelites came out from Egyptian bondage, no part of their camp was more than two thousand paces from the tabernacle. They were allowed to travel that distance to worship; therefore "a sabbathday's journey" was not more than two thousand paces. Also, according to Numbers 35:5, this was the extent of the suburbs of the Levitical cities.

The Mount of Olives was near Jerusalem, but on its eastern side the countryside for a considerable distance was known as the region of Bethany, and it was from this eastern side of the mountain that Jesus ascended—about two thousand paces from the temple area in the city of Jerusalem.

Verse 13: *"And when they were come in, they went up into an upper room, where abode both Peter, and James, and John, and Andrew, Philip, and Thomas, Bartholomew, and Matthew, James the son of Alphaeus, and Simon Zelotes, and Judas the brother of James."*

There was an "upper room" in almost all homes in the city of Jerusalem, especially the homes of Jewish leaders. It was a large room, designated as the upper chamber, and it was used for devotion and prayer. It was also the place where the dead were laid before burial. For instance, in Acts 9:36,37 we read of Dorcas, a woman "full of good works and almsdeeds which she did. And it came to pass in those days, that she was sick, and died: whom when they had washed, they laid her in an *upper chamber.*"

In Acts 20:7,8 we read where Paul preached "upon the first day of the week, when the disciples came together to break bread . . . And there were *many lights in the upper chamber,* where they were gathered together."

Luke 24:53 tells us that after the disciples returned to Jerusalem from the Mount of Olives where they had witnessed the ascension of Jesus, they were "continually in the temple, praising and blessing God," but there is no evidence that the "upper room" mentioned in our present verse was in the temple.

This room (probably the upper room used by our Lord and His disciples for the Passover feast) is mentioned as the *"abode"* of Peter, James, John, and the other disciples. This "abiding" was a temporary occupancy and does not mean that it was the house where they *lived.* This was the place where they tarried until the coming of the Holy Spirit, as promised by the Lord Jesus before His ascension.

Verse 14:   *"These all continued with one accord in prayer and supplication, with the women, and Mary the mother of Jesus, and with His brethren."*

The minds and hearts of these early Christians were dedicated to meditation and their whole attention was directed toward God in prayer. The only business for that hour was prayer and devotion, worship directed to God and to their Lord and Saviour Jesus Christ.

In Acts 6:4, where the first deacons were chosen, the twelve apostles said, "We will give ourselves *continually to prayer,* and to the ministry of the Word."

In Romans 12:12 Paul declared that we should be "rejoicing in hope; patient in tribulation; *continuing instant in prayer.*"

In I Thessalonians 5:17 Paul admonished the believers, *"Pray without ceasing."*

In Colossians 4:2 he instructs, *"Continue in prayer,* and watch in the same with thanksgiving."

These verses describe the attitude of the disciples in the upper room throughout the ten days of waiting for the coming of the Holy Spirit. They prayed *"with one accord,"* they were of one mind. There were no schisms in this group, they were in complete accord and perfect unity. This is the spirit which *should* prevail in the house of God at all worship services and prayermeetings today; but sad to say, such instances are rare indeed!

In the hearts and minds of the disciples there was but one great objective: *to be faithful to the instructions Jesus had given them,* to be in the right place, in the right spirit and the right attitude, at the moment when the promise of the Spirit's coming should be fulfilled. They continued *"in prayer and supplication,"* sending up petitions to God for the blessings He was about to pour out upon them. (I do not doubt that they were also sending up petitions concerning the days that lay ahead, for certainly they did not know what those days held for them.)

"The women" mentioned here were undoubtedly those who had followed Jesus from Galilee. We read of these women in Luke 8:2,3—*Mary Magdalene, Joanna* the wife of Chuza, *Susanna,* "and many others, who ministered unto Him of their substance" as He went throughout the cities and villages in Galilee.

We read of these women again in Luke 23:49 and 55, at the crucifixion: "And all His acquaintance, and *the women that followed Him from Galilee,* stood afar off, beholding these things. . . *And the women also, which came with Him from Galilee,* followed after, and beheld the sepulchre, and how His body was laid."

They are mentioned again in Luke 24:10, and in Matthew 27:55,56 we read, "And many women were there beholding afar off, *which followed Jesus from Galilee,* ministering unto Him: among which was Mary Magdalene, and Mary the mother of James and Joses, and the mother of Zebedee's children."

These women—along with others whose names are not mentioned—were present in the upper room that day, and *"Mary the mother of Jesus"* was there. This is the last time the New Testament Scriptures mention the mother of Jesus. It is most significant that she was among the company that waited in the upper room for the coming of the Spirit. There are those who make much about Mary in their religion, but from the few Scriptures we find about her in God's Word we know that she was but a sinner saved by grace, as were all the other women there. She waited in the upper room along with the others, and she had no more power than they.

Mary was highly honored of God in that the Holy Ghost overshadowed her and she brought forth God's only begotten Son; but insofar as making intercession for us is concerned, interceding to God on our behalf, *there is NO SCRIPTURE* for any such doctrine—and anyone who seeks to reach God through *Mary* will be sadly disappointed! There is but *ONE Mediator* between God and men, *"the Man Christ Jesus"* (I Tim. 2:5). Mary has no place of superiority among other women—or men.

Yes, the Virgin Mary was chosen by Almighty God to be the blessed vessel through whom He would send His Son into the world in a human body—but according to the Scriptures, that same blessed vessel *tarried along with the other women and the disciples* in the upper room to receive the outpouring of the Holy Spirit; and when the Holy Spirit was poured forth, Mary was baptized *by that Spirit* into the body of Christ. By the grace of God she became a member of the New Testament Church, just as did the disciples and all of those present in the upper room at Pentecost! Mary was fallible, a sinner saved by grace along with others who waited with her; and I would re-emphasize that not one time is she mentioned in any way after this first chapter of Acts. The epistles do not once record her name.

I believe the Lord's *"brethren"* mentioned here are the same brethren who, along with Mary His mother, attempted to interfere with the Lord's ministry in Mark chapter 3. As Jesus ministered, the multitudes pressed around Him in such magnitude that there was no time to eat, and the Scripture tells us that "when His friends heard of it, they went out to lay hold on Him: for they said, He is beside Himself. . .

"There came then *His brethren and His mother,* and, standing without, sent unto Him, calling Him. And the multitude sat about Him, and they said unto Him, Behold, *thy mother and thy brethren* without seek for thee. And He answered them, saying, Who IS my mother, or my brethren? And He looked round about on them which sat about Him, and said, Behold my mother and my brethren! *For whosoever shall do the will of God, the same is my brother, and my sister, and mother"* (Mark 3:21,31−35).

In John 7:5 we are told, *"Neither did His brethren BELIEVE in Him"*—but somewhere between that time and the time of our present passage, they were converted and believed on Him, because they were present here in the upper room with other believers, waiting for the coming of the Holy Ghost.

It would be interesting to know the feelings of these disciples when they left that blessed spot from whence the Lord Jesus had ascended bodily back to the Father. It would be most interesting to know their *conversation* as they traveled those two thousand paces back to Jerusalem. But the important thing is that they were obedient

to the command of Jesus. They did exactly as He had
instructed them, and went immediately to the upper
room to wait for the coming of the Holy Spirit.

This was a unique group. There has never been another assembly such as this was, and there never *will* be.
These believers were not the *Church* as yet, because the
Church was not born *until* Pentecost, until the coming
of the Holy Spirit for whom this group was waiting. No
assembly of believers in this Dispensation of Grace could
ever fill the position the disciples filled in that upper
room before Pentecost.

It is unscriptural for believers today to pray for the
outpouring of the Holy Spirit, for He has *already been
poured out* upon all believers. Persons who are praying
for and expecting a repetition of Pentecost will be disappointed, because *Pentecost will not be repeated* any
more than the day of *Christ's crucifixion* will be repeated!
Jesus died for the sins of the world at the very moment
it was foreordained of God that He *should* die. The
Holy Ghost came on the very day it was foreordained
of God that He *should* come, and He came just as Jesus
had *declared* that He would come.

Verses 15 and 16: *"And in those days Peter stood up
in the midst of the disciples, and said, (the number of
names together were about an hundred and twenty,) Men
and brethren, this Scripture must needs have been fulfilled, which the Holy Ghost by the mouth of David
spake before concerning Judas, which was guide to them
that took Jesus."*

Here we are told the number of believers who were
gathered in the upper room to wait for the coming of the
Spirit. Some may ask, "If more than five hundred brethren saw Jesus at one time after His resurrection, as Paul
states in I Corinthians 15:6, why were only *one hundred
and twenty* in the upper room?" We must consider that
the five hundred were probably from all over Galilee, and

many of those who saw the resurrected Lord had already returned to their own communities. The one hundred and twenty were very likely from the immediate vicinity of Jerusalem.

"Peter stood up in the midst of the disciples" and began to speak. It was *customary* for a speaker to *stand,* but someone may ask why *Peter* was the one to stand. Who gave *him* authority to be spokesman on that occasion? In the first place, we know from previous acquaintance with Peter that he was impulsive, the most ardent of the disciples, and often served as spokesman for the disciple band. Also, he was probably the oldest in the group, and this could have been one reason why he acted as spokesman on this particular occasion. Certainly he had walked with Jesus, and knew as much as any of the others about the matter at hand. It would be according to his nature to stand and introduce the motion to elect an apostle to take the place of Judas Iscariot.

Here we see the first group assembled to transact business concerning the Church which was about to be born. When electing or appointing someone to fill an important position in the church or assembly, such action should be transacted by the entire church, not by an individual; and no ecclesiastical group should have the right to place a minister at the head of a congregation. Acts 20:28 tells us that the *Holy Ghost* appoints the ministers who are to serve as God's undershepherds: "Take heed therefore unto yourselves, and to all the flock, over the which the Holy Ghost hath made you overseers, to feed the Church of God, which He hath purchased with His own blood."

Some have questioned the legitimacy of Peter's action here. Was it of the Lord? Was it of the Lord that the group elected an apostle to take the place of Judas? Or was it Peter's own idea and did he act of his own volition? I believe, with many outstanding Bible teachers, that Peter was a little premature in his action—that he should not have made this suggestion to the apostles at that time, and that they should not have elected Matthias to take the place of Judas. It seems that Peter was still thinking in terms of the earthly kingdom and the place the twelve apostles would occupy in that kingdom—for the Lord had told them, ". . . in the regeneration when the Son of man shall sit in the throne of His glory, *ye also shall sit upon twelve thrones, judging the twelve tribes of Israel*" (Matt. 19:28).   However, the kingdom had been *postponed*, and the election of a twelfth apostle was not necessary before the Church was born—but Peter had not accepted this idea of a postponed kingdom.

It seems to me that God did not recognize the choice of Matthias, because this man is never mentioned again in all the rest of the Bible. *I* believe that *Paul* should have been the one to replace Judas and become the twelfth apostle.   God apparently *ignored* man's ordination—and after Pentecost, when the Holy Ghost had come, God chose HIS man to fill the place vacated by the betrayer, Judas Iscariot.   He called *Paul* to be an apostle—a *singular* apostle, called for a very special ministry.   It was not man's choice, as was that of Matthias; but it was an outright call, commission, and ordination by God the Son—*the risen, glorified Christ*—for the office of apostleship: "Paul, *an apostle,* (not of men, neither by man, but *by Jesus Christ, and God the Father, who raised Him from the dead)*" (Gal. 1:1).

Paul's apostleship was entirely different from that of the other eleven.   *They* were called of the Lord Jesus and ordained by Him in connection with His earthly ministry; but the Apostle Paul was called *after* the birthday of the Church, was given a message which he called "*my* Gospel" (Rom. 2:16), and was anointed the *apostle to the Church*—the Gentile bride of Christ.   In Romans 11:13 he declared, "*I speak to you Gentiles,* inasmuch as *I am the apostle of the Gentiles,* I magnify mine office."

And I Timothy 2:7 declares that Paul was *"ordained a preacher, and an apostle . . . a teacher of the Gentiles in faith and verity."*

The Church, a mystery hidden through ages past, was revealed to the Apostle Paul:

"For this cause *I Paul, the prisoner of Jesus Christ for you Gentiles,* if ye have heard of the dispensation of the grace of God which is given me to you-ward: How that *by revelation He made known unto me the mystery;* (as I wrote afore in few words, whereby, when ye read, ye may understand my knowledge in the mystery of Christ) *which in other ages was not made known unto the sons of men, as it is now revealed unto His holy apostles and prophets by the Spirit; that the Gentiles should be fellowheirs, and of the same body, and partakers of His promise in Christ by the Gospel:* Whereof *I was made a minister,* according to the gift of the grace of God given unto me by the effectual working of His power" (Eph. 3:1—7).

"Men and brethren . . . ." Peter began his address to the other disciples, quoting Scripture which *"must needs have been fulfilled, which the Holy Ghost by the mouth of David spake before concerning Judas . . . ."* (Christ was to die on the cross, betrayed by one who was supposed to be His friend.) This is a direct reference to Psalm 41:9: "Yea, mine own familiar friend, in whom I trusted, which did eat of my bread, hath lifted up his heel against me."

In Psalm 109:1—8 David also prophesied of Judas Iscariot: "Hold not thy peace, O God of my praise; for the mouth of the wicked and the mouth of the deceitful are opened against me: they have spoken against me with a lying tongue. They compassed me about also with words of hatred; and fought against me without a cause. For my love they are my adversaries: but I give myself unto prayer. And they have rewarded me evil for good, and hatred for my love.

"Set thou a wicked man over him: and let Satan stand at his right hand. When he shall be judged, let him be condemned: and let his prayer become sin. *Let his days be few; and let another take his office.*"

In Psalm 69:20—25 David prophesied, "Reproach hath broken my heart; and I am full of heaviness: and I looked for some to take pity, but there was none; and for comforters, but I found none. They gave me also gall for my meat; and in my thirst they gave me vinegar to drink. Let their table become a snare before them: and that which should have been for their welfare, let it become a trap. Let their eyes be darkened, that they see not; and make their loins continually to shake. Pour out thine indignation upon them, and let thy wrathful anger take hold of them. *Let their habitation be desolate; and let none dwell in their tents.*"

Verse 17:   *"For he was numbered with us, and had obtained part of this ministry."*

Notice that Judas was "numbered" with the twelve, he took part of their ministry—but this certainly does not mean that he was a born again believer! Later in this series we will discuss whether or not Judas was saved and whether or not he fell from grace.

Verse 18:   *"Now this man purchased a field with the reward of iniquity; and falling headlong, he burst asunder in the midst, and all his bowels gushed out."*

"This man (Judas) *purchased a field."* In other words, Judas *acquired* a field—which may be said not only of one who *buys* a field, but of one who becomes the occasion of *another's* buying. The field was bought by the chief priests with the money which Judas returned to them:

"Then Judas, which had betrayed Him, when he saw that He was condemned, repented himself, and brought again the thirty pieces of silver to the chief priests and elders, saying, I have sinned in that I have betrayed the innocent blood. And they said, What is that to us? See thou to that.

"And he cast down the pieces of silver in the temple, and departed, and went and hanged himself. *And the chief priests took the silver pieces, and said, It is not lawful for to put them into the treasury, because it is the price of blood. And they took counsel, and bought with them the potter's field, to bury strangers in. Wherefore that field was called, The field of blood, unto this day"* (Matt. 27:3—8).

The chief priests could not take the money Judas returned and put it into the treasury because it was *blood money;* therefore the property they purchased would be looked upon as the property of the traitor, and the money thus used is referred to as *"the reward of iniquity."* The property purchased with this blood money was turned into a public burial ground, and the people of Jerusalem accepted it as such.

"And falling headlong, he burst asunder in the midst, and all his bowels gushed out." What a horrible picture! I believe Judas hanged himself in the place the chief priests eventually purchased with the money he received as the price of betraying Jesus. This place is spoken of by Matthew as the "potter's field," a place where potters obtained clay to make earthen vessels. It was undoubtedly a rugged place, desolate, with many jagged rocks. It is not unreasonable to think that Judas fell on one of these rocks when the rope broke, and the rocks cut his body. Thus he literally *"burst asunder"* as the Scripture tells us here.

This could easily have been such a place as is described in II Chronicles 25:12: "And other ten thousand left alive did the children of Judah carry away captive, and brought them unto the top of the rock, *and cast them down from the top of the rock, that they all were broken in pieces!"*

Although Matthew mentioned *one single incident* in the death of Judas, the Holy Spirit through the pen of Luke in our present study gives a more detailed account of the horrible death he died. The account here also coincides with the prophecy given by David in the Psalms to which Peter referred.

Verse 19: *"And it was known unto all the dwellers at Jerusalem; insomuch as that field is called in their proper tongue, Aceldama, that is to say, The field of blood."*

"And it was known"—that is, it *became* known. The news of the fate of Judas Iscariot spread rapidly, and since he died such a horrible death in the field which was purchased with the thirty pieces of silver, the name of the field was changed from *the potter's field* to *"the field of blood,"* a name that was very fitting.

"That field IS called . . . ." The present tense used in this verse indicates that we are dealing here with documents written *before* the destruction of Jerusalem by Titus in A. D. 70. The record books would show that the field purchased with the "blood money" was originally the potter's field, and the record was then changed to read "the field of blood."

"In their proper tongue" means the language spoken by the Jews. The addition of these words and the explanation of the name "Aceldama," point to this passage as an insertion made by Luke for the information of Theophilus, who was—as his name indicates—probably of *Greek* origin and was unacquainted with the language of the Jews in Palestine.

Verse 20: *"For it is written in the book of Psalms, Let his habitation be desolate, and let no man dwell therein: and his bishoprick let another take."*

Again Peter quotes from Psalms 69:25 and 109:8. Notice that the Holy Spirit changes the plural of the former verse into the singular. David was speaking of *many* enemies of his own, but he was also *prophesying* concerning Judas, through whom Jesus would be betrayed. The Holy Spirit makes no mistake; therefore the plural is changed to the singular here as Peter quotes.

Peter was speaking of the punishment of *Judas.* The punishment of the *Jewish nation* came later, although their days as a nation were few when Peter spoke these words—for in A. D. 70, Titus the Roman overran the city, and history tells us that he not only destroyed the city, but also killed more than a million Jews. When the destruction of the Jewish nation came, it was as horrible as was the destruction of *Judas* individually.

"Let his habitation be desolate"—or, "Let his habitation *become* (or be *made*) desolate."

"And his bishoprick let another take." In the Greek the word *"bishoprick"* means "office." In verse 25 "this ministry" is used in speaking of the same charge or position Judas held.

We have two quotations here, from two different Psalms. There is no contradiction between the two passages quoted by Peter, for though the habitation of Judas is to become desolate and there will be no one dwelling there, the *office* which he had filled was to be occupied by one chosen of God to take his place to complete the number of the disciples, making twelve instead of eleven. Psalm 69 pronounced his *curse,* and Psalm 109 that a successor was to fill his office.

Verses 21 and 22:   *"Wherefore of these men which have companied with us all the time that the Lord Jesus went in and out among us, beginning from the baptism of John, unto that same day that He was taken up from us, must one be ordained to be a witness with us of His resurrection."*

Peter now gives the essential qualification of the one to take the place of Judas. He declared that the new apostle was required *"to be a witness with us of His resurrection."* The resurrection, *bodily,* was the central truth to be known and declared by this new apostle. He must be an eyewitness of the resurrected Lord, one who had talked and communed with Him. For this qualification it should be carefully noted that Paul met Jesus on the road to Damascus (Acts 9:1—6), and he later told the Corinthians that he had seen the Lord (I Cor. 15:8).

The Holy Spirit is careful to relate exactly *how* the vacancy was filled, how the disciples chose Matthias to take the place of Judas; but we are not enlightened concerning the *ministry* of Matthias nor of any special duties appointed to him.

Verse 23:   *"And they appointed two, Joseph called Barsabas, who was surnamed Justus, and Matthias."*

Notice, *"THEY appointed two."* This could refer to the eleven apostles, or to the entire one hundred and twenty who were in the upper room. In either case, it was not left up to Peter alone (whom some religionists declare to have been the first apostolic pope or ruler over God's affairs on earth). I believe it was the eleven apostles who thus exercised their own judgment in this appointment. They selected and nominated two men— *"Joseph called Barsabas, who was surnamed Justus, and Matthias."* Thus they limited the Lord in His choice to *two* men whom *they* nominated. How did they know God had chosen *either* of these two? *They* chose two men and then asked the Lord which one He wanted. Many people today are too prone to make up their own minds first as to what they are going to do, and then they ask the Lord to put His endorsement upon *their* choice or decision.

Some teachers believe that *"Joseph"* mentioned here is identical with *"Joses"* of Acts 4:36, but there are actually no sufficient grounds for such identification. Concerning the previous history of Joseph we know nothing. The fact that he stands first in order of the two men mentioned here could indicate that he was better known among the disciples than Matthias was. Some Bible scholars tell us that *Matthias* was one of the seventy sent out by Jesus, but this cannot be proved by Scripture.

Verse 24: *"And they prayed, and said, Thou, Lord, which knowest the hearts of all men, shew whether of these two thou hast chosen."*

Whether Peter was right or wrong in what he was doing, his prayer was a beautiful example—direct, simple, and short. When we pray for the Lord's leadership we need not compose long, flowery prayers, we need not try to flatter God. We need simply to recognize the divine fact that God is omniscient, omnipotent, and omnipresent, and that *He knows the hearts of ALL men.* Not only does He know the *hearts* of all men, He also knows the *needs* of all men—and He is able to supply those needs. So let us, like these apostles, make our requests known to Him in a direct and simple way.

When the disciples prayed, *"Lord,"* I believe they were thinking of the Lord Jesus, from whom they had sought advice and wisdom when He walked with them in person. *"Shew whether of these two thou hast chosen."* Notice that they used the past tense—*"hast chosen"*— indicating that they knew the risen Lord had already made His choice. This is all the more reason they were out of place in choosing two men of their own choice.

This is the first example of prayer directed to the Lord Jesus Christ as the Exalted One, the Man Christ Jesus, seated at the right hand of the Majesty to make intercession for believers. This is but further proof of the divinity of Jesus, for these men were praying to *the same Jesus* spoken of in John 2:24,25; 21:15—17; and Revelation 2:23.

Was Judas Iscariot Born Again?

Verse 25: *"That he may take part of this ministry and*

apostleship, from which Judas by transgression fell, that he might go to his own place."

(The Greek reads here, "That he may take the place from which Judas transgressed and fell, that he might go to his own place.")

In the analysis of this verse of Scripture *we can learn much* about Judas Iscariot. First of all, we notice *that from which he fell: "ministry and apostleship."* There is no place in the Scripture which suggests that Judas was ever saved, or that he ever believed on Jesus and trusted Him as his Saviour. You may search the Gospels, but in their entire records you will find no place where Judas ever called Jesus *"Lord."* This is a very significant point, because in Paul's letter to the Corinthian church he said, "Wherefore I give you to understand, that no man speaking by the Spirit of God calleth Jesus accursed: *and that no man can say that Jesus is the Lord, BUT BY THE HOLY GHOST"* (I Cor. 12:3).

Judas was not with the eleven when Jesus breathed on them and said, "Receive ye the Holy Ghost." He *knew* Jesus was not his Lord, therefore he always called Him *"Master."* Not once did he refer to Him as "Lord." Judas was a devil, and Jesus knew it (John 6:70); but even the devil can call Jesus "Master," because *He IS Master of the devil!* James tells us that the devils *"believe,* and tremble" (James 2:19)—but certainly the devil and his demons are not saved.

John 6:67—71 is a very interesting passage concerning Judas: "Then said Jesus unto the twelve, Will ye also go away? Then Simon Peter answered Him, Lord, to whom shall we go? Thou hast the words of eternal life. And we believe and are sure that thou art that Christ, the Son of the living God.

"Jesus answered them, *Have not I chosen you twelve, and one of you is a DEVIL?* He spake of *Judas Iscariot* the son of Simon: for he it was that should betray Him, being one of the twelve."

Since Greek authorities maintain that there is no "a" in verse 70, then what Jesus really said was, "One of you is *devil*"—and there is no other place in all of the Word of God where Jesus ever called anyone else "devil." Actually, there is *only ONE devil*—Satan, the master deceiver; but there are *millions* of demons. Unbelievers are referred to in the Scripture as *"children* of the devil," but never as *devils*.

Another interesting Scripture concerning Judas is found in the Lord's intercessory prayer in John 17. In verse 12 of that chapter Jesus said, "While I was with (the disciples) in the world, I kept them in thy name: those that thou gavest me I have kept, *and none of them is lost, BUT THE SON OF PERDITION;* that the Scripture might be fulfilled." He referred, of course, to Judas Iscariot, the only person whom He ever called "the son of perdition."

Someone may say that *all* sinners are sons of perdition; but if that be true, then somewhere, sometime, Jesus would have said, "I have not come to call the righteous, but *sons of perdition*, to repentance!" But He did not say that. He said, "I came not to call the righteous, *but SINNERS* to repentance" (Matt. 9:13). And He said that "the Son of man is come to seek and to save *that which was lost*" (Luke 19:10). Yet He called Judas "the son of perdition."

This expression is found but twice in the entire New Testament. Jesus used it in John 17:12, and *Paul* used it in II Thessalonians with reference to the Man of Sin, the Antichrist: "Let no man deceive you by any means: for that day shall not come, except there come a falling away first, *and that Man of Sin be revealed, THE SON OF PERDITION"* (II Thess. 2:3).

The "son of perdition" is the son of Satan. *Jesus* was the Son of God, *God incarnate*. The Antichrist will be the son of the devil, *Satan* incarnate. For every good thing God has, the devil has a cheap counterfeit. Just as

Jesus was THE Son of God (not *"a"* son of God), so Judas was THE son of perdition, the son of Satan, the devil incarnate.

I know someone will ask *why* Jesus chose a devil among the twelve. In Deuteronomy 29:29 we read, *"The secret things belong unto the Lord our God:* but those things which are revealed belong unto us and to our children for ever . . . ." Aside from this passage I can give no answer as to why Jesus chose Judas among the twelve, beyond the facts laid down in our present study. We know from the words of Jesus Himself that Judas was a devil when He called him into the disciple band (John 6:70).   We know that verse 12 in John 17 declared that he was lost "that the Scripture might be fulfilled."   Both of these verses were spoken by the Lord Jesus, He who knows ALL things.   But enough is revealed to us to assure us that Judas was never a believer, he was never born again.

There is nothing in the Scripture to suggest that Judas ever produced one bit of fruit to testify that he knew *anything* about grace.   Everything revealed about him indicates that he never knew either the *grace* of God or the *love* of God.   The Scripture tells us that Judas *fell*— but he did not fall from *grace* because he was never *IN grace,* he had no grace from which to fall.   He fell from an *office,* from *apostleship.*

Oh, yes—Judas was a minister, and he held the office of treasurer of the disciples as a group; but that does not prove that he was saved.   He was a *follower*—and certainly anyone can be a follower of a religious leader and not be saved.   There are ministers in pulpits today— pastors, evangelists, perhaps even missionaries—who do not bear the fruits of grace, a fact which is proved by the following passages of Scripture:

In Matthew 7:21—23 Jesus declared, "Not every one that saith unto me, Lord, Lord, shall enter into the kingdom of heaven; but he that doeth the will of my Father which is in heaven. Many will say to me in that day, Lord, Lord, have we not prophesied in thy name? and in thy name have cast out devils? and in thy name done many wonderful works? *AND THEN WILL I PROFESS UNTO THEM, I NEVER KNEW YOU: DEPART FROM ME, YE THAT WORK INIQUITY!"*

In II Corinthians 11:13−15 the Apostle Paul speaks of these ministers: "For such are false apostles, deceitful workers, transforming themselves into the apostles of Christ. And no marvel; for Satan himself is transformed into an angel of light. Therefore it is no great thing if his ministers also be transformed as the ministers of righteousness; whose end shall be according to their works."

Such men may prophesy, they may do great works as ordained pastors and evangelists; but they are *ministers of Satan,* ordained of him. They are workers of iniquity, wolves in sheep's clothing. Judas Iscariot was such a person—and worse: *he was the son of perdition,* the devil incarnate.

We cannot understand *why* Judas was born a devil any more than we can understand why *Pharaoh* was born to be drowned in the Red Sea—*BUT THAT IS EXACTLY what God's Word declares:*

In Exodus 9:16 God told Moses to carry this message to Pharaoh: "In very deed *for this cause have I raised thee up,* for to shew in thee my power; and that my name may be declared throughout all the earth!" (*Paul* uses this reference in Romans 9:17.)

If you will study the account in Exodus concerning Moses and his dealings with Pharaoh, you will notice that on several occasions *God hardened Pharaoh's heart;* and then when Pharaoh and his army, in pursuit of the Israelites, were in the Red Sea attempting to cross on dry ground, God turned the waters loose and closed them in on Pharaoh and his army, drowning them all!

We cannot understand all of the statements in God's

Word, but neither can we *question* His Word. We cannot ask God *why* He does what He does. We must accept His wisdom, His actions, and His Word. As Paul declared in Romans 3:4, *"Let GOD be true, but every man a liar!"*

Our present verse contains another unique statement concerning Judas:

Judas *"by transgression fell, THAT HE MIGHT GO TO HIS OWN PLACE."* Such a statement occurs only this one time in the entire Bible. Judas went to *"his own place"*—but where was that place? Certainly it was not *hell,* for hell does not belong to Judas. According to the words of Jesus in Matthew 25:41, hell was *"PREPARED for the devil and his angels."* It was prepared to punish Lucifer when he was cast out of heaven:

"How art thou fallen from heaven, O Lucifer, son of the morning! How art thou cut down to the ground, which didst weaken the nations! For thou hast said in thine heart, I will ascend into heaven, I will exalt my throne above the stars of God: I will sit also upon the mount of the congregation, in the sides of the north: I will ascend above the heights of the clouds; I will be like the most High. *YET THOU SHALT BE BROUGHT DOWN TO HELL, TO THE SIDES OF THE PIT"* (Isa. 14:12—15).

In the beginning of creation, there was no hell and no *need* for hell. Genesis 1:1 tells us that "in the beginning God created *the heaven and the earth."* There is no mention of His creating hell. But there is a hell now; it was created for the devil and his angels—but it does not *belong* to the devil, nor does it belong to Judas Iscariot.

In the Word of God, when people depart this life they are spoken of as either lifting up their eyes in hell (as did the rich man in Luke 16:23), or being taken to Paradise where Jesus and all the redeemed are (like the beggar Lazarus in Luke 16:22). Jesus said to the penitent thief on the cross, *"TO DAY shalt thou be with me in Paradise"* (Luke 23:43).   No person except Judas is said to have gone to "his own place."

Now notice: Judas Iscariot *came* from a place to carry out his part in the eternal program of Almighty God concerning God's dear Son.   After betraying Jesus, he returned to the chief priests with whom he had bargained to sell the Lord for thirty pieces of silver, he threw the money at their feet, and went out and hanged himself— *"that he might go to his own place,"* the place from whence he came *that the Scripture might be fulfilled.* He has yet another task to fulfill, and one day, after the Rapture of the Church, the spirit of Judas will be incarnate in the body of a man who will be known as the Man of Sin, the Antichrist.

I know there are some people who will say that this is absurd, ridiculous, unreasonable, and that I am wrongly interpreting Scripture; but consider *this:*

In Malachi 4:5 we read, "Behold, *I will send you Elijah* the prophet before the coming of the great and dreadful day of the Lord." It is an accepted fact among Bible scholars that Elijah was taken out of the world hundreds of years before Malachi wrote those words. (Read II Kings 2:1—11.) But he has yet another task to perform in the end of time, and he will return to earth for that purpose.   We know that Elijah (together with Moses) appeared with Jesus on the Mount of Transfiguration (Matt. 17:3), and the *spirit* of Elijah was on John the Baptist, forerunner of the Lord Jesus (Matt. 17:12,13; Mark 9:12,13).   But he has a work yet to do in person, and he will be one of the two witnesses in Revelation 11:3—12.

I ask you, beloved, If God can send *Elijah* back to this earth in a body to perform a righteous act and fulfill the Word of God, would it be any more *difficult* for Him to ordain that Judas Iscariot be born of a harlot, and in a mortal body work the works of the Antichrist *that the Scripture be fulfilled?*

Now to sum up what we have just presented concerning Judas, we first of all declared that he was never saved, he was never in grace. The Scripture plainly testifies to this fact, for Judas was a devil (John 6:70), and as such would not have been born again.

This is further proved by the fact that Judas never called Jesus *"Lord."* He always referred to Him as "Master"—even in the betrayal (Matt. 26:49). He could not call Jesus "Lord" because he did not possess the Holy Ghost (I Cor. 12:3).

Judas was "the son of perdition" (John 17:12). The *Antichrist* is the son of perdition (II Thess. 2:3). The "son of perdition" will return "that the Scripture might be fulfilled."

In I Corinthians 2:10−14, Paul wrote of spiritual truths, "God hath revealed them unto us by His Spirit: for the Spirit searcheth all things, yea, the deep things of God. For what man knoweth the things of a man, save the spirit of man which is in him? Even so the things of God knoweth no man, but the Spirit of God. Now we have received, not the spirit of the world, but the spirit which is of God; that we might know the things that are freely given to us of God. Which things also we speak, not in the words which man's wisdom teacheth, but which the Holy Ghost teacheth; comparing spiritual things with spiritual. But the natural man receiveth not the things of the Spirit of God: for they are foolishness unto him: neither can he know them, because they are spiritually discerned."

In this brief study about Judas Iscariot we have taken the Scripture line upon line, truth upon truth, *comparing spiritual things with spiritual;* and with these scriptural facts in mind, who could suggest that Judas was ever saved, that he was ever a born again child of God? Yes, *Judas fell*—but he fell from the office of ministry and apostleship; he did not fall from grace!

Matthias Chosen

Verse 26: *"And they gave forth their lots; and the lot fell upon Matthias; and he was numbered with the eleven apostles."*

Casting lots was a Jewish mode of seeking divine direction, and was resorted to here. This mode of seeking divine guidance was one recognized under the Law (Lev. 16:8), and as such was a practice of immaturity. It should be noted that this event took place before *Pentecost*; after the Holy Spirit came the casting of lots was never mentioned again.

We might ask, "Would the same procedure be in order for believers *today?*" No, it would *not* be right for us to cast lots today. We have "the perfect law of liberty" (James 1:25); "that which is *perfect*" has come, and therefore "that which is in part" should be done away with (I Cor. 13:10). We have the complete Word of God, and we are living in the Dispensation of Grace when the Holy Spirit dwells in the hearts of believers and guides in all things. He reveals to us the will of God, and we have no need to cast lots in the election of a pastor, deacon, or in other matters of the church.

"And the lot fell upon Matthias." By the word "fell" here there can be no doubt that the passage speaks of "lots" rather than *voice votes*.

We are not told what *mode* of casting lots the disciples used in electing Matthias. Bible history tells us that this was usually done by writing the names of persons on pieces of stone or wood, putting them in an earthen jar, and then someone drew a name at random. *Blank* pieces of wood or rocks were also put in the jar with those on which a choice had been written, and the urn was shaken until one name fell out.

What a method to use to ask the risen Lord His choice in the replacement of Judas! Personally, I have my doubts that Jesus honored their request, and I feel that it was purely a matter of chance that Matthias was elected, and not divine guidance in the hearts of the disciples. Nevertheless, the lot fell on Matthias—and as a result, he was reckoned the twelfth apostle. We find no further record of him—where he ministered, what he did, or where he traveled in proclaiming the Gospel.

There is nothing in the Scriptures that says these disciples should choose men to be their successors. Ministers today are not successors of the apostles; we are called of God to preach the Gospel and feed the lambs and sheep of His fold during this Dispensation of Grace:

"There is one body, and one Spirit, even as ye are called in one hope of your calling; one Lord, one faith, one baptism, one God and Father of all, who is above all, and through all, and in you all.

"But unto every one of us is given grace according to the measure of the gift of Christ. Wherefore He saith, When He ascended up on high, He led captivity captive, and gave gifts unto men. (Now that He ascended, what is it but that He also descended first into the lower parts of the earth? He that descended is the same also that ascended up far above all heavens, that He might fill all things.) And He gave some apostles; and some, prophets; and some, evangelists; and some, pastors and teachers; *for the perfecting of the saints, for the work of the ministry, for the edifying of the body of Christ:* Till we all come in the unity of the faith, and of the knowledge of the Son of God, unto a perfect man, unto the measure of the stature of the fulness of Christ: That we henceforth be no more children, tossed to and fro, and carried about with every wind of doctrine, by the sleight of men, and cunning craftiness, whereby they lie in wait to deceive; but speaking the truth in love, may grow up into Him in all things, which is the head, even Christ: From whom the whole body fitly joined together and compacted by that which every joint supplieth, according to the effectual working in the measure of every part, maketh increase of the body unto the edifying of itself in love" (Eph. 4:4—16).

CHAPTER II

1. And when the day of Pentecost was fully come, they were all with one accord in one place.

2. And suddenly there came a sound from heaven as of a rushing mighty wind, and it filled all the house where they were sitting.

3. And there appeared unto them cloven tongues like as of fire, and it sat upon each of them.

4. And they were all filled with the Holy Ghost, and began to speak with other tongues, as the Spirit gave them utterance.

5. And there were dwelling at Jerusalem Jews, devout men, out of every nation under heaven.

6. Now when this was noised abroad, the multitude came together, and were confounded, because that every man heard them speak in his own language.

7. And they were all amazed and marvelled, saying one to another, Behold, are not all these which speak Galilaeans?

8. And how hear we every man in our own tongue, wherein we were born?

9. Parthians, and Medes, and Elamites, and the dwellers in Mesopotamia, and in Judaea, and Cappadocia, in Pontus, and Asia,

10. Phrygia, and Pamphylia, in Egypt, and in the parts of Libya about Cyrene, and strangers of Rome, Jews and proselytes,

11. Cretes and Arabians, we do hear them speak in our tongues the wonderful works of God.

12. And they were all amazed, and were in doubt, saying one to another, What meaneth this?

13. Others mocking said, These men are full of new wine.

14. But Peter, standing up with the eleven, lifted up his voice, and said unto them, Ye men of Judaea, and all ye that dwell at Jerusalem, be this known unto you, and hearken to my words:

15. For these are not drunken, as ye suppose, seeing it is but the third hour of the day.

16. But this is that which was spoken by the prophet Joel;

17. And it shall come to pass in the last days, saith God, I will pour out of my Spirit upon all flesh: and your sons and your

daughters shall prophesy, and your young men shall see visions, and your old men shall dream dreams:

18. And on my servants and on my handmaidens I will pour out in those days of my Spirit; and they shall prophesy:

19. And I will shew wonders in heaven above, and signs in the earth beneath; blood, and fire, and vapour of smoke:

20. The sun shall be turned into darkness, and the moon into blood, before that great and notable day of the Lord come:

21. And it shall come to pass, that whosoever shall call on the name of the Lord shall be saved.

22. Ye men of Israel, hear these words; Jesus of Nazareth, a man approved of God among you by miracles and wonders and signs, which God did by him in the midst of you, as ye yourselves also know:

23. Him, being delivered by the determinate counsel and foreknowledge of God, ye have taken, and by wicked hands have crucified and slain:

24. Whom God hath raised up, having loosed the pains of death: because it was not possible that he should be holden of it.

25. For David speaketh concerning him, I foresaw the Lord always before my face, for he is on my right hand, that I should not be moved:

26. Therefore did my heart rejoice, and my tongue was glad; moreover also my flesh shall rest in hope:

27. Because thou wilt not leave my soul in hell, neither wilt thou suffer thine Holy One to see corruption.

28. Thou hast made known to me the ways of life; thou shalt make me full of joy with thy countenance.

29. Men and brethren, let me freely speak unto you of the patriarch David, that he is both dead and buried, and his sepulchre is with us unto this day.

30. Therefore being a prophet, and knowing that God had sworn with an oath to him, that of the fruit of his loins, according to the flesh, he would raise up Christ to sit on his throne;

31. He seeing this before spake of the resurrection of Christ, that his soul was not left in hell, neither his flesh did see corruption.

32. This Jesus hath God raised up, whereof we all are witnesses.

33. Therefore being by the right hand of God exalted, and having received of the Father the promise of the Holy Ghost, he hath shed forth this, which ye now see and hear.

34. For David is not ascended into the heavens: but he saith himself, The Lord said unto my Lord, Sit thou on my right hand,

35. Until I make thy foes thy footstool.

36. Therefore let all the house of Israel know assuredly, that God hath made that same Jesus, whom ye have crucified, both Lord and Christ.

37. Now when they heard this, they were pricked in their heart, and said unto Peter and to the rest of the apostles, Men and brethren, what shall we do?

38. Then Peter said unto them, Repent, and be baptized every one of you in the name of Jesus Christ for the remission of sins, and ye shall receive the gift of the Holy Ghost.

39. For the promise is unto you, and to your children, and to all that are afar off, even as many as the Lord our God shall call.

40. And with many other words did he testify and exhort, saying, Save yourselves from this untoward generation.

41. Then they that gladly received his word were baptized: and the same day there were added unto them about three thousand souls.

42. And they continued stedfastly in the apostles' doctrine and fellowship, and in breaking of bread, and in prayers.

43. And fear came upon every soul: and many wonders and signs were done by the apostles.

44. And all that believed were together, and had all things common;

45. And sold their possessions and goods, and parted them to all men, as every man had need.

46. And they, continuing daily with one accord in the temple, and breaking bread from house to house, did eat their meat with gladness and singleness of heart,

47. Praising God, and having favour with all the people. And the Lord added to the church daily such as should be saved.

Never in the history of the Church—from its beginning until this present hour—has there been such drastic need for a prayerful study of this second chapter of Acts as there is at this time. Today there is much ignorance and gross misunderstanding among tens of thousands of church people concerning what happened on the Day of Pentecost. A great majority of church folk are totally ignorant of that which God in His greatness did on that day when the Holy Spirit was poured out; they know very little of the deep meaning of that momentous event. There are many *denominational* interpretations and "religious fads" concerning Pentecost; but there is but *one true meaning.*   So, by the grace of God, by comparing Scripture with Scripture and rightly dividing the Word, we will learn what we can from the Bible, not from books of denominational doctrine.

Before we go into our verse-by-verse study of this chapter, let us look briefly at what took place at Pentecost, and what was accomplished on that memorable day:

In Matthew 3:11, John the Baptist (forerunner of the Lord Jesus) declared, "I indeed baptize you with water unto repentance: but He that cometh after me is mightier than I, whose shoes I am not worthy to bear: He shall baptize you with the Holy Ghost, and with fire."

Also, on many occasions *Jesus* instructed His disciples about the coming of the Holy Spirit.   In Luke 11:13 He said to them, "If ye then, being evil, know how to give good gifts unto your children: *how much more shall your heavenly Father give the Holy Spirit to them that ask Him?"*

In John 7:37—39 we read, "In the last day, that great day of the feast, Jesus stood and cried, saying, If any man thirst, let him come unto me, and drink.   He that believeth on me, as the Scripture hath said, out of His belly shall flow rivers of living water. *(But this spake He of the Spirit, which they that believe on Him SHOULD RECEIVE: FOR THE HOLY GHOST WAS NOT YET GIVEN; because that Jesus was not yet glorified.)"*   At the time Jesus spoke these words, the promise pointed to the future.   This promise could not be fulfilled before the crucifixion and bodily resurrection of the Lord Jesus Christ.

During the forty days after the resurrection and just before the ascension of our Lord, He commanded the disciples to tarry in Jerusalem, to wait for the promise of the Father, the coming of the Holy Spirit; and when the Day of Pentecost arrived, all the promises Jesus had made to His disciples, together with God's promises in the book of Joel (and other places in the Old Testament) were once and for all fulfilled, never to be repeated. The Day of Pentecost can no more occur again than can the crucifixion of Jesus occur again. He died *once*, for all, forever. Through His one sacrifice He paid the sin-debt and satisfied every demand of God pertaining to the remission of sin and the believer's being made acceptable to the heavenly Father:

"By the which will we are sanctified through the offering of the body of Jesus Christ once for all. . . For by one offering He hath perfected for ever them that are sanctified" (Heb. 10:10,14).

All born again believers share in the accomplished promise of the heavenly Father and Jesus the Son, and all believers possess the Holy Spirit:

"For as the body is one, and hath many members, and all the members of that one body, being many, are one body: so also is Christ. *For by one Spirit are we all baptized into one body,* whether we be Jews or Gentiles, whether we be bond or free; and have been all made to drink into one Spirit" (I Cor. 12:12,13).

"But ye are not in the flesh, but in the Spirit, if so be that the Spirit of God dwell in you. *Now if any man have not the Spirit of Christ, he is none of His. . . For as many as are led by the Spirit of God, they are the sons of God.* For ye have not received the spirit of bondage again to fear; but ye have received the Spirit of adoption, whereby we cry, Abba, Father. *The Spirit itself beareth witness with our spirit, that we are the children of God"* (Rom. 8:9,14—16).

In Ephesians 4:30 Paul said, "Grieve not the Holy Spirit of God, *whereby ye are sealed* unto the day of redemption!"

The Bible fact that every believer possesses the Holy Spirit declares that the promise of God the Father has been fulfilled, and testifies to the efficacy of the shed blood of the Lamb of God. Furthermore, the Holy Spirit in our hearts testifies that Jesus is now glorified at the right hand of the Majesty on high, because before He finished His ministry on earth He said to His disciples, "I tell you the truth: It is expedient for you that I go away: for if I go not away, the Comforter will not come unto you; but if I depart, I will send Him unto you" (John 16:7).

It is unscriptural to beg God for the gift of the Holy Spirit because He has already *given* the Spirit. It is unscriptural to pray for God to fulfill promises which were *fulfilled literally* on the Day of Pentecost. The Holy Ghost is already here, and He will come into the heart of any and all who ask Him, in faith believing in the finished work of the Lord Jesus Christ. It is unscriptural to pray for *a mighty baptism* of the Holy Ghost, and it is certainly unscriptural to ask God to give us MORE of the Spirit because the Holy Spirit is a *Person*—not an "influence"—and we do not receive a person *in parts!* To possess the third Person of the Trinity is to possess ALL of that Person.

The book of Acts is NOT a book of doctrine CONCERNING the Holy Spirit, nor does it CONTAIN doctrine OF the Holy Spirit. It shows *revealed doctrine* in its practical side; it is the book of *the continued work and teaching* of the living Christ *by* the Holy Spirit *through* the body of Christ—the Church of the living God.

The *purpose* of the coming of the Holy Spirit is revealed in this chapter, and other purposes which are *indicated* here are fully revealed in the fourteen epistles penned by the Apostle Paul *under inspiration* of the Holy Spirit.

On the Day of Pentecost the Holy Spirit came upon the one hundred and twenty believers *individually*, but He also did a work in a *corporate* way. Each individual believer in the upper room was filled with the Holy Spirit and He *indwelt* each individual; but He also *filled the*

ROOM and all the house where the believers were gathered. Thus the group of one hundred and twenty people became one body through the baptism of the Holy Spirit. In *reality, one hundred and twenty believers went into the upper room, and in the spiritual aspect, only ONE came down!* They were all united into one body, as set forth in I Corinthians 12:13.

The Day of Pentecost was the birthday of the New Testament Church; and since that day, the split second a sinner believes in the finished work of the Lord Jesus Christ and accepts Him by faith, the Holy Spirit *baptizes* that individual into the New Testament Church, which is the body of Christ.

There are those who reject the teaching that the Day of Pentecost was the birthday of the Church. They maintain that the Church did not begin until after Paul began to preach to the Gentiles; but this is error. The Church began with the one hundred and twenty in the upper room — and according to the book of Ephesians, the New Testament apostles and prophets were the *foundation* of the Church (Eph. 2:20). Later the Gentiles were added to the body of Christ and became joint-heirs and joint partakers of the same promise.

Through the Apostle Paul, God's chosen vessel for the Church, the *mystery* of the Church, which was not known in past ages, was revealed: "Which in other ages was not made known unto the sons of men, as it is now revealed unto His holy apostles and prophets by the Spirit" (Eph. 3:5). The Church existed *before* Paul, even though its mystery was not clearly seen or understood *until God revealed it TO Paul.* In fact, Paul was not even converted until after the Church was born!

As Saul of Tarsus, he was traveling to Damascus to arrest Christians there, when a light from heaven shone down on him and a voice spoke: "Saul, Saul, why persecutest thou me?" Paul immediately asked, "Who *art* thou?" and Jesus replied, "I am Jesus whom thou persecutest." (Read Acts 9:1—19.)

We know Paul was not persecuting Jesus *personally*, because at that time Jesus was already seated at the right hand of the Father in heaven. But Paul was persecuting *believers*—and believers are members of the Church of the living God, *the body of Christ*. In I Corinthians 15:8,9 Paul testifies of himself, "Last of all (Jesus) was seen of me also, as of one born out of due time. For I am the least of the apostles, that am not meet to be called an apostle, because *I persecuted the Church of God.*" How could Saul of Tarsus persecute the Church if the Church did not *begin* until after Saul's *conversion?*

I repeat: The Church was born on the Day of Pentecost, and since that day every believer is united to that one body through the miracle of the new birth and the baptism of the Holy Spirit.

It is true that not all believers react the same emotionally or outwardly when they become children of God. There may be a variety of forms and a variety of measures in which His power is displayed when one rests upon the finished work of Christ. There may be a difference in the degree of joy and emotional stir—but there are no different degrees of possessing *the Holy Spirit* because He is a *Person,* and when He comes into the inner man He comes in *wholly*—not partially.

On the Day of Pentecost, people out of every nation of the known world were present in the city of Jerusalem; and after the Holy Spirit came upon the one hundred and twenty believers, every person present heard the Gospel in his own language—which testifies that the good news of the saving grace of God is for every nation under heaven, even though those who spoke that day were all *Jews*. Jesus commanded His disciples to preach the Gospel to every creature.

The events which occurred on the Day of Pentecost have a special Jewish significance. They proved that

Jesus Christ had risen, and the *signs* at Pentecost proved that Jesus of Nazareth, whom they had rejected, was then seated at the right hand of Jehovah, their God. Pentecost was the beginning of the second offer of mercy to the nation Israel. But they again rejected Him, and after the stoning of Stephen God called the Apostle Paul and commissioned him to carry the Gospel to the Gentiles.

The Gospel Given to the Jews; Peter's First Use of the Keys

Verse 1: *"And when the Day of Pentecost was fully come, they were all with one accord in one place."*

Pentecost, one of the Jewish feasts, was so called by the Jews because it occurred fifty days after the Passover. The offering in this feast (Pentecost) was the first two loaves made from the first portion of the wheat harvest of the year, and it was given as a "thank offering."

In the Old Testament this feast has three names:

In Exodus 23:16 it is called *"the feast of harvest."*

In Exodus 34:22 it is called *"the feast of weeks."*

In Numbers 28:26 it is called *"the day of the firstfruits."*

In the Old Testament era the feast of Pentecost commemorated the wheat harvest, and after the exile it became the traditional festival where Israel remembered the giving of the law to Moses.

In this present day, orthodox Jews still keep this feast. They offer prayers, and in their synagogues they read publicly the Old Testament account of the giving of the law to Moses as recorded in Exodus. Then from the prophets they read the first chapter of Ezekiel and the third chapter of Habakkuk, also the second chapter of Joel. They undoubtedly practiced this custom at the time the Holy Spirit was poured out fifty days after the resurrection of Jesus, and it is not without significance that some of the outward signs which occurred when the law was given also occurred at Pentecost—i. e., the sound as of a mighty wind, the fire, a voice of words. In Hebrews 12:18,19 we read, "For ye are not come unto the mount that might be touched, and that burned with fire, nor unto blackness, and darkness, and tempest, and the sound of a trumpet, and the voice of words; which voice they that heard intreated that the word should not be spoken to them any more."

The Day of Pentecost was the birthday of a new dispensation, and it occurred with signs and wonders *according to God's own will* (Heb. 2:4). There were also tremendous outward signs at the beginning of the Dispensation of Law, but these signs did not *continue* throughout that dispensation. The same is true concerning the beginning of this new Dispensation of Grace. It began with mighty signs and wonders—but these were *only* at the beginning. When the "perfect law of liberty" came, the signs ceased. We do not *need* signs and wonders today, because we have the completed Word of God —"that which is perfect" is come. The just shall live by faith; faith comes by hearing and hearing by the Word of God. We can depend upon what God's Word declares. We can claim God's promises with the assurance that He will *keep* those promises.

"When the Day of Pentecost was fully come . . . ." What is meant by Pentecost being *"fully come"*? *Pentecosto* is a Greek word signifying *the fifth part* of a thing or *the fiftieth in order.* Therefore on *the fiftieth day* after the resurrection of Jesus, *Pentecost occurred.* It was not the *forty-ninth* day after the resurrection, nor the *fifty-first* day after the resurrection. It was the *fiftieth* day. As previously stated, the feast of Pentecost under the Old Testament economy was in commemoration of the firstfruits, and Jesus was the firstfruits from the dead:

"But now is Christ risen from the dead, and become the firstfruits of them that slept. For since by man came death, by man came also the resurrection of the dead.

For as in Adam all die, even so in Christ shall all be made alive. But every man in his own order: *Christ the firstfruits;* afterward they that are Christ's at His coming" (I Cor. 15:20−23).

Verse 2: *"And suddenly there came a sound from heaven as of a rushing mighty wind, and it filled all the house where they were sitting."*

Surely the words of this verse must stir the heart of every believer who reads them. So picturesque, so dynamic, is the word-description here that it could have come only from one who witnessed it all.

"Suddenly there came a sound from heaven . . . ." The Church was *born* suddenly, and from the epistles we learn that it will *depart* this earth suddenly. In Revelation 22:20 Jesus declared, "Surely I come quickly!" One day—we know not the day nor the hour—"the Lord Himself shall descend from heaven with a shout, with the voice of the archangel, and with the trump of God: and the dead in Christ shall rise first: Then we which are alive and remain shall be caught up together with them in the clouds, to meet the Lord in the air: and so shall we ever be with the Lord" (I Thess. 4:16,17).

In I Corinthians 15:51−53 the Apostle Paul tells us, "Behold, I shew you a mystery: We shall not all sleep, but we shall all be changed, *in a moment, in the twinkling of an eye,* at the last trump: for the trumpet shall sound, and the dead shall be raised incorruptible, and we shall be changed. For this corruptible must put on incorruption, and this mortal must put on immortality."

The Greek word here translated *"sound"* applies to any noise or loud report, such as "the sound of a trumpet" in Hebrews 12:19. The sound that preceded the actual filling of the Spirit was a sound to arrest the attention of each member of the group in the upper room, a sound they could never forget.

Their attention was also attracted by the *direction*

from whence the sound came. Ordinarily, wind blows horizontally—from north to south, from east to west; but this "rushing" sound as of a mighty wind came down from the sky, and the waiting disciples knew it was from heaven—from God.

This sound was the outward sign of the descent of the Divine Person, the Holy Spirit, who would come to dwell in the hearts of these believers, and form the body of Christ, the New Testament Church, the building spoken of in Ephesians 2:19—22 as the "habitation of God through the Spirit."

The sound "as of a rushing mighty wind" prepared the company in the upper room for the coming of the Spirit, for to them, *wind* was a familiar *symbol* of the Holy Spirit. In Ezekiel 37:9,10 we read, "Then said He unto me, Prophesy unto the wind, prophesy, son of man, and say to the wind, Thus saith the Lord God; Come from the four winds, O breath, and breathe upon these slain, that they may live. So I prophesied as He commanded me, and the breath came into them, and they lived, and stood up upon their feet, an exceeding great army."

In the *New* Testament, *Jesus* used the wind as a symbol of the Spirit. Speaking to Nicodemus He said, "The wind bloweth where it listeth, and thou hearest the sound thereof, but canst not tell whence it cometh, and whither it goeth: so is every one that is born of the Spirit" (John 3:8). In John 20:22 Jesus *breathed* on the disciples and said to them, "Receive ye the Holy Ghost." (Please read Psalms 29; 104:3; 18:10; and I Kings 19:11.)

Notice, our Scripture does not say that this was "the sound of *wind*," but *"the sound AS OF* a rushing mighty wind." There is no suggestion that wind was actually present. This makes the miracle even more remarkable than if there had been a strong wind in the house which could have destroyed it. There was *a great sound "AS OF"* a *mighty wind,* but all was still, there was no wind.

The men in the upper room had seen many storms on the Sea of Galilee, but there was no storm around them now—no thunder and lightning, no wind; yet there was a powerful, rushing *sound* which came down from heaven—*"and it filled ALL THE HOUSE where they were sitting."*

In I Kings 8:10 we read that *the cloud* (in the Old Testament the sign of the presence of Jehovah) filled the whole house after the sacrifices had been brought to be offered to God when Solomon's temple was dedicated; but *Pentecost* was a much greater event than the dedication of the temple. The entire house where the one hundred and twenty believers were assembled was *filled* with the sound from heaven, thus signifying that a much greater and more noble building (the New Testament Church) was to be built on earth as the habitation of God.

Verse 3: *"And there appeared unto them cloven tongues like as of fire, and it sat upon each of them."*

Notice that the *sound* came before the visible *tongues of fire* appeared. Faith comes by hearing, and hearing by the Word of God (Rom. 10:17). The disciples *heard* the sound as of a mighty rushing wind—and even though the sound did not speak, the *wind* was to them a symbol of the Holy Spirit; and *the Holy Spirit must accompany the Word* or there can be no living faith. I believe the sound that came from heaven was the first step in establishing in the heart and mind of each of those individuals the fact that *God* was in this great miracle. They first *heard the sound,* it filled the whole house; and then came *visible* evidence of the coming of the Holy Spirit.

"There appeared unto them cloven tongues like as of FIRE!" Here *"cloven"* tongues means *parted* tongues—not that *each tongue* was parted, but that the tongues were separate one from another; and these tongues sat upon *each* of the one hundred and twenty people in the

upper room, testifying that not only did the Holy Ghost come upon the *entire company* and fill the whole house, He also came upon *each individual IN the company.* Each person present received Him.

The Holy Spirit was not given *by measure*—that is, the older disciples like Peter, James, and John did not receive *more* of the Spirit than did the younger (newer, or weaker) believers. I re-emphasize the divine fact that the Spirit is the third *Person* of the Trinity; He is not just a "power" or an "influence," *therefore He is NOT received in portions!* He came as the gift of God to all believers, as promised in both the Old and New Testaments.

The *"cloven* (parted) *tongues"* were symbols of the diverse languages in which the disciples would declare the grace of God to all present on the Day of Pentecost—and notice: the tongues were not *literal FIRE* as we know it in the natural realm. The Scripture very carefully declares that they were tongues *"LIKE as of fire,"* thus symbolic of the righteousness, holiness, and *judgment* of Almighty God:

"For the Lord thy God is a consuming fire, even a jealous God" (Deut. 4:24).

"For our God is a consuming fire" (Heb. 12:29).

Even though the tongues were not literal fire, they were *visible.* Those in the upper room saw them as they appeared—first filling the room and then coming to rest upon each of those gathered there.

"Tongues" is a word used often in the Scripture. Sometimes it denotes *the human tongue,* the instrument of taste and speech. Sometimes it denotes *language* or speech.   It is also used to denote an object which, in shape, *resembles* the human tongue—for example, in Joshua 7, verses 21 and 24, we read of "a *wedge* of gold," but in the Hebrew it is "a *tongue* of gold," evidently a piece of gold in a long, narrow shape resembling a human tongue.   In Isaiah 11:15 we read of "the tongue of the

Egyptian *sea"*; and in Isaiah 5:24 where we read, "Therefore as the fire devoureth the stubble, and the flame consumeth the chaff," the *Hebrew* language reads "the *tongue* of fire devoureth the stubble."

In the upper room, the "tongues like as of fire" no doubt resembled the human tongue, and this miracle put a new tongue (a new *language*) into the mouth of every person present, and they spoke words they had never spoken before.

On *many* occasions God had appeared to Israel (and to individual Jews) in a flame of fire. He manifested Himself to *Moses* in a flame:

"The angel of the Lord appeared unto (Moses) in a flame of fire out of the midst of a bush: and he looked, and, behold, the bush burned with fire, and the bush was not consumed. And Moses said, I will now turn aside, and see this great sight, why the bush is not burnt. And when the Lord saw that he turned aside to see, God called unto him out of the midst of the bush, and said, Moses, Moses. And he said, Here am I. And (God) said, Draw not nigh hither: put off thy shoes from off thy feet, for the place whereon thou standest is holy ground. Moreover He said, I am the God of thy father, the God of Abraham, the God of Isaac, and the God of Jacob. And Moses hid his face; for he was afraid to look upon God" (Ex. 3:2—6).

When God gave the Law to Moses, He descended to Mount Sinai in fire: "And it came to pass on the third day in the morning, that there were thunders and lightnings, and a thick cloud upon the mount, and the voice of the trumpet exceeding loud; so that all the people that was in the camp trembled. And Moses brought forth the people out of the camp to meet with God; and they stood at the nether part of the mount. And Mount Sinai was altogether on a smoke, *because the Lord descended upon it in fire:* and the smoke thereof ascended as the smoke of a furnace, and the whole mount quaked greatly"

(Ex. 19:16—18).

On the Day of Pentecost, only Jews were present in the upper room; they were familiar with Old Testament Scripture and with God's dealings with their forefathers. The sound "as of a rushing mighty *wind*" and the cloven tongues "like as of *fire*" were to them emblems of the presence of Jehovah God, emblems of the presence of the promised Holy Spirit. But the fire appeared here in such manner as it had never appeared before—*like a tongue*, indicating the *different languages* which they would presently become able to speak in the presence of people "from every nation under heaven."

Jesus had commanded them "Go ye therefore, and teach *all nations* . . . teaching them to observe all things whatsoever I have commanded you" (Matt. 28:19,20 in part). They were now to be endowed with tongues that would enable them to speak many languages which they themselves had not known and had never studied. They were now to be empowered to carry out His command.

The Baptism of the Holy Spirit

Verse 4: *"And they were all filled with the Holy Ghost, and began to speak with other tongues, as the Spirit gave them utterance."*

All four of the Gospel writers recorded the prophecy of John the Baptist when he spoke of the baptism of the Holy Ghost which was to come:

In *Matthew 3:11* he declared, "I indeed baptize you with water unto repentance: but He that cometh after me is mightier than I, whose shoes I am not worthy to bear: He shall baptize you with the Holy Ghost, and with fire."

Mark 1:8 records, "I indeed have baptized you with water: but He shall baptize you with the Holy Ghost."

In *Luke 3:16* John the Baptist prophesied, "I indeed baptize you with water; but One mightier than I cometh, the latchet of whose shoes I am not worthy to unloose: He shall baptize you with the Holy Ghost and with fire."

And in *John 1:33* we read, "I knew Him not: but He that sent me to baptize with water, the same said unto me, Upon whom thou shalt see the Spirit descending, and remaining on Him, the same is He which baptizeth with the Holy Ghost."

Then in Acts 1:5 Jesus Himself declared to His disciples, "John truly baptized with water; but ye shall be baptized with the Holy Ghost *not many days hence.*"

Now please notice: The passages just quoted cover about three and one-half years, during which time the baptism of the Spirit was still future; yet *during* that time the apostles achieved many remarkable results in their ministry. They preached the Gospel, healed the sick—even *demons* were subject unto them:

"And (the disciples) departed, and went through the towns, preaching the Gospel, and healing every where" (Luke 9:6).

"And they went out, and preached that men should repent. And they cast out many devils, and anointed with oil many that were sick, and healed them" (Mark 6:12,13).

"And the seventy returned again with joy, saying, Lord, even the devils are subject unto us through thy name" (Luke 10:17).

All of these miracles took place BEFORE Pentecost, therefore before the baptism of the Holy Spirit! However, Matthew 17:14—21 records *one* occasion on which the disciples *failed*—and it also records the *reason* for their failure, as stated by Jesus Himself:

A man brought his son to Jesus, saying, "Lord, have mercy on my son: for he is lunatick, and sore vexed: for ofttimes he falleth into the fire, and oft into the water. *And I brought him to thy disciples, and they could not cure him.*" Jesus healed the boy immediately, and then the disciples asked Him why *they* could not cast out the demons and heal him. Jesus replied, *"Because of your UNBELIEF:* for verily I say unto you, If ye have faith as a grain of mustard seed, ye shall say unto this mountain, Remove hence to yonder place; and it shall remove; and nothing shall be impossible unto you."￼ He did not say that the disciples failed to heal the boy because they had not received the baptism of the Holy Spirit, but because of unbelief.

These passages furnish unquestionable proof that the baptism of the Spirit was not necessary in order to accomplish miracles, perform wonders, and effectually preach the Gospel while the Lord was here on earth. The baptism of the Spirit came to pass at a definite time *after* Jesus had ascended back to heaven and was seated at the Father's right hand.

If we keep this fact in mind as we study the baptism of the Spirit, we will not be carried away by false doctrines which are based on Scripture taken out of context and wrongly interpreted by those who misunderstand the baptism of the Holy Spirit as to why it occurred, and the meaning of it in the New Testament Church.

What Is Meant by Being Baptized with Fire?

There is much misunderstanding concerning the words of John the Baptist when he spoke of Jesus baptizing "with the Holy Ghost and *with FIRE.*"￼ What John meant was that each person who heard him speak would be baptized with one or the other—i. e., those who were baptized in the Holy Ghost *would not be baptized in fire,* but those who *refused* to receive Jesus and the Holy Ghost *would be* baptized in fire.

What did this "fire" signify? In the third chapter of Matthew, *fire* is mentioned three times:

In verse 10: "Every tree which bringeth not forth good fruit is hewn down, and cast into the fire."

In verse 11, the Lord Jesus Christ would baptize "with the Holy Ghost, and with fire."

In verse 12: "He will burn up the chaff with unquenchable fire."

You will notice that in each of these verses, *fire* definitely and specifically points to *judgment*. Could "fire" mean one thing in verses 10 and 12, and mean something entirely different in verse 11?- Indeed not!

Someone may ask why John the Baptist would speak so much of judgment. This is easily understood when we consider that those to whom he spoke were "a generation of vipers":

"But when he saw many of the Pharisees and Sadducees come to his baptism, he said unto them, *O generation of vipers, who hath warned you to flee from the wrath to come? Bring forth therefore fruits meet for repentance"* (Matt. 3:7,8). Unless these people repented they would be baptized in *fire*—engulfed in the *lake of fire.* In other words, they would receive *a baptism of judgment!* (Heb. 10:27; 12:29).

Luke also speaks of baptism with fire (Luke 3:16), but by contrast *Mark* makes no mention of it (Mark 1:8). Why? Mark wrote of a group who were confessing their sins, they were not "a generation of vipers." In Mark 1:5 we read, "And there went out unto him (John the Baptist) all the land of Judaea, and they of Jerusalem, *and were all baptized of him in the river of Jordan, CONFESSING THEIR SINS."* The Pharisees and Sadducees whom John called "a generation of vipers" came to him to request baptism, but he refused to baptize them because *they were NOT confessing their sins* nor repenting of their iniquities!

At the time John the Baptist declared that Jesus would baptize with the Holy Ghost and with fire, *both baptisms were future.* The baptism of the Spirit came within four years after John made the prophetic statement, and the prophecy of the baptism of fire was probably fulfilled in part when Titus overran Jerusalem and destroyed the city, burning the temple and killing more than a

million Jews.   That was indeed a baptism of fire, but
the *ultimate* fulfillment of that prophecy points to the
lake of fire which will engulf all who are not recipients
of God's grace and possessors of the Holy Spirit.   When
the Lord Jesus sits in judgment, those who know not
God will be baptized in fire:

"And to you are troubled rest with us, when the Lord
Jesus shall be revealed from heaven with His mighty
angels, *in flaming fire taking vengeance on them that
know not God, and that obey not the Gospel of our
Lord Jesus Christ"* (II Thess. 1:7,8).

"And I saw a great white throne, and Him that sat
on it, from whose face the earth and the heaven fled
away; and there was found no place for them.   And I
saw the dead, small and great, stand before God; and
the books were opened: and another book was opened,
which is the book of life: and the dead were judged out
of those things which were written in the books, according to their works.   And the sea gave up the dead which
were in it; and death and hell delivered up the dead
which were in them: and they were judged every man
according to their works.   And death and hell were cast
into the lake of fire.   This is the second death.   *And
whosoever was not found written in the book of life was
cast into the lake of fire"* (Rev. 20:11–15).

The fire of judgment is definite. John the Baptist did
not say that Jesus would baptize with the Holy Spirit
and with a baptism *"LIKE as OF fire."* He made no
suggestion that this baptism would simply *resemble* fire.
He declared that Jesus would baptize with the Holy
Ghost *"and with FIRE"*—not with "tongues *like* as of
fire."

"*And they were ALL filled with the Holy Ghost."*
Every person in the upper room was entirely under the
sacred influence and power of the Holy Ghost.   To be
filled denotes that all faculties are controlled *by that
which FILLS*.   Therefore, when each individual was

filled with the Holy Spirit, each individual began to speak with other tongues *"as the Spirit gave them utterance."*

I think it would be well for us to look at the Corinthian church and study some enlightening Scripture given to the Corinthians (and to all believers) through the inspired pen of the Apostle Paul:

I Corinthians 12:12,13 is a very helpful passage concerning the baptism of the Holy Spirit: "For as the body is one, and hath many members, and all the members of that one body, being many, are one body: so also is Christ. *For BY ONE SPIRIT are we ALL baptized into ONE BODY,* whether we be Jews or Gentiles, whether we be bond or free; and have been *all* made to drink into one Spirit."

In this passage, we notice two things of special importance:

First, *ALL of the Corinthian believers* were baptized in the Holy Ghost, they *ALL drank into one Spirit.* Yet some of them were quarrelsome and sectarian in spirit: "For it hath been declared unto me of you, my brethren, by them which are of the house of Chloe, that there are contentions among you. Now this I say, that every one of you saith, I am of Paul; and I of Apollos; and I of Cephas; and I of Christ. Is Christ divided? Was Paul crucified for you? or were ye baptized in the name of Paul?" (I Cor. 1:11—13).

Others in the Corinthian church were *carnal.* Paul said to them, "I have fed you with milk, and not with meat: for hitherto ye were not able to bear it, neither yet now are ye able. *For ye are yet carnal:* for whereas there is among you envying, and strife, and divisions, are ye not carnal, and walk as men?" (I Cor. 3:2,3).

Still others among them were going to law against each other, thus hurting their testimony before unbelievers. Paul said, "I speak to your shame! Is it so, that there is not a wise man among you? no, not one that shall be able to judge between his brethren? *But brother goeth to law with brother, and that before the unbelievers"* (I Cor. 6:5,6).

In the church in Corinth, the Lord's Supper had been turned into a time of drinking and feasting, and because of that sinful practice, some of the members were sick and some of them had died:

"When ye come together therefore into one place, this is not to eat the Lord's supper. For in eating every one taketh before other his own supper: and one is hungry, and another is drunken. What? Have ye not houses to eat and to drink in? or despise ye the church of God, and shame them that have not? What shall I say to you? Shall I praise you in this? I praise you not. . . For this cause many are weak and sickly among you, and many sleep. For if we would judge ourselves, we should not be judged. But when we are judged, we are chastened of the Lord, that we should not be condemned with the world. Wherefore, my brethren, when ye come together to eat, tarry one for another. And if any man hunger, let him eat at home; that ye come not together unto condemnation. And the rest will I set in order when I come" (I Cor. 11:20−22, 30−34).

A careful study of both of the Corinthian epistles will reveal that Paul rebuked these people again and again for their carnal, fleshly ways; but in spite of all their failures, shortcomings, and lack of spirituality *they had truly believed on the Lord Jesus Christ,* they were saved, washed in the blood, justified, sanctified, and baptized in the Holy Ghost. This we know from the Scriptures:

"Crispus, the chief ruler of the synagogue, believed on the Lord with all his house; *and many of the Corinthians hearing believed,* and were baptized" (Acts 18:8).

In I Corinthians 6:9−12 Paul wrote, "Know ye not that the unrighteous shall not inherit the kingdom of God? Be not deceived: neither fornicators, nor idolaters, nor adulterers, nor effeminate, nor abusers of themselves with mankind, nor thieves, nor covetous, nor drunkards, nor revilers, nor extortioners, shall inherit the kingdom of God. *AND SUCH WERE SOME OF YOU: BUT YE ARE WASHED, BUT YE ARE SANCTIFIED, BUT YE ARE JUSTIFIED IN THE NAME OF THE LORD JE-SUS, AND BY THE SPIRIT OF OUR GOD.* All things are lawful unto me, but all things are not expedient: all things are lawful for me, but I will not be brought under the power of any."

The *second* outstanding teaching in our Corinthian passage concerns the formation of the body of Christ. *ALL born again believers* are baptized into the body of Christ. They cease to be merely a group of individuals brought together and bound by a common bond of love, fellowship, worship, and interest. They are much more than that. True believers are baptized with the Holy Spirit *and united into ONE BODY.*

The Holy Spirit always uses illustrations that we can grasp and understand. Here He uses the human body as a figure of the New Testament Church, which is *the body of Christ.* The human body is not an "organization"; it is an *organism* with many members—hands, feet, eyes, ears. The same is true of the Church of the living God. The *Church* is not an organization, but *a living organism* made up of born again, blood-washed believers. In the human body, every member is *alive,* every member *functions,* every member is *needed*—and the same is true in the Church. Jesus is the head; the head governs the body—and believers are *members* of His body, bone of His bone, flesh of His flesh (Eph. 5:30).

I insist that in the book of Acts *no ONE person alone* is ever said to have been baptized with the Holy Ghost, nor is *an individual* ever invited to *seek* the baptism of the Holy Ghost. *Always* we find a *group* baptized. On the Day of Pentecost, the group was composed of Jews; not a Gentile was present. At another time, all were Samaritans. And in the house of Cornelius all were

Gentiles. In Acts 19:1—7 the disciples of John the Baptist were baptized with the Holy Spirit, and this also was a *group*—twelve men. In every instance these were groups, never an individual alone.

Baptism or Filling?

We do not find the word *"baptize"* in this second chapter of Acts, but we do find a detailed account of *the fulfillment of the promise of Jesus* to His disciples: *"Ye shall be baptized* with the Holy Ghost not many days hence"* (Acts 1:5). But even though the actual words "baptize" and "baptism" are not found in this second chapter, the occurrence described is, beyond any shadow of doubt, the fulfillment of that which Jesus promised.

There are those today who confuse the *baptism* of the Holy Ghost with the *filling* of the Holy Ghost. In Ephesians 5:18 Paul admonishes, *"Be not drunk with wine,* wherein is excess; but *BE FILLED with the Spirit."* According to this verse, if it is a sin to be drunk with wine, it is also a sin *NOT to be filled* with the Spirit; but the *filling* of the Spirit is altogether different from the *baptism* of the Spirit, as we will learn a little later in this series. We are *commanded* to be *filled,* but there is no place in the New Testament which commands present-day believers to wait for the baptism of the Spirit, as Jesus told the disciples to do. The very second one believes on the Lord Jesus Christ and trusts in His shed blood for salvation, that person is *born* of the Spirit (John 3:3,5,7), *indwelt* by the Spirit (Rom. 8:9,14,16), *baptized* in the Spirit (I Cor. 12:12,13), *sealed* by the Spirit (Eph. 4:30)—and if one is obedient and completely yielded to Jesus he is *filled* with the Spirit (Eph. 5:18).

Thousands today seek a mighty baptism of the Holy Ghost with outward evidence (such as speaking in tongues) in order to receive power to perform great miracles or other remarkable service. But we have already learned that the *disciples* performed great miracles *before* the coming of the Holy Ghost.

Jesus said, "If ye have *faith* as a grain of mustard seed . . . nothing shall be impossible unto you" (Matt. 17:20).   We are *saved* by grace through faith; we *overcome* by faith; we *live* by faith; *and whatsoever is NOT of faith is sin!*   But not many ministers today invite people to pray for *more faith.*   Faith comes by hearing, and hearing by the Word of God (Rom. 10:17).   One reason so many church people have so little faith today is because they hear so little *Gospel* — and the average church member rarely — if ever — takes time to study the Bible.   What church folk know about the Bible today is what they hear from the pulpit in Sunday services and at an occasional Wednesday night prayermeeting.

I readily admit that there are outstanding ministries today where extraordinary things are accomplished, but this does not necessarily signify a life of real communion with God or complete love to the Lord Jesus Christ.   According to Numbers 24:2, *Balaam* was controlled by the Spirit of God.   The Lord put words in his mouth and he was forced to utter wonderful things — but he was a vile, evil man, a lover of gain — and in Jude 11 we read, "Woe unto them! for they have gone in the way of Cain, *AND RAN GREEDILY AFTER THE ERROR OF BALAAM FOR REWARD,* and perished in the gainsaying of Core."   Then in Revelation 2:14, in the message to the church in Pergamos, we read, "I have a few things against thee, because thou hast there them that hold the doctrine of Balaam, *who taught Balac to cast a stumblingblock* before the children of Israel, to eat things sacrificed unto idols, and to commit fornication."   Thus we see that Balaam was not only corrupt, he also corrupted others.

Saul, king of Israel, was a man possessed on one occasion by the mighty power of the Spirit of God.   (Read I Samuel 10:6—10.)   Saul was "turned into another man"

—he was changed from a poor, insignificant, country youth into a kingly man who sat on the throne with dignity. He who had been a clumsy country boy, opened his mouth and *prophesied.* As King of Israel, Saul performed deeds just as outstanding as some men perform today—but he continued going further and further from God until the Lord repented having made him king over Israel (I Sam. 15:35), and in the end Saul died by his own hand (I Sam. 31:4).

Comparing spiritual things with spiritual as we have been doing, I declare on the basis of the Scripture that according to the examples of Balaam, Saul, and others which we have not the time and space to name here, *possession of power to perform signs and wonders is no proof of holiness or real dedication to God, nor real surrender to the will of God.*

The question may be asked, "Why did God allow tongues at Pentecost, and in Samaria, in the house of Cornelius, and in the case of the twelve disciples of John the Baptist? Why did *they* speak with tongues, and why did God work special miracles by the hands of the *apostles?*" These mighty signs and wonders were sent by God "according to His own will" (Heb. 2:4), and they continued through most of the lifetime of the apostles. They occurred during the transition period, and ushered in a new dispensation, a new era.

The same was true when God called Israel as His chosen nation. Israel's birth as a nation and the deliverance of that nation from Gentile tyranny were marked by great signs and wonders:

"He sent Moses His servant; and Aaron whom He had chosen. They shewed His signs among them, and wonders in the land of Ham. He sent darkness, and made it dark; and they rebelled not against His word. He turned their waters into blood, and slew their fish. Their land brought forth frogs in abundance, in the chambers of their kings. He spake, and there came divers sorts of

flies, and lice in all their coasts. He gave them hail for
rain, and flaming fire in their land. He smote their vines
also and their fig trees; and brake the trees of their
coasts. He spake, and the locusts came, and caterpillars,
and that without number, and did eat up all the herbs
in their land, and devoured the fruit of their ground. He
smote also all the firstborn in their land, the chief of all
their strength. He brought them forth also with silver
and gold: and there was not one feeble person among
their tribes. Egypt was glad when they departed: for the
fear of them fell upon them.

"He spread a cloud for a covering; and fire to give
light in the night. The people asked, and He brought
quails, and satisfied them with the bread of heaven. He
opened the rock, and the waters gushed out; they ran in
the dry places like a river. For He remembered His holy
promise, and Abraham His servant. And He brought
forth His people with joy, and His chosen with gladness"
(Psalm 105:26—43).

In the future, when this Dispensation of Grace comes
to a close and the Millennium begins, there will again
be mighty signs and wonders. The beginning of the Millennium will be marked by a great outpouring of the
Holy Ghost, accompanied by miraculous signs and marvelous wonders:

"And it shall come to pass afterward, that I will pour
out my Spirit upon all flesh; and your sons and your
daughters shall prophesy, your old men shall dream
dreams, your young men shall see visions: And also upon
the servants and upon the handmaids in those days will
I pour out my Spirit. And I will shew wonders in the
heavens and in the earth, blood, and fire, and pillars of
smoke. The sun shall be turned into darkness, and the
moon into blood, before the great and the terrible day
of the Lord come" (Joel 2:28—31).

We will be dealing with the transition period throughout the book of Acts—especially in the first twelve chap-

ters.   That period was marked by outstanding miracles
and wonders (speaking with tongues and many other
signs) which confirmed the message of the apostles.   In
Hebrews 2:3,4 Paul speaks of our "great salvation, which
at the first began to be spoken by the Lord, and was
confirmed unto us by them that heard Him; *God also
bearing them witness, both with signs and wonders, and
with divers miracles, and gifts of the Holy Ghost,* according to His own will."

God sent the signs to prove to unbelievers that He had
sent the apostles, and that they were preaching *His Word.*
Since they did not have the Gospels or the Epistles (the
perfect law of liberty had not yet come) "signs and wonders" were given to confirm the message and to declare
that these men were appointed and anointed of God for
those days.   But nowhere in the instructions to the New
Testament Church are we told to seek the baptism of
the Holy Ghost.

We are, however, told to *"be FILLED with the Spirit"*
(Eph. 5:18), and the *evidences* of a Spirit-filled life are
clearly spelled out in verses 19 through 21 of that same
chapter in Ephesians: "Speaking to yourselves in psalms
and hymns and spiritual songs, singing and making melody in your heart to the Lord; giving thanks always for
all things unto God and the Father in the name of our
Lord Jesus Christ; submitting yourselves one to another
in the fear of God."

When the one hundred and twenty believers in the
upper room were filled with the Holy Ghost at Pentecost,
they spoke *"AS THE SPIRIT GAVE THEM UTTER-
ANCE."*   As the Holy Spirit filled each of them, He
gave them power to speak, and the *words* they should
speak.   It is noteworthy that no one spoke in an "unknown" tongue on the Day of Pentecost. The "unknown"
tongue was born in the church at *Corinth.*   At *Pentecost,*
each person spoke a language that was understood perfectly by *someone* who was hearing the message that

day—and Pentecost used no interpreters! Interpretations were unnecessary because they spoke languages of those who were present from other nations, languages named in verses 9 through 11 of this chapter.

It was prophesied in Isaiah 28:11 that such a miracle would occur in the times of the Messiah, and in Mark 16:17 *Jesus Himself* said that these men would speak with tongues: "These signs shall follow them that believe: In my name shall they cast out devils; *they shall speak with new tongues.*"

Nothing could have happened on the Day of Pentecost that could have stirred the people so miraculously and thoroughly as the power of conveying their message in all the languages of the earth. Those who carry the Gospel to other lands today must overcome the language barrier by highly specialized study and months of untiring labor, because *the gift* of this miracle has been withdrawn. We are commanded to carry this good news to every nation and individual, and I believe if God gave the gift of languages to *anyone* today, it would surely be to missionaries who are willing to leave the comforts of home and the fellowship of loved ones and friends, to face the dangers and uncertainties of foreign fields, to labor under adverse conditions, suffering deprivations and hardships, giving their lives to preach the Gospel in the far corners of the earth. Yes, if *anyone* could receive a gift such as the apostles received on the Day of Pentecost, it would undoubtedly be the dedicated missionaries. But no such gift is given them. They must spend from four to six years in college before going to the field, and then struggle for months to become proficient enough in the native language to deliver one simple Gospel message.

It is true that there were some in the Corinthian church who truly possessed the gift of speaking *other languages* (NOT an "unknown tongue"). In I Corinthians 12:10,11 we read, "To another the working of miracles; to another prophecy; to another discerning of spirits; to another *divers kinds of tongues;* to another the *interpretation* of tongues: but all these worketh that one and the selfsame Spirit, dividing to every man severally as He will." Then in verse 28 of that same chapter we read, "God hath set some in the church, first apostles, secondarily prophets, thirdly teachers, after that miracles, then gifts of healings, helps, governments, *diversities of tongues.*"

The fact that the men at Pentecost spoke every language under heaven at that time is within itself a tremendous miracle. In Genesis chapter 11 we learn that the corruption of language was because of sin. At the time Nimrod attempted to build a tower to heaven, the whole world was of *one language!* But the people said, "Let us build . . . a tower, whose top may reach unto heaven . . . And the Lord came down to see . . . the tower, which the children of men builded. And the Lord said, Behold, the people is one, and they have all *one language;* and this they begin to do: *and now nothing will be restrained from them, which they have imagined to do. Go to, let us go down, and there confound their language, that they may not understand one another's speech.* So the Lord scattered them abroad from thence upon the face of all the earth..." (Gen. 11:1−9 in part).

There are hundreds upon hundreds of dialects and languages on earth today. What a conglomeration of tongues we have! But Pentecost and the fact that God gave one hundred and twenty men the ability to preach the Gospel in every tongue on earth at that time, proved that His power can overcome all evil. The Jews who spoke so many languages that day were clearly understood by all who heard them speak.

Verse 5: *"And there were dwelling at Jerusalem Jews, devout men, out of every nation under heaven."*

The Greek word translated *"dwelling"* means to have

a fixed and permanent residence or habitation. In addition to the visitors, there were Jews in Jerusalem at that time who had taken up permanent dwelling there, having come from all over the known world. Some Bible authorities believe that many wealthy, devout Jews from other parts of the world had purchased residences in Jerusalem near the temple, for to a Jew it was a thing much to be desired that he might die and be buried near the Holy City.

The Holy Spirit points out that these people were *"JEWS"* (signifying that they were of Jewish descent or birth) and that they were Jewish in their religion—they were *"devout* men." The Greek word means "discreet or cautious." Luke used the same word in Luke 2:25, and it is also used in Acts 8:2, in each instance meaning "good, or godly men." According to Webster, the word "devout" means "yielding a solemn and reverential attention to God in religious exercises, particularly in prayer." The meaning in our present verse is simply that these men lived circumspect lives, they lived in a prudent manner. They were *deeply religious* people, extremely cautious concerning the keeping of the commandments, afraid of offending their God.

These "devout men," these Jews, were *"out of every nation under heaven"*—that is, they were from all parts of the known world at that time. The countries from which they came are named in verses 9 through 11 of this chapter. The Jews were scattered almost to the four corners of the earth (as it was then known), but on special occasions they traveled to the Holy City to attend various feasts and ceremonies.

At that particular time there would be an unusually great number of Jews in Jerusalem, because most of those who came to observe the feast of the Passover would remain to attend the feast of Pentecost. History tells us that Titus the Roman besieged the city at about the time of the feast of the Passover, and at that time there were approximately three million Jews there.   Josephus the historian, in his book on Jewish Wars, mentions an instance in which great multitudes of Jews from other nations were present at the feast of Pentecost.

Verse 6:   *"Now when this was noised abroad, the multitude came together, and were confounded, because that every man heard them speak in his own language."*

"When this was noised abroad . . . ."   Naturally the news of such a miracle traveled rapidly, spreading across the city and into the surrounding communities.

"The multitude came together, and were confounded." The Greek word used here means "confused."   The same word is used in Acts 21:27, where the Jews *"stirred up all the people."*   It is also used in Acts 9:22 in speaking of Paul's preaching of the Gospel: "But Saul increased the more in strength, and *confounded the Jews* which dwelt at Damascus, proving that this is very Christ." The same word is sometimes used with reference to people who were utterly *amazed,* and I think that is its real meaning here in verse 6.   When the news spread abroad that the one hundred and twenty Jews in the upper room had been empowered to speak with other tongues and were speaking many languages, a miracle of such magnitude would naturally cause much confusion, amazement, and perplexity among those who did not understand the power of God—and certainly it could not be accounted for from the standpoint of human reason.

"Every man heard them speak in his own language." This was what so perplexed and amazed the people. Great revival under the power of God has always amazed the masses.   When revival breaks it will be "noised abroad," and multitudes will come to see what is taking place.   God often uses this to bring great crowds together in order to get the Gospel message to them.   Such gatherings took place in the days of Billy Sunday, Charles Spurgeon, Dwight L. Moody, and other great men of God.

I do not doubt that there were many curiosity seekers on the Day of Pentecost; that was probably the reason for the multitudes coming together—but many *sincere* persons were there, too, and the same is true today. Many people who attend mass religious meetings just out of curiosity *hear the Gospel* and are born again. To be exposed to the Word of God is to be exposed to the *power* of God that brings salvation. The Gospel has not lost its power; it will still reach hearts and open them to the message of the cross of Jesus.

On the Day of Pentecost, the one hundred and twenty people in the upper room were all baptized into one body, the cloven tongues sat upon *each* of them, and by a powerful and sudden inspiration of the Holy Spirit (poured out upon them by God the Eternal Father) each of them spoke with other languages. They uttered words not of their own minds—perhaps not even of their own *understanding*—as each of them became the mouthpiece of the Holy Spirit and praised God in languages which up to that time he had not known and had never spoken! It is possible that these Galilaeans did not realize what they were saying, but *those who heard them understood.*

Thus was it made known that the good news of the Gospel of the grace of God, purchased through the death, burial, and resurrection of Jesus Christ, would be preached to all nations under heaven, to the uttermost parts of the earth; and even though no Gentiles *spoke* at Pentecost, every Gentile present there heard the Gospel in his own language, spoken by Jews under the power of the Holy Spirit.

I am sure many have asked, "What did these disciples *say* when they spoke in other languages? What was the message they proclaimed?" The Scripture does not give us the words spoken by the one hundred and twenty that day, but since *Peter's* message which *followed* that experience brought three thousand souls to Jesus, it seems to me that *whatever* was said when the entire group began to speak with other tongues, their words brought deep conviction to the hearts of those who listened sincerely with an open heart and mind. Peter's message then drew in the net.

Of one thing we can be sure: Whatever message was given in the various languages at Pentecost, all was done "decently and in order" (I Cor. 14:40). There was no confusion. The gift of the Holy Spirit bestowed upon those in the upper room that day did not create a Gospel service filled with disorder and confusion. Wherever the Holy Ghost is in charge, things are done in decency and order. This is not true today in some of the modern "miracle meetings," so-called.

There is no scriptural record where such an outpouring of the Spirit ever occurred again with so great a crowd present. If the one hundred and twenty continued to preach and teach in tongues, it is not recorded in Acts nor in any of the epistles.

Acts records four instances where groups received the baptism of the Holy Spirit, but only three of the groups spoke with tongues:

The first of these was at Pentecost, where all were Jews and all spoke with other tongues (other languages). The gift of tongues here was a sign of the keeping of God's promise to send the Spirit, and also a sign to the multitude gathered there.

Acts chapter 8 records the ministry of Philip in Samaria, and the receiving of the Holy Ghost by the Samaritans when Peter and John laid their hands on them, but no mention is made of the gift of tongues.

In the tenth chapter of Acts, the Holy Ghost fell on the household of Cornelius when Peter preached the Gospel to them, and they spoke with tongues, which gave evidence to Peter and the other Jewish apostles that the Gentiles had received the Holy Spirit, the same as they. In Acts 11:15 Peter said of those in the house of Cornelius, "As I began to speak, the Holy Ghost fell on them, *as on us at the beginning."*

Then in chapter 19, the disciples of John received the baptism of the Holy Spirit "and they spake with tongues, and prophesied" (v. 6). But in *none* of these instances were the groups *seeking* the gift of tongues, nor were they *instructed* to do so.

The apostles visited many cities and preached the Word of God in many places, but the Scripture records not one word about anyone speaking with other tongues. *Philip* was a great evangelist; but when he led the Ethiopian eunuch to salvation nothing was said about the gift of tongues (Acts 8:26—39). Lydia was converted under *Paul's* preaching, but he did not instruct her concerning the baptism of the Spirit or the gift of tongues (Acts 16:14,15). *Paul and Silas* led the Philippian jailer and all his household to salvation, but they made no mention of tongues, no mention of the baptism of the Spirit (Acts 16:25—34). Yet there are many today who teach and preach that to be born of the Spirit, washed in the blood, and saved by grace one must seek the baptism of the Holy Ghost evidenced by speaking with other tongues. I ask in all sincerity, *If such should be taught, then why did not Philip so instruct the Ethiopian eunuch? and why did Paul not give such instruction to the Philippian jailer and to many others who were converted under his ministry?*

There are many ministers today—not only in the Pentecostal movements but in other denominational groups as well—who declare that each believer is to seek his own Pentecost, with the mighty baptism of the Spirit evidenced by speaking in tongues. On the basis of the Word of God I declare that such teaching is unscriptural! The book of Acts gives record of thousands being saved; but not one word is said of their speaking with other tongues or tarrying for the baptism of the Spirit. We are told that *Stephen* was a man of faith, *full of the Spirit,* full of wisdom, a powerful man of God; but there is no suggestion that he ever spoke one word in a language other than his own, or that he ever sought the baptism of the Holy Spirit as it is taught today.

What About I Corinthians Chapter 14?

It is true that the entire fourteenth chapter of I Corinthians is given over to the discussion of *tongues*, but if you will compare that chapter with our present study you will discover that there is *no resemblance* between the tongues in Acts 2 and the tongues in I Corinthians 14. Even in I Corinthians chapter 12, where the gifts of the Spirit are named, the gift of tongues is at the end of the list (and must be accompanied by *interpretation*), indicating its inferior place in spiritual gifts.

The Apostle Paul penned the letters to the Corinthian church, and it was also Paul whom God used to organize the church at *Ephesus*. But there was a vast difference in the two churches:

Concerning the church at Ephesus we read where Paul called the elders together and said to them, "Ye know, from the first day that I came into Asia, after what manner I have been with you at all seasons, serving the Lord with all humility of mind, and with many tears, and temptations, which befell me by the lying in wait of the Jews: *And how I KEPT BACK NOTHING THAT WAS PROFITABLE UNTO YOU,* but have shewed you, and have taught you publickly, and from house to house, testifying both to the Jews, and also to the Greeks, *repentance toward God, and faith toward our Lord Jesus Christ. . . FOR I HAVE NOT SHUNNED TO DECLARE UNTO YOU ALL THE COUNSEL OF GOD"* (Acts 20:17—27 in part).

Now according to this portion of God's infallible Word, Paul preached *everything that was profitable* to the Ephesians, he declared *ALL the counsel of God;* and yet when we read every word in *the entire book* of Ephesians we find absolutely no mention of tongues or new languages!

He *did* say, ". . . speaking to yourselves in psalms and hymns and spiritual songs, singing and making melody in your heart to the Lord" (Eph. 5:19), which things are evidence of a Spirit-filled life.

In the *Corinthian* church, however, Paul had much to say about tongues. The Corinthian Christians were carnal, divided, sectarian. They sought vainglory, their spiritual understanding and knowledge were very limited. He plainly told them that he had found it necessary to feed them with *milk* rather than with *meat* because of their lack of spiritual growth (I Cor. 3:1—3).

The book of Ephesians contains only six chapters and was written to Spirit-filled believers. Paul's first epistle to the Corinthian church contains *sixteen* chapters, and the greater part of the entire book is given over to correcting the evil practices and carnal walk of the Corinthian church!

On the Day of Pentecost, the one hundred and twenty people in the upper room were not *seeking* the mighty baptism of the Holy Spirit or the gift of tongues. They were *waiting,* as Jesus had instructed them to do, until they should be endued with power from on high.

The *Samaritans* were not seeking the Holy Ghost or the gift of tongues. Philip preached the Word, they received the Word, and the mighty baptism of the Spirit was poured out upon them.

The Gentiles in the house of *Cornelius* were not seeking the baptism of the Holy Spirit or the gift of tongues. Cornelius sent for Peter that he might hear *words of salvation,* and when he heard and believed the words of salvation, the Holy Ghost fell upon all his household.

The disciples of John were not seeking the baptism of the Holy Ghost, they were not seeking Pentecost. They had gone as far as they *could* go with the light and limited understanding they had, and when Paul heard about these sincere seekers of truth he simply went to them and asked them if they had received the Holy Ghost.

They replied, "We have not so much as heard whether there *be* any Holy Ghost." Paul then asked them, "Unto what then were ye baptized?" They replied, "Unto John's baptism." Paul then told them, "John verily baptized with the baptism of repentance, saying unto the people, that they should believe on Him which should come after him, that is, on Christ Jesus." When they heard this, they were baptized in the name of the Lord Jesus, and then when Paul laid his hands upon them, "the Holy Ghost came on them; and they spake with tongues, and prophesied." (Read the account in Acts 19:1—7.)

If you will study I Corinthians you will find that the believers there were seeking the gift of the *"unknown"* tongue—and a careful reading of chapter 14 will reveal that the *women* in the church were in the foreground. Paul reprimanded them:

"Let your women keep silence in the churches: for it is not permitted unto them to speak; but they are commanded to be under obedience, as also saith the law. And if they will learn any thing, let them ask their husbands at home: for it is a shame for women to speak in the church" (I Cor. 14:34,35).

I believe my readers will agree that in our modern "tongues" movements, the women are definitely in the foreground, making more show and more noise than the men do in services where tongues are practiced. Yet the Scripture plainly tells us that man is head of the woman *as CHRIST is head of the CHURCH* (Eph. 5:23,24).

In the early days of my ministry, in sincerity and for my own information I attended meetings where people sought the gift of tongues. I saw women become hysterical, fall on the floor, utter all kinds of queer noises, and then cry out, "O God, send the power! Send the Holy Ghost!" We know God *did* send the power, He *did* pour out the Holy Ghost on the Day of Pentecost—but there was no such hysterical, uncontrolled emotional behaviour in the Pentecostal miracle, or in any other place in the book of Acts where an account is given of the baptism of the Holy Spirit—"for God is not the author of confusion, but of peace, as in all churches of the saints" (I Cor. 14:33). The Greek word translated "confusion" literally means *tumult.*

According to the passage we are studying in I Corinthians 14, speaking in an "unknown" tongue is unintelligible to those who hear, and even if the tongue is *genuine,* only GOD knows what is being said and therefore the speaker does not edify the assembly:

"For he that speaketh in an unknown tongue speaketh not unto men, but unto God: for no man understandeth him; howbeit in the spirit he speaketh mysteries" (I Cor. 14:2).

In verses 1 and 3 of that same chapter we read, "Follow after charity (love), and *desire* spiritual gifts, but rather that ye may *prophesy.* . . He that prophesieth speaketh unto men to edification, and exhortation, and comfort."

Furthermore, tongues are strictly forbidden in the church if no interpreter is present:

"If any man speak in an unknown tongue, let it be by two, or at the most by three, and that by course; *and let one interpret. BUT IF THERE BE NO INTERPRETER, LET HIM KEEP SILENCE IN THE CHURCH; AND LET HIM SPEAK TO HIMSELF, AND TO GOD"* (I Cor. 14:27,28).

The gift of interpretation of tongues is mentioned in I Corinthians 12:10, and the only way the assembly could *benefit* from hearing someone speak in tongues would be for an interpreter to make known what was said. According to Ephesians 4:29 we are to speak "that which is good to the use of edifying, that it may minister grace unto the hearers." He who speaks with tongues without an interpreter speaks to no profit because nothing is revealed; therefore there is no knowledge imparted, no clear prophesying, no revelation of doctrine (I Cor. 14:6).

In the assembly we are to speak "words easy to be understood" (I Cor. 14:9), for Paul declares, "If I know not the meaning of the voice, I shall be unto him that speaketh a barbarian, and he that speaketh shall be a barbarian unto me. Even so ye, forasmuch as ye are zealous of spiritual gifts, seek that ye may excel *to the edifying of the church*" (I Cor. 14:11,12).

Paul suggests that speaking with tongues when no interpreter is present may even *damage* the cause of Christ instead of helping it:

"If therefore the whole church be come together into one place, and all speak with tongues, and there come in those that are unlearned, or unbelievers, *will they not say that ye are mad?*

"But if all *prophesy,* and there come in one that believeth not, or one unlearned, he is convinced of all, he is judged of all: and thus are the secrets of his heart made manifest; *and so falling down on his face HE WILL WORSHIP GOD, and report that God is in you of a truth*" (I Cor. 14:23—25).

There is no doubt in my mind that when Paul said, *"Let your women keep silence in the churches"* he was speaking specifically of the practice of speaking with tongues, because nowhere in Paul's writings do we find a suggestion that a woman is not to give her testimony, or pray, or worship with freedom as do the men of the congregation. I firmly believe he was speaking of the women "keeping silent" in the church as having to do with the unknown tongue.

Paul declared that he himself spoke with tongues more than any or all of the Corinthian believers, yet it is plain that he placed no high spiritual value on the gift of tongues, because he fervently declared, "In the church I had rather speak *five* words with my *understanding,* that by my voice I might teach others also, than *ten thousand* words in an unknown tongue!" Then in the next verse he described those who sought the gift of tongues as being childish in understanding: "Brethren, *be not children* in understanding: howbeit in malice be ye children, *but IN UNDERSTANDING BE MEN*" (I Cor. 14:18—20).

From our study in I Corinthians chapter 14 we clearly see that the practice of tongues does not serve to edify others. On the contrary, such practice has a tendency to cause disorder in the church, opening the door to dangerous confusion, entrance of evil spirits, and religious impostors who copy the *genuine* and thus cause division in the local church and hinder the cause of Christ.

Then in his *second* letter to the church at Corinth, Paul went a step further and acquainted the believers with the sad fact that the devil has ordained ministers who pass themselves off as ministers of righteousness:

"Such are false apostles, deceitful workers, transforming themselves into the apostles of Christ. And no marvel; for Satan himself is transformed into an angel of light. Therefore it is no great thing if his ministers also be transformed as the ministers of righteousness; whose end shall be according to their works" (II Cor. 11:13—15).

In John's first epistle, God's "little children" are warned against these apostate teachers and evil spirits: "Beloved, believe not every spirit, but try the spirits whether they are of God: because many false prophets are gone out into the world" (I John 4:1). There were many false teachers and false prophets in John's day and there are many more today. We must be careful which spirit we follow—whether the genuine, or the counterfeit.

We know that the true gift of tongues was given in the apostolic church, the first century of Christianity, and certainly I do not doubt God's ability to give the gift of languages *today,* that the Gospel might be preached in a foreign tongue; but I do *not* believe that the gift of tongues as it came upon the apostles on the Day of Pentecost was to abide in the Church up to this present time. I believe the Scripture indicates what I have just stated.

In I Corinthians 13:9,10 Paul said, "For we know in part, and we prophesy in part. *But when that which is perfect is come, then that which is in part shall be done away."* He was speaking here of "the perfect law of liberty"—the Word of God in its entirety; and we do have the completed Word of God now.

In Ephesians 4:7—16 Paul named the spiritual gifts which God gave the New Testament Church:

"Unto every one of us is given grace according to the measure of the gift of Christ. Wherefore He saith, When He ascended up on high, He led captivity captive, and gave gifts unto men. (Now that He ascended, what is it but that He also descended first into the lower parts of the earth?   He that descended is the same also that ascended up far above all heavens, that He might fill all things.)   And He gave some, apostles; and some, prophets; and some, evangelists; and some, pastors and teachers; for the perfecting of the saints, for the work of the ministry, for the edifying of the body of Christ: Till we all come in the unity of the faith, and of the knowledge of the Son of God, unto a perfect man, unto the measure of the stature of the fulness of Christ: That we henceforth be no more children, tossed to and fro, and carried about with every wind of doctrine, by the sleight of men, and cunning craftiness, whereby they lie in wait to deceive; but speaking the truth in love, may grow up into Him in all things, which is the head, even Christ: From whom the whole body fitly joined together and compacted by that which every joint supplieth, according to the effectual working in the measure of every part, maketh increase of the body unto the edifying of itself in love."

Notice, there is no mention of speaking in an unknown tongue. We are to speak the truth in love, be stable in our experience instead of being tossed about with every wind of doctrine.   It is plain that God gave the Church apostles, prophets, evangelists, pastors and teachers, but it is not said that He gave the church at Ephesus (or any church thereafter) those who had the gift of tongues or the gift of *interpretation* of tongues. Not one of the epistles teaches that the miraculous sign-gifts will continue until the Rapture of the Church. With this in mind, I admonish all believers to "give the more earnest heed to the things which we have heard, lest at any time we should let them slip. For if the word spoken by angels was stedfast, and every transgression and disobedience received a just recompence of reward; how shall we escape, if we neglect so great salvation; which at the first began to be spoken by the Lord, and was confirmed unto us by them that heard Him; God also bearing them witness, both with signs and wonders, and with divers miracles, and gifts of the Holy Ghost, according to His own will?" (Heb. 2:1–4).

During the transition period (the apostolic days), God did give special signs, divers miracles, and gifts of the Holy Ghost; but He did it *"according to His own will."* Through the apostles He also gave the perfect law of liberty, His Word, *complete,* the last writer being John the Beloved who, from the Isle of Patmos, penned The Revelation. We now have the Word of God, *"that which is perfect";* and we do not *need* signs or miracles such as were experienced on the Day of Pentecost and in the apostolic era.

Jesus promised to give the Holy Spirit to all who ask Him (Luke 11:13); therefore when a sincere seeker of truth asks the Lord Jesus to save his soul, to let the Holy Spirit come into his heart, *it is nothing less than an insult to God* to immediately demand a "sign" such as a feeling, a tongue, a bright light, or a clap of thunder. What God promises, God will *do*; and to refuse to *believe* Him is to offer insult to Him.

Some suggest that the wide-spread movement of "tongues" today is a sign that the Lord's coming is near.

They say that just before His coming the gift of tongues and other signs will be seen again in the churches; but according to the teaching of the Scriptures, this is error. God's Word declares that "evil men and seducers shall wax worse and worse, deceiving, and being deceived" (II Tim. 3:13). If you will study verses 1 through 13 of this chapter in II Timothy you will see that in the last days there will *not* be a tendency for world conditions to get better. The Church will *not* become more powerful. The opposite will be true: evil will become more and more rampant and the visible church will become lukewarm. The darkest days this world will ever know this side of the Great Tribulation period will be the days just preceding the Rapture. Every book in the New Testament teaches that there will be a spiritual decline and apostasy, rather than the restoration of apostolic power and spiritual gifts.

Verses 7 and 8: *"And they were all amazed and marvelled, saying one to another, Behold, are not all these which speak Galilaeans? And how hear we every man in our own tongue, wherein we were born?"*

The apostles—who were undoubtedly quite prominent in this group in the upper room—had been known as *Galilaeans* before Jesus was crucified. (Read Matthew 26:69—73 and Luke 22:59.) The Galilaeans were ignorant, rude people (John 1:46). The dialect of people from Galilee was somewhat corrupt, as we see from the statement about Peter in Mark 14:70: "And a little after, they that stood by said again to Peter, Surely thou art one of them: *for thou art a Galilaean, and thy SPEECH agreeth thereto!"* In John 7:52, when Nicodemus offered protest to the illegality of condemning Jesus without proper trial, the Pharisees said to him, "Art thou *also* of Galilee? Search, and look: *for out of Galilee ariseth no prophet!"*

Since the Galilaeans were thought of as rough, uncouth, ignorant people by other nations, it is not surpris-

ing that the people should be amazed when they heard
these uneducated men speaking many languages and
praising God in words understandable to all other nationalities represented there.

The miracle at Pentecost bears out the teaching of
I Corinthians 1:26—31:

"For ye see your calling, brethren, how that *not many
wise men after the flesh, not many mighty, not many
noble, are called: But God hath chosen the foolish things
of the world to confound the wise; and God hath chosen
the weak things of the world to confound the things
which are mighty;* and base things of the world, and
things which are despised, hath God chosen, yea, and
things which are not, to bring to nought things that are:
that no flesh should glory in His presence. But of Him
are ye in Christ Jesus, who of God is made unto us wisdom, and righteousness, and sanctification, and redemption: That, according as it is written, *HE THAT GLORI-
ETH, LET HIM GLORY IN THE LORD!"*

In II Corinthians 4:7 Paul wrote, *"But we have this
treasure in earthen vessels, THAT THE EXCELLENCY
OF THE POWER MAY BE OF GOD, and not of us!"*

*"How hear we every man in our own tongue, wherein
we were born?"* This certainly does not describe a conglomeration of incoherent speech! The languages spoken
by those in the upper room were languages to which
these visitors had been born, languages they had spoken
from their youth, in their own nations.

I maintain that those who claim to have the Pentecostal baptism *today* should act and talk as the people
did on the Day of Pentecost! Let's not claim a Pentecostal experience *unless we claim it ALL!* Let's not
claim *tongues*—and leave out the sound "as of a rushing
mighty wind," filling the whole church, room, tent, or
auditorium where the people sit. Let's not leave out the
"cloven tongues like as of fire" that sat upon each one
who received the mighty baptism and infilling, and

tongues spoken in order and clearly understood by all
who hear! Yes, those who claim Pentecostal experience
should testify to *all* of it, not just to the experience of
"tongues."

Verses 9—11: *"Parthians, and Medes, and Elamites,
and the dwellers in Mesopotamia, and in Judaea, and
Cappadocia, in Pontus, and Asia, Phrygia, and Pamphylia, in Egypt, and in the parts of Libya about Cyrene,
and strangers of Rome, Jews and proselytes, Cretes and
Arabians, we do hear them speak in our tongues the
wonderful works of God."*

The *Parthians* occupied the country south of the Caspian Sea, from which they were separated by Hyrcania.
In the apostolic days they occupied the land from India
to the Tigris river, and they were very famous among
other nations at that time—which is probably the reason
they are named ahead of other nationalities here.

The country of the *Medes* lay east of Assyria, north-
west of Persia, and south and southwest of the Caspian
Sea.   In the Old Testament Scriptures these people are
often mentioned in connection with the Persians.

The land of the *Elamites* lay at the north of the Persian Gulf, was bounded on the west by the Tigris river,
and touched Media on the north and Persia on the south
and east.   These were Semitic people, perhaps taking
their name from Elam, son of Shem (Gen. 10:22).   *Shu-
shan* in the province of Elam is mentioned in Daniel 8:2.

Mesopotamia was the country between the Euphrates
and Tigris rivers.

The *Judaeans,* of course, were Jews from the neighboring towns around Jerusalem.

There were people from Cappadocia, Pontus, Asia,
Phrygia, and Pamphylia—all countries within Asia Minor.
When we read of Asia—in this present verse and else-
where in Acts—it means the Roman province known as
proconsular Asia, which made up all the western coast of

Asia Minor and embraced such countries as Mysia, Lycia, and Caria. Its capital was Ephesus, and in this district were the seven churches mentioned in Revelation.

Egyptians were there. A great number of Jews lived in Egypt at that time, especially in the city of Alexandria.

Libya was the name applied to the African continent at the time of Pentecost. It lay east of the Syrtis Major and contained five chief cities, of which Cyrene was the best known. Matthew 27:32 tells us that it was Simon, *a man of Cyrene,* who was compelled to carry the cross of Jesus when He was led out to Golgotha to be crucified. *Josephus* tells us that during the time of the dispersion of the Jews, many thousands of them moved into Egypt and parts of Libya about Cyrene.

"Strangers of Rome, Jews and proselytes" means *sojourners* from Rome, *including* both Jews and proselytes. We learn from historians and Latin writers that there were many Jews living in Rome at that time. It is most likely that converts from among the Romans were founders of the church of which we read in Acts 28:14,15, for the church in Rome was already flourishing when Paul first went to that city. *"Proselytes"* comes from a Greek word meaning "one who has come over." The general meaning of "proselyte" in the New Testament is one who has been converted from heathenism to the religion of the Jews—Judaism.

The *Cretes* lived in the well-known island of Crete, which lies south of the Cyclades in the Mediterranean Sea. The same place is now called Candia. It is possible that Christianity spread to Crete from converts on the Day of Pentecost when Peter preached. We do know that *Titus* was left in charge of the church in Crete by the Apostle Paul: "For this cause left I thee in Crete, that thou shouldest set in order the things that are wanting, and ordain elders in every city, as I had appointed thee" (Titus 1:5).

Arabians were the inhabitants of the great peninsula

which stretches between the Red Sea and the Persian Gulf.

There are at least sixteen different groups named here, indicating an equal number of different dialects or variations of speech; yet each of these people heard the Gospel in his own native tongue, spoken by the Jews under the power of the Holy Spirit.

Verse 12: *"And they were all amazed, and were in doubt, saying one to another, What meaneth this?"*

The original language in this verse indicates *anxiety*, hesitancy, as of one traveling but not knowing exactly which way to go or which path to follow. These people were perplexed, filled with anxiety. They were *astonished* at what they saw and heard, they did not understand or know how to explain what was going on.

Verse 13: *"Others mocking said, These men are full of new wine."*

The Greek word translated *"mocking"* means "to deride, jeer, scoff," and the only other time it is used in the New Testament is in Acts 17:32: "And when they heard of the resurrection of the dead, *some mocked*: and others said, We will hear thee again of this matter."

Men have *always* mocked when the power of God brings great revival. Even though the majority of the community may believe in the power of God and acknowledge revival to be genuine, there are always a few who will mock—or "deride." But God promises that one day He will laugh at the calamity of such people:

"How long, ye simple ones, will ye love simplicity? and the scorners delight in their scorning, and fools hate knowledge? Turn you at my reproof: behold, I will pour out my spirit unto you, I will make known my words unto you.

"Because I have called, and ye refused; I have stretched out my hand, and no man regarded; but ye have set at nought all my counsel, and would none of my reproof: *I also will laugh at your calamity; I WILL MOCK WHEN YOUR FEAR COMETH;* when your fear cometh as desolation, and your destruction cometh as a whirlwind; when distress and anguish cometh upon you. Then shall they call upon me, *but I will not answer;* they shall seek me early, *but they shall not find me: FOR THAT THEY HATED KNOWLEDGE, AND DID NOT CHOOSE THE FEAR OF THE LORD"* (Prov. 1:22—29).

Yes, a minority has always mocked God and the *power* of God—and that minority will always be with us. On the Day of Pentecost when the disciples and others spoke with tongues and magnified God, the *majority* of the people who heard them believed that a great miracle had taken place; but there were some skeptics who claimed, *"These men are full of new wine!"* In other words, "These men are *drunk."*

"New wine" literally reads *"sweet* wine," wine which was made of the juice-drippings from clusters of grapes before they were completely crushed and distilled. Sweet wine is mentioned in the Old Testament (Isa. 49:26; Amos 9:13). There could have *been* no *new* wine at Pentecost because *August* was the time for gathering grapes, and Pentecost occured only fifty days after the resurrection. Therefore no grapes could possibly have been ready to be gathered and turned into wine at that time of year.

Peter's Sermon on the Day of Pentecost

Verse 14:   *"But Peter, standing up with the eleven, lifted up his voice, and said unto them, Ye men of Judaea, and all ye that dwell at Jerusalem, be this known unto you, and hearken to my words."*

We know the Holy Spirit gave Peter the message he delivered that day, the theme of which is clearly stated in verse 36:

"Therefore let all the house of Israel know assuredly,
THAT GOD HATH MADE THAT SAME JESUS, WHOM
YE HAVE CRUCIFIED, BOTH LORD AND CHRIST!"

It is interesting that Peter did not *announce* his theme
until he had thoroughly covered every possible Jewish
objection and had given the truth concerning the coming
of Messiah—first as *Saviour,* later as King of kings and
Lord of lords.   He could not have delivered a message
that would have been more unwelcome to his audience!
The Jews had rejected their Messiah.   They had chosen
Barabbas and demanded that Jesus be crucified.   They
were looking for and expecting a powerful King who
would deliver them from the rule of Rome, and they
failed to understand why Jesus came in humility and
meekness when their Old Testament Scriptures had prophesied of a Messiah who would gather Israel from every
nation under heaven and from the islands of the sea and
establish them in their own land, giving them a grand
and glorious kingdom.

There are those today who spiritualize the kingdom,
they spiritualize God's promises to Abraham and David;
but in his message on the Day of Pentecost—especially
in verses 25 through 32 of this chapter—Peter showed how
David understood that the Messiah would be crucified
and rise again; that He would eventually *fulfill* God's
covenant to Abraham and his seed; and that *as King He*
would sit on the throne of David and reign over the
house of Judah, as set forth in the Annunciation:

"He shall be great, and shall be called the Son of the
Highest: and the Lord God shall give unto Him the
throne of His father David: and He shall reign over the
house of Jacob for ever; and of His kingdom there shall
be no end" (Luke 1:32,33).

It was natural that Peter should be the one who came
forward and delivered the message at Pentecost. He was
bold, he was alert, he was zealous; and he rose to defend the name of Jesus and to defend the apostles from

the charge of drunkenness. The ridicule and criticism of the skeptics did not disturb him, for he saw in this crowd the glorious opportunity to deliver a message concerning the Christ. True, not long ago in the temple court, he had trembled before the accusation of a little maid and had denied his Lord; but he was of different character now, and with the courage of his Spirit-filled heart he could look the Jews in the face and declare that Jesus, whom they crucified, *GOD had raised and exalted,* making Him both Lord and Christ.

Peter stood up *"with the eleven... and said unto them, Ye men of Judaea, and all ye that dwell at Jerusalem . . . ."* Peter was addressing those who were Jews by birth, whether or not they were permanent residents of Judaea and Jerusalem. They were members of Jewish families, and the literal Greek here reads, "Men, *Jews."*

"Hearken to my words." Notice how carefully Peter selected his words. Under inspiration of the Holy Spirit he spoke respectfully, yet firmly. He was not *excited* as he had been on the night he had denied his Lord. He calmly but firmly set about to convince these men that they were in error and needed to *repent* of their sins and believe on the Lord Jesus Christ.

Later, in his first epistle, Peter wrote as the Holy Spirit directed, "Sanctify the Lord God in your hearts: and be ready always to give an answer to every man that asketh you a reason of the hope that is in you with meekness and fear: having a good conscience; that, whereas they speak evil of you, as of evildoers, they may be ashamed that falsely accuse your good conversation in Christ" (I Pet. 3:15,16).

Verse 15: *"For these are not drunken, as ye suppose, seeing it is but the third hour of the day."*

It was not reasonable to even *suppose* that the disciples were drunk since it was only *"the third hour of the day."* The Jews reckoned their day from sunrise to sunset, and the *third hour* would be nine o'clock in the morning as *we* reckon time. Undoubtedly then, as now, men who were guilty of drunkenness got drunk at night, for in I Thessalonians 5:7 we read, "They that sleep sleep in the night; *and they that be DRUNKEN are drunken in the night!*" (Some authorities say that wine was drunk by the Jews with *flesh only*—and, founding the custom on Exodus 16:8, they ate bread in the morning and *flesh* in the *evening*, and so took no wine till late in the day.)

Not only was this too early an hour for drunkenness, it was also the hour devoted to public worship; and even *before Pentecost* these men were devout Jews and they certainly would not have been intoxicated at the hour of worship! The religious Jews made a practice of not eating or drinking anything until *after* the third hour of the day, especially on the Sabbath and on all feast days. Bible history and antiquity tell us that *many* of them abstained from food and drink *until the noon hour.*

All Jews were considered to be "religious" from the standpoint of ritual and tradition; and though they might be very wicked in daily life, when the Sabbath and feast days came, they adhered strictly to the customs of their forefathers to the letter of the law. Knowing this, Peter appealed to them by pointing them to their own customs and religious practices, because these mockers knew that even a *careless* Jew would not drink wine before the third hour of the morning. One Jewish historian of that day tells us, "It was the custom of pious people in ancient times that each one should offer his morning prayers, with additions in the synagogue, and *then return home* to take refreshment."

Joel's Prophecy Fulfilled

Verse 16: *"But this is that which was spoken by the prophet Joel."*

Here Peter presented the *second* part of his argument

of proof that these men were not drunk. In a sense, he accused the Jews of ignorance concerning their own Scriptures; for if they had known prophecy as they should have known it, they would have recognized this as the fulfillment of the words of their own prophet Joel. The reference is to Joel 2:28—32:

"And it shall come to pass afterward, that I will pour out my Spirit upon all flesh; and your sons and your daughters shall prophesy, your old men shall dream dreams, your young men shall see visions: And also upon the servants and upon the handmaids in those days will I pour out my Spirit. And I will shew wonders in the heavens and in the earth, blood, and fire, and pillars of smoke. The sun shall be turned into darkness, and the moon into blood, before the great and the terrible day of the Lord come. And it shall come to pass, that whosoever shall call on the name of the Lord shall be delivered: for in Mount Zion and in Jerusalem shall be deliverance, as the Lord hath said, and in the remnant whom the Lord shall call."

Verse 17: *"And it shall come to pass in the last days, saith God, I will pour out of my Spirit upon all flesh: and your sons and your daughters shall prophesy, and your young men shall see visions, and your old men shall dream dreams."*

"It shall come to pass"—meaning "It shall happen (or occur)." The very things these men were witnessing had been declared by Joel as coming to pass *"in the last days"*—an expression used many times in the Old Testament. For example, in Genesis 49:1 Jacob gathered his sons together that he might instruct them concerning what should happen to them *"in the last days"*—that is, in the future that lay ahead of them. Isaiah 2:2 also speaks of *"the last days."*

To the Jew, the coming of the Messiah was the most important event in the coming ages, and *"the last days"* to the Jew was a statement that stood in contrast to the days of the patriarchs, kings, and prophets. The Jews did not think of the last days as *the end of the world;* they were looking for that glorious rule of their Messiah when there would be peace on earth and good will among men.   They were awaiting—and expecting—a powerful ruler to deliver them from their enemies and restore Israel to greater glory than they had ever known.

In the *true sense* of the word, we have been *living* in the "last days" since the coming of the Lord Jesus Christ. *These* are the last days, these days of God's marvelous grace. This is plainly stated in Hebrews 1:1,2:

"God, who at sundry times and in divers manners spake in time past unto the fathers by the prophets, *hath in these last days spoken unto us BY HIS SON,* whom He hath appointed Heir of all things, by whom also He made the worlds."

I Peter 1:20 testifies that Christ "verily was foreordained before the foundation of the world, *but was manifest IN THESE LAST TIMES" for us.*

II Peter 3:3 declares "that *there shall come IN THE LAST DAYS scoffers,* walking after their own lusts."

Jude 18 speaks of *"mockers IN THE LAST TIME,* who should walk after their own ungodly lusts"; and in I John 2:18 we read, "Little children, *IT IS THE LAST TIME:* and as ye have heard that antichrist shall come, even now are there many antichrists; *whereby we know that it is THE LAST TIME."*

We must always observe a distinction between "the last days" with reference to *Israel,* and "the last days" with reference to *the Church.* In addition to the passages already quoted, please study I Timothy 4:1—3, II Timothy 3:1—8, I Peter 1:3—5, II Peter 3:1—9.

We must also distinguish between "the last *days"* (plural), and "the last *day"* (singular). *"The last DAY"* refers to the final resurrection and the white throne judgment: "He that rejecteth me, and receiveth not my words, hath one that judgeth him: *the word that I have spoken, the same shall judge him IN THE LAST DAY"* (John 12:48).

"The last days" *for the Church* began when Jesus was born.   He came into the world to declare the Father (John 1:18). He came to lay His life down that we might have life (John 10:18). He came to pay the sin-debt, to die for the Church (Eph. 5:25—32).

We have been *living* in "the last days" for almost two thousand years.   Surely the Rapture of the Church is imminent.   Jesus could come at any second of any minute. *Are YOU ready* for His coming?

"I will pour out of my Spirit upon all flesh." This conveys the idea of communicating freely and abundantly, as water is poured from a fountain: "Not by works of righteousness which we have done, but according to His mercy He saved us, by the washing of regeneration, and renewing of *the Holy Ghost; which He shed on us ABUN-DANTLY through Jesus Christ our Saviour"* (Tit. 3:5,6).

In Job 36:27,28 we read, "He maketh small the drops of water: they pour down rain according to the vapour thereof: which the clouds do drop and distil upon man *abundantly."*

In Isaiah 44:3 we find the prophecy, "I will pour water upon him that is thirsty, and *floods* upon the dry ground: I will pour my *Spirit* upon thy seed, and *my blessing* upon thine offspring."

In Malachi 3:10, concerning the tithe and giving to God what rightfully belongs to Him, He promises, ". . . *Prove me now herewith, saith the Lord of hosts, if I will not open you the windows of heaven, and pour you out a blessing, THAT THERE SHALL NOT BE ROOM ENOUGH TO RECEIVE IT!"*

"I will pour out my *Spirit"* therefore signifies *abundance of blessing,* the immeasurable influence of the Holy Ghost's coming on the Day of Pentecost.

The Holy Spirit, third Person of the Holy Trinity, is

the source of all blessings which believers experience. He convicts us of sin, draws us to the Saviour, "borns" us into the family of God, indwells and enlightens us. He leads us, seals us, and produces Christian graces in our lives (John 3:5; 6:44; 16:7—9; Rom. 8:9,14,16; Gal. 5:22—25; Tit. 3:5—7; Eph. 4:30; I John 3:24; 4:13). The Holy Spirit is our teacher (I John 2:20,27).

That the Spirit would be poured out *"upon all flesh"* does not mean every *individual,* but *every class or rank* of men—i. e., the outpouring of the Holy Spirit was not to be limited to the *Jews.* In the Old Testament economy, Israel was the elect nation; and even in the days of the apostles, *Gentiles* were referred to as "dogs." But on the Day of Pentecost the Holy Ghost came into the world *to indwell the hearts of ALL who believe*—Jews or Gentiles, rich or poor, bond or free, wise or unwise, slave or master—*ALL persons* who believe on and receive the Lord Jesus Christ. That is why Paul exhorts believers to pray for all men:

"I exhort therefore, that, first of all, supplications, prayers, intercessions, and giving of thanks, be made for all men; for kings, and for all that are in authority; that we may lead a quiet and peaceable life in all godliness and honesty. For this is good and acceptable in the sight of God our Saviour; who will have all men to be saved, and to come unto the knowledge of the truth. For there is one God, and one Mediator between God and men, the Man Christ Jesus; *who gave Himself a ransom for ALL,* to be testified in due time" (I Tim. 2:1—6).

"And your sons and your daughters shall prophesy." Young men and young women shared in this remarkable blessing of the empowering of the Holy Spirit. In Acts 21:8,9 we learn that Philip the evangelist had four daughters who prophesied:

"The next day we that were of Paul's company departed, and came unto Caesarea: and we entered into the house of Philip the evangelist, which was one of the seven; and abode with him. And the same man had four daughters, virgins, which did prophesy."

In Scripture, the word *"prophesy"* is used with a variety of applications. It means *to predict* (or foretell) future events, as in Matthew 11:13 and 15:7. In general, it denotes *speaking under divine influence or divine power*, whether prophesying future events, instructing others, or forthtelling what has already been *foretold*. In Acts 19:6, when Paul laid his hands on the disciples of John and they received the Holy Ghost, they prophesied.

In one sense, *ALL ministers* are prophets (and the same can be said of all *teachers*):

"Follow after charity, and desire spiritual gifts, *but rather that ye may PROPHESY*. For he that speaketh in an unknown tongue speaketh not unto men, but unto God: for no man understandeth him; howbeit in the spirit he speaketh mysteries. But *he that prophesieth* speaketh unto men to edification, and exhortation, and comfort. He that speaketh in an unknown tongue edifieth himself; *but he that prophesieth edifieth the Church*. I would that ye all spake with tongues, *but rather that ye prophesied: FOR GREATER IS HE THAT PROPHESIETH than he that speaketh with tongues*, except he interpret, that the Church may receive edifying" (I Cor. 14:1−5).

"Your young men shall see visions." During the Old Testament economy, God spoke to the fathers by the prophets—and in various other ways, such as visions and dreams. Because of this, the prophets were known as *"seers,"* that name being superceded by the term "prophet":

"(Beforetime in Israel, when a man went to enquire of God, thus he spake, Come, and let us go to the *seer: for he that is now called a Prophet was beforetime called a Seer.)* . . . And as they went up the hill to the city, they found young maidens going out to draw water, and said unto them, Is the *seer* here? . . . Then Saul drew near to Samuel in the gate, and said, Tell me, I pray thee, where the *seer's* house is" (I Sam. 9:9,11,18). Read also II Samuel 24:11.

The name *"seer"* was given because of the manner in which the divine will of God was communicated to the prophet. Usually while the prophet was in a state of ecstasy, God caused a vision (the appearance of objects or events) to come into his mind or pass before him, and thus he received what God wanted to communicate to him. When we reach chapter 10 of Acts we will study the vision God gave Peter to reveal to him the inclusion of the Gentiles in the "whosoever" of the Gospel of grace.

Sometimes God gave visions to prophets while they slept. At other times, the vision appeared while the prophet was definitely awake; and at still other times the vision was given during a prophetic ecstasy. Study Daniel 2:28; 7:1,2,15; 8:2; Ezekiel 1:1; 8:3; 11:24; Genesis 15:1; Numbers 12:6; Job 4:13; 7:14.

In the transition period, God gave visions to several of His prophets. In Acts 9:10 He appeared to *Ananias* in a vision. In Acts 9:12, *Paul saw Ananias* in a vision. In Acts 10:3 the angel of God spoke to *Cornelius* in a vision.

In Revelation 1:9,10 we read, "I John, who also am your brother, and companion in tribulation, and in the kingdom and patience of Jesus Christ, was in the isle that is called Patmos, for the word of God, and for the testimony of Jesus Christ. *I WAS IN THE SPIRIT on the Lord's day, and heard behind me a great voice,* as of a trumpet."

In Revelation chapter 1, verses 1 through 20, John the seer is on the earth—but *in the Spirit* he is looking at the vision of the Man Christ Jesus, the Lord.

In Revelation chapter 2, verse 1, through chapter 3, verse 22, John is on earth *looking forward* through the Church Age and up to the Rapture.

In Revelation 4:1 to chapter 11, John (in the Spirit) is observing things in heaven *and* things on earth.

In Revelation 11, verses 1 through 12, John is in the

Holy City Jerusalem, with the two witnesses, beholding the things that occur *there.*

And in chapter 11 verse 13 through chapter 22 verse 21, John is in heaven *observing and recording* things in heaven and things simultaneously taking place on *earth.* But bear in mind that *John was the LAST prophet,* the last seer. We do not *need* prophets today because we have the revealed will of God laid down in the Word of God, and the Word of God was completed with John's inspired recording of *The Revelation.*

"Your old men shall dream dreams." Again I point out that during the Old Testament economy the will of God was often made known through visions and *dreams.* There are several such instances recorded in the Old Testament Scripture:

In Genesis 20:3 God warned *Abimelech* that Sara was Abraham's wife: "God came to Abimelech *in a dream by night,* and said to him, Behold, thou art but a dead man, for the woman which thou hast taken; for she is a man's wife."

In Genesis 31:11 God spoke to *Jacob*: "And the angel of God spake unto me *in a dream,* saying, Jacob: And I said, Here am I."

In Genesis 31:24 God spoke to *Laban*: "And God came to Laban the Syrian *in a dream by night,* and said unto him, Take heed that thou speak not to Jacob either good or bad."

In Genesis 37:5 God spoke to *Joseph*: "And *Joseph dreamed a dream,* and he told it his brethren: and they hated him yet the more."

In Genesis 40:5 God spoke to *Pharaoh's butler and baker*: "And they *dreamed a dream both of them,* each man his dream in one night, each man according to the interpretation of his dream, the butler and the baker of the king of Egypt, which were bound in the prison."

In Genesis 41:1−7 God spoke to *Pharaoh*: "And it came to pass at the end of two full years, that Pharaoh *dreamed* . . . So Pharaoh awoke. And he slept and *dreamed the second time* . . . And Pharaoh awoke, and, behold, it was a dream." In verses 1 through 44 we find the story of Joseph's interpretation of this dream of Pharaoh's, which brought him into the king's favor and lifted him to power, next to the king in authority.

In I Kings 3:5 God spoke to *Solomon*: "In Gibeon the Lord appeared to Solomon *in a dream by night*: and God said, Ask what I shall give thee." It was in answer to this question that Solomon asked for "an understanding heart to judge thy people, that I may discern between good and bad." His request was granted. God gave him "a wise and understanding heart . . . so that there shall not be any among the kings like unto thee all thy days." (Read verses 5 through 15.)

In Numbers 12:5,6, "the Lord came down in the pillar of the cloud, and stood in the door of the tabernacle, and called Aaron and Miriam: and they both came forth. And He said, Hear now my words: If there be a prophet among you, *I the Lord will make myself known unto him in a VISION, and will speak unto him in a DREAM.*"

Moving on into the New Testament era during the transition period, God spoke to *Joseph* in a dream: "But while (Joseph) thought on these things, behold, the angel of the Lord appeared unto him *in a dream*, saying, Joseph, thou son of David, fear not to take unto thee Mary thy wife: for that which is conceived in her is of the Holy Ghost" (Matt. 1:20). In Matthew 2:13 the angel of the Lord *again* appeared to Joseph in a dream, warning him to take Mary and the child Jesus and flee into Egypt to escape Herod's slaughter of all the children under two years of age. Again in verses 19 and 22 of that chapter, God spoke to Joseph in dreams, calling him out of Egypt and leading him back to Nazareth.

In Matthew 27:19 God spoke to an unbelieving woman (Pilate's wife) concerning Jesus: "When (Pilate) was set down on the judgment seat, his wife sent unto him, say-

ing, Have thou nothing to do with that just Man: for I
have suffered many things this day *in a dream* because
of Him."

But in this day of God's marvelous grace when we
have *the complete Word of God,* He no longer speaks
as He did "in sundry times and divers manners." All
we need to know about time and eternity, heaven and
hell, God and the devil, the *love* of God and the *wrath*
of God, salvation *from* sin and victory *over* sin, we can
find in the Word of God. *Ours* is a *"more excellent way"*
(I Cor. 12:31)—*the way of FAITH:* "But without faith it
is impossible to please Him: for he that cometh to God
must believe that He is, and that He is a rewarder of
them that diligently seek Him" (Heb. 11:6).

"And Jesus answering saith unto them, *Have faith
in God"* (Mark 11:22).

Verse 18: *"And on my servants and on my handmaidens I will pour out in those days of my Spirit; and
they shall prophesy."*

Here Joel's prophecy points out that the power of the
Holy Spirit would not be confined to any particular class
or rank of society, but that servants and handmaidens—
as well as masters—would be recipients of this power.

The meaning is *not* that the Holy Ghost would be
poured out upon *all persons,* both good and evil, but
that a king's *servant* can receive the Holy Spirit just as
surely as the king *himself* can receive Him. In this Day
of Grace the invitation is to *"whosoever will."* The
message is no longer to "the lost sheep of the house of
Israel," as when Jesus came and offered the kingdom and
the Gospel "to the Jew first" (Rom. 1:16). *NOW* the
Holy Spirit is poured out upon all who will believe on
Jesus, whether king, peasant, servant, or master. The
servant who *believes* receives the Holy Spirit just as
surely as does his believing master.

"Handmaidens" here means female servants. The term

was applied to pious women in many places in the Psalms, and is also used in Luke 1:38 and 48:

"And Mary said, Behold the handmaid of the Lord; be it unto me according to thy word.   And the angel departed from her. . . For He hath regarded the low estate of His handmaiden: for, behold, from henceforth all generations shall call me blessed."

In this Dispensation of Grace, "whosoever will" may drink of the water of life freely, "whosoever will" may call upon the name of the Lord and be saved—and with salvation the Holy Spirit comes into the heart to abide (John 3:5; Rom. 8:9).

"And they shall prophesy."   A partial fulfillment of this can be seen in Acts 19:6, where the disciples of John prophesied; in Acts 21:9, where the daughters of Philip prophesied; and in Acts 11:28, where Agabus prophesied. During the transition period there were men who had *the specific GIFT* of prophecy, and this gift was given to them by the Holy Spirit.

Verses 19 and 20:   *"And I will shew wonders in heaven above, and signs in the earth beneath; blood, and fire, and vapour of smoke: The sun shall be turned into darkness, and the moon into blood, before that great and notable day of the Lord come."*

"I will shew wonders" reads literally, "I will give signs."   The word in the Hebrew means "wonderful occurrences"—miracles wrought by God or His messengers. It is the common word to denote a miracle in the Old Testament.   Examples of this may be found in Exodus 4:21 where God said to Moses, "When thou goest to return into Egypt, see that thou do *all those wonders before Pharaoh, which I have put in thine hand . . . ."* and in Exodus 7, verses 3 and 9: "And I will harden Pharaoh's heart, *and multiply my signs and my wonders* in the land of Egypt. . . When Pharaoh shall speak unto you, saying, Shew a miracle for you: then thou shalt say

unto Aaron, Take thy rod, and cast it before Pharaoh, *and it shall become a serpent.*"

Then in Exodus 11:9 God said to Moses, "Pharaoh shall not hearken unto you; *that my wonders may be multiplied* in the land of Egypt," and in Deuteronomy 4:33,34 we read, "Did ever people hear the voice of God speaking out of the midst of the fire, as thou hast heard, and live? or hath God assayed to go and take Him a nation from the midst of another nation, by temptations, *BY SIGNS, AND BY WONDERS*, and by war, and by a mighty hand, and by a stretched out arm, and by great terrors, according to all that the Lord your God did for you in Egypt before your eyes?"

Here—and in other places in the New Testament, such as John 4:48—it means "something strange, causing the beholder to marvel, is always used in the plural, and generally joined with the word 'signs' in the New Testament. A sign is intended to appeal to the understanding, a wonder appeals to the imagination, a power (dunamis) indicates its source as supernatural. 'Wonders' are manifested as Divine operation in thirteen occurrences (nine times in Acts); three times they are ascribed to the work of Satan through human agents (Matt. 24:24; Mark 13:22; and II Thess. 2:9)" (Vine's Dictionary of New Testament Words).

There has been much misunderstanding of verses 19 and 20 of our present chapter. Some theologians and professors in the field of religion have missed the meaning by a wrong interpretation of *"THAT GREAT AND NOTABLE DAY OF THE LORD."* Certainly not all the events recorded here occured on the Day of Pentecost, for at Pentecost there was no *"blood, and fire, and vapor of smoke."* The sun did not turn to darkness and the moon did not turn to blood, but these things *will* occur literally in the future, "in the last days" (v. 17).

The *"day of the Lord"* is that day in the future when Almighty God will manifest Himself in a definite, powerful, and peculiar manner, the day when judgment will be poured out upon wicked men, and the Lord Jesus Christ will be glorified. In that day He will come—not as a Lamb, not as a Babe in a manger—but as King of kings and Lord of lords:

"For as the lightning, that lighteneth out of the one part under heaven, shineth unto the other part under heaven; *so shall also the Son of man be in His day*" (Luke 17:24).

"For yourselves know perfectly that *the day of the Lord* so cometh as a thief in the night" (I Thess. 5:2).

"Being confident of this very thing, that He which hath begun a good work in you will perform it until *the day of Jesus Christ*" (Phil. 1:6).

"But the day of the Lord will come as a thief in the night; in the which the heavens shall pass away with a great noise, and the elements shall melt with fervent heat, the earth also and the works that are therein shall be burned up" (II Pet. 3:10).

"That great and notable day of the Lord" refers to the time, yet future, when God will manifest Himself in mighty judgment upon the enemies of the Gospel and the enemies of the Lord Jesus. That will be the day when these *"wonders in heaven above, and signs in the earth beneath"* will take place, the day described by Amos in chapter 5, verses 16 through 20 of his prophecy:

"Therefore the Lord, the God of hosts, the Lord, saith thus: Wailing shall be in all the streets; and they shall say in all the highways, Alas! alas! and they shall call the husbandman to mourning, and such as are skilful of lamentation to wailing. And in all vineyards shall be wailing: for I will pass through thee, saith the Lord. Woe unto you that desire *the day of the LORD!* to what end is it for you? *The day of the Lord is darkness,* and not light. As if a man did flee from a lion, and a bear met him; or went into the house, and leaned his hand on the wall, and a serpent bit him. *Shall not the day*

*of the Lord be darkness, and not light? even very dark,
and no brightness in it?"*

Joel's prophecy therefore relates to the last days and
will have its ultimate fulfillment in the Messiah, when
He shall come as King and establish His kingdom here
on earth.   It is in this sense that Peter uses the phrase
here.   He tells the assembled multitude that something
similar to that which they were now witnessing, God had
promised in connection with the days of Messiah—with
His coming as King, when the Spirit was to be poured
out upon all flesh.   That which they saw and heard was
indeed the outpouring of the Holy Spirit, but not in the
full sense as given in the prophecy of Joel.   What took
place on the Day of Pentecost was an evidence that Jesus, whom they had crucified, is the true Messiah; and
as the prophecy was thus partially fulfilled, it was a
pledge that in due time *all* the prophecy contained in
the book of Joel would be fulfilled.

"*Blood . . . fire . . . vapour of smoke.*"   Blood is commonly used as an emblem of war and slaughter, and *there
was no blood* on the Day of Pentecost; but during the
terrible time when judgment will be poured out upon
the earth, *there WILL BE blood:*

The *moon* will become as blood: "And I beheld when
he had opened the sixth seal, and, lo, there was a great
earthquake; and the sun became black as sackcloth of
hair, *and the MOON became as blood*" (Rev. 6:12).

At the battle of Armageddon, *blood will run to the
horses' bridles:* "And I looked, and behold a white cloud,
and upon the cloud one sat like unto the Son of man,
having on His head a golden crown, and in His hand a
sharp sickle.   And another angel came out of the temple,
crying with a loud voice to Him that sat on the cloud,
Thrust in thy sickle, and reap: for the time is come for
thee to reap; for the harvest of the earth is ripe.   And
He that sat on the cloud thrust in His sickle on the
earth; and the earth was reaped.

"And another angel came out of the temple which is in heaven, he also having a sharp sickle. And another angel came out from the altar, which had power over fire; and cried with a loud cry to him that had the sharp sickle, saying, Thrust in thy sharp sickle, and gather the clusters of the vine of the earth; for her grapes are fully ripe. And the angel thrust in his sickle into the earth, and gathered the vine of the earth, and cast it into *the great winepress of the wrath of God.* And the winepress was trodden without the city, *and BLOOD came out of the winepress, EVEN UNTO THE HORSE BRIDLES, BY THE SPACE OF A THOUSAND AND SIX HUNDRED FURLONGS"* (Rev. 14:14—20).

As the vials of God's wrath are poured out upon the earth, *men will be given blood to drink*: "For they have shed the blood of saints and prophets, *AND THOU HAST GIVEN THEM BLOOD TO DRINK;* for they are worthy" (Rev. 16:6).

The *sea* will turn to blood: "And the second angel poured out his vial upon the sea; *and IT BECAME AS THE BLOOD OF A DEAD MAN:* and every living soul died in the sea" (Rev. 16:3).

The rivers and fresh fountains of water will be changed into blood: "And the third angel poured out his vial upon the rivers and fountains of waters; *AND THEY BECAME BLOOD"* (Rev. 16:4).

Please study the entire sixteenth chapter of Revelation in connection with these quotations.

After the Rapture of the Church, the false messiah will appear and there will be three and one-half years of peace on earth. *Then*—according to Revelation 6:3,4— this earth will become a literal hell:

"And when He had opened the second seal, I heard the second beast say, Come and see. *And there went out another horse that was red: and power was given to him that sat thereon to take peace from the earth, and that they should kill one another: and there was given unto him a great sword."*

". . . FIRE, and vapour of smoke." Fire is also an emblem of war. The Greek language here suggests that columns and pillars of smoke will rise—another sign of a terrible, terrible holocaust of war, with smoke rising from burning towns and countryside. Since the *beginning* of wars it has been the custom to burn the habitations of the enemy, destroying the food supplies and commodities of war. During the time prophesied in Scripture here, there will be fires with great columns of smoke ascending, accompanied by such pain and misery as this world has not yet known.

The destruction of Jerusalem by Titus the Roman in A. D. 70 was a *forerunner* of this terrible judgment, but it was not its total fulfillment because the things spoken of here were not all present then, and certainly there was no such display as will take place when God pours out His wrath upon Antichrist and upon the multi-billions of people who will be led astray by him!

In the Olivet discourse Jesus speaks of the time when He will be glorified as King of kings and Lord of lords:

"For as the lightning cometh out of the east, and shineth even unto the west; so shall also the coming of the Son of man be. For wheresoever the carcase is, there will the eagles be gathered together.

"Immediately after the tribulation of those days shall the sun be darkened, and the moon shall not give her light, and the stars shall fall from heaven, and the powers of the heavens shall be shaken: And then shall appear the sign of the Son of man in heaven: and then shall all the tribes of the earth mourn, and they shall see the Son of man coming in the clouds of heaven with power and great glory. And He shall send His angels with a great sound of a trumpet, and they shall gather together His elect from the four winds, from one end of heaven to the other" (Matt. 24:27—31).

Verse 20 in our present study tells us that *"the sun*

shall be turned into darkness." In the Word of God, the shining of the sun is an emblem of prosperity and of God's blessings upon the people. In contrast, the sun's *withdrawing* of its light is a symbol of calamitous judgment and is often spoken of in the Scriptures:

In Jeremiah 15:9 we read, "She that hath borne seven languisheth: she hath given up the ghost; *her sun is gone down while it was yet day:* she hath been ashamed and confounded: *and the residue of them will I deliver to the sword before their enemies,* saith the Lord."

Ezekiel 32:7 declares, "When I shall put thee out, I will cover the heaven, and make the stars thereof dark; *I will cover the sun with a cloud,* and the moon shall not give her light."

Amos 8:9 also declares, "It shall come to pass in that day, saith the Lord God, that *I will cause the sun to go down at noon,* and I will darken the earth in the clear day."

Going on over into the New Testament we read:

"And the fourth angel sounded, *and the third part of the sun was smitten,* and the third part of the moon, and the third part of the stars; so as the third part of them was darkened, and the day shone not for a third part of it, and the night likewise" (Rev. 8:12).

"And He opened the bottomless pit; and there arose a smoke out of the pit, as the smoke of a great furnace; *and the sun and the air were darkened* by reason of the smoke of the pit" (Rev. 9:2).

"And the fourth angel poured out his vial upon the sun; and power was given unto him to scorch men with fire. And men were scorched with great heat, and blasphemed the name of God, which hath power over these plagues: and they repented not to give Him glory" (Rev. 16:8,9).

Please read Revelation 6:12—17. Time and space will not permit the quoting of the entire passage here, but it will shed a great deal of light on our present passage.

Peter used Joel's prophecy to let the men of Judah know that the miracle of Pentecost was just the *beginning* of a series of wonders and signs which would take place during the times of the Messiah. He did not suggest that Pentecost would be the end of these mighty signs and wonders. There are many signs yet future which will occur when "that great and notable day of the Lord" shall come—but *only the Father in heaven* knows when that day will be.

The summarized meaning of verses 19 and 20 is simply this: Before Jesus comes as King of kings and Lord of lords to sit on the throne of David and reign in right- eousness forever, great wonders and signs will occur in heaven and on earth. The sun will be turned to dark- ness, the moon will become as blood, and the earth will receive a blood-bath as well as a bath of "fire, and va- pour of smoke." All these things will occur before Jesus comes to reign in glory.

However, *not all* of these things will take place before the *Millennium.* Jesus will reign for one thousand years, and the saints of God will reign with Him. Then *at the consummation of all things* He will take the throne *to reign FOREVER:* "Of the increase of His government and peace there shall be no end, upon the throne of Da- vid, and upon His kingdom, to order it, and to establish it with judgment and with justice from henceforth even for ever. The zeal of the Lord of hosts will perform this" (Isa. 9:7).

II Peter 3:12 describes the introduction of the day of eternity, "the coming of the day of God, *wherein the heavens being on fire shall be dissolved, and the ele- ments shall melt with fervent heat."* Every sign of sin will then be gone! There will be a new, glorious earth filled with holiness, and God Himself will be the center of all:

"And there shall be no more curse: but the throne of God and of the Lamb shall be in it; and His servants shall serve Him" (Rev. 22:3).

"And when all things shall be subdued unto Him, then shall the Son also Himself be subject unto Him that put all things under Him, *that God may be ALL IN ALL"* (I Cor. 15:28).

God's day of perfection and completion will never end. It will continue through all ages, eternity through eternities; *but before that day comes,* every detail of Joel's prophecy will be literally fulfilled. We are moving toward that day moment by moment, and we should live in such a way that we can sincerely pray, "Even so, *come quickly,* Lord Jesus!"

Verse 21: *"And it shall come to pass, that whosoever shall call on the name of the Lord shall be saved."*

How refreshing these words must have been to the ears of Peter's audience at Pentecost, for this was not true under the Old Testament economy. Under Levitical law, the people were continually bringing animals to be sacrificed, *year after year.* Paul tells us in Hebrews 10:11 that many times they brought the same sacrifice for the same sins again and again. But Peter declared in his Pentecostal message that *Jesus paid the sin-debt,* once and for all, that He has been exalted at the right hand of the Father and is now both Lord and Christ. In other words, the *sin-question* has been settled. It is now the *SON-question:* "What think ye of *Christ?* Whose Son is He?" If we believe that He is the Son of God—crucified, buried, risen, ascended, exalted and seated at the right hand of God, then we receive Him, call upon His precious name, and we are assured of salvation.

To call upon the Lord for salvation does not mean that a person who, for instance, has been the victim of a fatal accident and has only a few minutes to live, can cry out, "O Lord! O Lord!" and be saved. It does not mean that at all. To call on the name of the Lord unto salvation means that the individual who calls *has heard and believed the Word.* Jesus said, "He that *heareth my word,* and *believeth on Him that sent me,* hath ever-lasting life, and shall not come into condemnation; but is passed from death unto life" (John 5:24).

James 1:18,21 declare, "Of His own will begat He us *with the Word of truth,* that we should be a kind of firstfruits of His creatures. . . Wherefore lay apart all filthiness and superfluity of naughtiness, and *receive with meekness the ENGRAFTED WORD, which is able to save your souls!"*

Then in I Peter 1:23—25 we read, *"Being born again, not of corruptible seed, but of incorruptible, by the WORD OF GOD, which liveth and abideth for ever.* For all flesh is as grass, and all the glory of man as the flower of grass. The grass withereth, and the flower thereof falleth away: *BUT THE WORD OF THE LORD ENDURETH FOR EVER. And this is the WORD which by the Gospel is preached unto you."*

There can *be* no salvation until one hears *the Word.* Hearing the Word brings *faith.* The individual then exer-cises faith in the Christ of whom the Word speaks—*the Lord Jesus Christ,* crucified, buried, risen, ascended, and seated at the Father's right hand. When such a person, hearing and believing the record God has given of His Son, calls upon the Lord Jesus Christ for salvation, God will certainly save that individual.

In Romans 10:13—17 the Apostle Paul gives a clear explanation of what it means to call on the name of the Lord unto salvation:

"Whosoever shall call upon the name of the Lord shall be saved.   How then shall they call on Him in whom they have not *believed*? and how shall they *believe* in Him of whom they have not *heard*? and how shall they *hear* without a preacher? *and how shall they preach, except they be sent*?   As it is written, How beautiful are the feet of them that preach the Gospel of peace, and bring glad tidings of good things!   But they have not all obeyed the Gospel. For Esaias saith, Lord, who hath believed our report? *So then FAITH cometh by hearing, and hearing by THE WORD OF GOD.*"

In this passage, penned under inspiration by God's apostle to the Gentiles, we are clearly taught that God's grace *saves* us—but saving grace becomes ours *by FAITH;* and since faith comes by hearing the Word of God, *the only possible way* for anyone to exercise faith in the finished work of Jesus is to hear the Gospel message.

BUT—"how shall they call on Him *in whom they have not BELIEVED?*" So *believing* precedes *calling*—but "how shall they believe in Him *of whom they have not HEARD?*" Believing precedes calling, *hearing* precedes *believing*—but *"how shall they HEAR without a PREACHER?"* The Word of God *must* be preached, and it has pleased God in this Dispensation of Grace to call men to preach His Word to the unsaved; and when sinners *hear the Word and believe on Jesus,* they will call on His name for salvation—and we have Bible assurance that salvation will be granted:

In John 6:37 Jesus promised, "Him that cometh to me I will *in no wise* cast out."

In Matthew 11:28 He invited, "Come unto me, all ye that labour and are heavy laden, *and I will give you rest.*"

The last invitation in the Bible is found in Revelation 22:17: "The Spirit and the bride say, COME. And let him that heareth say, COME. And let him that is athirst COME. And *WHOSOEVER WILL, let him take the water of life FREELY!*" Thank God, *it HAS* "come to pass" that any and all who call on the name of the Lord Jesus, believing in His shed blood, are saved.

The Wonderful Works of Jesus
Proved Him Lord and Christ

Verse 22: *"Ye men of Israel, hear these words: Jesus of Nazareth, a Man approved of God among you by mir-*

*acles and wonders and signs, which God did by Him in
the midst of you, as ye yourselves also know."*

"*Ye men of Israel, hear these words.*" The men of
Israel addressed here were descendants of Jacob, primarily
the Jews.   Peter set about to prove to them that what
had occurred at Pentecost was divine proof that Jesus
had risen from the dead, that He had ascended to the
right hand of God, from whence He had sent the Holy
Spirit as He had promised.

"*Jesus of Nazareth, a Man approved of God . . . by
miracles and wonder and signs . . . .*" Jesus had shown
by His miracles and works that He was *sent* from God,
empowered of God, and *was indeed God.* The miracles
He wrought, the wonderful things He did, the signs He
showed, proved that He was more than man.   Even some
of the religious leaders confessed that He was a Man sent
from God.   *Nicodemus*—perhaps the outstanding teacher
in all Israel—declared, "*Rabbi, we know that thou art a
teacher come from God: for NO MAN can do these miracles that thou doest, except God be with him*" (John
3:2).

On various occasions Jesus told the Jews that He came
from God.   He declared that God sent Him into the
world, and that the *works* He did were works the Father
had given Him to do. He further declared that His *words*
were words God had given Him to speak. (Read John
5:19—30.)   So Peter here *reminded* the Jews that it was
God who wrought the miracles by Jesus, and then he
added, "*as ye yourselves also KNOW.*"

The mighty works which God wrought *from the very
beginning*—in creation as well as in redemption—He
wrought by His only begotten Son:

"*In the beginning was the Word, and the Word was
with God, and the Word was God. The same was in the
beginning with God.   All things were made by Him; and
WITHOUT Him was not anything made that was made*"
(John 1:1—3).

Jesus is "the image of the invisible God, the firstborn of every creature: *For by Him were ALL things created, that are in heaven, and that are in earth, visible and invisible, whether they be thrones, or dominions, or principalities, or powers: ALL things were created by Him, and FOR Him: And He is BEFORE all things, and BY HIM all things consist"* (Col. 1:15—17).

"God, who at sundry times and in divers manners spake in time past unto the fathers by the prophets, hath in these last days spoken unto us *by His Son, whom He hath appointed heir of all things, BY WHOM ALSO HE MADE THE WORLDS"* (Heb. 1:1,2).

In Peter's sermon at Pentecost the Jews were given to understand that Jesus was their Messiah, that He came in fulfillment of the prophecies penned down by their Old Testament prophets, and that everything He did and said *proved* Him to be their promised Messiah. In John 15:24,25 *Jesus Himself* declared, "If I had not done among them the works which none other man did, they had not had sin: but now have they both seen and hated both me and my Father. But this cometh to pass, that the word might be fulfilled that is written in their law, *They hated me without a cause.*"

The manifold miracles of Jesus were so outstanding that Peter appealed to the Jews to *remember* those miracles and consider that *only GOD* could have performed them. In their very presence He had raised the dead, opened the eyes of the blind, and cleansed the lepers— miracles such as they had never seen before. "But though He had done so many miracles before them, *yet they believed not on Him"* (John 12:37). Peter appealed to them to recognize and confess that they had *crucified* their Messiah, and must therefore repent of their terrible sin.

Verse 23:   *"Him, being delivered by the determinate counsel and foreknowledge of God, ye have taken, and by wicked hands have crucified and slain."*

The word here translated *"delivered"* is used many times of those who are "surrendered" into the hands of enemies — and if God had not surrendered Jesus into the hands of His enemies and allowed them to take Him, they could never have laid hands on Him! When Pilate said to Jesus, "Knowest thou not that I have power to crucify thee, and have power to release thee?" Jesus replied, *"Thou couldest have no power at all against me, EXCEPT IT WERE GIVEN THEE FROM ABOVE"* (John 19:10,11).

Jesus was surrendered (delivered) to His enemies to be crucified only because it was foreordained of God that it should be so in order for Him to pay the sin-debt. In Mark 10:33,34 Jesus told His disciples, "Behold, we go up to Jerusalem; *and the Son of man shall be delivered unto the chief priests, and unto the scribes;* and they shall condemn Him to death, and shall deliver Him to the Gentiles: and they shall mock Him, and shall scourge Him, and shall spit upon Him, and shall kill Him: *and the third day He shall rise again."*

The *chief priests* delivered Jesus to Pilate: "When they had bound Him, they led Him away, and delivered Him to Pontius Pilate the governor" (Matt. 27:2).

Pilate delivered Him to be crucified: "Then released he Barabbas unto them: and when he had scourged Jesus, he delivered Him to be crucified" (Matt. 27:26). "Then delivered he Him therefore unto them to be crucified. And they took Jesus, and led Him away" (John 19:16).

In this manner the death of Jesus (foreordained of God before the foundation of the world) *was accomplished.* We can now more fully understand the meaning of John 3:16: *"For God so loved the world, that HE GAVE His only begotten Son,* that whosoever believeth in Him should not perish, but have everlasting life!"

Also, in I John 4:8—10 we are told, "He that loveth not knoweth not God; *for God is love.* In this was manifested the love of God toward us, because that *GOD*

SENT HIS ONLY BEGOTTEN SON into the world,
that we might live through Him.   Herein is love, *not
that WE loved GOD, but that HE loved US, and SENT
HIS SON to be the propitiation for our sins!"*

Peter made it clear to the Jews that what they did to
Jesus they did *"by the determinate counsel of God."* The
Greek word translated *"determinate"* means "defined,
marked out, or bounded," as we would define or mark
the boundary of a plot of ground.   The same word is
used in Acts 10:42 where it is translated "ordained," denoting God's purpose that it should be so.   It is used
again in Luke 22:22 where Jesus said, "Truly the Son of
man goeth, as it was *determined . . . ,"* meaning of
course that God purposed (or determined) before ever
the world was, that Jesus should die on the cross.

The death of Jesus was no accident.   In the *beginning,*
before the dawn of creation, God designed and perfected
the plan of salvation; and the members of the Godhead
agreed that Jesus the Son would take the place of poor,
lost mankind, and in a body of humiliation He would
pay the sin-debt.   He did exactly that—and even though
I cannot understand it or explain it, *I DO believe it* because the Word of God *declares* it!

I know there are those who will say that the *Jews*
killed Jesus.   Some will say that the *Romans* killed Him.
Still others will declare that *WE killed Him,* that *our
sins* brought about His death.   It is true that sin demanded His death—it was a divine necessity that one
die if sinners were to be saved and made acceptable unto
God.   But what God demanded, only God could provide.
Therefore He provided a body and occupied that body
in the Person of the Lord Jesus.   *"God was in Christ,*
reconciling the world unto Himself" (II Cor. 5:19).   Yes,
Jesus was God in flesh.

However, according to the Scriptures, *NO MAN killed
Jesus.*   Isaiah 53:4 declares that it was *Jehovah God* who
smote the Lamb.   *Jesus* said, *"NO MAN taketh (my life)*

from me, but I lay it down of myself. I have power to
lay it down, and I have power to take it again. This
commandment have I received of my Father" (John 10:18).
Jesus laid His life down willingly, smitten of God. He
literally took His life in His own hands and passed it
back to God: "And when Jesus had cried with a loud
voice, He said, *Father, into thy hands I commend my
spirit:* and having said thus, He gave up the ghost"
(Luke 23:46).

Beloved, *God was not compelled* to surrender His Son
to die on the cross for us! It was the *grace* of God that
brought the *love* of God down to man. *Jesus* was God's
love wrapped up in flesh (Heb. 2:9; I John 4:8—10). *God*
did not go away from man; *MAN went away from GOD.*
Therefore man had no claim on Jesus. *Only God* had
the right to plan when and how the sin-debt should be
paid; *only God* had the right to determine when and how
Jesus would die. The fact that His death (and the *manner* of His death) was declared by the prophets in the
Old Testament furnished indelible proof that His death
was foreordained and fixed before the world began—
*otherwise, the prophecies in the Old Testament could
not have been fulfilled!*

The Greek word rendered *"counsel"* denoted "decree,
will, or purpose." It was God's *decree,* it was His *will,*
it was in His plan and *purpose* to provide redemption
for a lost world. It was God's decree, it was His will
and His purpose, that Jesus should be delivered into the
hands of wicked men, and crucified.

In Acts 4:28 we read, "For to do whatsoever thy hand
and thy COUNSEL determined before to be done."

In Ephesians 1:11 Paul wrote, "In whom (Christ) also
we have obtained an inheritance, being predestinated
*according to the purpose of Him who worketh all things
AFTER THE COUNSEL of His own will."*

In Hebrews 6:17 we read, "Wherein God, willing more
abundantly to shew unto the heirs of promise *the im-*

mutability of HIS COUNSEL, confirmed it by an oath."

The divine plan in the life and death of Jesus was insisted on by Peter in an effort to convince the Jews that Jesus was *not* delivered into their hands because of personal weakness, nor did they take Him because He was unable to defend Himself. Rather, He was delivered by the deliberate purpose of God. When Jesus reprimanded Peter for drawing his sword and cutting off the ear of the high priest's servant when they came to arrest Him in the garden, He said to Peter, "Thinkest thou that I cannot now pray to my Father, *and He shall presently give me MORE THAN TWELVE LEGIONS OF ANGELS?* But how then shall the Scriptures be fulfilled, that thus it must be?" (Matt. 26:53,54).

The Jews must come to understand that Jesus was delivered into their hands by Almighty God, it being God's eternal plan that His Son be nailed to a cross in order that sinners (*including* the Jews) might be saved by believing in His shed blood and finished work. Since the death of Jesus was *in accordance with God's will,* since it was in God's plan and design *to provide salvation,* then His death in no way interfered with His claims of messiahship.

The Greek word translated *"foreknowledge"* denotes "seeing beforehand an event that is yet to take place." Thus, Peter declares here the omniscience of God and of Jesus. *"Foreknowledge"* as used here implies that God did what He did because He foresaw what would be best for mankind; He foresaw the best time, place, and manner of doing what must be done if He were to be just and yet justify the ungodly:

"But now the righteousness of God without the law is manifested, being witnessed by the law and the prophets; even the righteousness of God which is by faith of Jesus Christ unto all and upon all them that believe: for there is no difference: for all have sinned, and come short of the glory of God; being justified freely by His grace through the redemption that is in Christ Jesus: Whom God hath set forth to be a propitiation through faith in His blood, to declare His righteousness for the remission of sins that are past, through the forbearance of God; to declare, I say, at this time His righteousness: that He might be just, and the justifier of him which believeth in Jesus.

"Where is boasting then? It is excluded. By what law? of works? Nay: but *by the law of faith. THERE-FORE WE CONCLUDE THAT A MAN IS JUSTIFIED BY FAITH WITHOUT THE DEEDS OF THE LAW"* (Rom. 3:21—28).

Since God is omniscient, He knew the death of Jesus— ghastly as it was—would prove to be the greatest blessing that could possibly come to man. Therefore, regardless of what man may *do* or may *not* do, *the eternal counsel of God will stand.* God will work out His plan and will for the salvation of all who will come to Him by and through the finished work of the Lord Jesus Christ. In Isaiah 46:8—13 He declared:

"Remember this, and shew yourselves men: bring it again to mind, O ye transgressors. Remember the former things of old: *for I am God, and there is none else; I am God, and there is none like me, declaring the end from the beginning, and from ancient times the things that are not yet done, saying, MY COUNSEL SHALL STAND, and I will do all my pleasure:* Calling a ravenous bird from the east, the man that executeth my counsel from a far country: yea, I have spoken it, I will also bring it to pass; I have *purposed* it, *I will also do it.* Hearken unto me, ye stouthearted, that are far from righteousness: I bring near my righteousness; it shall not be far off, and my salvation shall not tarry: and I will place salvation in Zion for Israel my glory."

Although Jesus was "delivered by the determinate counsel and foreknowledge of God," Peter declared to the Jews, *"Him . . . ye have taken, and by wicked hands have crucified and slain.''* It could be that among those to whom Peter was speaking were some who had been present when Jesus was arrested and led away to be tried—possibly some of those in Peter's audience had even cried out, ''Crucify Him! Crucify Him!''

Peter did not deal in generalities here, nor in general accusations. He brought the charge *directly and specifically* to the Jewish people, declaring that with wicked hands *they* had taken Jesus and led Him away to be crucified. This plain preaching was as it *should be* with preachers *today*. We need not deal in generalities. We need to preach to *people*, to the *individual*, because *salvation is a personal matter*, each of us is personally guilty of sin, and we need to be dealt with as individuals.

In the Greek, *''wicked hands''* reads ''through or by the hands of the lawless, the wicked.'' The Jews did not nail Jesus to the cross with their own hands, but they *demanded His death* and the Roman soldiers carried out their demand. The Jews did not have the *authority* to put anyone to death, and if they *could* have executed the death sentence it would have been by stoning. Death by crucifixion was definitely Roman. But even though it was the Roman soldiers who actually nailed Jesus to the cross, they did it because the Jews demanded it. The person who commits a deed through the instrumentality of another person is *responsible* for that deed. The Jews planned the death of Jesus, they demanded it—even over the protest of the Roman governor; therefore *they were guilty of His death.*

Peter charged the crime directly to them—and rightly so. The fact that they did not actually nail Jesus to the cross did not lessen their guilt.

In this particular passage, the Holy Spirit gives a striking illustration of the doctrine that the foreknowledge of God does not interfere with the free will of mortal man. The crucifixion of Jesus was divinely determined beforehand—nothing in the Word of God is clearer than this truth; but the Word *also* clearly declares that the Jews with "wicked hands" *took Him and crucified Him.* Because of the gracious plan and purpose of God the Eternal Father, He decreed in His own mind that His only begotten Son should come into this world born of a virgin, that He should occupy a body of humiliation, and in that body He should die at the appointed time, in the appointed manner.

The crucifixion of Jesus was divinely decreed just as surely as were the circumstances surrounding His birth and His life, and *ALL circumstances* having to do with His birth, life, ministry, death, burial, and resurrection were foretold by the prophets in the Old Testament Scriptures.   But in spite of the decreed, foreordained plan of God, *the Jews did what they CHOSE to do.*   There is no inconsistency between the divine decrees of God and the free will of man.   God never compels man to act contrary to his own will, for then there would be no such thing as *the free will of man.*

The crucifixion of Jesus was the most horrible crime ever committed, and yet it brought the greatest blessing to the greatest number of people of anything that has ever happened, or ever *will* happen.   The purpose of God in permitting wicked hands to lay hold on Jesus, lead Him away to Calvary and crucify Him, does not destroy the *nature* of the crime nor exonerate those who committed it.   The purpose of God does not change the character of what men do.   God's predetermination and foreordination of the death of Jesus will not lessen man's responsibility for his own acts, and if those acts deserve punishment *you may rest assured God will mete out that punishment at the appointed time!*

The case before us here meets all the *excuses* of all *sinners* of *all ages.*   NO ONE can be absolved from guilt on the plea of being "innocent because God is sovereign," and because His predetermined counsel must be

carried out. Those who would make excuses in the day
of judgment will find those excuses of no avail, just as
Adam's excuse was no good in the Garden of Eden when
he said to God, "The woman whom thou gavest to be
with me, she gave me of the tree, and I did eat" (Gen.
3:12).   God rejected Adam's excuse—and the same will
be true with *all* who make excuses at the judgment.

God so loved *the world* that He gave His only begotten Son *to pay the sin-debt* for the whole world, and
since God's righteousness and holiness were satisfied in
the life, ministry, death, burial and resurrection of His
Son, *man HAS no excuse before God:*

*"THEREFORE THOU ART INEXCUSABLE, O MAN,
WHOSOEVER THOU ART THAT JUDGEST: for wherein
thou judgest another, thou condemnest thyself; for thou
that judgest doest the same things. . . FOR THERE IS
NO RESPECT OF PERSONS WITH GOD"* (Rom. 2:1,11).

In another chapter of his letter to the Romans, Paul
plainly declares that God's mercy is under His sovereign
will:

"What shall we say then? Is there unrighteousness
with God?   God forbid!   For He saith to Moses, *I will
have mercy on whom I will have mercy, and I will have
compassion on whom I will have compassion.* So then
it is not of him that willeth, nor of him that runneth, but
of God that sheweth mercy. For the Scripture saith unto
Pharaoh, *Even for this same purpose have I raised thee
up, that I might shew my power in thee, and that my
name might be declared throughout all the earth.*

"Therefore hath He mercy on whom He will have mercy, and whom He will He hardeneth.   Thou wilt say
then unto me, Why doth He yet find fault?   For who
hath resisted His will?   Nay but, O man, who art thou
that repliest against God?   Shall the thing formed say
to Him that formed it, Why hast thou made me thus?
Hath not the potter power over the clay, of the same
lump to make one vessel unto honour, and another unto

dishonour?

"What if God, willing to shew His wrath, and to make His power known, endured with much longsuffering the vessels of wrath fitted to destruction: and that He might make known the riches of His glory on the vessels of mercy, which He had afore prepared unto glory, even us, whom He hath called, not of the Jews only, but also of the Gentiles?" (Rom. 9:14—24).

Verse 24: *"Whom God hath raised up, having loosed the pains of death: because it was not possible that He should be holden of it."*

Peter now gives the main point in his message. Everyone in Jerusalem, Judaea, and throughout that part of the world knew of the horrible death Jesus had died on the cross, but Peter here declares that *God raised Him up* from the dead, thus using the resurrection as *divine proof* that Jesus was Messiah, very God in flesh, that Prophet whom the Old Testament Scriptures promised would come.

God the Eternal Father *"loosed the pains of death"* and brought Jesus back from the grave. The Greek word translated "loosed" means "to set free or to liberate." The same word is used in Luke 13:16 and in I Corinthians 7:27.

The Greek word translated *"pains"* denotes extreme sufferings; severe, excruciating pain. The same word in Hebrew means "extreme agony under bands or cords closely drawn, tightly binding the victim, binding and constricting the limbs, thereby producing terrible, almost unbearable pain." The death of Jesus is represented under this kind of pain. The idea in both Greek and Hebrew pictures a man *tightly bound* with cords, completely wrapped from head to foot with bands, making it utterly impossible for him to escape a horrible death. This is a true picture of the death of Jesus. He suffered the most horrible agony ever suffered, or ever *to be* suffered. Jesus was *God*, but He was also *man*, made like unto His brethren in all things. Yet if the sin-debt was to be paid, it was impossible for Him to *escape* this horrible death. That was His purpose in coming into the world. From infancy to manhood He moved ever toward the cross.

The suffering of the Lord Jesus Christ took place before He said, "It is finished" and commended His spirit to God. He did not suffer *after* death. The grave could not hold Him; God loosed the bonds (or cords) which held Him, and delivered Him from death *"because it was not possible that He should be holden of it."* Since Jesus was God in flesh, it was impossible for Him to remain in the grave. Because of the circumstances foreordained before the foundation of the world (circumstances having to do with His death), if Jesus had remained in the grave, *prophecies concerning His resurrection* would have been broken—and that cannot be. *The Scriptures CANNOT be broken,* it is impossible for God to lie (Heb. 6:18; Tit. 1:2).

Jesus had clearly said that no man could take His life, but that He had power to lay it down, and He had power to take it again (John 10:18). He was "the Prince of life" (Acts 3:15), and "as the Father hath life in Himself; so hath He given to the Son to have life in Himself" (John 5:26). Jesus came into this world "that He by the grace of God should taste death for every man" (Heb. 2:9). He came "that through death He might destroy him that had the power of death, that is, the devil" (Heb. 2:14).

Since Jesus came to conquer death, hell, and the grave, and since He was very God in flesh, it was impossible for Him to be defeated. Death could not hold Him. In Revelation 1:18 He proclaimed, *"I am He that liveth, and was dead; and, behold, I am alive for evermore, Amen; AND HAVE THE KEYS OF HELL AND OF DEATH!"*

David Prophesied Concerning
the Messiah's Kingship After His Resurrection

Verse 25: *"For David speaketh concerning Him, I foresaw the Lord always before my face, for He is on my right hand, that I should not be moved."*

As proof of our Lord's resurrection, Peter here used Scripture familiar to the Jews—the Old Testament prophecy given to David through the Holy Spirit. In what sense this Psalm applies to Christ will be seen as we examine Peter's quotation from Psalm 16:8—11, which reads:

"I have set the Lord always before me: because He is at my right hand, I shall not be moved. Therefore my heart is glad, and my glory rejoiceth: my flesh also shall rest in hope. For thou wilt not leave my soul in hell; neither wilt thou suffer thine Holy One to see corruption. Thou wilt shew me the path of life: in thy presence is fulness of joy; at thy right hand there are pleasures for evermore."

"I foresaw the Lord" in the Hebrew reads literally, "I expected, I waited for, the Lord." This is the cry, the prayer, of one who is helpless, dependent upon another, the prayer of one who waits for help from God. The statement is used often in the Old Testament.

"I foresaw the Lord *always before my face"*—that is, the Lord is always present to help, a very present help in time of trouble or need. He is there to deliver us out of trouble, to lift us up from the miry clay and plant our feet on the solid rock. David knew the Lord and trusted in Him with his whole heart. He believed in God as being able to supply his every need. After all, it was David who declared, *"The Lord is my shepherd; I SHALL NOT WANT"* (Psalm 23:1).

"He is on my right hand, that I should not be moved." In Scripture, the "right hand" denotes dignity and honor. Thus David declared that his Lord held the highest

place in his affections, the place of highest honor and revered dignity. In Psalm 109:31 David wrote, "For He shall stand at the right hand of the poor, to save him from those that condemn his soul."

We who are believers, children of God by faith in the finished work of the Lord Jesus, should exalt Him *above ALL things.* It is true that He is our "helper"—and certainly we could do nothing *without* Him; but we should honor Him by giving Him the highest place in our lives. We should allow Him to occupy the throne of our heart, and whatever we do—*ALL that we do*—should be done to the glory of God and for the sake of our Lord and Saviour Jesus Christ.

David's Lord was always before his face—ever present. He was always on his right hand—a place of dignity, honor, and highest affection, as well as the place of help. And then David declares, *"that I should not be moved."* That is, "that no great evil could happen to me." The Hebrew language here denotes sinking into a horrible pit or being overcome by calamity, falling prey to the power of mighty enemies. The habits and desires of *David's* enemies are described in Psalm 56:6:

"They gather themselves together, they hide themselves, they mark my steps, when they wait for my soul!" The words of David—used by Peter here in his Pentecostal message—expressed the unshakable confidence of one who stands in great danger, and *IN that hour of danger* places complete and unquestioning trust in the Lord God Almighty, knowing that God can and will deliver him in such an hour.

Verses 26 and 27: *"Therefore did my heart rejoice, and my tongue was glad; moreover also my flesh shall rest in hope: because thou wilt not leave my soul in hell, neither wilt thou suffer thine Holy One to see corruption."*

"Therefore"—that is, "because of the preceding, the following is true." Peter ascribes these expressions to

the Lord Jesus, the Messiah.   He argues that it could not be of *himself* that the Psalmist there spoke, for the Jews had evidence that the words could not be truly said of David, since David *did* die and see corruption; but the Psalmist spoke of *Him who was to be born of his (David's) line,* and thus identified with himself.   The reason for the Saviour's rejoicing was His absolute confidence that He would be preserved in the midst of sorrows, indescribable pain and woe that would come upon Him.   He was looking beyond the darkness of Calvary, seeing the great and glorious victory on the other side. Jesus did not *enjoy* the cross, but He *endured* it, "despising the shame, and is set down at the right hand of the throne of God" (Heb. 12:2).

In Philippians 2:5—9 Paul speaks of "Christ Jesus: who, being in the form of God, thought it not robbery to be equal with God: but made Himself of no reputation, and took upon Him the form of a servant, and was made in the likeness of men: and being found in fashion as a man, He humbled Himself, and became obedient unto death, even the death of the cross.

"Wherefore God also hath highly exalted Him, AND GIVEN HIM A NAME WHICH IS ABOVE EVERY NAME."

Paul also speaks of the working of God's mighty power, "which He wrought in Christ, when He raised Him from the dead, and set Him at His own right hand in the heavenly places, *far above all principality, and power, and might, and dominion, and every name that is named, not only in this world, but also in that which is to come"* (Eph. 1:20,21).

Thus we see that throughout the New Testament the sufferings and sorrows of Jesus are always connected with His victory and His glory.   In this Jesus has set us an example to follow.   We are *assured of tribulation* in *this* world (John 16:33), and if we "live godly in Christ Jesus" we shall *surely* suffer persecution (II Tim. 3:12);

but *"the sufferings of this present time are not worthy to be compared with the glory which shall be revealed in us"* (Rom. 8:18).

"Therefore did my heart rejoice" — or, literally, *"My heart rejoices."* The "heart" of course speaks of the *individual.* In this also Christ set an example. The born again believer is the only person who can weep and rejoice at the same time. He is the only person who can endure pain and misery, and *rejoice* while he *endures!* The reason for this is that he has a *new heart* (Ezek. 36:26), *divine nature* (II Pet. 1:4). God has promised never to leave us nor forsake us, "so that we may boldly say, The Lord is my helper" (Heb. 13:5,6). Yes, the true believer can say with David, *"Yea, though I walk through the valley of the shadow of death, I will fear no evil: FOR THOU ART WITH ME!"* (Psa. 23:4).

"My tongue was glad." From the heart are the issues of life (Prov. 4:23) — but the tongue *utters* what is in the heart! In Psalm 30:12 the word "glory" is used expressly for *tongue* — "to the end that my glory (my tongue) may sing praise to thee and not be silent." With the tongue we sing praises to God and glorify Him when our heart is filled with His presence.

"Moreover also my flesh shall rest in hope." Flesh here refers to the body. The passage means "My body will I commit to the grave with a confident expectation of the future; that is, with a firm belief that it will not see corruption." It thus expresses the confidence of the crucified Saviour that His repose in the grave would not be long. Verse 31 of this chapter carries the same message: "He seeing this before spake of the resurrection of Christ, that His soul was not left in hell, neither His flesh did see corruption."

The death of a Christian is represented in the New Testament as a *sleep* or repose (Acts 7:60, I Cor. 15:6, I Thess. 4:13). That *"flesh"* is the *body* we see in I Corinthians 5:5, where Paul instructed the Corinthian Christians to deliver one of their brethren "unto Satan for the destruction of the *flesh,* that the spirit may be saved in the day of the Lord Jesus."

We see here that the body is definitely separate from the soul. When a believer dies, the body goes back to dust and the spirit returns unto God who gave it (Eccl. 12:7). But because Jesus was resurrected, the body will rest (or sleep) in the grave in hope until Jesus comes in the Rapture and the first resurrection (I Thess. 4:13—18). Then the bodies of saints will be raised incorruptible and living believers will be changed "in a moment, in the twinkling of an eye" (I Cor. 15:51,52). And our resurrection body will be exactly like the glorified, resurrection body of Jesus (I John 3:1—3).

Since Jesus conquered the world, the flesh, the devil, death, hell, and the grave, then ascended, and (in a body of flesh and bones) sat down at the right hand of the Majesty on high, *there is a MAN in heaven* (Heb. 1:3; I Tim. 2:5), and every believer has this same hope. We know that when He shall appear, we shall be like Him, for we shall see Him as He is. "For this corruptible must put on incorruption, and this mortal must put on immortality" (I Cor. 15:53).

In verse 27, the Hebrew word translated "soul" is *nephesh,* and means the immortal, invisible part of man. The meaning is, "Thou wilt not *resign* me to, or *give me over* to, or *allow* me to be held *under the power of HELL.*"

The Greek word translated "hell" is *hades,* the region of departed spirits of the lost (but including the blessed dead in periods preceding the ascension of Christ). In the New Testament, *hades* is the place where the wicked spirits now are, and where they will remain until death and hell shall be cast into the lake that burns with fire and brimstone—the last (and *everlasting*) abode of the wicked. In Revelation 20:13,14 we read, "And the sea gave up the dead which were in it; and death and hell (hades) delivered up the dead which were in them: and they were judged every man according to their works. *And death and hell were cast into the lake of fire. This is the second death.*" The same word is used in Revelation 1:18 and 6:8.

"Thou wilt not leave my soul in hell" is the Lamb of God speaking. (Now I hear someone immediately exclaim, "Do you mean to tell me that the soul of Jesus actually *went into hell*?") The soul of Jesus descended into *the Paradise side* of hell. In the Old Testament, hell had two compartments—and between the *torment* side and the *Paradise* side, a *great gulf* was fixed.

This is effectively illustrated in the account given in Luke 16:19—31, where a certain rich man fared sumptuously every day, and dressed in purple and fine linen. A beggar named Lazarus lay at the rich man's gate and begged for the crumbs which fell from the rich man's table.

"And it came to pass, that the beggar died, and was carried by the angels into Abraham's bosom: the rich man also died, and was buried; *and in hell he lift up his eyes,* being in torments, and seeth Abraham afar off, and Lazarus in his bosom." The rich man cried out to Abraham for mercy, begging him to "send Lazarus, that he may dip the tip of his finger in water, and cool my tongue; for I am tormented in this flame!"

But Abraham said, *"Son, REMEMBER that thou in thy lifetime receivedst thy good things, and likewise Lazarus evil things: BUT NOW he is comforted, and thou art tormented!"* Please notice: Abraham said, "NOW." This *one verse alone* destroys the doctrine of soul-sleep, a man-made doctrine entirely foreign to the Word of God.

Abraham then said to the rich man, "Beside all this, *between us and you there is A GREAT GULF fixed:* so that they which would pass from hence to you cannot; neither can they pass to us, that would come from thence."

The rich man then begged Abraham to send Lazarus back to warn his five brothers, lest they also come to the place of torment where he now was. Abraham said to him, "They have Moses and the prophets; let them hear them." But the rich man insisted that if one went to his brothers *from the dead* and warned them, they would repent. Abraham then said to him, "If they hear not Moses and the prophets, *neither will they be persuaded, though one rose from the dead.*"

The purpose in giving this account is to point out that in the Old Testament era, the spirits of the righteous *and* the spirits of the wicked went to hell, but the spirits of the wicked were in a place of fire and torment, and the spirits of the righteous were in Paradise. Furthermore, between those two places a great gulf was fixed, but the unrighteous could see over into Paradise, just as the rich man saw Lazarus *and recognized him.*

Jesus said to the penitent thief on the cross, *"TO DAY shalt thou be with me in Paradise"* (Luke 23:43). When Jesus died, it was still the Old Testament era— the Day of Grace had not begun. Therefore when Jesus spoke of Paradise, He spoke of the heart of the earth. That is where He went, and that is where the penitent thief went. (The other thief entered the torment side of hades where there was fire, and weeping and wailing.)

Jesus descended into the heart of the earth as He had declared He would: *"For as Jonas was three days and three nights in the whale's belly; so shall the Son of man be three days and three nights IN THE HEART OF THE EARTH"* (Matt. 12:40).

He announced to the spirits in prison (the Old Testament saints) that the sin-debt had been paid, the victory had been won, and that He would now liberate them from Paradise *in the heart of the earth* and take them with Him to the Paradise *far above all heavens:*

"For Christ also hath once suffered for sins, the just for the unjust, that He might bring us to God, being put to death in the flesh, but quickened by the Spirit: *By which also HE WENT AND PREACHED UNTO THE SPIRITS IN PRISON;* which sometime were disobedient, when once the longsuffering of God waited in the days of Noah, while the ark was a preparing, wherein few, that is, eight souls were saved by water" (I Pet. 3:18—20).

Paul tells us in Ephesians 4:7—10, "Unto every one of us is given grace according to the measure of the gift of Christ.   Wherefore He saith, When He ascended up on high, *He led captivity captive,* and gave gifts unto men.   (*Now that He ascended, what is it but that He also descended first into the lower parts of the earth? He that descended is the same also that ascended up far above all heavens,* that He might fill all things.)"

Since the resurrection of Jesus, hell has been the abode of the wicked only.   When Jesus brought the spirits of the righteous out of the Paradise side of hell, the great gulf was dissolved and the entire center of this earth became a burning inferno where the spirits of the wicked are now—and where they will *remain* until hell itself is cast into the lake that burns with fire and brimstone: *"THEREFORE HELL HATH ENLARGED HERSELF, AND OPENED HER MOUTH WITHOUT MEASURE: AND THEIR GLORY, AND THEIR MULTITUDE, AND THEIR POMP, AND HE THAT REJOICETH, SHALL DESCEND INTO IT"* (Isa. 5:14).

At the consummation of all things, when the eternity of eternities begins, Jesus will *personally* see to it that death and hell are cast into the lake of fire: "And death and hell were cast into the lake of fire.   This is the second death.   And whosoever was not found written in the book of life was cast into the lake of fire" (Rev. 20:14,15).

The *devil* will be in the lake of fire, the *beast* and the *false prophet* will be there, *all the wicked* will be there.   There will be no more sin, no more sorrow, no more disappointment in that long, eternal day of peace when we will dwell with Jesus in the Pearly White City. All things will be created new. There will be a new earth where will be no more sin. The heavens will be renovated and there will be no evil spirits in the atmosphere. Righteousness will *fill* God's new creation. Beloved, *that is the day believers are looking for!*

"*Neither wilt thou suffer thine Holy One to see corruption.*" We need not wonder who the *"Holy One"* is here. The Scriptures make it crystal clear:

In Mark 1:23,24 we read, "And there was in their synagogue a man with an unclean spirit; and he cried out, saying, Let us alone; what have we to do with thee, thou Jesus of Nazareth? Art thou come to destroy us? *I know thee who thou art, the HOLY ONE OF GOD.*"

In Acts 3:14 Peter said, "*Ye denied the HOLY ONE and the Just,* and desired a murderer to be granted unto you."

In Luke 1:35 the angel Gabriel announced to the Virgin Mary, "The Holy Ghost shall come upon thee, and the power of the Highest shall overshadow thee: *therefore also that HOLY thing which shall be born of thee shall be called the SON OF GOD.*"

"*Corruption*" here means putrefaction in the grave. The same word is used in Acts 13:34−37: "And as concerning that He raised Him up from the dead, now no more to return to corruption, He said on this wise, I will give you the sure mercies of David. Wherefore he saith also in another psalm, Thou shalt not suffer thine Holy One to see corruption. For David, after he had served his own generation by the will of God, fell on sleep, and was laid unto his fathers, and saw corruption: *but He, whom God raised again, saw no corruption.*"

Verse 28: *"Thou hast made known to me the ways of life; thou shalt make me full of joy with thy countenance."*

The preceding verses refer to the death and burial of

the Lord Jesus Christ, the Messiah. This verse speaks of
His resurrection from the dead—Jesus *restored to life* after
His crucifixion and entombment.   The quotation Peter
used here is from Psalm 16:11:

"Thou wilt shew me the path of life: in thy presence
is fulness of joy; at thy right hand there are pleasures
for evermore."   The prophecy is related to the Messiah,
and means "Thou wilt *restore* me to life, thou wilt *make
known to me LIFE ITSELF.*"   It was impossible for
death to hold Him, because *He IS life:* To Martha He
declared, "I am the resurrection, and the life: he that
believeth in me, though he were dead, yet shall he live:
and whosoever liveth and believeth in me shall never
die" (John 11:25,26).

"Thou shalt make me full of joy."   This speaks of
the feelings of Messiah in view of the fact that He would
be raised from the dead and given the seat at the right
hand of God the Father. Jesus was omniscient; He knew
death could not hold Him, and it was the foreknowledge
of His resurrection that brought joy: "Wherefore seeing
we also are compassed about with so great a cloud of
witnesses, let us lay aside every weight, and the sin
which doth so easily beset us, and let us run with patience the race that is set before us, looking unto Jesus
the author and finisher of our faith; *who for the JOY
that was set before Him ENDURED the cross, DESPIS-
ING THE SHAME, and is set down at the right hand
of the throne of God"* (Heb. 12:1,2).

It was for the joy set before Him that He endured
the cross and suffered its terrible shame, *willingly taking
our place* that we might have life in Him: ". . . God
hath given to us eternal life, *and this life is in His Son.
He that hath the Son hath life; and he that hath NOT
the Son of God hath not life"* (I John 5:11,12).

"With thy countenance" literally reads, "with thy
face"—that is, "in thy presence, *beholding thy face,"*
which signifies favor, joy, honor, and happiness afforded

the Lord Jesus Christ because of the exalted position He now occupies in the presence of God the Eternal Father.

In view of the glories that were set before Him, *Jesus rejoiced* in spite of the suffering, pain, and misery that lay ahead of Him. Surely, then, *believers* should rejoice, because Jesus is our Redeemer and "we know that, when He shall appear, *we shall be like Him;* for we shall see Him as He is" (I John 3:2). We should rejoice because He has promised that we will sit with Him on His throne *as HE overcame* and is set down with the Father *on HIS throne* (Rev. 3:21). Such hope should give us absolute assurance; it should sustain and encourage us when we are persecuted or when we face fiery trials. We should rejoice, knowing that one day we will be with Him where He is, and since we will be *like* Him we will have fulness of joy as *He* had fulness of joy!

In verses 22 through 28, Peter unfolded before his congregation the whole story of the Messiah whom they had rejected and crucified. In John 6:69 Peter had confessed Jesus as the "Christ, the Son of the living God," but in our present study he referred to Him as "Jesus of Nazareth" (v. 22), using the humble, lowly name by which the Jews had known Him. Jesus *did* come out of Nazareth; that name was written above His cross, and the very *name* was an offence to the Jews. Peter used it here—and rightly so—in showing the guilt of the nation Israel, proving to them that they were guilty of the death of their Messiah. The main theme of Peter's address on the Day of Pentecost was "The crucified One is Lord and Christ"; therefore "Jesus of Nazareth" was the only name that *could* be used here.

Actually, it is improper for us today—nineteen hundred years this side of Christ's resurrection—to refer to Him as Jesus the Nazarene. We should call Him by His resurrection name: *the Lord Jesus Christ.* Peter declared, "Let all the house of Israel know assuredly, that *God hath made THAT SAME JESUS*, whom ye have crucified,

BOTH LORD AND CHRIST" (v. 36). We should speak of Jesus today as the Lord Jesus Christ *who conquered the world, the flesh, the devil, death, hell, and the grave, and who is now seated* at the right hand of God the Father to make intercession for us (Rom. 8:34).

In these verses Peter covered the events of the past three years briefly — events which were familiar to all of those who were present that day. Since God the Father witnessed to Jesus the Nazarene through the *works* He did, through the *power* He demonstrated, and through the wonderful *signs and miracles* He wrought, there is no doubt in my mind that many who heard Peter's sermon at Pentecost had also heard *Jesus* speak and were eyewitnesses of the miracles wrought by the power of God *through Him.*

Jesus Himself declared that He was more than man, that He was sent from God and was doing the works God had sent Him to do:

"I have greater witness than that of John (the Baptist): for the works which the Father hath given me to finish, *the same works that I do, bear witness of me, that the Father hath sent me. . .* Believe me that I am in the Father, and the Father in me: *OR ELSE BELIEVE ME FOR THE VERY WORKS' SAKE"* (John 5:36; 14:11).

But He who had claimed to be very God had been nailed to a cross. Could He *possibly* be Messiah, as He claimed to be? It was true that He had performed mighty miracles such as they had never before witnessed, yet He had surrendered to their insults and mockery, He had yielded to a crown of thorns instead of a crown of glory, and instead of taking the throne of David He had finally come to a shameful death by crucifixion on Mount Calvary! Could this Person, this Nazarene, possibly *be* the expected King of the Jews, their Messiah?

By such reasoning the cross became a stumblingblock to the Jews, and now, speaking under inspiration of the

Holy Spirit, Peter tells them *why* Jesus was nailed to a cross.   He declared that the death of Jesus of Nazareth was the result of *the determinate counsel and foreknowledge of God*—the God of Abraham, Isaac, and Jacob. The *sufferings* of Messiah were fully foretold in the Old Testament, and if the Jews had understood Isaiah chapter 53 they would have known that He must be led as a lamb to the slaughter *and so enter into glory*—but suffering *MUST precede* the glory.

Peter then declared that all of this had come to pass exactly as prophesied, and in perfect accordance with the foreknowledge of God.   All that had happened to Jesus of Nazareth had been predetermined and arranged in the eternal council of Almighty God (I Pet. 1:18—20); but the Jews were the instruments *used* in the death of their Messiah, therefore they were *guilty* of His death.

Abraham spoke of Jesus, but these were lawless, wicked men who had not heard the Law of Moses in their hearts and they had demanded the death of the lowly Nazarene. They were responsible for what happened to Him, regardless of the predetermination and foreknowledge of God.   This was the divine truth Peter's sermon laid before the Jews that day.   Then he brought his message to a climax by thundering out the prophecies of the *resurrection* of Him who had been nailed to the cross! True, the Jews had been guilty of His death, but the God of their fathers had *raised* Him from the dead because it was impossible that death should hold Him.   He conquered death and rose again, *the "firstfruits,"* declaring victory over death, hell, and the grave.

Thank God, Jesus was "made a little lower than the angels . . . *that He by the grace of God should taste death for every man. . .* Forasmuch then as the children are partakers of flesh and blood, He also Himself likewise took part of the same; *that through death He might destroy him that had the power of death, that is, the devil; and deliver them who through fear of death were all their lifetime subject to bondage"* (Heb. 2:9,14,15). Now, *all believers* can shout, "O death, where is thy sting? O grave, where is thy victory?" (I Cor. 15:55).

There were three major points in Peter's sermon at Pentecost, three positive proofs that Jesus the Nazarene was Messiah:

His LIFE proved that He was Messiah, for certainly no mortal ever lived (or ever *could* live) as Jesus lived.

His DEATH proved that He was Messiah, for He died *exactly* as the Old Testament Scriptures had *prophesied.*

His RESURRECTION proved that He was Messiah.

He came as promised, His life and His works were evidence of His identity, He openly and clearly *told* the people who He was—but they rejected Him and crucified Him.

Peter plainly showed his congregation the path Jesus walked—from the humiliation of death on the cross, to His resurrection and ascension to the right hand of God the Father. Then having established *unquestionable proof* that this was their Messiah, he continued his sermon by *showing* Jesus exalted and seated at the right hand of the Majesty on high. God the Eternal Father was put on display in the Person of Jesus Christ. It was by God's determinate counsel that Jesus was delivered unto death, it was by God's mighty power that He was raised from the dead, and finally, by the power of God the Eternal Father He ascended and was made *"both Lord and Christ"* (v. 36).

Verse 29: *"Men and brethren, let me freely speak unto you of the patriarch David, that he is both dead and buried, and his sepulchre is with us unto this day."*

Peter now begins to explain to the Jews *why* the passage quoted from Psalms could not possibly relate to *David,* but must be prophetically applied to the Messiah.

"Men and brethren...." Only a few minutes earlier, these men had declared that Peter and the other believers

were drunk; but notice he here addressed them as *"BRETHREN."* In spite of their accusation he respected them because they were his brethren *according to the flesh.* We should apply this example to our own lives, because if we hope to convince sinners that we are children of God, our attitude toward them *cannot* be one of contempt. *Those whom we desire to win for Christ* we must treat with respect.

"Let me freely speak." The tone of the Greek is, "It is proper and lawful for me to speak boldly respecting David. Even though he was a righteous man and a king, yet it is proper to say he is dead, buried, and his body has returned to dust."

Since the *"Holy One"* of whom David wrote should not *"see corruption,"* he could not have been speaking of himself. The Jews had great respect for David. Peter knew this, and if he hoped to get his message across to them, he dared not show disrespect for the king whom they held in such high regard. Therefore he paid respect to David as a godly man and a king of Israel—but he was also bold in defending the Scriptures by declaring that the Old Testament passage he had just quoted *could not* refer to David, because *"the patriarch David . . . is both dead and buried, and his sepulchre is with us unto this day."*

"Patriarch" speaks of the head or ruler of a family, or of an illustrious ancestor. It denotes the chief men in the tribes of the nation Israel (I Chron. 24:31; II Chron. 19:8). The term is used with reference to Abraham, Isaac, Jacob, founders and heads of the Jewish nation. (Study Hebrews 7:4 and Acts 7:8,9.) Peter used the word here to show honor and respect for King David, Israel's most illustrious king and founder of the royal family through whose lineage their Messiah was to come.

But the Old Testament Scripture declared that David was dead, that he "slept with his fathers" in Jerusalem (I Kings 2:10), and there was no suggestion that he had *risen* from the dead.   In Jerusalem—even today—historians and archeologists point out his sepulchre.   I visited the tomb of David when I was in the Holy Land, and I can personally testify that it is still known and honored by the Jews.   They will not enter the sepulchre without wearing a head-covering, and they leave an offering each time they go there.

Solomon buried David in Jerusalem, with all the honor and magnificence possible to bestow upon him. Josephus the historian tells us that immense wealth—much gold and money—was buried with him. Some time later (also according to Josephus), one of the rooms in the sepulchre was opened and three thousand talents removed—which would amount to quite a sum of money. Some years later, Herod opened *another* room and took away a great sum of money. *This is a matter of history.*

The tomb of David was familiar to the Jews, and certainly no Jew would have suggested—or even *supposed*—that he had been raised from the dead! In view of this fact, Peter could assure them that in the Old Testament Scripture he had used, David was not speaking of himself but of their Messiah whom they had crucified and buried, but God had raised Him from the dead.

Verse 30:   *"Therefore being a prophet, and knowing that God had sworn with an oath to him, that of the fruit of his loins, according to the flesh, He would raise up Christ to sit on his throne."*

"Therefore being a prophet . . . ." There is no doubt that David was inspired of God. He gave this in personal testimony in II Samuel 23:2 where, as "the sweet psalmist of Israel" he declared, *"The Spirit of the Lord spake by me, and His word was in my tongue."* The Psalms contain many prophetic passages concerning the coming of Jesus, and the Jews *accepted* David as a prophet.

We might take time here to compare some of the

prophecies of David relating to the Messiah, and the *fulfillment* of those prophecies in the New Testament:

Psalm 22:1: "My God, my God, why hast thou forsaken me? Why art thou so far from helping me, and from the words of my roaring?"

Compare this with Matthew 27:46: "And about the ninth hour Jesus cried with a loud voice, saying, Eli, Eli, lama sabachthani? That is to say, My God, my God, why hast thou forsaken me?"

Psalm 22:18: "They part my garments among them, and cast lots upon my vesture."

Compare this with Matthew 27:35: "And they crucified Him, and parted His garments, casting lots: *that it might be fulfilled which was spoken by the prophet,* They parted my garments among them, and upon my vesture did they cast lots."

Psalm 69:25: "Let their habitation be desolate; and let none dwell in their tents."

Compare this with Acts 1:20: "For it is written in the book of Psalms, Let his habitation be desolate, and let no man dwell therein: and his bishoprick let another take." (This, of course, refers to Judas.)

"Knowing that God had sworn with an oath to him . . . ." God made promises to David in regard to his posterity—that is, *"that of the fruit of his loins, according to the flesh, He would raise up Christ to sit on his throne."* Insofar as the *human* nature of Jesus is concerned, He was prophesied to descend from David, or through the *seed* (lineage) of David.

In *Psalm 89:3,4* God said, "I have made a covenant with my chosen. I have sworn unto David my servant, *Thy seed will I establish for ever, and build up thy throne to all generations."*

In *Psalm 132:11* we read, "The Lord hath sworn in truth unto David; He will not turn from it: *Of the fruit of thy body will I set upon thy throne."*

In *II Samuel 7:12—16* God sent the following message

to David, through Nathan: "And when thy days be fulfilled, and thou shalt sleep with thy fathers, I will set up thy seed after thee, which shall proceed out of thy bowels, and I will establish his kingdom. He shall build an house for my name, and I will establish the throne of his kingdom for ever. I will be his Father, and he shall be my son. If he commit iniquity, I will chasten him with the rod of men, and with the stripes of the children of men: But my mercy shall not depart away from him, as I took it from Saul, whom I put away before thee. *And thine house and thy kingdom shall be established for ever before thee: thy throne shall be established for ever.*"

These promises made to David were repeated when Gabriel announced to Mary that she would be the mother of the Son of God:

"And the angel said unto her, Fear not, Mary: for thou hast found favour with God. And, behold, thou shalt conceive in thy womb, and bring forth a Son, and shalt call His name JESUS. He shall be great, and shall be called the Son of the Highest: *and the Lord God shall give unto Him THE THRONE OF HIS FATHER DAVID: and He shall reign over the house of Jacob for ever; AND OF HIS KINGDOM THERE SHALL BE NO END*" (Luke 1:30—33).

The Old Testament references we have studied here have immediate reference to *Solomon,* David's son who reigned after him; but the ultimate reference is to the Lord Jesus Christ, the Messiah, and the Jews *understood* that their Messiah was to come through the lineage of David (Matt. 12:23; 21:9; 22:42—45; Mark 11:10; John 7:42); but they were not looking for a humble, submissive *Saviour* made like unto man, who would suffer death and be crowned with a crown of thorns. They were looking for a powerful ruler who would deliver them from the bondage of Rome.

Just how the Jews understood these prophecies to

apply to their Messiah, we cannot fully understand nor determine; *but they did believe in the FACT of the coming Messiah,* and they also believed that He would come as a descendant of David, to rule over an unending kingdom as promised in Isaiah 9:6,7:

"For unto us a Child is born, unto us a Son is given: and the government shall be upon His shoulder: and His name shall be called Wonderful, Counsellor, The mighty God, The everlasting Father, the Prince of Peace. *Of the increase of His government and peace THERE SHALL BE NO END, upon the throne of David, and upon his kingdom, to order it, and to establish it with judgment and with justice from henceforth, even for ever.* The zeal of the Lord of hosts will perform this."

God's promise to David was made *only* to David, never to another king or kingdom. In his message on the Day of Pentecost, Peter declared that David was *fully aware* of all that he had prophesied concerning the Messiah, and made it clear that David believed God's promise to point forward—not only to Solomon, but *beyond Solomon to the Messiah.* The Old Testament contains a commentary of David's views of the promises God gave him. Please study these *entire chapters:* Psalm 2, Psalm 22, Psalm 45, and especially Psalm 16.

David looked forward to the coming of Messiah. He understood that the promises made to him *pointed to* the Messiah and the time when King Jesus would occupy the *throne* of David and would reign over the whole earth.

Yes, the Lord Jesus Christ will one day sit on the throne of David—and beloved, the throne of David is a *historical* throne just as surely as the throne of *Caesar* is a historical throne. Some commentators and teachers declare that this Scripture speaks of a *spiritual* throne, but not so. *David* did not sit on a spiritual throne. *He sat on a LITERAL throne in a literal PLACE—Jerusalem;* and so will the Lord Jesus Christ sit on a literal throne,

in the temple which will be rebuilt in Jerusalem after
the Rapture of the Church.   In connection with this,
please read Acts 15:13—18, which we will study in detail
when we reach that passage.

Israel asked for a king, and God gave them Saul (I
Sam. chapters 8 and 9).   But Saul's kingdom was taken
from him and his descendants, and given to David.   God
then declared and ordained that the kingdom should *continue* through the lineage of David.   *One fact* distinguished David from all other earthly kings: *HE
REIGNED OVER ISRAEL, THE CHOSEN PEOPLE
OF GOD.*   And since he reigned over God's chosen people, the Holy One who would one day come as King of
kings and Lord of lords should also reign over the people
of God, and should occupy the throne of David.   One
glorious day a literal King Jesus will sit on the literal
throne of David, and will reign over this earth, as promised in the Scriptures.

Verse 31:   *"He seeing this before spake of the resurrection of Christ, that His soul was not left in hell,
neither His flesh did see corruption."*

"He seeing this before" means that David, by the Spirit of prophecy, spoke of the resurrection of Jesus. Through
the eyes of the Holy Spirit, he foresaw the resurrection of
the Messiah—*"that His soul was not left in hell, neither
His flesh did see corruption."*   The statement in this
verse clearly teaches that David had unusual spiritual in-
sight, and God made known to him in a very special way
the great doctrines pertaining to the coming of Messiah—
not only His coming as King of kings and Lord of lords,
but also His coming to suffer and wear the crown of
thorns, that *we* might wear the crown of life.   These
prophecies were then given to the fathers through the
inspired pen of David.   *Jesus* told His disciples after His
resurrection, "These are the words which I spake unto
you, while I was yet with you, that all things must be

fulfilled, which were written in the law of Moses, and in the prophets, *and in the psalms, concerning me"* (Luke 24:44).

The Bodily Resurrection of Jesus
Proves That He Is Lord and Christ

Verse 32: *"This Jesus hath God raised up, whereof we all are witnesses."*

Peter had clearly set before the Jews the fact that the resurrection of Jesus was a matter of Old Testament prophecy recorded in their Scriptures, and to deny that truth was to deny the Scripture given to the fathers through such prophets as David, whom they so highly revered and respected.   Since the resurrection was a matter of Old Testament prophecy, Peter then set about to present *further* undeniable evidence that Jesus of Nazareth *had risen* from the dead.

"Whereof we all are WITNESSES." Peter could have been speaking here of the apostles only, but it is more probable that he referred to the entire group of one hundred and twenty people who were present in the upper room when the Holy Spirit came, and who were now witnessing to the glorious Gospel of the grace of God—and the Gospel is the death, burial, and resurrection of Jesus "according to the Scriptures" (I Cor. 15:1—4).   Peter's aim now was to prove to the Jews that Jesus was *seen alive* after His crucifixion and burial, and God appointed the apostles *to bear witness* to the resurrection.

Paul also gives a brief commentary on the assurance of the bodily resurrection of Jesus:

"Moreover, brethren, I declare unto you *the Gospel* which I preached unto you, which also ye have received, and wherein ye stand; by which also ye are *saved. . .* For I delivered unto you first of all that which I also received, how that *Christ died* for our sins according to the Scriptures; and that *He was buried,* and that *He rose again* the third day according to the Scriptures: And that He was *seen of Cephas,* then of *the twelve*: After that, He was seen *of above FIVE HUNDRED brethren at once:* of whom the greater part remain unto this present, but some are fallen asleep. After that, He was seen *of James;* then of *all the apostles.* And last of all He was seen *of me also,* as of one born out of due time" (I Cor. 15:1—8).

Paul here declared that five hundred believers saw Jesus at one time, and I believe the one hundred and twenty witnesses in the upper room were *part* of that five hundred. The Jews might deny *Peter's* testimony, they might deny the testimony of the *apostles;* but the testimony of five hundred people could not be easily set aside. If the Jews refused to believe the testimony of five hundred brethren—or even the testimony of the one hundred and twenty—then there was *no way* to prove any fact to them.

Peter did not say that the apostles had witnessed the actual *resurrection.* He was attempting to establish in the minds of the Jews the fact that he and many others had seen Jesus *AFTER the resurrection.* He had walked and talked with them, He had eaten with them, and He had invited them to touch Him and be convinced that He was not a *spirit,* as some supposed when they first saw Him after His resurrection (Luke 24:39).

It was *a matter of record* that Jesus died on the cross; the fact of His death was already established. Peter wanted the Jews to know *just as surely* that He whom they called "Jesus of Nazareth" *had also RISEN* from the tomb, that many of His followers had seen Him after His resurrection, and to this they were willing to bear witness.

It should have been evident to the Jews that Peter and the other believers at Pentecost were not seeking fame or fortune, because *Jesus* had been put to death for preaching the very Gospel *they* were now preaching.

They were risking their very lives by declaring that they had seen Jesus alive after His crucifixion. They were subjecting themselves to sufferings, persecution, perhaps even death on a cross as Jesus had died; but regardless of personal risk, Peter boldly declared, "Jesus the Nazarene is *alive. We KNOW He is alive because we SAW Him, and we testify to the FACT of His BODILY resurrection.*"

Verse 33: *"Therefore being by the right hand of God exalted, and having received of the Father the promise of the Holy Ghost, He hath shed forth this, which ye now see and hear."*

To the Hebrews, *"the right hand"* denoted power, and Peter's declaration that Jesus was at that very moment sitting *at GOD'S right hand* was also a declaration that He was seated *in the place of POWER*, in the same position He had occupied before the world was created by Him and for Him (Heb. 1:1−3; John 17:5).

The use of the term "right hand" to denote power is common in the Scriptures:

In *Psalm 17:7* David wrote, "Shew thy marvellous lovingkindness, O thou that savest *by thy right hand* them which put their trust in thee from those that rise up against them."

In *Psalm 18:35* he wrote, "Thou hast also given me the shield of thy salvation: and *thy right hand* hath holden me up, and thy gentleness hath made me great."

Then in *Psalm 20:6* we read, "Now know I that the Lord saveth His anointed; He will hear him from His holy heaven with *the saving strength of His right hand.*"

In *Psalm 21:8* we read, "Thine hand shall find out all thine enemies: *thy right hand* shall find out those that hate thee."

Psalm 44:3 says, "For they got not the land in possession by their own sword, neither did their own arm save them: but *thy right hand,* and thine arm, and the light of thy countenance, because thou hadst a favour unto them."

"And having received of the Father the promise of the Holy Ghost . . . ." The Holy Ghost was promised to the disciples by the Lord Jesus before He was crucified:

"But the Comforter, which is the Holy Ghost, whom the Father will send in my name, He shall teach you all things, and bring all things to your remembrance, whatsoever I have said unto you. . . When the Comforter is come, whom I will send unto you from the Father, even the Spirit of truth, which proceedeth from the Father, He shall testify of me. . . When He, the Spirit of truth, is come, He will guide you into all truth: for He shall not speak of Himself; but whatsoever He shall hear, that shall He speak: and He will shew you things to come. He shall glorify me: for He shall receive of mine, and shall shew it unto you. All things that the Father hath are mine: therefore said I, that He shall take of mine, and shall shew it unto you" (John 14:26; 15:26; 16:13 — 15).

Peter was here announcing that the promises made by Jesus before His crucifixion had been literally fulfilled. The gift of the Holy Ghost had now been bestowed, and surely those who witnessed the extraordinary occurrences at Pentecost must realize this. The one hundred and twenty in the upper room were God's chosen vessels through which the Gospel of the death, burial, and resurrection of Jesus would be proclaimed — not only to the nation Israel, but to the uttermost parts of the earth.

"Hath shed forth this" speaks of the different languages spoken by the Jews that day, so that all who were present heard the Gospel in their own tongue. Such a miracle could only come through the fulfillment of Joel's prophecy that the Holy Spirit would be poured out. It was *not* the result of drinking "new wine" as

the scoffers claimed. It was undeniable proof that the Holy Ghost had come as promised, to empower these witnesses to spread the Gospel of God's grace to all men everywhere.

Verses 34 and 35: *"For David is not ascended into the heavens: but he saith himself, The LORD said unto my Lord, Sit thou on my right hand, until I make thy foes thy footstool."*

Peter knew—as did all of the Jews—that David had neither risen from the dead nor ascended into heaven. No Israelite would dare suggest such a thing. This fact *alone* was sufficient to prove that Psalm 16 did not refer to David, but to the Lord Jesus Christ, the Messiah, and Peter here reminds the Jews that *David himself* gave testimony to the exalted character and divine dignity of the Messiah, exaltation and dignity far beyond what David had known or ever *could* know.

(This does not mean that David was not saved, that his spirit did not go into Paradise when he departed this life. It means that he was not *raised from the dead* as Jesus was, and that he was not *exalted in the heavens* in the same sense that Jesus was exalted.)

"But he saith himself . . . ." What David said is recorded in Psalm 110:1: "The LORD said unto my Lord, Sit thou at my right hand, until I make thine enemies thy footstool." Notice the first *"LORD"* in this Scripture is in capitals, denoting that in the original language the word was *Jehovah.* The Jews regarded *Jehovah* as the peculiar name of Almighty God, and it was never applied to anyone *except* God the Father. Therefore we see that David was quoting what Jehovah God had said— that is, "Jehovah said to the Person whom I, David, readily acknowledge to be greater than I in dignity and power, my superior and Sovereign, *'Sit thou on my right hand until I make thy foes thy footstool.'"* Even though David prophesied of Jesus as *descending FROM him*

(through his lineage according to the flesh), he regarded the Messiah as his superior, his Lord.

Jesus Himself used this passage when He answered one of the questions put to Him by the Pharisees:

"While the Pharisees were gathered together, Jesus asked them, saying, What think ye of Christ? Whose Son is He? They say unto Him, *The son of David.*

"He saith unto them, *How then doth David in spirit call Him Lord,* saying, The LORD said unto my Lord, Sit thou on my right hand, till I make thine enemies thy footstool? *If David then call Him Lord, how is He his son?* And no man was able to answer Him a word, neither durst any man from that day forth ask Him any more questions" (Matt. 22:41—46).

Jesus applied this passage in such a manner as to show that this was the accepted doctrine of the Jews— i. e., Messiah would reign until He put all of His enemies under His feet, making them His footstool. *He would then become King of kings and Lord of lords.* The Jewish nation looked forward to the coming of such a King.

Verse 36: *"Therefore let all the house of Israel know assuredly, that God hath made that same Jesus, whom ye have crucified, both Lord and Christ."*

"Therefore"—since the Old Testament prophecies concerning Messiah were literally fulfilled in Jesus; and since Peter and the other disciples witnessed *the mighty miracles* of Jesus throughout His earthly ministry; and since such remarkable miracles had been exhibited on the Day of Pentecost— *"let all the house of Israel know ASSUREDLY"* that Jesus is now seated at the right hand of God the Father—no longer the lowly Nazarene, but *GOD'S CHRIST and Lord of all!*

"House of Israel" includes the entire Jewish nation. Of course such an appeal can be made only to Israel, for they alone had known the prophecies and received

the promises. Let them *"know ASSUREDLY"* (beyond any shadow of doubt) that this *"SAME JESUS"* whom they crucified had *by the power of God* been raised from the dead, exalted to God's right hand, and made *"both LORD and CHRIST"*—rejected of men, but *received of Jehovah God* and given the seat on God's right hand.

The word here translated *"Lord"* denotes sovereignty. Therefore the meaning is clear: *God exalted Jesus to be King,* He has given Him dominion in the heavens and made Him ruler of all things:

"These words spake Jesus, and lifted up His eyes to heaven, and said, Father, the hour is come; glorify thy Son, that thy Son also may glorify thee: *AS THOU HAST GIVEN HIM POWER OVER ALL FLESH, that He should give eternal life to as many as thou hast given Him"* (John 17:1,2).

Paul speaks of the working of God's mighty power, "which He wrought in Christ, when He raised Him from the dead, and set Him *at His own right hand in the heavenly places, FAR ABOVE ALL PRINCIPALITY, AND POWER, AND MIGHT, AND DOMINION, AND EVERY NAME THAT IS NAMED, NOT ONLY IN THIS WORLD, BUT ALSO IN THAT WHICH IS TO COME"* (Eph. 1:20,21).

In the future, Jesus will come to judge the world, He will judge in righteousness, and His judgment will be *according to His WORD:*

"He that rejecteth me, and receiveth not my words, hath one that judgeth him: *THE WORD THAT I HAVE SPOKEN, THE SAME SHALL JUDGE HIM IN THE LAST DAY"* (John 12:48).

Peter made his declaration that Jesus was now "both Lord and Christ" in an attempt to bring the Jews to repentance and cause them to return to the Lord, instead of going further and further from Him. *Amos* had warned the Jewish people in *these* words:

"I have overthrown some of you, as God overthrew

Sodom and Gomorrah, and ye were as a firebrand plucked out of the burning: *yet have ye not returned unto me, SAITH THE LORD.* Therefore thus will I do unto thee, O Israel: and because I will do this unto thee, *prepare to meet thy God, O Israel"* (Amos 4:11,12).

Yes, the Jews had good reason to fear, and to dread the day when Jesus would come in vengeance and judgment to punish them for their sins. They had crucified the hope of their nation—the One of whom their prophets had written, the One in whom their fathers had hoped. *No wonder* they were disturbed when they realized the shame they had brought upon their nation and the guilt that hung heavily over them. *No wonder* they cried out, *"Men and brethren, WHAT SHALL WE DO?"*

There was *a definite purpose* in Peter's enlarging on the prophecy of David in this message of the Day of Pentecost: *That prophecy was the foundation of Peter's appeal to the Jews.* They had never thought of applying the sixteenth Psalm to their coming Messiah, but thought the passage referred to David personally; but Peter showed them that such a traditional belief was wrong and explained *why* the words of the Psalm could not refer to David. They all knew of David's tomb, they all knew David had not risen from the dead. He was buried, and his body saw corruption. Therefore it was *impossible* for the prophecy to be applied to *him.* *"He* (David) *seeing this before spake of the resurrection of Christ."* Seeing it by the Word of God, David spoke concerning the resurrection of Messiah, and *in Christ alone* could these words have been fulfilled.

There are tens of thousands today who deny the bodily resurrection of Jesus, but *in order to be saved* it is a divine imperative that we *believe* in His bodily resurrection: "If thou shalt confess with thy mouth the Lord Jesus, *and shalt believe in thine heart that God hath RAISED HIM FROM THE DEAD, thou shalt be saved"*

(Rom. 10:9).

Paul tells us, "If Christ be not risen, then is our preaching vain, and your faith is also vain. . . If Christ be not raised, your faith is vain; ye are yet in your sins. Then they also which are fallen asleep in Christ are perished" (I Cor. 15:14−18).

The coming of the Holy Spirit on the Day of Pentecost (as prophesied by Joel and promised by Jesus) was divine evidence and proof positive that Jesus *was exalted* to His place at the right hand of the Father. The very fact that the Holy Spirit *had come* was proof that Jesus had returned to the Father, because He promised that when He *did* return to the Father He would send the Comforter. Thus the Holy Spirit's coming proved the ascension and exaltation of Jesus.

The Jews *could* have asked Peter, "If the crucified Nazarene was really Messiah, why does He not come and sit on the throne of David *now*? Why is He not reigning over His kingdom?" The answer is in Psalm 110: Jesus was to return to the Father, take His seat at the Father's right hand, and remain there until His enemies be made His footstool. Then−and *not until* then−He will sit on the throne of David and reign over the earth, in keeping with God's plan and program.

The *theme* of the pure Gospel of God's marvelous grace is that *Jesus has been made both Lord and Christ.* He died for our sins "according to the Scriptures." He rose again the third day "according to the Scriptures." He is now exalted−Lord and Christ−in glory seated at the right hand of the Father "according to the Scriptures," and *He is coming again,* King of kings and Lord of lords, "according to the Scriptures." Paul told Titus that the grace of God teaches us to *look* for "that blessed hope, and the glorious appearing of the great God and our Saviour Jesus Christ; who gave Himself for us . . ." (Tit. 2:13,14). This message will stir *anyone* who will listen with an open heart and an open mind. It stirred the Jews on the Day of Pentecost, and they cried out, "Men and brethren, *what shall we do?*"

What Israel Must Do

Verse 37:   *"Now when they heard this, they were pricked in their heart, and said unto Peter and to the rest of the apostles, Men and brethren, what shall we do?"*

When the Jews heard Peter's message and his final declaration, convinced that they had crucified their Messiah *"they were pricked in their heart."* The Greek word translated *"pricked"* is not used anywhere else in the New Testament. Literally, it means *"to pierce or penetrate,* as with a needle or a sharp instrument, also *to pierce with grief or acute pain."*

The implication here is that after Peter's sermon the Jews were deeply *pierced with fear* because of the things he had proved from their own Old Testament Scriptures. Not *all* who were present on that day were grieved because they realized they had put their Messiah to death, but *many* of them did feel a deep sense of guilt because of what they had done. They became keenly aware that the Nazarene whom they had crucified as an impostor was truly their Messiah, and the result of that realization was a sudden anguish and alarm. God might pour out some kind of terrible wrath upon them *immediately!* Jesus was alive, exalted to the right hand of God. He was now Lord, and He had *power.*   They feared His vengeance, lest He immediately mete out judgment and pour out His vengeance upon them.

"Men and brethren, what shall we do?"   In other words, "Please tell us what we can do to cause God to withhold His wrath!"

"Men and brethren" is an expression of love, earnestness, and devotion. But minutes earlier, this same crowd had mocked the disciples and accused them of drunken-

ness. Peter's sermon enlightened them and brought them under such deep conviction for their great sin, that here they addressed the disciples with acceptance and respect. They were no longer mocking, no longer hypocritical. They sincerely wanted to know what they could do to keep God from unleashing His holy wrath upon them!

Verse 38: *"Then Peter said unto them, Repent, and be baptized every one of you in the name of Jesus Christ for the remission of sins, and ye shall receive the gift of the Holy Ghost."*

"REPENT!" True repentance is sorrow for sin committed against a holy God—and not only sorrow *for* sin, but *turning from* sin, forsaking sin and turning to God. To do again the same thing supposedly repented of is not true repentance.

Repentance is *not* fear of the consequences of sin and damnation in hell. It is *not* fear of the wrath of God that is to be poured out upon the wicked. *True repentance in the heart* looks upon sin in its true light and recognizes sin as having nailed Jesus to the cross. *True repentance* is such hatred for sin that the penitent one forsakes sin and turns "about face" to walk with God. Sin is evil. God hates sin. Sin nailed the Saviour to the cross—and certainly that fact alone is sufficient reason why all who have genuinely *repented* hate sin and forsake sinful ways.

Some people mistake *conviction* for repentance, but there is a vast difference between conviction and *repentance with faith toward God.* Conviction may pass quickly and leave a soul as lost and hopeless as before. A man may fear God—even *the devils* believe and tremble (James 2:19), but certainly they are not saved! *Fear of the consequences of ungodly living* is not repentance. The drunkard in jail the morning after he was arrested for drunkenness and disorderly conduct repents of his deed, he is sorry he is in jail; but *ninety-nine times out of a hundred he will do the same thing again when he gets out!* To be sorry because we are caught in wrong-doing, or to be fearful because we know "the wages of sin is death" is NOT true heart-repentance which leads us to forsake sin and follow righteousness. *Many* people are *alarmed* about their sins, but they never repent. They live in fear and trembling—but they never know godly sorrow for their sins, they never turn to God in true repentance. To *turn TO God* is to automatically *turn FROM sin.* This is the only repentance that will bring peace to the heart and mind of man.

Ministers today can learn a vital lesson here if they will but listen to the Word of God: When the Jews cried out, "What shall we do?" Peter immediately answered, *"Repent!"* He did not tell them to lay aside their sin and try to reform. He did not tell them to "turn over a new leaf" and promise to live better; nor did he suggest that they postpone a decision until a more "convenient" time. We should warn those to whom we minister that *today* is the day of salvation, *now* is the accepted time (II Cor. 6:2). We have no promise of tomorrow, and when we deal with those who are convicted of sin we should urge them to repent immediately and exercise faith in the finished work of the Lord Jesus Christ.

All *men of God* preach repentance. John the Baptist came on the scene preaching, *"Repent ye: for the kingdom of heaven is at hand"* (Matt. 3:2). *Jesus Himself* preached repentance: *"Except ye repent,* ye shall all likewise perish"* (Luke 13:3,5). On the Day of Pentecost, *Peter* preached repentance. I realize that in this day and hour it is not *"popular"* to tell sinners to repent and cry out to God for mercy, but unpopular as we know the doctrine of repentance to be, it is *profitable,* because *"except ye repent—*Jew, Gentile, bond, free, wise, unwise—*YE SHALL PERISH in the lake of fire!"*

"Repent and be baptized, every one of you . . . ."

Jesus gave His disciples their commission to go "and teach all nations, baptizing them in the name of the Father, and of the Son, and of the Holy Ghost" (Matt. 28:19). The people to whom Peter preached at Pentecost had not been baptized, but please notice he urged them to *repent*—and *then* be baptized. Repentance *precedes* baptism.

Baptism is an outward confession that we are *dead* with Christ, buried with Christ, and *raised* with Him to walk in newness of life. Peter commanded the Jews to repent, and then follow Christ in baptism, thus denoting their break with Judaism and their acceptance of the Lord Jesus Christ. By accepting Christian baptism they testified that they had embraced Jesus as their Messiah and Saviour.

Water baptism has nothing to do with redemption. *Obedience?* Yes. We should obey the Lord Jesus, we should follow Him in baptism; but the water does not wash away sin, it does not help to save us, it does not cause us to be any better (or more fully) saved. There are tens of thousands of people today who are depending on baptism to get them to heaven—and they are headed for tragic disappointment! If they have not been washed in the precious blood of Jesus, certainly the washing of the water in the baptistry will not make them fit for the kingdom of God.

Nicodemus was a master teacher in the religion of the Jews; yet Jesus told him, "Except a man be *born again,* he cannot see the kingdom of God." Nicodemus then asked, "How can a man be born when he is *old?*" and Jesus replied, "Except a man be born *of water and of the Spirit,* he cannot enter into the kingdom of God. That which is born of the flesh is flesh; and that which is born of the Spirit is spirit" (John 3:1—6 in part).

There are those who teach that the *"water"* of which Jesus spoke refers to the baptistry, and that baptism washes away sins; but by carefully studying the Word

and comparing Scripture with Scripture we readily see
that Jesus did not tell Nicodemus that he must be baptized *IN water* and IN the Spirit, or that he must be
born IN water and IN the Spirit, in order to enter the
kingdom of heaven.

In Scripture, *water* is a type or symbol of the Word
of God.   For instance, in John 15:3 Jesus said to His
disciples, "Now ye are *clean* through *the WORD* which
I have spoken unto you."

In James 1:18 we read, "Of His own will begat He us
with the *WORD of truth,* that we should be a kind of
firstfruits of His creatures."

In Ephesians 5:25,26 Paul tells us that Christ loved
the Church "and gave Himself for it; *that He might sanctify and cleanse it with the washing of water BY THE
WORD.*"

In I Peter 1:23 we are told that we are "born again,
not of corruptible seed, but of incorruptible, *BY THE
WORD OF GOD,* which liveth and abideth for ever."

Now coming back to the words of Jesus in John 3:6
where He told Nicodemus, "That which is born of the
flesh is *flesh;* and that which is born of the Spirit is
spirit," He was actually saying to Nicodemus, "It is not
a *flesh-birth* but a *spiritual* birth by which you must
enter the kingdom of God."   Beloved, *the water in the
baptistry does not touch the SPIRIT, it touches only the
FLESH—that which is NOT born of God!*

If we die before the Rapture, our flesh is destined to
corrupt and return to dust.   If we live to see the Rapture, we will be changed *in a moment* and the corruptible will put on incorruption, the mortal will put on
immortality (I Cor. 15:51—53).   It is the inner man, *the
spirit,* that is born of God through the incorruptible seed
of the Word.

In John 5:24 Jesus declared, "Verily, verily, I say unto
you, He that heareth my Word (*not* he that is baptized
in water), and believeth on Him that sent me, hath ever-

lasting life, and shall not come into condemnation; but is passed from death unto life."

John 3:18 declares, "He that believeth on Him is not condemned: but he that believeth not is condemned already, *because he hath not believed in the name of the only begotten Son of God!*" Nothing is said here about being condemned because we are not *baptized,* or being *saved* because we *are* baptized. People are saved *by believing on Jesus Christ.* They are *lost* by *refusing* to believe.

In Romans 11:13 Paul declared that God called him as a special apostle to the Gentiles. In Ephesians chapter 3 he makes known the marvelous truth that God had revealed unto him the mystery of the New Testament Church, a mystery hidden from eternity but made known to Paul by revelation. Then in I Corinthians 1:17 this spiritual giant cried out, *"CHRIST SENT ME NOT TO BAPTIZE, but to preach the Gospel:* not with wisdom of words, lest the cross of Christ should be made of none effect!"

I ask you, beloved—if baptism is essential to salvation, if water washes away sins, *WHY did Paul say, "Christ sent me NOT to baptize"?* In Galatians 6:14 he said, *"God forbid that I should glory, SAVE IN THE CROSS OF OUR LORD JESUS CHRIST, by whom the world is crucified unto me, and I unto the world."*

To the Corinthian church he said, *"I determined not to know any thing among you, SAVE JESUS CHRIST, AND HIM CRUCIFIED!"* (I Cor. 2:2). So—Paul, God's chosen vessel to carry the Gospel to the Gentiles, plainly declared that *the cross and the shed blood of Jesus* is the message that makes men clean and fit for the kingdom of God. John the Beloved *also* taught that *the blood of Jesus cleanses from ALL sin* (I John 1:7). This being true, then *there IS no sin* for *water* to wash away!

Baptism is a symbol: it signifies death, burial, and resurrection. When we exercise faith in the Lord Jesus

Christ, we become children of God—dead to sin but alive
unto God, new creations in Christ:

"Therefore we are buried with Him by baptism into
death: that like as Christ was raised up from the dead
by the glory of the Father, even so we also should walk
in newness of life" (Rom. 6:4).

Water baptism has nothing to do with redemption, it
does not wash away sins. God's Holy Word plainly declares, *"Without shedding of blood is NO REMISSION"*
(Heb. 9:22).

"In the name of Jesus Christ . . . ." Many today
declare that for a person to be saved, water baptism must
be administered *in the name of Jesus ONLY,* but such a
doctrine is heresy and not according to Scripture rightly
divided. I am sure someone will ask, "Why did Peter
use the name *Jesus* instead of using *Father, Son, and
Holy Ghost?"* The answer is simple and easy to see if
we study the Word of God with an open mind:

The Jews believed in *God the Father*—Jehovah God.
They believed in the Holy Spirit, they knew He came upon men in the Old Testament era. But to them, *Jesus
the Nazarene* was an impostor, a false prophet who sowed
sedition. Therefore Peter instructed them to be baptized
in the name of Jesus Christ.

The miracle of Pentecost *occurred* because Jesus of
Nazareth had been raised from the dead, He had ascended unto the Father, and at that moment He was seated
at the right hand of Jehovah God. The Jews must now
accept Jesus Christ as well as the Father and the Holy
Spirit, or spend eternity in hell, because *"Christ is the
END of the law for righteousness to every one that believeth"* (Rom. 10:4). "Therefore by the deeds of the
law there shall no flesh be justified in His sight . . ."
(Rom. 3:20). These Jews must be baptized—not only in
the name of the Father and in the name of the Holy
Ghost, *but also in the name of JESUS CHRIST.*

Jesus told His disciples to go into all the world and

preach the Gospel, baptizing converts in the name of the Father, and of the Son, and of the Holy Ghost. Peter wanted the Jews to realize that it was *absolutely imperative* for them to embrace the Trinity—Father, Son, and Holy Ghost—if they hoped to be in the kingdom in that glorious day when King Jesus reigns from the throne of David.

All true believers are baptized into the body of Christ by the Holy Ghost the very moment they believe (I Cor. 12:13), but we should also follow Christ in baptism. Some believers have never *had* Christian baptism. They "joined the church" while they were still sinners, they were *baptized* while they were still sinners, and they *lived* like sinners until the time when they finally accepted Jesus and were born again. Therefore, if they have not been baptized *since* they believed, they have not had believers' baptism. We must repent and believe before we can receive *Christian baptism.*

These Jews were concerned primarily about their sin of having crucified Jesus—they were afraid God would pour out His wrath upon them immediately; but Peter said, "Repent and be baptized . . . *for the remission of SINS*"—not only the sin of crucifying their Messiah but all other sins as well. "If we confess our sins, He is faithful and just to forgive us our sins, and to cleanse us from all unrighteousness" (I John 1:9).

"And ye shall receive the gift of the Holy Ghost." How simple! Repent, believe on Jesus, trust Him for salvation, and you will receive the gift of the Holy Ghost. Yet today sincere, well-meaning believers go to a mourners' bench and beg, pray, and cry for the coming of the Holy Ghost—and then go home disappointed in heart because they did not have the experience they *expected* to have, an experience their minister or counselor told them they *should* have as a recipient of the Holy Ghost!

The Word of God is clear on this: "If ye then, being evil, know how to give good gifts unto your children:

how much more shall your heavenly Father give the Holy Spirit TO THEM THAT ASK HIM" (Luke 11:13). No man will *ask* for the Holy Spirit unless he is convicted of sin and truly repentant, seeking salvation by faith in the finished work of the Lord Jesus Christ. Therefore, God *gives* the Spirit to those who *ask* for the Spirit —and His infallible Word declares that all born again believers are *possessors* of the Holy Spirit (Rom. 8:9,14,16; Eph. 4:30).

When the one hundred and twenty in the upper room at Pentecost were baptized with the Holy Ghost they spoke with other tongues "as the Spirit gave them utterance." Verse 41 declares that three thousand were saved at the close of Peter's sermon that day, but there is no suggestion that any of them spoke with other tongues— nor did Peter give any indication that they *should.* He simply instructed them to repent, follow Jesus in baptism, and they would receive *remission of sins and "the gift of the Holy Ghost."*

There are many believers who do not yield themselves wholly to the Spirit, they are not *filled* with the Spirit, nor are they completely *led* by the Spirit. They take God's second best for their lives instead of allowing Him to give them *abundant* life (John 10:10), but the Holy Spirit *abides* in the heart of all true believers, whether or not He is allowed *complete control* of the believer's life. He abides to give us power, to comfort us, to enlighten us, to bring to mind the things we need to know spiritually, and to give us peace. He leads us in the paths of righteousness for Jesus' sake, He fills us if we will allow Him to do so, and He seals us until the day of redemption.

The Holy Spirit ministers a very definite ministry in the heart of the believer. Paul lists the *fruit* of the Spirit in Galatians 5:22,23:

"The fruit of the Spirit is love, joy, peace, longsuffering, gentleness, goodness, faith, meekness, temperance:

against such there is no law."

How sad it is that many well-meaning Christians pray and beg for the Holy Spirit. How *grieved* He must be, because even while they plead and weep, begging Him to come, *He already abides in their hearts!* Any person who has repented of sin and received Jesus by faith is a possessor of the Holy Spirit. He baptizes every believer into the body of Christ, He leads every believer, He seals every believer, He is our Comforter—and when we are so burdened that we cannot pray as we ought to pray, the Holy Spirit prays *for* us, telling God what we would like to tell Him but do not know how:

"Likewise the Spirit also helpeth our infirmities: for we know not what we should pray for as we ought: but the Spirit Himself maketh intercession for us with groanings which cannot be uttered. And He that searcheth the hearts knoweth what is the mind of the Spirit, because *He maketh intercession for the saints according to the will of God"* (Rom. 8:26,27).

Verse 39: *"For the promise is unto you, and to your children, and to all that are afar off, even as many as the Lord our God shall call."*

In Romans 11:1—5 we find that the promise is *still* to the Jews and to their children:

"I say then, *Hath* God cast away His people? *God forbid!* For I also am an Israelite, of the seed of Abraham, of the tribe of Benjamin. *God hath NOT cast away His people which He foreknew.* Wot ye not what the Scripture saith of Elias? how he maketh intercession to God against Israel, saying, Lord, they have killed thy prophets, and digged down thine altars; and I am left alone, and they seek my life.

"But what saith the answer of God unto him? *I have reserved to myself seven thousand men, who have not bowed the knee to the image of Baal. EVEN SO THEN AT THIS PRESENT TIME ALSO THERE IS A REM-*

NANT ACCORDING TO THE ELECTION OF GRACE!"
In a day yet future, the Holy Spirit will be poured
out upon the nation Israel and there will be national
repentance.   *As a nation* they will mourn because they
will realize that they crucified their Messiah:

"And it shall come to pass in that day, that I will
seek to destroy all the nations that come against Jerusalem.   And I will pour upon the house of David, and
upon the inhabitants of Jerusalem, the Spirit of grace
and of supplications: *and they shall look upon me whom
they have pierced, and they shall mourn for Him, as
one mourneth for his only son, and shall be in bitterness
for Him, as one that is in bitterness for his firstborn.*

*"In that day shall there be a great mourning in Jeru-
salem,* as the mourning of Hadadrimmon in the valley
of Megiddon.   And the land shall mourn, every family
apart; the family of the house of David apart, and their
wives apart; the family of the house of Nathan apart,
and their wives apart; the family of the house of Levi
apart, and their wives apart; the family of Shimei apart,
and their wives apart; all the families that remain, every
family apart, and their wives apart" (Zech. 12:9—14).

In Ezekiel 39:28,29 we read, "Then shall they know
that I am the Lord their God, which caused them to be
led into captivity among the heathen: but I have gathered them unto their own land, and have left none of
them any more there.   *Neither will I hide my face any
more from them: for I have poured out my Spirit upon
the house of Israel, saith the Lord God."*

Yes, the promise was to the very Jews who had crucified Jesus, and to their children (their descendants). Joel's
prophecy had declared that their sons and daughters
would prophesy, their young men would see visions, and
their old men would dream dreams.   Isaiah also had
proclaimed, "Thus saith the Lord . . . I will pour my
Spirit *upon thy seed,* and my blessing upon *thine offspring"* (Isa. 44:2,3 in part).

In Isaiah 59:20,21 God promised, "The Redeemer shall come to Zion, and unto them that turn from transgression in Jacob, saith the Lord. As for me, this is my covenant with them, saith the Lord: *My Spirit that is upon thee, and my words which I have put in thy mouth, shall not depart out of thy mouth, nor out of the mouth of thy seed, nor out of the mouth of thy seed's seed, saith the Lord, from henceforth and for ever.*"

The promise of God was—and still is—to Israel and the descendants of Israel, but NOW the invitation is not to the Jews only, but to whosoever will believe. God gave His Son to die for the sins of the whole world, and Gentiles are no longer aliens from the commonwealth, strangers to the covenants and promises. We are fellow-heirs with Israel. God loves the Jew, He loves the Gentile. Christ died for all, therefore *the invitation* is to all—*to the whole human race.*

"*And to all that are afar off*" means even to the ends of the earth, to all lands. Peter was speaking under inspiration of the Holy Ghost and probably did not fully understand what he was saying. It was not until God sent him to carry the Gospel to the house of Cornelius that he realized that the message was to the Gentiles as well as to the Jew, and that no man cleansed by God is to be called unclean. We will study this more fully when we reach chapter 10 where the Scripture records Peter's call and ministry to the household of Cornelius.

The Gentiles were included in those who were "*afar off.*" In Ephesians 2:11—18 *Paul* speaks of the Gentiles as having been "*without Christ, being aliens from the commonwealth of Israel, and strangers from the covenants of promise, having no hope, and without God in the world: but NOW in Christ Jesus ye who sometimes were FAR OFF are made nigh by the blood of Christ.*" Jesus broke down the "middle wall of partition" between Jew and Gentile, and reconciled us both unto God "*in one body by the cross,*" and now, through Him, both Jew and

Gentile "have access by one Spirit unto the Father."

"Even as many as the Lord our God shall call" does not mean that some are called and others are not called. It does not mean that some are "elected" to be *saved* and others are "elected" to be *lost.* God does not predestine part of mankind to spend eternity in hell and others to spend eternity in Paradise with Him. Indeed not! Jesus commanded His disciples to go into *ALL the world* and preach the Gospel *to EVERY creature.* They were to preach first at home—in Jerusalem and Judaea— and then *to the uttermost parts of the earth.*

How does God *"call"* men to repentance? In all the Word of God there is no better illustration of how God calls men than Romans 10:13—17:

"Whosoever shall CALL upon the name of the Lord shall be saved"—the invitation is to *whosoever,* not to a small, select group. But *believing* on Jesus precedes *calling* on Him for salvation, and one must *hear the Word* before he can *believe.* In order for the Word to be *heard,* it must first be *preached.*

In this Dispensation of Grace it has pleased God to call men to preach the Word in order that sinners may *hear* the Word, *believe* the Word, and call upon the name of Jesus for salvation. *BUT—"How shall they PREACH except they be SENT?"*

The responsibility for spreading the Gospel rests upon born again believers in the Church of the living God. We who have heard the message and have been born again are obligated to send ministers and missionaries to the ends of the earth to preach this glorious Gospel, so that those who are still in the darkness of sin may hear the Gospel, be convicted of sin and convinced of their need of a Saviour. God will then call them to repentance *through* the Gospel, they will repent of their sins, believe on the Lord Jesus Christ, and call on His name for salvation.

It is impossible for anyone to be saved apart from

hearing the Word of God, but *the first step* is for the Church to send preachers to *preach* the Word. God calls men through His Word, and *hearing* the Word, sinners then call upon the name of the Lord *according* to the Word—thus *"whosoever shall call upon the name of the Lord shall be SAVED."*

God has not called the heathen today *because the Church has not carried the Gospel to the heathen!* God is certainly not limited in His provisions of grace, but according to His divine plan He cannot call men to repentance except through His Word. His promise of grace is free *to all,* it is all-sufficient, and it is *fitted* to all. The invitation is to everyone, everywhere, and God is *able to save* to the ends of the earth any and all who come to Him by faith; but the only way they *can* come to Him by faith is by hearing the message of the Word! The plan of salvation is applicable to all mankind, and it is God's purpose and plan in this Day of Grace to *send* His message to all men. *GOD has not failed,* but the *CHURCH* has failed *both God and men!*

Verse 40: *"And with many other words did he testify and exhort, saying, Save yourselves from this untoward generation."*

Notice: *It was with "WORDS"*—not with signs and wonders—that Peter testified concerning God's promise to mankind. The *"many other words"* he spoke are not recorded here, but *enough* of his words are written down to show us that salvation comes by hearing the Word of God. Peter testified (bore witness) to the promises of God to all men, pointing out the danger of sin, inviting men to come to Jesus in repentance and be delivered from sin's *penalty.*

His exhortation and warning entreated them, *"Save yourselves from this untoward generation."* This does not mean that they could redeem their own souls, but rather that they should *preserve themselves from the*

FATE of that generation by coming out from among them. In other words, "Do not allow yourselves to come under the influence of their habits and practices of life."

God created man a free moral agent and gave him the right to choose his way of life; and He still deals with men as free moral agents. He gave *Adam* the right to choose, He gives *all* men the right to choose. Man was created in the image of God, and though he *lost much* of that image in the fall he still has body, soul, and spirit. Man can *reason,* he can *plan,* and he is the highest creation of Almighty God.

We can count on God to do for us anything and everything we cannot do for ourselves, but He *will not* do for us what we *can* do for ourselves. For example, Paul called upon the Romans to present their bodies "a living sacrifice, holy, acceptable unto God," *which was their REASONABLE service* (Rom. 12:1). God does not *force* obedience and dedication upon His children; He gives us the right to *choose*—and those who choose obedience and wholehearted service, *complete devotion to HIM,* are blessed above anything mortal man can think or dream of. Those who choose—as many do—to follow self-will and hold back part of their lives unto themselves are never blessed as God would *like* to bless them if only they would permit Him to do so.

Jesus said to His disciples, "So likewise ye, when ye shall have done *ALL those things which are commanded you,* say, We are unprofitable servants: *we have done that which was our DUTY to do"* (Luke 17:10).

"Untoward" (according to Webster) means "perverse, refractory, not easily guided or taught." The *"generation"* to which Peter referred was corrupt, perverse, wicked and ungodly. Such was the character of the group described in Matthew 11:16—19:

Jesus said, "Whereunto shall I liken *this generation?* It is like unto children sitting in the markets, and calling unto their fellows, and saying, We have piped unto you, and ye have not danced; we have mourned unto you, and ye have not lamented. For John (the Baptist) came neither eating nor drinking, and they say, He hath a devil. The Son of man came eating and drinking, and they say, Behold a man gluttonous, and a winebibber, a friend of publicans and sinners. But wisdom is justified of her children."

There are many other passages in the Gospels that describe the *"untoward generation"* of which Peter spoke. (Read Matthew 12:30; 16:4; and Mark 12:38–40, for examples.) These men were wicked, cunning, energized by the devil. Outwardly they wore sheep's clothing, but inwardly they were "ravening wolves"—corrupt in principle, with hearts as black as the walls of hell. Therefore we might well wonder *why* Peter gave such a warning to those who cried out, *"What must we DO?"*

We must remember that the Pharisees in that day had almost *absolute* influence over the people. It was not the majority of the Jewish people who crucified Jesus. (Mark 12:37 declares, "The *common* people heard Him *gladly.*") It was the *rulers*—the Pharisees, chief priests, and scribes—who demanded that Jesus be put to death. Peter now exhorts those who repent of their sins, to *break away and save themselves* from that group and have no fellowship with them, take no part in their way of life.

I repeat—God does not *force* men to serve Him any more than He forces men to be saved; but when one hears the Gospel, repents of sin and trusts the Lord Jesus, he will automatically have a *desire* to break relations with his former way of life and former associations. Sometimes that means breaking with relatives or closest friends, but the born again Christian has a new heart, he is a new creation in Christ, he walks in the light, and therefore he *seeks fellowship* with the *children* of light. (Read I Thessalonians 5:1–10.)

God commands His children today to come out from

the world.   Ephesians 5:11 tells us to "have no fellowship with the unfruitful works of darkness, but rather
reprove them."

In II Corinthians 6:14—18 we are commanded, *"Be ye
not unequally yoked together with unbelievers:* for what
fellowship hath righteousness with unrighteousness? and
what communion hath light with darkness? and what
concord hath Christ with Belial?   Or what part hath he
that believeth with an infidel? And what agreement hath
the temple of God with idols? For ye are the temple of
the living God; as God hath said, I will dwell in them,
and walk in them; and I will be their God, and they
shall be my people.   *WHEREFORE COME OUT FROM
AMONG THEM, AND BE YE SEPARATE,* saith the
Lord, *AND TOUCH NOT THE UNCLEAN THING;
AND I WILL RECEIVE YOU, and will be a Father
unto you, and ye shall be my sons and daughters,* saith
the Lord Almighty."

And finally, John the Beloved admonishes, *"Love not
the world, neither the things that are IN the world.   IF
ANY MAN LOVE THE WORLD, THE LOVE OF THE
FATHER IS NOT IN HIM.* For all that is in the world,
the lust of the flesh, and the lust of the eyes, and the
pride of life, is not of the Father, but is of the world.
And the world passeth away, and the lust thereof: but
he that doeth the will of God abideth for ever" (I John
2:15—17).

Verse 41:   *"Then they that gladly received his word
were baptized: and the same day there were added unto
them about three thousand souls."*

"Gladly" means *freely.*   Those who heard the Word
preached by Peter were not compelled to receive it, but
they received it freely, joyfully, and were baptized, thus
signifying that they received the Gospel message and
acknowledged Christ as Messiah and Saviour.

The same is true today. Christianity is not *compulsory,*

but *it IS the one and only true religion.* Those who come to Jesus do it cheerfully and of their own free will, rejoicing in the privilege of becoming Christians through faith in His shed blood and finished work.

The *"word"* mentioned here is not *Peter's* word, but the Word of God spoken *through* Peter under the power of the Holy Ghost, declaring that repentance and faith in God bring pardon from sin through Jesus Christ.

They that gladly received the Word *"were baptized."* This certainly suggests that these converts were baptized the same day they were saved. However, I do not advocate that people be baptized the split second they are born again. On the contrary, I think it would be far better in many instances if churches would wait at least thirty days before baptizing converts, because if they are truly born again they will walk with the Lord and will *want* to be baptized, and if they fall away it is far better that they *not be* baptized. True salvation puts within the heart a desire to obey Jesus, and baptism is in obedience to His command. We are not baptized *in order to BE saved,* we are baptized *because we ARE saved.*

The Holy Spirit did not see fit to tell us *where* these people were baptized, nor in what manner. God had His reasons for not revealing this information. Personally, I believe in immersion as the proper form of baptism. I believe the Scripture teaches that *Jesus* was baptized by immersion in the river Jordan—however, if I should travel to the Holy Land and be immersed in Jordan it would not make me one whit more saved than I am now! It would not help my state of redemption one iota! I do not quarrel with my fellow Christians over the mode of baptism. I do believe Jesus was immersed; I also believe the Ethiopian eunuch was immersed when Philip led him to the Lord *"and they went down both INTO the water,"* and Philip baptized the eunuch. Then we are told that *"when they were COME UP OUT OF the water,* the Spirit of the Lord caught away Philip, that

the eunuch saw him no more: and he went on his way
rejoicing."   You can read the entire account in Acts 8:
26—39.   We will learn more about this when we reach
that portion of our study.

I do not maintain that if Christians are not immersed
they are not saved—not at all. I do believe that insofar
as possible we should obey the Scriptures, and the one
hundred and twenty believers at Pentecost could have
baptized three thousand people within a reasonable length
of time.   I repeat—God had His own reasons for not
giving us further information on the baptism of these
three thousand new converts.

*"The same day there were added unto them about
three thousand souls."*   When a person repents of sin,
receives the Lord Jesus as Saviour, and experiences the
new birth through the miracle wrought by the Holy Spirit,
that person should unite with a local assembly—but only
with an assembly where God's anointed and appointed
minister feeds the flock with the pure Word of God. Paul
admonished the Thessalonian believers, *"KNOW THEM
WHICH LABOUR AMONG YOU,* and are over you in
the Lord, and admonish you; and to esteem them very
highly in love for their work's sake . . ." (I Thess. 5:
12,13).

No Christian should unite with a church—or *stay* in
a church—unless the pastor of that assembly preaches
"Thus saith the Lord!"   It is dangerous and expensive
to support a man who does not preach the Word of God.
John warns in his second epistle:

"Many deceivers are entered into the world, who confess not that Jesus Christ is come in the flesh.   This is
a deceiver and an antichrist.   Look to yourselves, that
we lose not those things which we have wrought, but
that we receive a full reward.

*"Whosoever transgresseth, and abideth not in the
doctrine of Christ, hath not God.* He that abideth in the
doctrine of Christ, he hath both the Father and the Son.

*If there come any unto you, and bring not this doctrine,
receive him not into your house, neither bid him God
speed: FOR HE THAT BIDDETH HIM GOD SPEED
IS PARTAKER OF HIS EVIL DEEDS"* (II John 7—11).

According to verse 15 of Acts chapter 2, Peter began
his message that morning about nine o'clock. We do not
know how long he preached, but the *recorded* portion of
his sermon is very brief; it can easily be read in five
minutes. But regardless of how long he preached, about
three thousand individuals became members of the church
in Jerusalem. I suppose no other church has over grown
so rapidly—from a congregation of one hundred and twenty members, to more than *three thousand* members in
one day!

From the practical aspect, I do not believe that three
thousand people walked forward and stood in a group
while Peter prayed with them. I believe these people
came from all over the city of Jerusalem as the one hundred and twenty believers spread out over the city and
delivered messages to many groups gathered in various
parts of Jerusalem; and *as a result of that first day's
ministry* three thousand souls were saved and added to
the Church of the living God. The Word of God is *the
power of God* unto salvation, and when it is faithfully
preached and the Holy Spirit has His way, the Church
grows as men's hearts are changed and they become new
creations in Christ.

The fact that the Holy Spirit on the Day of Pentecost
began to form the body of Christ (the New Testament
Church) was not revealed to the disciples at that moment.
It is beyond the mind of man to *imagine* what would
be taking place today if the ministers of the Church had
been as faithful down through the years as the one hundred and twenty Christians were that day. If we had
continued to evangelize and win souls at such a rapid
pace we would be living in Paradise today, instead of
living in a world steeped in sin, ungodliness, and wretch-

edness! May God help us to realize that it is still through the "foolishness" of preaching the Gospel that God saves sinners. He cannot call them except through His Gospel, and it is His command that we preach the Gospel to the ends of the earth. We cannot all go to foreign fields, we cannot all pastor churches; but we *can* evangelize at home, and *without exception we can PRAY for those who are on mission fields.*

This first church with its increase from only a few members to more than three thousand was the result of one day's labor of no more than one hundred and twenty Christians, delivering the Gospel as they were empowered of the Holy Spirit; and *the teaching of the apostles*—the Word of God which they declared concerning the crucified, buried, risen, ascended, and coming-again Lord—*became the foundation of the great spiritual building:*

"Now therefore ye are no more strangers and foreigners, but fellowcitizens with the saints, and of the household of God; *and are built upon the foundation of the APOSTLES AND PROPHETS,* Jesus Christ Himself being the chief corner stone; *in whom all the building fitly framed together groweth unto AN HOLY TEMPLE IN THE LORD: In whom ye also are builded together for an habitation of God through the Spirit"* (Eph. 2:19—22).

The First Local Church

Verse 42: *"And they continued stedfastly in the apostles' doctrine and fellowship, and in breaking of bread, and in prayers."*

There was nothing ordinary about this first church. It was unusual in every respect. The converts who made up its membership were converted *suddenly,* and as far as the record tells us *not one* backslid, not one *apostatized.*   Each one who professed faith in the risen Lord that day *continued* in the faith, following Jesus day by day.

That they *"continued stedfastly"* means that these early Christians got in the yoke with Jesus and walked side by side with Him. In Matthew 11:29,30 He invited, "Take my yoke upon you, and learn of me; for I am meek and lowly in heart: and ye shall find rest unto your souls. *For my yoke is easy, and my burden is light."*

They continued *"in the apostles' doctrine and fellowship."* This does not mean that they followed doctrine decreed or declared by the apostles. The word translated *"doctrine"* means literally *teaching,* and the statement simply means that they followed the apostles' teaching and instruction, obeying the Word of God as the apostles taught them day by day and from house to house. One evidence of true conversion is the desire of the individual to be instructed in the Word of God, to learn the believer's duties to God and to mankind.

The Greek word here rendered *"fellowship"* is often translated *communion.* It denotes having things in common—after all, "Can two walk together, except they be agreed?" (Amos 3:3). Born again believers will agree on the fundamentals of the faith. We may not agree on all *minor* doctrines, but we *do agree* on such *major* doctrines as the verbal inspiration of the Scriptures, the deity of Christ, the blood atonement, salvation by grace, and the second coming of Jesus. Born again believers have these things in common because the grace of God that saves us also *teaches* us (Tit. 2:11—14).

Believers have *the same HOPE.* We are looking forward to that glorious day when we will see Jesus in heaven. All believers who live godly in Christ Jesus will suffer persecution; therefore we have the same enemies. Yes, true believers have *many* things in common, and "if we walk in the light, as He is in the light, *we have fellowship one with another"* (I John 1:7).

"And in breaking of bread . . . ." It is impossible to determine whether the statement here is speaking of

ordinary food or of the Lord's Supper. *"Breaking"* bread seems to indicate Jewish bread, which was baked in small, thin wafers or little cakes, hard, thin, and brittle. I am inclined to believe that these Christians ate their *regular meals* together, so close was their communion and fellowship with each other. They broke bread together day by day. Actual *breaking* of the bread was performed by the head of the family, and took place immediately after the blessing.

"And in prayers." The first church was a *praying* church—they continued stedfastly in prayer. If a pastor wants to know the spiritual temperature of his church, he should take that temperature on prayermeeting night—not on homecoming Sunday or at Sunday morning worship service. A praying church is a growing church, a productive church; and Christians who do not love prayermeeting are not where they should be spiritually. They may be born again children of God; but they are not fully surrendered to His will.

Verse 43: *"And fear came upon every soul: and many wonders and signs were done by the apostles."*

"Fear" here is not fear such as a little child has for the dark. The early Church lived in great reverence and awe. These Christians had been disbelieving, mocking, accusing the apostles of drunkenness; but now the power of God was so great in their lives that it silenced their mocking and produced repentance and godly fear. A mighty work of the Holy Spirit—whether in a community, in a home, or in an individual life—will produce solemnity and reverential fear. Many times a mighty outpouring of God's power in a community, some mighty stirring of the Spirit, will cause even the most ungodly sinners to stand in awe and wonder, and though they may not embrace Christianity, they will admit that the working of the Spirit has been evident. God's power restrains, subdues, and many times *silences* opposition.

"Many wonders and signs were done by the apostles."
God performed many outstanding miracles by the hands
of the apostles. As we continue in our study, we will
learn that they wrought miracles such as no ordinary
mortal could perform. This is in accordance with the
promise Jesus gave them in Mark 16:17,18:

"And these signs shall follow them that believe: In
my name shall they cast out devils; they shall speak with
new tongues; they shall take up serpents; and if they
drink any deadly thing, it shall not hurt them; they shall
lay hands on the sick, and they shall recover."

In John 14:12 He said to His disciples, ". . . He that
believeth on me, the works that I do shall he do also;
and GREATER WORKS than these shall he do; because
I go unto my Father."

Verses 44 and 45: *"And all that believed were together, and had all things common; and sold their possessions and goods, and parted them to all men, as every
man had need."*

"All who believed" simply means those who heard
the Gospel message and put their faith in Jesus for salvation. These believers *"were together"*—not that they
all lived in the same house or under the same roof, but
that they were *united,* joined together in the bond of
love and Christian unity. All believers are one in Christ,
baptized into one body by one Spirit, hid with Christ in
God, *COMPLETE in Jesus.*

These people were all followers of Jesus, they were
interested in making disciples by giving out the good
news that Jesus saves. They were "together" in thought
and aim, in every aspect of living. They had prayer and
praise together daily. I would emphasize the fact that,
more than anything else, *fellowship and prayer with God's
people* will strengthen new converts. It is through such
fellowship, as well as through prayer and study of the
Word, that new Christians are built up and helped to

grow in grace.   That is why we are admonished, "Let us consider one another to provoke unto love and to good works: *not forsaking the assembling of ourselves together,* as the manner of some is; but exhorting one another: and so much the more, as ye see the day approaching" (Heb. 10:24,25).

These first believers *"had all things common."* They sold their property and put their money in a common fund.   (Study chapter 4, verses 32—37, and chapter 5, verses 1—10. We will study these passages in detail when we reach them, but it will be helpful to read them now in connection with verse 45.)

The *disciples* had their money in a common fund, with Judas as secretary-treasurer (John 12:6; 13:29), and since *they* lived after this manner as they walked with Jesus, it is possible that they led the early believers to follow their steps to this extent, though they certainly did not *compel* them to do so. Later, however, as new churches were founded throughout Asia Minor and in other places, believers owned property and supported the Church through free-will offerings, as the Lord's work is supported today. We *know* John the Beloved owned property, because after the crucifixion he took the mother of Jesus to "his own home" (John 19:27). Jesus did not command John to sell his property, and the apostles did not command the believers here to sell their property (Acts 5:4).

The members of this first church looked upon themselves as one big family, united in fellowship, in love, and in common needs. Therefore they put their wealth together and shared alike. They sold whatever was necessary to provide for the need of the group.

The Greek word translated *"possessions"* indicates property, particularly real estate. It points to *fixed property,* such as houses, lands, and vineyards. *"Goods"* refers to *personal* property, items which could be moved or carried about. They sold their possessions and goods *"and parted them to all."*

Some of the believers were no doubt very poor. On the Day of Pentecost people were present from every nation, and some of them who decided to *remain* in Jerusalem had not brought sufficient funds to supply their needs over an extended time, because they had not planned to stay. The believers who lived in and near that area therefore sold their property, put their money into a common fund, and shared with others until they could find a means of support for themselves.

"As every man HAD need" suggests that they perhaps sold enough property to supply the need day by day. One believer sold property one day, and when those funds were exhausted another believer sold property to bring in funds to take care of the needs of brethren who were less fortunate.

Our Scripture does not necessarily suggest that these people sold *all* that they had, or that they relinquished the title to all of their belongings. They sold *as the need arose,* and thus brought in funds to *meet* that need. The handling of such funds was given over to the disciples, as we read in chapter 4, verses 34 and 35:

"Neither was there any among them that lacked: for as many as were possessors of lands or houses sold them, *and brought the prices of the things that were sold, and laid them down at the apostles' feet: and distribution was made unto every man according as he had need."*

There is a lesson plainly taught here: *Property* is one of the things in life that is hardest to let go when one becomes a Christian. When a man sells his business and his home in order to prepare for life on the mission fields or for the preaching of the Gospel, you may rest assured that he has experienced a real miracle of God's grace in his heart! The love of property is one of the strongest of man's affections, and salvation is the only thing that will cause him to willingly break with all earthly possessions. When these first Christians were put to the test, they proved themselves *true believers.*

I believe this passage also teaches that the Church of the living God should provide for the needs of the poor. Sad but so, many secular organizations today are getting praise, honor, and glory that should be going to the Church.   Certainly the Church is not seeking *praise of men,* but what the true Church does is done in the name of Jesus, to the honor and glory of God.   Instead of civic organizations getting credit for taking care of the poor and providing for orphans and for the homeless, the Church should be taking that responsibility; for by feeding the poor we would open the door to preach the Gospel of grace to many who do not know the Lord Jesus as Saviour (I John 3:16—18).

There are many in our communities today who need help, and by helping them the Church would preach an illustrated sermon, proving that Christians do possess the love of God. God proved His love for us by giving His only begotten Son. Jesus proved His love for us by giving His life. We should certainly prove *that WE possess the love of God* by giving materially (as well as spiritually) to those less fortunate than we.

The Scriptures do not indicate that this practice continued for very long.   Having *"all things common"* is mentioned again in chapter 4, verses 32—37 and in chapter 5, verses 1—10—references already given. It is not mentioned again, and there is no evidence that the believers practiced this common sharing in the churches in Antioch, Philippi, Rome, Ephesus, or any of the other churches established by Paul and others, although taught that Christians should be liberal toward those who are less fortunate.   (Study I Corinthians 16:2; Galatians 2:10.)

Christianity does not demand that we sell our possessions and sever relations with all business and property holdings; but we *should be willing* to let go of anything the Lord calls upon us to give up, anything that would hinder Christian service. We must be willing to put God first if we would be effective soul-winners. God loves a cheerful giver (II Cor. 9:6—15), and if we give cheerfully He will reward us. He is able to supply our every need, and He *will supply* our needs if we trust Him.

Verse 46: *"And they, continuing daily with one accord in the temple, and breaking bread from house to house, did eat their meat with gladness and singleness of heart."*

In chapter 1, verse 14, we noted that as the disciples waited for Pentecost as Jesus had told them to do, they "continued *with one accord* in prayer and supplication." In verse 1 of our present chapter, "they were all *with one accord* in one place." And now they *continued* day by day *"with one accord in the temple."* No wonder this church grew so rapidly and accomplished such miracles to the glory of God!

The temple was the place of public worship for the Jews; the disciples had gone there with Jesus many times, and they were not disposed to leave the place where their forefathers had met to worship Jehovah God. This does not mean that they spent twelve or twenty-four hours a day in the temple. They were there at the hours of prayer and worship—nine o'clock in the morning and three o'clock in the afternoon—according to the religion of their fathers; for even though these disciples were born again believers, they were new in the Christian way and they had not completely broken with the traditional hour of prayer.

In verse 1 of chapter 3 we read where Peter and John "went up together into the temple *at the hour of prayer,* being the ninth hour." Many churches today do not even *have* a midweek prayermeeting—or a Sunday night prayermeeting either, for that matter. Every church should have appointed times of prayer. Paul said we should "pray without ceasing" (I Thess. 5:17), which means that we should be in an *attitude* of prayer at all times; but there should also be days and hours appointed when God's people meet together *in one accord* to pray.

"Breaking bread from house to house." Some scholars and commentators of the past have translated this *"breaking bread at home."* I personally believe this breaking of bread has nothing to do with the Lord's Supper, but simply means that they ate their meals in homes, from house to house. That they ate "their *meat"* also implies that this was a regular meal, because *there IS no meat* in connection with the ordinance of the Lord's Supper. When the Bible speaks of *meat* it does not necessarily mean flesh, but in this particular instance it is plainly implied that the people broke bread and *ate meat.*

In connection with this passage, it would be well to study I Corinthians 11:17—34. We quote verses 33 and 34 here: When Paul reprimanded the Corinthian church for disorderly conduct at the Lord's table he said, "Wherefore, my brethren, when ye come together to eat, tarry one for another. And *if any man hunger, let him eat at home;* that ye come not together unto condemnation. And the rest will I set in order when I come."

The first church was a happy church—the members ate their bread and meat in unity, of one accord, *"with gladness."* Rejoicing is one of the fruits of salvation. Peter tells us that believers rejoice with joy that cannot be described in words (I Pet. 1:8). The believers in the first church were happy, thankful, satisfied, filled with joy because they had found their Messiah, the Saviour. Secondary things no longer mattered to them. They thanked God for whatever they had—whether little or much—and ate their food with a thankful, sincere heart, dedicated to God. Food and raiment are necessary—we must eat, we must have clothes to wear; but *if we put GOD first, He will ADD these necessary things.*

Jesus promised, "Seek ye first the kingdom of God, and His righteousness; *and all these things shall be added unto you"* (Matt. 6:33). In Philippians 4:19 the Apostle

Paul declared, "My God shall supply all your need *according to His riches in glory by Christ Jesus.*"

Verse 47: *"Praising God, and having favour with all the people. And the Lord added to the Church daily such as should be saved."*

"Praising God" does not mean that these believers shouted, clapped their hands, or ran up and down the streets shouting praises. There are *many ways* to praise God. Some people laugh when they are happy, others *cry;* but those who cry are just as happy as those who laugh. They simply react differently under emotional pressure. It is wrong for us to attempt to fit others into our own mold when it comes to praising God, or in the joy and happiness of salvation. *We are all SAVED alike* —there is but one way of salvation; but we do not all display the same outward reactions. We should never criticize another believer because he or she does not praise God exactly as *we* praise Him.

Above all, our praise—whether it be in prayer, in quiet words of testimony to the goodness and mercy of God, or in loud exclamations of adoration and joy—should be *genuine,* from an honest heart.

The first believers were not only happy and praising God, but they lived and conducted themselves in such a way that they *"found favour with all the people."* This does not mean that they found favor with each and every individual, but with the mass of people in general. Nor does it mean that the multitudes were *converted,* but that they recognized in these believers a humble, serious, devoted life which they were forced to respect. Paul admonished the Romans, "Let not then your good be evil spoken of" (Rom. 14:16). We should live in such a way that our lives will enable us to win people to Christ, rather than alienating them from Christianity.

"AND THE LORD ADDED TO THE CHURCH DAILY SUCH AS SHOULD BE SAVED." The *LORD*

added believers to this first church, and the Lord *still* adds to His Church all who are saved. We will study the Church fully when we reach chapter 20.

There is but ONE true Church. The *local* church is of the Lord, and I believe every Christian should unite with the local church—but if joining a local assembly is the extent of one's spiritual experience, that person is lost! Through the new birth and the baptism of the Holy Ghost, *the Lord* adds members to the body of Christ the moment they exercise faith in Jesus; but *no man* has the power to add members to the Church of the living God.

In Acts 20:28 Paul warned the Ephesian elders, "Take heed therefore unto yourselves, and to all the flock, over the which the Holy Ghost hath made you overseers, to feed the Church of God, *which He hath purchased with His own blood!*" The Church of God is made up of all born again, blood-washed believers, but we are *added TO* God's Church, we do not "join" it. We join the *local* church and the church clerk adds our name to the membership; but only the Lord God Almighty can add our name to heaven's register when we are born again— and thus we become members of the body of Christ.

The Greek word translated *"church"* means *"called out ones."* Believers are called out and separated from the world—*new creations in Christ Jesus.* The word is found only three times in the Gospels—once in Matthew 16:18, twice in Matthew 18:17. "Church" occurs many times in other parts of the New Testament and in most places it speaks of the followers of the Lord Jesus—true believers. (Read Acts 5:11; 8:1–3; 9:31; 11:22,26; 12:1.)

In old English literature the church is mentioned many times in speaking of an *assembly,* not necessarily an assembly of believers. It is used twice in Acts in this manner: In chapter 19 verse 39 we read, "If ye enquire any thing concerning other matters, it shall be determined in *a lawful assembly.*" Then in verse 41 of the same chapter, "when he had thus spoken, he dismissed the *assembly."*

"*Such as should be saved"* in the literal Greek reads,
"such as were in the way of salvation." Day by day,
those who *believed* were added to the Church that very
day. Today, some local assemblies receive members at
revival time—and they have only one revival effort each
year. Other churches have several revivals yearly, and
still other churches invite members into fellowship each
Sunday.

Some churches have *baptismal services* every Sunday
night. I have no criticism for the minister who wants
to baptize new members every Sunday night—or every
night of a revival if he so desires; there is no Scripture
against such practice. But there is no real point in rushing the matter, and I believe most pastors will agree
that had they waited to baptize *some* of their members
they would not have baptized them at all. It is much
easier to reach a poor, lost sinner who has never been
baptized and affiliated with a church, than it is to reach
a sinner who is a member of the local church, having
been baptized and taken into membership without the
experience of the new birth.

The New Testament Church is not an "organization,"
but *a living organism;* and this chapter proves beyond
any shadow of doubt that the Church began with the
miraculous event which took place at Pentecost. Peter
gave testimony to the people concerning the Nazarene
whom they had rejected and crucified, but whom God
had raised from the dead and made both Lord and Christ.
Those who heard and believed the message were saved
and added to the body of Christ by the Holy Spirit.

In Paul's last letter to Timothy, he warned the young
preacher that men would depart from the faith and from
the doctrine of Christ. It might be helpful to look at
Paul's admonition before we close this chapter dealing
with the foundation and building of the New Testament
Church. In II Timothy 4:1—5 Paul said:

"I charge thee therefore before God, and the Lord Jesus Christ, who shall judge the quick and the dead at His appearing and His kingdom: *Preach the Word; be instant in season, out of season; reprove, rebuke, exhort with all longsuffering and doctrine. For the time will come when they will not endure sound doctrine; but after their own lusts shall they heap to themselves teachers, having itching ears; and they shall turn away their ears from the truth, and shall be turned unto fables. But watch thou in all things, endure afflictions, do the work of an evangelist, make full proof of thy ministry.*"

Certainly we know that this prophecy has been fulfilled. Tens of thousands today refuse to receive sound doctrine. They hire teachers who will tickle their ears with what they want to hear. They have turned from the truth, and men who pastor such churches are blind guides leading the blind, headed for certain destruction.

If you are wondering how you can know whether or not you are supporting a preacher who preaches the doctrine of Jesus Christ, the Scripture tells how you can know:

I Peter 2:6: "Wherefore also it is contained in the Scripture, *Behold, I lay in Sion a chief corner stone, elect, precious: AND HE THAT BELIEVETH ON HIM SHALL NOT BE CONFOUNDED.*"

John 14:26: "But the Comforter, which is the Holy Ghost, whom the Father will send in my name, *HE SHALL TEACH YOU ALL THINGS, and bring all things to your remembrance, whatsoever I have said unto you.*"

And finally, *Romans 8:16* declares, *"THE SPIRIT ITSELF BEARETH WITNESS WITH OUR SPIRIT, THAT WE ARE THE CHILDREN OF GOD,"* and the same Spirit who witnesses to our being born again, the same Spirit who dwells in the heart of every believer, will witness to the truth of the message being preached from the pulpit!

CHAPTER III

1. Now Peter and John went up together into the temple at the hour of prayer, being the ninth hour.

2. And a certain man lame from his mother's womb was carried, whom they laid daily at the gate of the temple which is called Beautiful, to ask alms of them that entered into the temple;

3. Who seeing Peter and John about to go into the temple asked an alms.

4. And Peter, fastening his eyes upon him with John, said, Look on us.

5. And he gave heed unto them, expecting to receive something of them.

6. Then Peter said, Silver and gold have I none; but such as I have give I thee: In the name of Jesus Christ of Nazareth rise up and walk.

7. And he took him by the right hand, and lifted him up: and immediately his feet and ankle bones received strength.

8. And he leaping up stood, and walked, and entered with them into the temple, walking, and leaping, and praising God.

9. And all the people saw him walking and praising God:

10. And they knew that it was he which sat for alms at the Beautiful gate of the temple: and they were filled with wonder and amazement at that which had happened unto him.

11. And as the lame man which was healed held Peter and John, all the people ran together unto them in the porch that is called Solomon's, greatly wondering.

12. And when Peter saw it, he answered unto the people, Ye men of Israel, why marvel ye at this? or why look ye so earnestly on us, as though by our own power or holiness we had made this man to walk?

13. The God of Abraham, and of Isaac, and of Jacob, the God of our fathers, hath glorified his Son Jesus; whom ye delivered up, and denied him in the presence of Pilate, when he was determined to let him go.

14. But ye denied the Holy One and the Just, and desired a murderer to be granted unto you;

15. And killed the Prince of life, whom God hath raised from

the dead; whereof we are witnesses.

16. And his name through faith in his name hath made this man strong, whom ye see and know: yea, the faith which is by him hath given him this perfect soundness in the presence of you all.

17. And now, brethren, I wot that through ignorance ye did it, as did also your rulers.

18. But those things, which God before had shewed by the mouth of all his prophets, that Christ should suffer, he hath so fulfilled.

19. Repent ye therefore, and be converted, that your sins may be blotted out, when the times of refreshing shall come from the presence of the Lord;

20. And he shall send Jesus Christ, which before was preached unto you:

21. Whom the heaven must receive until the times of restitution of all things, which God hath spoken by the mouth of all his holy prophets since the world began.

22. For Moses truly said unto the fathers, A prophet shall the Lord your God raise up unto you of your brethren, like unto me; him shall ye hear in all things whatsoever he shall say unto you.

23. And it shall come to pass, that every soul, which will not hear that prophet, shall be destroyed from among the people.

24. Yea, and all the prophets from Samuel and those that follow after, as many as have spoken, have likewise foretold of these days.

25. Ye are the children of the prophets, and of the covenant which God made with our fathers, saying unto Abraham, And in thy seed shall all the kindreds of the earth be blessed.

26. Unto you first God, having raised up his Son Jesus, sent him to bless you, in turning away every one of you from his iniquities.

The first two chapters of Acts contain the record of the instructions Jesus gave His disciples just before His ascension. He told them to tarry in Jerusalem until the Holy Spirit should come upon them and endue them with power from on high. This happened on the Day of Pentecost. They were all baptized in the Holy Ghost, they received power to speak with boldness and with other tongues so that every person present that day heard the Gospel in his own language. Thus the first church, made up of about one hundred and twenty born again, Spirit-filled believers, began the ministry of preaching the Gospel to every creature, making disciples of all men; and as a result about three thousand souls were saved and baptized into the church in Jerusalem.

Now in chapter 3 we find the record of the healing of the lame man, a miracle which presents a beautiful picture of the conversion of a sinner.

Also in this chapter we find Peter's second address and appeal to Israel. In this message he spoke to the Jews—nationally and individually—and appealed to them to repent of their sins and receive Jesus as the Christ, the Son of God, their promised Messiah. He promised *national blessing* to Israel if they would repent, and spoke of "the times of refreshing" and the "restitution of all things" (vv. 19,21). These two expressions are used in connection with the kingdom promised to Abraham and his descendants in Old Testament Scriptures; but in order to *receive* the "times of refreshing" and the "restitution of all things," Israel must repent as a nation.

Also, in verses 20 and 21 of this chapter we find the first declaration of the second coming of Christ after the account of His ascension in chapter 1.

The First Miracle Wrought by the Apostles

Verse 1: *"Now Peter and John went up together into the temple at the hour of prayer, being the ninth hour."*

In verse 46 of the preceding chapter we learned that the disciples visited the temple daily for prayer and worship, as their custom had been; and from Luke 24:53 we learned that they were continually in the temple praising God. This is understandable because the temple was the place where, for centuries, their fathers had met to worship God, and since this was the transition period these men as yet did not fully understand the new Dispensation of Grace into which they had moved. True, they had walked with Jesus while *He* was on earth, but they had not fully realized that the temple belonged to the old economy and must be left behind.

In this Day of Grace, we do not worship in "temples made with hands" because *WE are God's temple.* The Holy Spirit dwells within our hearts and "where two or three are gathered together" in the name of Jesus, He is there to own and bless. *Every believer* is a high priest and can meet God in worship anywhere, any time, in the name of *our* Great High Priest, the Lord Jesus Christ.

"Peter and John *went up together* into the temple." We find Peter and John together on several occasions—we might call them "prayer partners"; but at this particular time these two disciples went to the temple at the hour of prayer. This does not necessarily mean that they went *inside* of the building, but rather *into the court* where prayer was made by those who came to worship. (See also Matthew 21:12.)

Please notice that these men had a definite hour for prayer, and they prayed *more* than once a day. We should "pray without ceasing" (I Thess. 5:17), but we should also have a *specific time and place* where we meet God in prayer.

Daniel prayed three times a day before his open window facing toward the Holy City, Jerusalem. He prayed at his regular time and place even when it meant facing death by the king's decree: *"Now when Daniel knew that the writing was signed, he went into his house; and his windows being open into his chamber toward Jerusalem, he kneeled upon his knees three times a day, and prayed, and gave thanks before his God, as he did aforetime"* (Dan. 6:10). God honored Daniel's faithfulness, and even though he was sentenced to the lions' den, the angel of God came and closed the lions' mouths so that they did the prophet no harm.

"The ninth hour" would be about three o'clock in the afternoon, and this was the time of the *evening* prayer. *Morning* prayers were offered at nine o'clock each morning. The Psalmist declared, "Evening, and morning,

and at noon, will I pray, and cry aloud: and He shall
hear my voice" (Psa. 55:17).

A Picture of the Unbeliever

Verse 2: *"And a certain man lame from his mother's
womb was carried, whom they laid daily at the gate of
the temple which is called Beautiful, to ask alms of them
that entered into the temple."*

Verse 43 of chapter 2 told us that *"many* wonders
and signs were done by the apostles." This suggests that
they performed many outstanding miracles, but the Holy
Spirit selected *one* out of *many* and gave us a more detailed account of this miracle of the healing of a lame
man who sat daily at the Beautiful gate of the temple,
begging alms.

This man presents a perfect picture of the sinner.
First of all, we note that he could not *walk,* he had
never walked, he had been lame since birth. Many times
in His Word God calls men *to walk in His ways*—but
this is as impossible for the unbeliever as it was impossible for this man to walk *physically.*

In Exodus 18:20 Moses was commanded, "Thou shalt
teach (the people) ordinances and laws, and shalt shew
them *the way wherein they must WALK, and the WORK
that they must do."*

Deuteronomy 5:33 commanded, "Ye shall walk *in ALL
the ways* which the Lord your God hath commanded
you, that ye may live, and that it may be well with you,
and that ye may prolong your days in the land which
ye shall possess."

In I Kings 6:11,12, "the Word of the Lord came to
Solomon, saying, Concerning this house which thou art
in building, if thou wilt *walk in my STATUTES,* and
execute my judgments, and *keep all my commandments
to walk in them;* then will I perform my word with thee,
which I spake unto David thy father."

In Psalm 84:11, God commands men to walk *uprightly:* "For the Lord God is a sun and shield: the Lord will give grace and glory: *no good thing will He withhold from them that walk uprightly."* Proverbs 2:7 promises, "He layeth up sound wisdom for the righteous: He is a buckler to them that *walk uprightly."*

In Isaiah 2:5, God commands His people to *"walk in the light of the Lord."*

In Romans 4:12, through the inspired pen of the Apostle Paul we are commanded to walk "in *the steps of that faith* of our father Abraham . . . ."

Romans 8:1 commands us to *"walk not after the flesh, but after the SPIRIT"*—and the only way *any* man can walk in the Spirit is to be *BORN of the Spirit!*

It is utterly impossible for the unbeliever—"the natural man"—to fulfill these commands of God and walk in His ways. He *cannot* walk according to the Spirit; he can only walk according to the *flesh,* "because the carnal mind is enmity against God: for it is not *subject to the law of God,* neither indeed *can* be" (Rom. 8:7).

To the unbeliever, the things of God are foolishness because he has no capacity to appreciate or comprehend them: "The *natural man* receiveth not the things of the Spirit of God: for they are foolishness unto him: *neither can he know them, because THEY ARE SPIRITUALLY DISCERNED"* (I Cor. 2:14).

This lame man, unable to walk under his own power or of his own will, was carried about by the will and the power of another. The sinner is *in like condition:* he, too, is controlled and led by the power of another, held captive by Satan and subject to Satan's will:

Jesus said to the Pharisees, "Ye are of your father the devil, and *the lusts of your father ye will do . . ."* (John 8:44).

In Colossians 1:13 Paul speaks of the *believer* having been *delivered "FROM the power of darkness,"* and translated into the kingdom of God's Son.

In Acts 26:18, in Paul's defense before King Agrippa, he speaks of being sent to the Gentiles, "to open their eyes, and to turn them *from darkness to light, and FROM THE POWER OF SATAN unto God.*"

In II Timothy 2:26 Paul speaks of those who are held in the snare of the devil, "*who are taken captive by him AT HIS WILL.*"

There are only two classes of people on earth: sinners who have been *saved by the grace of God*, and sinners who are *not* saved and are therefore children of the devil:

"*And you hath He QUICKENED, who were DEAD IN TRESPASSES AND SINS: Wherein in time past ye walked according to the course of this world, ACCORDING TO THE PRINCE OF THE POWER OF THE AIR, the spirit that now worketh in THE CHILDREN OF DISOBEDIENCE: among whom also WE ALL had our conversation in times past in the lusts of our flesh, fulfilling the desires of the flesh and of the mind; and were BY NATURE the children of wrath, even as others*" (Eph. 2:1−3).

In our present verse, a person (or persons) carried the lame man each day to "*the gate of the temple, which is called Beautiful.*" (They probably placed him on the steps that led *up to the gate.*) Historians tell us that this gate was truly *most* beautiful. It was made of solid gleaming brass, glistening in great beauty when the sun's rays glinted upon it. But notice—the lame man was only "*at*" (or *by*) the gate, *he was not inside.*

In the spiritual aspect, this gate is typical of Jesus, the only Door to heaven. In John 10:9 He declared, "*I AM THE DOOR: by me if any man enter in, he shall be saved . . . .*" But those who have not *accepted* Jesus are outside the Door, just as the lame man was outside the Beautiful gate; and, like him, *they have no power of their own* by which they can enter the kingdom! According to the Word of God, no man can come to God except he be drawn by the power of the Holy Spirit

(John 6:44). However, when the sinner is drawn by the
Spirit, convicted of his sins, and exercises faith in the
Lord Jesus Christ, he is *born* of the Spirit and saved
by God's grace. He then enters through the Door, by
the miracle of the new birth wrought by the Holy Spirit.

I have heard people say, "I will be saved when I am
ready to be saved"—*but not so!* You will be saved when
you hear the Gospel and the Holy Spirit *calls* you; and
if you refuse to let Jesus come into your heart when
you are called through the Gospel and the power of the
Holy Spirit, *you certainly will NOT be saved* when you
finally make up your mind to accept Jesus in order to
escape the damnation of hell! *Salvation* is not a fire-
insurance policy against the flames of hell. Salvation is
God's gift to man—and it is for all who hear the Gospel
and *believe on the Lord Jesus Christ* (Acts 16:31).

As you read these words, if you are not saved and
you hear the voice of God calling you through the Gospel, *believe* on Jesus and be saved *this moment.* "Behold, *now* is the accepted time; behold, *NOW is the day
of salvation*" (II Cor. 6:2b). Proverbs 27:1 warns, *"Boast
not thyself of to morrow; for thou knowest not what a
day may bring forth."* And in James 4:14 we read, *"Ye
know not what shall be on the morrow. For what is
your life? It is even a vapour, that appeareth for a little
time, and then vanisheth away!"*

Verse 3:   *"Who seeing Peter and John about to go
into the temple asked an alms."*

This poor man was not only lame—he was also *a
beggar.* Each day he sat by the temple gate and begged
alms from those who passed. *All unbelievers* are beggars.
Granted, they may be worth *millions* in this world's
goods; but they are beggars nonetheless, because Jesus
said, "Whosoever will save his life shall lose it: and
whosoever will lose his life for my sake shall find it. *For
what is a man profited, if he shall gain THE WHOLE*

*WORLD, AND LOSE HIS OWN SOUL? or what shall
a man give IN EXCHANGE for his soul?"* (Matt. 16:
25,26).

Better never to be born than to gain the whole world
and lose one's own soul. Luke 16:19−31 gives the account of one such man—a man so rich in this world's
goods he had *everything he wanted.* He was clothed
in "purple and fine linen"—the raiment of royalty. His
food was the best that could be bought—he "fared *sumptuously* every day." But in the midst of his pomp and
splendor this rich man *died,* "and in hell he lift up his
eyes, being in torments, and secth Abraham afar off,
and Lazarus in his bosom. And he cried and said, Father Abraham, have mercy on me, and send Lazarus,
*that he may dip the tip of his finger in water, and cool
my tongue; for I AM TORMENTED IN THIS FLAME!"*

Sad beyond words! A multi-millionaire one minute;
the *next* minute, unable to purchase *one little drop of
water* to ease his torments. All unbelievers are beggars;
and unsaved friend, if you do not learn this fact on this
side of death, you will be assured of it thirty seconds
after you reach the *other* side!

Verse 4: *"And Peter, fastening his eyes upon him
with John, said, Look on us."*

We notice two particularly outstanding things in this
verse: First, we notice Peter and John did not simply
give this beggar a casual glance and then pass on by.
They *fastened their eyes upon him*—that is, they looked
at him stedfastly. Being thus interested in him, they
saw him for what he really was—lame, helpless, needing
far more than money or alms could provide.

On the Day of Pentecost, these disciples had yielded
themselves *completely* to the Lord; they had yielded their
members (including their *eyes*) "servants to righteousness
unto holiness" (Rom. 6:19). If believers today would
follow that example and surrender their eyes to the Lord

Jesus, they would see many more opportunities to lead sinners into the way of salvation. The Christian should at all times be seeking the lost, seeing unbelievers for what they are—blind and helpless, as the beggar was *physically* helpless to enter the beautiful gate.

All sinners are blind: "(For) if our Gospel be hid, it is hid to them that are lost: in whom the god of this world hath blinded the minds of them which believe not, lest the light of the glorious Gospel of Christ, who is the image of God, should shine unto them" (II Cor. 4:3,4).

Seeing the sad plight of the unbeliever—blind, helpless, walking in the way of destruction and damnation, the Christian will be touched with compassion and he will sound out warning of danger and death ahead: "For the wages of sin is death . . . sin, when it is finished, bringeth forth death" (Rom. 6:23; James 1:15).

In John 4:35 *Jesus* stressed the ministry of the eyes: He stopped to rest at Jacob's well while His disciples went into the city to buy food. A woman came to the well to draw water, Jesus asked her for a drink, and the conversation led to her salvation. When the disciples returned from the city, Jesus was not hungry; and when they insisted that He eat, He told them, "I have meat to eat that ye know not of." The disciples then wondered among themselves if someone had brought their Master something to eat while they were away, but discerning their thoughts Jesus said to them, *"MY meat* is to do the will of Him that sent me, and to finish His work." And then He gave them this lesson:

"Say not ye, There are yet four months, and then cometh harvest? Behold, I say unto you, *LIFT UP YOUR EYES, and look on the fields; for they are white already to harvest!"*

Anywhere on this earth today, the believer who lifts up his eyes and looks around him will see a harvest white unto reaping—with laborers so pitifully few! Fellow

Christian, if you have not dedicated your eyes to Jesus, I urge you to do it now, for the most profitable business on earth is winning souls.

God's Word declares, "The fruit of the righteous is a tree of life: and *HE THAT WINNETH SOULS IS WISE*" (Prov. 11:30). *"And they that be WISE shall shine as the brightness of the firmament; and they that turn many to righteousness as the stars for ever and ever"* (Dan. 12:3).

The second outstanding thought in this verse is found in Peter's words to the lame man: *"Look on us."* Believers today are *challenged* by these words. Do we live in such a way and are our lives so consistently Christ-like that we can invite unbelievers to "look on *us*"? Christians should so live that sinners who watch our daily habits and manner of life will see Jesus in what we do and say. They should know from our daily conduct that we, like the apostles, *have been with Jesus.* Every believer should be a living epistle, read of men (II Cor. 3:2).

Verse 5: *"And he gave heed unto them, expecting to receive something of them."*

The fact that the lame man *"gave heed unto them"* suggests that there was something in the voice and manner of these men that commanded his attention in an unusual way. Normally, he was not interested in *looking* at men, nor in listening to them. He was interested in what they would *give* him. But when Peter and John said, "Look on us," his attention was arrested and he gave heed to what they were saying, although he no doubt still "expected to receive something of them."

Believers should speak with authority—but also with compassion; and what we say should be backed up by a life that commands sufficient respect from unbelievers to cause them to listen to what we say. This man could have said to Peter, "I am not interested in *looking* at

you. I am interested in what you will contribute toward
my living expenses." But he did not say that. Throughout the book of Acts we will notice that the apostles
were threatened, arrested, imprisoned, beaten; but in
spite of the persecution they endured, their enemies were
aware that these were no ordinary men—*"they took
knowledge of them, that they had been with JESUS"*
(Acts 4:13). Believers today should live so close to Jesus
and walk so closely in His steps that by appearance,
words, and actions we can arrest the attention of those
to whom we witness concerning the grace of God and
salvation by grace. We have something to give to those
who do not know the Christ. We cannot *save* them—
but we can give them the message that WILL save them
if they will only accept it. The world *needs* this message. The harvest truly is plenteous, but the laborers
are so few!

Verse 6:   *"Then Peter said, Silver and gold have I
none; but such as I have give I thee: In the name of
Jesus Christ of Nazareth rise up and walk."*

Notice the power of the spoken Word. Peter could
have performed a miracle here, but he did not. Instead,
he spoke WORDS. The same was true when he carried
the Gospel to the Gentiles in the household of Cornelius.
God sent an angel who told Cornelius to send to Joppa
and ask for Simon Peter, *who would tell him WORDS
whereby he and all his house could be saved* (Acts 11:14).

Jesus declared, "Verily, verily, I say unto you, *He that
heareth my WORD, and believeth on Him that sent me,*
hath everlasting life, and shall not come into condemnation; but is passed from death unto life" (John 5:24).

Peter wrote in his first epistle, "Being born again, not
of corruptible seed, but of incorruptible, *by the WORD
of God,* which liveth and abideth for ever" (I Pet. 1:23).

We are saved by grace through faith; *faith comes by
hearing, and hearing by the WORD of God* (Rom. 10:17).

The lame man gave heed to Peter and John, *"expecting to receive something of them"*—but instead of the silver or gold he expected to receive, *they gave him WORDS,* and what a change those words wrought in his life!

"Silver and gold have I none—but such as I have, give I thee: IN THE NAME OF JESUS CHRIST OF NAZARETH rise up and walk." The name of *Jesus!* The angel of the Lord appeared to Joseph and said to him, "Fear not to take unto thee Mary thy wife: for that which is conceived in her is of the Holy Ghost. *And she shall being forth a Son, and thou shalt call His name JESUS: for He shall save His people from their sins"* (Matt. 1:20,21).

The name *Jesus* means *Saviour*—and in Acts 4:12 we read, "Neither is there salvation in any other: for there is *none other NAME* under heaven given among men, whereby we must be saved." There was great significance in the wording of Peter's command to the lame man—*"in the name of JESUS the Saviour,* rise up and walk."

Peter had an opportunity here to become a famous healer if he had been *personally ambitious;* but he was a true minister of the Gospel and he coveted none of the glory that should go to Jesus. He gave all credit, honor, and glory to *the name of JESUS,* and to the *power* of that name. The lame man *believed* the words Peter spoke—otherwise he would have made no attempt to stand on his feet. He had faith in the name of Jesus, and he obeyed Peter's command.

If ever a man had the right to argue, this man had that right. According to chapter 4, verse 22, he was past forty years of age, he had been lame "from his mother's womb," and, understandably, he could have said to Peter, "Who do you think you *are?* How *can* I stand up? I have never walked a step in my life." But that is where *faith* stepped in: The only possible way for a sinner to become a child of God is by exercising faith in God's ability to do what He *promises*. The sinner cannot save himself, no minister of the Gospel can save him; but *Jesus* can—and when we give out the Word of God, declaring that *the blood of Jesus Christ cleanses from all sin and whosoever shall call* upon *the NAME of Jesus* shall be saved, sinners who *believe* the Word are born again and become new creations in Christ Jesus. *FAITH is believing God because God IS God.* If God *said* it we can *believe* it, because *"God CANNOT lie"* (Tit. 1:2; Heb. 6:18).

Verse 7:   *"And he took him by the right hand, and lifted him up: and immediately his feet and ankle bones received strength."*

Since *God* worked the miracle here, *why* was it necessary for Peter to take this man by the hand? *It was NOT necessary.* God could have raised him up without Peter's touching him; but I believe the Lord would have us see here that by giving unbelievers a helping hand we can prove to them that we have a practical interest in them. Certainly we cannot *isolate* ourselves from unsaved people if we hope to win them for Christ; but we *can* refuse to partake of their sinful habits of life. We should help them and show interest in them in a practical way when we can do so without compromising with their sins and ungodliness.

The touch of Peter's hand assured this crippled beggar that the apostle had a personal interest in him and caused him to put forth an effort to stand on his feet. There was no *power* in Peter's touch, there is no power in the touch of *any* mortal; but by extending our hand we show the sinner that we are interested in him, that we want to lend a helping hand if he is in need.

Jesus took *Jairus' daughter* by the hand when He restored her to life (Matt. 9:25). He took the blind man by the hand and led him out of the town of Bethsaida before He healed his blindness (Mark 8:23). After He

cast out the evil spirit from a young man, the boy was
"as one dead." Jesus took him by the hand "and lifted
him up" (Mark 9:27).

Peter took the beggar "by the right hand and lifted
him up, *and IMMEDIATELY his feet and ankle bones
received strength"* — not gradually, not a little today and
a little more tomorrow, but *IMMEDIATELY the man
was made whole*. I believe in *this kind* of divine healing.
I believe that when God works a miracle of healing, He
heals instantaneously and perfectly — not step by step,
not partially. Even in *this present day* He heals. Why
He does not heal in all cases, I do not know: but I *do*
know He is always *able*. God is omniscient and omnipotent; and poor, finite creature that I am, I cannot fathom
the depth of His ways. On occasion I myself have prayed
for healing, and God healed — or *did not* heal — as He saw
fit. But *however* he answers prayer, I know that Romans
8:28 is mine to claim: "We know that all things work
together for good to them that love God, to them who
are the called according to His purpose."

According to the words of Jesus, the sickness of *Lazarus* was "for the glory of God, that the Son of God
might be glorified thereby" (John 11:4). If Lazarus could
be sick to the glory of God, then *every believer* can be
sick to the glory of God — and many times God gets more
glory from the illness of His saints than He gets when
they are well! We should always remember to pray,
"Thy will be done."

Just as God does not *heal* gradually, He does not *save*
gradually. We are saved instantaneously, completely,
the moment we exercise faith in the finished work of Jesus — His death, burial, resurrection, and ascension; and
when we are born again we are just as redeemed as we
will *ever* be. We *grow in grace* after we are born into
the family of God (I Pet. 2:2); but we do not become
more fully redeemed. If you have been saved for forty
years or more, you are no more fully saved now than

you were the first hour you believed. When we are born into God's family we are *fully* born, new creations in Christ and possessors of divine nature (II Cor. 5:17; II Pet. 1:4); but we grow in grace as we feed upon the milk, bread, and meat of the Word of God.

The name of JESUS stands for authority and power, it stands for all that He accomplished on the cross, *and for all that He IS on our behalf* before God today. Salvation is *by* the name of Jesus, *through* the name of Jesus, *and ONLY by and through His precious name.* (Please study Acts 3:16; 4:10; I Corinthians 6:11; and I John 3:23.) When we come to God by faith in the name of Jesus Christ, we claim all for which that name stands—the redemptive value of the blood He shed on Golgotha, His risen life, and all the graces of salvation. When we come to God in the name of Jesus, claiming Him as our Saviour, we put God on His covenant honor— His faithfulness and the integrity of His promised Word; and He promises that all who receive Jesus will be saved:

"As many as received Him, to them gave He power to become the sons of God, even to them that believe on His name: which were born, not of blood, nor of the will of the flesh, nor of the will of man, but of God" (John 1:12,13).

Verse 8: *"And he leaping up stood, and walked, and entered with them into the temple, walking, and leaping, and praising God."*

This man, more than forty years old and never having walked, in obedience to Peter's command and in response to the apostle's extended hand *leaped up, stood, and walked!* There was new power within him—and when God *saves a sinner* He immediately puts the power of the Holy Spirit within that person's heart; and from that moment forward, the Holy Spirit *indwells, leads, assures,* and *seals* that child of God (Rom. 8:9,14,16; Eph. 4:30), thus denoting that he is *God's property* and no longer belongs to the devil. And the new power *within* the believer will lead him into paths of right living, into paths of newness of life.

Notice the first place the lame man went after he was healed: he *"entered with them into the TEMPLE."* The truly born again believer will attend the house of God; he will not need to be *persuaded* to join the local church. (Those who must be begged and coaxed to attend church have never been born again.) His first thought will be to unite with God's people to worship and praise God for salvation, just as *this* dear man praised God.

The man in our study was physically handicapped—he was crippled, unable to stand on his feet and walk; but a miracle happened, freeing him from his malady, enabling him to stand and run and leap for joy. *Unbelievers* are *spiritually* handicapped, crippled and scarred by sin, blinded by Satan; and when they are *saved,* liberated from the power of the devil, they experience *the greatest of ALL miracles* and are able to stand up in "the stature of the fulness of Christ" (Eph. 4:13). (Please study Galatians 5:1; Philippians 1:27; 4:1; and I Thessalonians 3:8 in connection with this.)

The man who had *never* walked was now walking, running, and leaping—proof positive that a great miracle had been wrought in his life. Born again people prove the miracle of *the new birth* by walking with Jesus, whereas *before they were saved* they walked in the way of the world, in sin; but as new creations in Christ, we have a new walk:

"Therefore we are buried with Him by baptism into death: that like as Christ was raised up from the dead by the glory of the Father, even so we also should walk in newness of life" (Rom. 6:4).

Believers walk after the Spirit, not after the world: "There is therefore now no condemnation to them which are in Christ Jesus, who walk not after the flesh, *but after the Spirit"* (Rom. 8:1).

Believers walk by faith: "Therefore we are always confident, knowing that, whilst we are at home in the body, we are *absent from the Lord: (for we walk by FAITH, not by SIGHT)*" (II Cor. 5:6,7).

Believers *prove* the new birth by good works: "For we are His workmanship, created in Christ Jesus *unto good works,* which God hath before ordained that we should walk in them" (Eph. 2:10).   "For as the body without the spirit is dead, so *faith without works is dead also"* (James 2:26).

Believers are children of God and should walk worthy of that vocation: Paul said, "I therefore, the prisoner of the Lord, beseech you that ye walk worthy of the vocation wherewith ye are called" (Eph. 4:1).

Believers should walk worthy of the Lord: "That ye might walk worthy of the Lord unto all pleasing, being fruitful in every good work, and increasing in the knowledge of God" (Col. 1:10).

Believers should walk honestly: "Let us walk honestly, as in the day; not in rioting and drunkenness, not in chambering and wantonness, not in strife and envying" (Rom. 13:13).   "That ye may walk honestly toward them that are without, and that ye may have lack of nothing" (I Thess. 4:12).

Believers should walk in the light, as *children* of light: "For ye were sometimes darkness, but now are ye light in the Lord: walk as children of light" (Eph. 5:8).   "If we walk in the light, *as HE is in the light,* we have fellowship one with another, and the blood of Jesus Christ His Son cleanseth us from all sin" (I John 1:7).

Believers should walk in truth: John the Beloved said, "I have no greater joy than to hear that my children walk in truth" (III John 4).

Believers should walk in wisdom because "Christ . . . is made unto us wisdom, and righteousness, and sanctification, and redemption" (I Cor. 1:30).   "Walk in wisdom toward them that are without, redeeming the time"

(Col. 4:5).

In other words, believers are sons of God, indwelt by divine nature and led by the Holy Spirit; therefore *believers should walk as JESUS walked*: "He that saith he abideth in Him ought himself also so to walk, *even as HE walked*" (I John 2:6).

The man who was healed of his lameness "entered *with them* into the temple." He immediately walked with the apostles. New converts should immediately unite with other believers; they should find companionship and fellowship with the people of God. A person who is truly born again *cannot find fellowship* with any other group. Christians cannot find fellowship in the world because the world holds nothing of interest to them — and they cannot *afford* to walk with the world. The Word of God makes this very clear:

"*Love not the world,* neither the things that are *in* the world. If any man love the world, the love of the Father is not in Him. For all that is in the world, the lust of the flesh, and the lust of the eyes, and the pride of life, is not of the Father, but is of the world. And the world passeth away, and the lust thereof: but he that doeth the will of God abideth for ever" (I John 2:15 — 17).

I Corinthians 15:33 declares, "Be not deceived: *evil communications corrupt good manners*" — and this is certainly true.

Christians are further commanded to *separate themselves FROM the world,* insofar as fellowship is concerned:

"Wherefore *come out from among them, and be ye separate,* saith the Lord, and touch not the unclean thing; and I will receive you" (II Cor. 6:17).

The believer will turn his steps to the house of God and rejoice with the people of God in fellowship and worship. He will say with David, "I was glad when they said unto me, Let us go into the house of the Lord!"

(Psa. 122:1).

Notice that the man in our Scripture not only *entered* the house of God with Peter and John, he also *praised* God. I do not believe in foolishness in God's house— putting on a religious "show," as it were; but *praise* is the loftiest function of the born again soul. The book of Psalms is *filled* with praises.

When Jesus made His triumphal entry into Jerusalem, the multitudes who welcomed Him rejoiced and praised God, shouting hosannas. The Pharisees commanded Jesus to *rebuke* the disciples and stop their shouting of praise; but Jesus replied, "I tell you that, if these should hold their peace, *the stones* would immediately cry out" (Luke 19:40).

God WILL BE PRAISED—and believers *should* praise Him: "By Him therefore let us offer the sacrifice of praise to God *continually*, that is, the fruit of our lips giving thanks to His name" (Heb. 13:15).

"Rejoice in the Lord, O ye righteous: for praise is comely for the upright" (Psa. 33:1).

"I will bless the Lord at all times: His praise shall continually be in my mouth" (Psa. 34:1).

"Enter into His gates with thanksgiving, and into His courts with praise: be thankful unto Him, and bless His name" (Psa. 100:4).

"And a voice came out of the throne, saying, *Praise our God, all ye His servants, and ye that fear Him, both small and great. AND I HEARD AS IT WERE THE VOICE OF A GREAT MULTITUDE, AND AS THE VOICE OF MANY WATERS, AND AS THE VOICE OF MIGHTY THUNDERINGS, SAYING, ALLELUIA: FOR THE LORD GOD OMNIPOTENT REIGNETH"* (Rev. 19:5,6).

Beloved, *believe* me when I say that we are in the quietest world we will ever *be* in, right here on earth! *HEAVEN is a place of rejoicing, and HELL is a place of weeping, wailing, and gnashing of teeth.* If you are not born again, give your heart to Jesus now, put your faith in His shed blood and finished work, and prepare for the place where we will praise God perfectly throughout all eternity!

Verse 9: *"And all the people saw him walking and praising God."*

The transformation in this man was so marked that *everyone* noticed it—and the same is true in the spiritual aspect. When a *sinner* becomes a *believer,* everyone who has known that person will immediately recognize the complete change in him. He turns to God from sin and Satan, he turns to righteousness from unrighteousness, he is a new creature in Christ; therefore *ALL things become new, OLD things pass away.* The truly born again person does not need to carry a sign advertising his conversion, because the language he uses, the songs he sings, the places he goes, and the company he keeps—his entire change of habits of life—will be all the advertising he needs! It is impossible to keep Christ hidden when we come to know Him as personal Saviour.

Verse 10: *"And they knew that it was he which sat for alms at the Beautiful gate of the temple: and they were filled with wonder and amazement at that which had happened unto him."*

"They KNEW that it was he." This man was well known. The people in that community had been accustomed to seeing him in the same place year after year as he sat by the temple gate and begged for alms. There was no doubt of it, this was the same man—but there was a striking difference about him. His face was now smiling, radiant with happiness and joy. His limbs were no longer twisted and deformed; they were straight and strong, and the man was walking on them, leaping for joy. They heard the same voice—not begging for alms, but lifted in praise to God!

Yes, this was the man they knew (and had known for many years), but he was a man made new, and the people were convinced that a truly great miracle had been wrought. They saw the effects of it, there was indisputable evidence that the man was completely healed of his lameness. Even those who had no interest in Jesus, no interest in the power of God or in things religious, saw him walking, leaping, and praising God.

Just so will excitement be created by the church in which the power of the Lord Jesus is manifested, where souls are brought into the fold and into the true knowledge of salvation. Such a church will create excitement and interest among unbelievers, it will be visited by those who hear the reports of people being saved and miracles being wrought. (By "miracles" I mean that when a *drunkard* becomes a consistently sober man; when a *dope addict* is cured of the dope habit; when a *gambler* gives up gambling; when a *thief* becomes completely honest—and all of these transformations are due to the fact that sinners have been born again—*THAT is a MIRACLE!*) And the church where revival breaks out, where souls are saved and lives are changed, will become the center of interest. Such a church cannot be hidden; it is like "a city set on a hill."

Verse 11: *"And as the lame man which was healed held Peter and John, all the people ran together unto them in the porch that is called Solomon's, greatly wondering."*

The man who had been so miraculously healed held to Peter and John, refusing to be separated from them—and small wonder! It is perfectly natural for a person to have a tender spot in his heart for the one who shows him the way of salvation. I know I shall never cease to thank God for the man who led *me* to the Lord, nor will I ever cease to thank Him for those who prayed for me when I had no desire to become a Christian.

Peter and John were used of God to bring about the miracle in this man's life, and it is understandable that he did not want to part company with them.

A crowd soon gathered in Solomon's porch—*excited* people, filled with curiosity: *"And ALL the people ran together unto them . . . greatly wondering."* People have always "wondered" when the power of God is displayed in miracles; but if we believe God is omnipotent, omniscient, and omnipresent—(and He IS)—why should we be amazed at what He can *do?* He "is able to do exceeding abundantly above all that we ask or think" (Eph. 3:20), but unbelievers do not realize this great truth. God wrought mighty miracles in the Old Testament era and the prophets recorded those miracles; but the sad truth was that these people were ignorant of the Scripture in the same way the majority of church members *today* are ignorant of the Scripture. If mighty revival broke out in the average church today, most of the members would be amazed. They would not understand what was taking place.

People gathered to see for themselves this amazing miracle that had been wrought, and the great crowd furnished a wonderful opportunity for Peter and John to preach the Gospel of God's marvelous grace.

"The porch that is called Solomon's" was a covered passage—we might call it a wide hallway—on the east side of the temple. In this porch crowds gathered to hear different speakers, to hold discussions and religious ceremonies. It was here that the religious leaders gathered to question Jesus, as recorded in John 10:23—29.

Peter's Second Sermon

Verse 12: *"And when Peter saw it, he answered unto the people, Ye men of Israel, why marvel ye at this? or why look ye so earnestly on us, as though by our own power or holiness we had made this man to walk?"*

"When Peter saw it, he answered unto the people."

Peter was alert, and when he saw the people assembling in Solomon's porch he took immediate advantage of the opportunity to make known to them that every covenant God had made with Abraham and the fathers would be literally and completely fulfilled.

The statement that Peter *"answered"* suggests that a question had been asked; but here the word *answer* is used in a different way. In the Bible it is often used—not when a question had been asked, but rather when an occasion arose for remarks, or when an occasion was offered to make a statement. Peter saw just such an occasion and he said, *"Ye men of Israel, why marvel ye at this?"*

The people looked on Peter and John as if the apostles had healed this man through their own power. The Jews should have *known* better; they should have known that only Almighty God could perform such a miracle. The Old Testament is *filled* with miracles, and the Jews, of all people, should have been the last to be astonished by such a miracle.

"Why look ye so earnestly on US?" That is, "Why do you gaze with such amazement on us, as though *we* could do what you have seen here?" If Peter and John had been self-centered, anxious to make a name for themselves, this was certainly the opportunity for it. But they ministered to the glory of God and the success of their ministry was ascribed to *Him,* not to their own power or ability. They knew that by their own accomplishments, talents, or personal holiness they could accomplish nothing. Paul expresses this very clearly in his second epistle to the Corinthian church:

"Such trust have we through Christ to God-ward: Not that we are sufficient of ourselves to think any thing as of ourselves; but our sufficiency is of God; who also hath made us able ministers of the new testament; not of the letter, but of the spirit: for the letter killeth, but the spirit giveth life" (II Cor. 3:4—6).

Verse 13: *"The God of Abraham, and of Isaac, and of Jacob, the God of our fathers, hath glorified His Son Jesus; whom ye delivered up, and denied Him in the presence of Pilate, when he was determined to let Him go."*

"The God of Abraham ... Isaac ... and Jacob." In Romans 4:3 Paul tells us, "Abraham *believed God,* and it was counted unto him for righteousness," and James 2:23 speaks of Abraham as "the friend of God."

In Genesis 26:24 God spoke to *Isaac:* "And the Lord appeared unto him the same night, and said, I am the God of Abraham thy father: fear not, for I am with thee, and will bless thee, and multiply thy seed for my servant Abraham's sake."

In Genesis 28:13 God spoke to *Jacob:* "And, behold, the Lord stood above it, and said, I am the Lord God of Abraham thy father, and the God of Isaac: the land whereon thou liest, to thee will I give it, and to thy seed." (Please read Exodus 3:6—15 in connection with these passages.)

In John 8:56 Jesus said to the Jews, "Your father Abraham rejoiced to see my day: and he saw it, and was glad." Peter was trying to show his people that the lame man had been made whole by the *same* God who had wrought miracles in the days of Abraham, Isaac, and Jacob, the SAME God from whom Abraham received the promises with which all Jews were familiar:

"Now the Lord had said unto Abram, Get thee out of thy country, and from thy kindred, and from thy father's house, unto a land that I will shew thee: *And I will make of thee a great nation, and I will bless thee, and make thy name great; and thou shalt be a blessing: And I will bless them that bless thee, and curse him that curseth thee: AND IN THEE SHALL ALL FAMILIES OF THE EARTH BE BLESSED"* (Gen. 12:1—3).

In Galatians 3:16 we read, "Now to *Abraham and his seed* were the promises made. He saith not, And to *seeds,* as of *many;* but *as of ONE,* And to thy *SEED, which is Christ."*

The God of Abraham, Isaac, and Jacob *"hath glorified His Son Jesus."* This does not sound like the same man who on the night of the Lord's arrest sat by the devil's fire, cursing and declaring that he had never *known* Jesus. Here, in clear, understandable words, Peter boldly declares to the Jews, "You denied Jesus, you hated Him and had Him crucified; but in spite of your terrible sin, the God of our fathers raised Him from the dead and placed Him in an exalted position at His right hand. And the miracle you have just witnessed was done *in the name of Jesus and through His power.* Thus has Jehovah God shown that He *approved* the ministry and the finished work—yes, even the *death*—of His Son, the Lord Jesus Christ!"

In John 17:1 Jesus prayed, "Father, the hour is come; *glorify thy Son,* that thy Son also may glorify thee."

Paul explained to the Philippian church the same truth Peter was offering the Jews in our present verse. Paul explained that because of the complete obedience of Jesus, "God also hath *highly exalted* Him, and given Him a name which is above every name: That at the name of Jesus every knee should bow, of things in heaven, and things in earth, and things under the earth; and that every tongue should confess that Jesus Christ is Lord, to the glory of God the Father" (Phil. 2:9—11).

Then in Hebrews 2:9 we read, "We see Jesus, who was made a little lower than the angels for the suffering of death, *crowned with GLORY AND HONOUR;* that He by the grace of God should taste death for every man."

"Whom ye delivered up . . . ." The question sometimes arises, "Who *really* was guilty of crucifying Jesus— the Jews or the Romans?" The answer is clear in the Scriptures: The Jews demanded His death and surrendered Him to the Romans. The Romans crucified Him.

The Jews could not put a person to death because they had no government of their own at that time; they were under Roman rule. But they were *guilty* of the death of Jesus; they *crucified* Him, even though they did not literally nail Him to the cross. No *man*—Roman, Jew, or anyone else—actually killed Jesus! *God* struck the fatal blow, according to Isaiah 53:4: "Surely He hath borne our griefs, and carried our sorrows: yet we did esteem Him stricken, SMITTEN OF GOD, and afflicted." *Jesus* said, "Therefore doth my Father love me, because *I lay down my life,* that I might take it again. *NO MAN taketh it from me, but I LAY IT DOWN OF MYSELF. I have power to lay it down, and I have power to take it again.* This commandment have I received of my Father" (John 10:17,18). Nevertheless, the guilt lies at the feet of the Jews.

"And denied Him in the presence of Pilate, when he was determined to let Him go." This of course refers to the trial of Jesus, and the fact that Pilate knew Jesus was innocent; but—weak in character and fearful of the Jews—he yielded to their demands and gave their Messiah into their hands to be crucified. (Study Matthew 27:17—25 and Luke 23:13—25.)

Verse 14: *"But ye denied the Holy One and the Just, and desired a murderer to be granted unto you."*

Yes, Jesus was *"the Holy One."* Psalm 16:10 declares, "Thou wilt not leave my soul in hell; neither wilt thou suffer *thine Holy One* to see corruption." He was the Faultless One, the Sinless One. He invited His enemies, "Which of you convinceth me of sin?" (John 8:46a). *Three times* Pilate examined and cross-examined Him, and three times declared, *"I find NO FAULT in Him!"*

"Pilate saith unto Him, What is truth? And when he had said this, he went out again unto the Jews, and saith unto them, *I find in Him no fault* at all. . . Pilate therefore went forth again, and saith unto them, Behold,

I bring Him forth to you, that ye may know that *I find no fault in Him*. . . When the chief priests therefore and officers saw Him, they cried out, saying, Crucify Him, crucify Him.   Pilate saith unto them, Take ye Him, and crucify Him: *FOR I FIND NO FAULT IN HIM!"* (John 18:38; 19:4,6).

Jesus was *"the Just One."* The Greek word here translated "just" means "the Innocent One."   The Jews charged Jesus with blasphemy (Matt. 26:65); the Sanhedrin brought this charge against Him—but they had no proof of the charge, and since Pilate would not accept the charge of blasphemy the Jews changed their accusation to *sedition:*   "And they began to accuse Him, saying, We found this fellow perverting the nation, and forbidding to give tribute to Caesar, saying that He Himself is Christ a King" (Luke 23:2); but that charge, too, was without proof.   He was "the Just One," and they could not prove Him *unjust,* which fact greatly aggravated the seriousness of the crime they committed against Him in demanding His death.

Verse 15:   *"And killed the Prince of life, whom God hath raised from the dead; whereof we are witnesses."*

The Greek word translated *"prince"* denotes a military leader or commander.   The same word is used in Hebrews 2:10, where it is rendered "captain," (speaking of Jesus as "the *Captain* of our salvation"), and in Hebrews 5:9, where Paul speaks of Him as "the *Author* of eternal salvation."

A military captain or commander who leads his soldiers to victory is given *credit* for his leadership.   Thus God's Word points out the One who is the Captain (or Author) of victory (Acts 5:31; Heb. 12:2).

Jesus is not only *"the PRINCE of life,"* He is *LIFE itself.*   Thomas asked Him, "How can we come where you are going when we do not know the way?"   Jesus answered, *"I am the Way, the Truth, and the LIFE:*   no man cometh unto the Father, but by me" (John 14:6). We who have life *have Christ,* because *Christ IS our life* (Col. 3:4).

"And this is the record, that *God hath given to us eternal life, and this life is in His SON. He that hath the SON hath LIFE; and he that hath NOT the Son of God HATH NOT LIFE.* These things have I written unto you that believe on the name of the Son of God; *that ye may KNOW that ye have eternal life,* and that ye may believe on the name of the Son of God" (I John 5:11—13).

In John 5:26 Jesus declared, "As the *Father* hath life in Himself; so hath He given to the *Son* to have life in Himself."

Yes, Jesus is *the Prince of life,* and He offered life to the Jews; but they chose Barabbas (who *destroyed* life), and demanded the death of the Author of life (Luke 23:18,19).

"*Whom God hath raised from the dead, whereof we are witnesses.*" God raised Jesus from the dead, and the apostles were witnesses to the *fact* of His resurrection. Paul declared "that Christ died for our sins according to the Scriptures; and that He was buried, *and that HE ROSE AGAIN THE THIRD DAY according to the Scriptures: and that He was SEEN of Cephas* (Peter), *then of the TWELVE: After that, He was seen of above FIVE HUNDRED brethren at once:* of whom the greater part remain unto this present, but some are fallen asleep. After that, *He was seen of JAMES; then of ALL THE APOSTLES.* And last of all *He was seen of ME also,* as of one born out of due time" (I Cor. 15:3—8).

Verse 16: "*And His name through faith in His name hath made this man strong, whom ye see and know: yea, the faith which is by Him hath given him this perfect soundness in the presence of you all.*"

"*His name*" speaks of Jesus Himself, as if Peter had

said, *"Through faith in JESUS,* who was very God in flesh, this man has been given *perfect soundness."*

The name "Jesus" means *Saviour;* "neither is there salvation in any other: *for there is none other name under heaven given among men, whereby we MUST be saved"* (Acts 4:12). Peter did not mean that the power was in the *name,* but in *the PERSON,* Jesus. It was He who had power to heal, and *through faith in HIM* the lame man was made whole. The healing was by the *authority and power* of Jesus.

"Through faith in His name"—(or by means of faith in the *Person,* Jesus) does not refer to the faith *the lame man* had in Him, for there is no evidence that he believed in Jesus, or that he even knew anything *about* Him. It was through the faith exercised by Peter and John that this miracle was wrought. This is a fulfillment of the promise Jesus made in Matthew 17:20 when He said, "If ye have faith as a grain of mustard seed, ye shall say unto this mountain, Remove hence to yonder place; and it shall remove; *and nothing shall be impossible unto you."*

There was no doubt that a great miracle had been wrought in this healing of the lame man, for the people declared, "What shall we do to these men? for that *indeed a notable miracle hath been done by them is manifest to all them that dwell in Jerusalem; and we cannot deny it"* (Acts 4:16). But Peter and John refused to take any credit for the miracle, declaring that only by the power of the Lord Jesus had this man been "given *perfect soundness."*

When Jesus heals, He heals perfectly. *HE was perfect,* and perfection cannot produce imperfection. Jesus could do nothing except He do it perfectly. The Greek word used here speaks of "integrity of parts, free from defect," and is not found anywhere else in the New Testament. It means that this man was made *perfectly whole, completely free of deformity,* as though he had never been paralyzed.

The same is true when a sinner is saved. No matter how wretchedly wicked an unbeliever may be, no matter if his soul and spirit are *paralyzed* by sin, when he exercises faith in the Lord Jesus Christ he is *perfectly saved.* The new birth is perfect and *complete,* for God does not stop short of perfection. He does not "partially" save. It is true that we become *stronger* in faith as we grow in grace through study of the Word; but when Jesus saves us we are just as completely saved as we will ever be. Believers make mistakes after they are born again, sometimes they stumble; but you may rest assured that *there are no flaws in salvation!* Christ is our salvation, and Christ is perfect. And when we are born into God's family, we are *perfectly born.*

Verse 17:   *"And now, brethren, I wot that through ignorance ye did it, as did also your rulers."*

In spite of the fact that the Jews had been guilty of crucifying their Messiah, Peter showed compassion in dealing with them—he addressed them as *"brethren."* He still regarded them as his brethren in the flesh, of the same nation as himself, entitled to claim the same promises, the same privileges, the same hope. He was not disposed to exalt himself above his brethren from the natural standpoint, he was not "holier than thou." He realized that the difference between himself and his nation was that *he* had *received* the Messiah, *THEY had REJECTED Him and demanded His death.*

Peter could have sternly rebuked the Jews for crucifying Jesus; but instead, he stated their guilt, proved their wickedness, and then in kindness and love he begged them to repent and receive the Lord Jesus Christ as their Saviour.

There is a time to "reprove, rebuke, exhort with all longsuffering and doctrine" (II Tim. 4:2), but we will win more people to God through *love* than we can win through reproof and rebuke.   Christians should be reproved for careless living, but *sinners* need to be called to God through the message of the cross—a message of love, for Jesus on the cross was *God's love* on display.

"*I wot* (I know) *that through ignorance ye did it.*" Peter did not mean that the Jews were *innocent* in what they had done, but rather that they had crucified Jesus because of *ignorance in their hearts* concerning Him. They did not recognize Him because they did not believe the Old Testament prophecies concerning His coming. If they had believed Moses they would have believed Jesus.

In John 5:45—47 Jesus Himself said to these people, "Do not think that I will accuse you to the Father: there is one that accuseth you, *even Moses,* in whom ye trust. *For had ye believed MOSES, ye would have believed ME: for he wrote of me.   But if ye believe not his writings, how shall ye believe my words?*"

On the cross, Jesus prayed, "Father, forgive them; for *they know not what they do*" (Luke 23:34).   Ignorance has many degrees, and it arises from many causes.   For example, the *Jewish multitudes* were ignorant from want of teaching.   The religious rulers among the Jews were looking at only one part of the prophecies concerning Messiah—i. e., they were expecting a powerful ruler who would deliver them from Roman tyranny and establish their promised kingdom; but Isaiah had declared that the Messiah would be led as a Lamb to the slaughter, and made it plain that the cross must precede the crown. Still the Jews refused to believe that the lowly Nazarene could be their Messiah, and because of this lack of knowledge they crucified Jesus.

The Apostle Paul declared practically the same thing in his personal testimony concerning his persecution of the Church.   As Saul of Tarsus he had murder in his heart and blood on his hands.   He consented to the death of Stephen, and persecuted all who were followers of Jesus. He declared in his testimony before King Agrippa, "I verily thought with myself, that I ought to do many things contrary to the name of Jesus of Nazareth. Which thing I also did in Jerusalem: and many of the saints did I shut up in prison, having received authority from the chief priests; and when they were put to death, I gave my voice against them. And I punished them oft in every synagogue, and compelled them to blaspheme; and being exceedingly mad against them, I persecuted them even unto strange cities" (Acts 26:9—11).

Then in I Timothy 1:13 he cried out, *"BUT I OBTAINED MERCY, because I did it ignorantly IN UNBELIEF!"* This was what Peter wanted the Jews to see. In spite of their great sin against a holy God in the crucifixion of His Son, they could obtain mercy if they would only repent and acknowledge Jesus as Saviour, their Messiah.

There is no doubt that the great majority of the Jewish people were ignorant of the identity of Jesus. They believed that He was a great teacher—but they did not believe Him to be their Messiah. The outstanding *religious leaders and rulers* certainly did not believe Jesus was Messiah, for in I Corinthians 2:7,8 Paul declared, "We speak the wisdom of God in a mystery, even the hidden wisdom, which God ordained before the world unto our glory: *which none of the princes of this world knew: FOR HAD THEY KNOWN IT, THEY WOULD NOT HAVE CRUCIFIED THE LORD OF GLORY!"*

The scribes and Pharisees carried a burning hatred for Jesus and were determined to find some means whereby they could put Him to death. They had many opportunities to know His true character and to recognize Him as the One for whom they waited. They were exposed to miracles such as no mortal could perform, but they were blinded, willingly ignorant, refusing to recognize in those miracles the unmistakable evidence that Jesus was their promised Messiah—and the Scripture makes it *clear* that they did not believe Him to be *the Son of God*, for in John 19:7, when they brought Him before Pilate, they said, "We have a law, and by our law He ought to die, *because He made Himself THE SON OF GOD!*"

Even the Sanhedrin was influenced by the hatred of the chief priests and other religious leaders (and the members of that body who *did* think Jesus was being unjustly condemned lacked the courage to resist the chief priests and Pharisees). Please read John 7:50—53 in connection with this.

Peter by no means considered the Jews free from blame in crucifying their Messiah; he was simply holding out to them hope and mercy from a longsuffering God. If they would repent of their sins and believe on Jesus, God would forgive them and save them through the shed blood of His beloved Son.

Verse 18: *"But those things, which God before had shewed by the mouth of all His prophets, that Christ should suffer, He hath also fulfilled."*

"Those things" were *everything* that actually occurred pertaining to the life and death of the Lord Jesus Christ on earth—His birth, His ministry, His miracles, His suffering, His death, and His resurrection.

"Which God before had shewed" simply means that centuries before these things happened, God announced *through the prophets* everything that *would* happen to Jesus; and if the Jews had known and understood the prophecies concerning Messiah, they could not have failed to recognize Jesus because everything the Old Testament prophesied concerning Him happened *literally and to the letter AS* prophesied.

"By the mouth of all His prophets." Peter does not name any specific prophet, but speaks of *all* the prophets and their prophecies concerning the coming of the Lord Jesus Christ as foretold in the Old Testament Scriptures.

God revealed to *Adam* the manner of Christ's coming—that He would be the Seed of the woman: "And I will put enmity between thee and the woman, and between thy seed and her Seed; it shall bruise thy head, and thou shalt bruise His heel" (Gen. 3:15).

God revealed to *Abraham* that Christ should be from the nation (Israel) of which he was head (Gen. 12:1—3).

To *Jacob* God made known that Christ would come through the tribe of Judah: "The sceptre shall not depart from Judah, nor a lawgiver from between his feet, until Shiloh come; and unto him shall the gathering of the people be" (Gen. 49:10).

To *David* God made known that Christ would be born through his lineage: "Now therefore so shalt thou say unto my servant David, Thus saith the Lord of hosts, I took thee from the sheepcote, from following the sheep, to be ruler over my people, over Israel . . . And when thy days be fulfilled, and thou shalt sleep with thy fathers, I will set up thy seed after thee, which shall proceed out of thy bowels, and I will establish his kingdom. He shall build an house for my name, and I will establish the throne of his kingdom for ever. . . And thine house and thy kingdom shall be established for ever before thee: thy throne shall be established for ever" (II Sam. 7:8,12,13,16).

To *Micah* God revealed that Christ would be born in the obscure little village of Bethlehem: "But thou, Bethlehem Ephratah, though thou be little among the thousands of Judah, yet out of thee shall He come forth unto me that is to be ruler in Israel; whose goings forth have been from of old, from everlasting" (Micah 5:2).

To *Malachi* God made known that Christ would be preceded by a forerunner who would announce His coming: "Behold, I will send my messenger, and he shall prepare the way before me: and the Lord, whom ye seek, shall suddenly come to His temple, even the messenger of the covenant, whom ye delight in: behold, He shall come, saith the Lord of hosts" (Mal. 3:1).

To *Daniel* was made known the TIME Christ should appear to be cut off in death—that is, at the end of the sixty-ninth week of the seventy weeks of years: "And after threescore and two weeks shall Messiah be cut off, but not for Himself: and the people of the prince that shall come shall destroy the city and the sanctuary . . ." (Dan. 9:26).

To *Zechariah* God made known that Christ would be betrayed for thirty pieces of silver: "And I said unto them, If ye think good, give me my price; and if not, forbear. So they weighed for my price thirty pieces of silver. And the Lord said unto me, Cast it unto the potter: a goodly price that I was prised at of them. And I took the thirty pieces of silver, and cast them to the potter in the house of the Lord" (Zech. 11:12,13).

To *Isaiah* it was unveiled that Christ should suffer and die for the sins of the people:

"Who hath believed our report? and to whom is the arm of the Lord revealed? For He shall grow up before Him as a tender plant, and as a root out of a dry ground: He hath no form nor comeliness; and when we shall see Him, there is no beauty that we should desire Him. He is despised and rejected of men; a man of sorrows, and acquainted with grief: and we hid as it were our faces from Him; He was despised, and we esteemed Him not.

"Surely He hath borne our griefs, and carried our sorrows: yet we did esteem Him stricken, smitten of God, and afflicted. But He was wounded for our transgressions, He was bruised for our iniquities: the chastisement of our peace was upon Him; and with His stripes we are healed. All we like sheep have gone astray; we have turned every one to his own way; and the Lord hath laid on Him the iniquity of us all.

"He was oppressed, and He was afflicted, yet He opened not His mouth: He is brought as a lamb to the slaughter, and as a sheep before her shearers is dumb, so

He openeth not His mouth. He was taken from prison and from judgment: and who shall declare His generation? for He was cut off out of the land of the living: for the transgression of my people was He stricken. And He made His grave with the wicked, and with the rich in His death; because He had done no violence, neither was any deceit in His mouth.

"Yet it pleased the Lord to bruise Him; He hath put Him to grief: when thou shalt make His soul an offering for sin, He shall see His seed, He shall prolong His days, and the pleasure of the Lord shall prosper in His hand. He shall see of the travail of His soul, and shall be satisfied: by His knowledge shall my righteous servant justify many; for He shall bear their iniquities. Therefore will I divide Him a portion with the great, and He shall divide the spoil with the strong; because He hath poured out His soul unto death: and He was numbered with the transgressors; and He bare the sin of many, and made intercession for the transgressors" (Isaiah 53).

To *the Psalmist* was revealed the manner of Christ's death—that it would be by crucifixion: "For dogs have compassed me: the assembly of the wicked have inclosed me: *they pierced my hands and my feet*" (Psa. 22:16); and that Christ would rise from the dead: "For thou wilt not leave my soul in hell; neither wilt thou suffer thine Holy One to see corruption. Thou wilt shew me the path of life: in thy presence is fulness of joy; at thy right hand there are pleasures for evermore" (Psa. 16:10,11).

Thus, in these and many other Scriptures God made known His plan and purpose regarding His Son, the Lord Jesus Christ. *All these prophesies were fulfilled to the letter,* every jot and tittle of every one of them.

"Those things" which God had shown by His prophets *"He hath so fulfilled."* Jesus fulfilled every jot and tittle of the law and the prophets, He completed the work He came to do (Matt. 5:17; John 19:30). Everything the prophets had foretold concerning Jesus had happened exactly as prophesied; and Peter reminds the Jews of this —not to *excuse* them, but to exhort them to repent of their terrible sin. Ignorance was no excuse for what they had done, but Peter was laying before them the eternal plan of God—that it was *foreordained* of God that sinners should be saved through the precious blood of the Lamb, "slain from the foundation of the world" (Rev. 13:8). Since what they had done was known to God in the beginning, and since the crucifixion of Jesus was a divine necessity in order for sinners to be saved, God would pardon their sin and forgive them if they would sincerely repent.

Verse 19: *"Repent ye therefore, and be converted, that your sins may be blotted out, when the times of refreshing shall come from the presence of the Lord."*

Interesting words—and of great importance; but they can be understood in the right way only if we keep in mind the fact that *they were spoken to Israel,* not to Gentiles. Peter was preaching to his own people, and these words were the heart of his message.

"Repent . . . and be converted, that your sins may be blotted out." The repentance Peter speaks of here is the acknowledgment of the wrong they had done in denying Jesus, the Holy and Righteous One. They must repent of their sin and confess that His blood was on their hands. Then God would blot out their sins and forgive them, as promised in Isaiah 43:25:

"I, even I, am He that blotteth out thy transgressions for mine own sake, and will not remember thy sins."

Sin cannot be forgiven before the sinner *repents* of his sin. Repentance must precede pardon. John the Baptist came on the scene, preaching *"Repent ye:* for the kingdom of heaven is at hand" (Matt. 3:2). *Jesus* preached repentance: in Luke 13:3,5 He declared, *"Except ye repent,* ye shall all likewise perish."

In His sovereignty, God knows that the glorious day will come when Israel *will* receive Messiah, they will look on Him whom they pierced (Zech. 12:10), they will recognize and claim Him as their own (Zech. 14:4—9). Knowing this, God said, *"I HAVE blotted out,* as a thick cloud, thy transgressions, and, as a cloud, thy sins: return unto me; *for I HAVE redeemed thee.* Sing, O ye heavens; for the Lord hath done it: shout, ye lower parts of the earth: break forth into singing, ye mountains, O forest, and every tree therein: *for the Lord HATH REDEEMED Jacob, and glorified Himself in Israel"* (Isa. 44:22,23). So sure are God's promises that they are recorded here as having *already been fulfilled!*

The preaching of repentance is unpopular in the average church today. Many preachers have outlawed repentance and simply invite people to unite with the church and be baptized. They do not invite them to an old-fashioned altar to repent of their sins. *Repentance* is "turning face-about"; that is, *turning TO God and AWAY from the devil.* It is not "turning *around,"* for if one turns *around* he will still be going in the same direction; but if he turns *TO God,* he will automatically turn *FROM sin.* Paul expresses the true meaning of repentance in I Thessalonians 1:9:

"For they themselves shew of us what manner of entering in we had unto you, and *how ye turned TO GOD FROM IDOLS to serve the living and true God."*

To "blot out" sins is taken from the practice of creditors in Old Testament times. A debt was recorded on wax, and when debtors paid their accounts the debt was not only *cancelled,* it was entirely removed from the record. By use of a flat instrument, the debt was removed from the wax tablet, leaving the wax as smooth as if nothing had been recorded there. That is what happens when sinners repent and believe on Jesus as Saviour. God *removes* the record, completely *blots out* every trace of sin up to that very moment when the

sinner is born again—and that is the moment he begins
to live, insofar as God's record is concerned. Everything
up to the new birth is blotted out, cast into the depths
of the sea, and God remembers those sins no more. Thank
God for a Saviour who not only *forgives* our sins, but
blots them out, as though they had never been!

We notice that in his second message Peter does not
mention the gift of the Holy Spirit—and this is in keeping with the heart of this address, which is *national*.
The Holy Spirit had been given on the Day of Pentecost,
the Church was born and the body of Christ had its beginning at that time. But Peter's *second* sermon has to
do with *the nation Israel* and the future of that nation.
Therefore the Holy Spirit (as He came on the Day of
Pentecost) is not mentioned in this message; but the
promise of the Spirit in future outpouring upon Israel as
a nation is included in "the times of refreshing"—a future
time of unusual blessing which is in store for that nation.

So numerous are the blessings and promises to be
fulfilled in the "times of refreshing" and the "restitution
of all things" (v. 21) that it would be utterly impossible
to mention all of them in this study; but we will consider just a few of them, which I trust will cause my
readers to search the Old Testament Scriptures and study
fully the blessings to be poured out upon Israel during
the Kingdom Age.

If we interpret the Old Testament prophecies of
Christ's *second* coming as literally as we interpret the
prophecies of His *first* coming, we will have no difficulty
in seeing the full meaning of "the times of refreshing...
the times of the restitution of all things"—which two
expressions mean practically the same thing.

In dealing with the nation Israel, God regulates all
things according to His eternal plan, and His blueprint
will be literally fulfilled *in detail* as having to do with
that nation. The Old Testament Scriptures are filled
with God's precious promises of a glorious future for

Israel, and *every jot and tittle* of those promises will be fulfilled (Matt. 5:18).

In Romans 11:26,27 Paul said, *"And so ALL ISRAEL SHALL BE SAVED: as it is written,* There shall come out of Sion the Deliverer, and shall turn away ungodliness from Jacob: For this is my covenant unto them, *when I shall take away their sins."*

The book of Ezekiel contains many prophecies concerning the future of Israel and God's plans for that nation, prophecies marked by one peculiarity: *the CERTAINTY of their fulfillment.* In Ezekiel we find more than three hundred *"I WILL'S,"* a few of which have already been fulfilled; but the majority are to be fulfilled in the future.

Ezekiel 11:16,17 records God's plan for Israel and the land promised to faithful Abraham:

"Therefore say, *THUS SAITH THE LORD GOD:* Although I have cast them far off among the heathen, and although I have scattered them among the countries, yet will I be to them as a little sanctuary in the countries where they shall come. Therefore say, *THUS SAITH THE LORD GOD: I will even gather you from the people, and assemble you out of the countries where ye have been scattered, and I will give you the land of Israel."*

There are three particularly noteworthy things in this passage:

First—the fact of the dispersion (the scattering) of the nation Israel. We know that the Jews *have* been scattered to every land and island on the face of the earth; and until that nation was born in May, 1948, there *was* no Israel. They were a people without a government or a land of their own. We are now living in the days of *the budding of the fig tree,* but for twenty-five centuries the Jews have been "far off among the heathen . . . scattered among the countries" from one end of earth to the other.

In the *second* place, God promised His people "a little sanctuary"—that is, He assured them of His love, protection, and care in spite of their suffering, their distress, and their disloyalty to Him.

In the *third* place, God promised to gather His chosen people back into their own land, even as a mother hen gathers her chickens under her protective wings. There was no chance of failure, for God said, *"I WILL be a sanctuary . . . I WILL gather . . . I WILL give you the land of Israel."* When God says, *"I WILL"* we can rest assured that *He WILL.* The promise is *sure* because God pledged Himself to fulfill it: *"Thus saith the Lord God!"* God the Immutable One will bring to pass all that He has promised.

In Ezekiel 20:34, 41 God said, "I will bring you out from the people, and will gather you out of the countries wherein ye are scattered, with a mighty hand, and with a stretched out arm, and with fury poured out. . . I will accept you with your sweet savour, when I bring you out from the people, and gather you out of the countries wherein ye have been scattered; and I will be sanctified in you before the heathen."

What God has done for Israel *in the past* is a divine guarantee of what He will do for that nation in the future. The reference to His "mighty hand" and His "stretched out arm" reminds us of His deliverance of Israel from Egyptian bondage:

"Wherefore say unto the children of Israel, I am the Lord, and I will bring you out from under the burdens of the Egyptians, and I will rid you out of their bondage, and *I will redeem you with a STRETCHED OUT ARM,* and with great judgments" (Ex. 6:6).

"And remember that thou wast a servant in the land of Egypt, and that the Lord thy God brought thee out thence *through a MIGHTY HAND and by a STRETCHED OUT ARM:* therefore the Lord thy God commanded thee to keep the sabbath day" (Deut. 5:15).

Notice in the passage from Ezekiel that God promises to bring Israel into their own land—"I will give you *the land of Israel.*" Centuries ago, God made a covenant with Abraham, as recorded in Genesis 15:18, saying, *"Unto thy seed have I given this land, from the river of Egypt unto the great river, the river Euphrates."* But the land possessed by Israel never reached the limits given in that covenant. The expression "from Dan to Beersheba" became a familiar term for the land Israel possessed (I Sam. 3:20), and that area from Dan to Beersheba covered approximately 30,000 square miles. According to Ezekiel 48:13−21, the promised land is to extend far beyond the boundaries heretofore possessed by Israel. The boundaries promised Abraham will cover about *300,000* square miles. Thus the land Israel will occupy during the Millennium, as compared to the land they occupied in the Old Testament, will be ten times as large as it was before the people of Israel were dispersed. When that glorious day comes and Israel occupies the land of promise, God's promises to them will be fulfilled literally and fully:

"When I have brought them again from the people, and gathered them out of their enemies' lands, and am sanctified in them in the sight of many nations; then shall they know that I am the Lord their God, which caused them to be led into captivity among the heathen: but I have gathered them unto their own land, and have left none of them any more there. Neither will I hide my face any more from them: for I have poured out my Spirit upon the house of Israel, saith the Lord God" (Ezek. 39:27−29).

This is one of God's most glorious promises—the gathering of His chosen people into the land He promised Abraham. He *pledged* to gather them from the nations of the heathen, therefore He speaks of it as *an accomplished fact* because it is just as sure to happen as if it had already taken place. We are seeing this in a small way today, but the great gathering will occur after the Rapture. The fig tree is budding today, but it will blossom to full fruition after the Church is caught up to meet Jesus in the clouds in the air; and the gathering of Israel will be complete—*none will be left* among the heathen nations.

The *"times of refreshing"* and "the times of restitution of all things" (v. 21) will be God's final restoration of Israel. They will be gathered back into their own land never to be scattered again:

"And I will make with them a covenant of peace, and will cause the evil beasts to cease out of the land: and they shall dwell safely in the wilderness, and sleep in the woods. And I will make them and the places round about my hill a blessing; and I will cause the shower to come down in his season; there shall be showers of blessing.

"And the tree of the field shall yield her fruit, and the earth shall yield her increase, and they shall be safe in their land, and shall know that I am the Lord, when I have broken the bands of their yoke, and delivered them out of the hand of those that served themselves of them.

"And they shall no more be a prey to the heathen, neither shall the beast of the land devour them; but they shall dwell safely, and none shall make them afraid" (Ezek. 34:25—28).

The promises in these verses proclaim the unending blessings—both earthly and spiritual—which God will pour out upon His chosen people Israel, and in Ezekiel 43:7 He said, "Son of man, the place of my throne, and the place of the soles of my feet, *where I will dwell in the midst of the children of Israel for ever,* and my holy name, shall the house of Israel no more defile, neither they, nor their kings, by their whoredom, nor by the carcases of their kings in their high places."

Joel 3:20 tells us, "Judah shall dwell for ever, and Jerusalem from generation to generation," and in Amos

9:15 we find the promise, *"I will plant them upon their land, AND THEY SHALL NO MORE BE PULLED UP OUT OF THEIR LAND WHICH I HAVE GIVEN THEM, saith the Lord thy God."*

In that glorious day, Jesus will sit on the throne of David in Jerusalem, the knowledge of the Lord will cover the earth as the waters cover the sea, men will beat their swords into plowshares and their spears into pruning hooks and will study war no more. (Please study II Samuel 7:4—29.)

In Ezekiel 37:24,25 we read, "David my servant shall be king over them; and they all shall have one shepherd: they shall also walk in my judgments, and observe my statutes, and do them. And they shall dwell in the land that I have given unto Jacob my servant, wherein your fathers have dwelt; and they shall dwell therein, even they, and their children, and their children's children for ever: and my servant David shall be their prince for ever."

When this prophecy is fulfilled, then will be fulfilled the prophecy given to the Virgin Mary in Luke 1:32,33: "He shall be great, and shall be called the Son of the Highest: and the Lord God shall give unto Him the throne of His father David: and He shall reign over the house of Jacob for ever; and of His kingdom there shall be no end."

The Jews denied their King when He came the first time. At His crucifixion they said to Pilate, *"Write not, THE KING OF THE JEWS;* but that *He SAID,* I am King of the Jews" (John 19:21). But in the glorious day when "the times of refreshing" come, they will not deny Him. All Israel will cry out:

"O clap your hands, all ye people; shout unto God with the voice of triumph. For the Lord most high is terrible; *He is a great King over all the earth.* He shall subdue the people under us, and the nations under our feet. He shall choose our inheritance for us, the excellency of Jacob whom He loved. Selah.

"God is gone up with a shout, the Lord with the sound of a trumpet. Sing praises to God, sing praises: *sing praises unto our KING,* sing praises. *For God is the King of all the earth:* sing ye praises with understanding. *God reigneth over the heathen: God sitteth upon the throne of His holiness.* The princes of the people are gathered together, even the people of the God of Abraham: for the shields of the earth belong unto God: He is greatly exalted" (Psalm 47).

In Genesis 12:3 God said to Abraham, "In thee shall all families of the earth be blessed." The same truth is declared in Ezekiel 39:21 and in Zephaniah 3:20. Then in Romans 11:15 the Apostle Paul wrote, *"For if the casting away of (Israel) be THE RECONCILING OF THE WORLD, what shall the receiving of them be, but life from the dead?"*

Paul explains in Romans, chapters 9 through 11, that God *has not* forgotten His people Israel. They are blinded "for a season," but the day is coming when *the entire nation of Israel will be saved.* God declared to His chosen people, *"Yea, I have loved thee WITH AN EVERLASTING LOVE: therefore with lovingkindness have I drawn thee"* (Jer. 31:3).

Verse 20:   *"And He shall send Jesus Christ, which before was preached unto you."*

Peter was here appealing to Israel *as a nation.* In chapter 2, verses 37 through 40, those *individuals* who were "pricked in their hearts" and convicted of sin were exhorted to save themselves from the "untoward generation" in which they lived; but in our present passage Peter was pleading for *national* repentance. If Israel would repent as a nation they would be delivered. God would *"send Jesus Christ"* to bring in the times foretold by the prophets. This was to remind them of God's promises to Abraham, promises which had not been fulfilled and could *be* fulfilled only in and through their Messiah. They had missed Him because they did not understand the clear and oft-repeated prophetic promises in the Old Testament—promises of a re-gathered Israel established in their own land, under their own government, with their own King seated on the throne of David in Jerusalem. (Study Isaiah chapter 11; Jeremiah 23:5—8; Ezekiel 37:21—28.)

"Which before was preached unto you" in the original text reads "which before was *designated or appointed* unto you." God designated (appointed) the Messiah, and He came as designated. He did the things the prophets declared He *would* do. Therefore Israel had no excuse for their sin of crucifying Him. They should have recognized Him as the Promised One, so plainly foretold and described in their Scriptures.

Verse 21: *"Whom the heaven must receive until the times of restitution of all things, which God hath spoken by the mouth of all His holy prophets since the world began."*

The Jews expected their promised Messiah to reign here on earth forever. They made this plain by their question in John 12:34. When Jesus explained that He must be lifted up from the earth to die on a cross, they cried out, *"We have heard out of the law that CHRIST ABIDETH FOR EVER:* and how sayest thou, The Son of man must be lifted up? *Who IS this Son of man?"* Because of this belief, they failed to see the clear prophecy in Isaiah 53 that Jesus would be crowned with thorns and suffer death before He was crowned with glory. They failed to understand that He would come as a lamb to the slaughter before He came as King of kings, and therefore they rejected Him, declaring that such a person could not possibly be their Messiah.

This made it necessary for the apostles to first establish the fact that Jesus had been raised from the dead and had *ascended back to the Father.* They could then proceed with the message they were to deliver to Israel. The fact that *they saw Him* when He ascended (Acts 1:9,10) was the evidence they presented to the Jews as proof that Jesus *did* return to God from whence He came.

"Whom the heaven must receive" means that it was "fit and proper" that Jesus ascend back into heaven, into the presence of the Father; and the *reason* His ascension was fit and proper is given in His own words in John 16:7 as He explained to His disciples, "Nevertheless I tell you the truth: *It is expedient for you that I go away: for if I go not away, the Comforter will not come unto you; but if I depart, I will send Him unto you."*

Acts 20:28 tells us that God purchased the Church *"with His own blood."* It was therefore "fit and proper" that Jesus return to the right hand of the Father in order to direct the affairs of the universe and see to the welfare of His Church. In Ephesians 1:20−23 we are told that God set Jesus "at His own right hand in the heavenly places, far above all principality, and power, and might, and dominion, and every name that is named, not only in this world, but also in that which is to come: *And hath put all things under His feet, AND GAVE HIM TO BE THE HEAD OVER ALL THINGS TO THE CHURCH*, which is His body, the fulness of Him that filleth all in all."

It was "fit and proper" that Jesus return to the right hand of the Father in order to exercise His office as our Great High Priest in making intercession for us:

"For there is one God, and *one Mediator between God and men, THE MAN CHRIST JESUS"* (I Tim. 2:5).

"My little children, these things write I unto you, that ye sin not. *And if any man sin, we have an Advocate with the Father, JESUS CHRIST THE RIGHTEOUS"* (I John 2:1).

"Wherefore He is able also to save them to the uttermost that come unto God by Him, *SEEING HE EVER*

LIVETH TO MAKE INTERCESSION FOR THEM"
(Heb. 7:25).

"For Christ is not entered into the holy places made
with hands, which are the figures of the true; but into
heaven itself, *NOW TO APPEAR IN THE PRESENCE
OF GOD FOR US"* (Heb. 9:24).

"Who is he that condemneth? *It is CHRIST that
died,* yea rather, that is risen again, *who is even at the
right hand of God, WHO ALSO MAKETH INTERCES-
SION FOR US"* (Rom. 8:34).

"Until the times of restitution of all things" certainly
implies that Jesus *will* return to earth at the appointed
time; and *UNTIL that time* He is "on the right hand
of God; angels and authorities and powers being made
subject unto Him" (I Pet. 3:22).

The Greek word translated *"restitution"* occurs only
here and in Acts 1:6 (there translated *restore*). The meaning in our present verse is limited by the words "which
God hath spoken by the mouth of all His holy prophets."
The prophets spoke of the restoration of Israel to the
land (Palestine). In connection with this read Genesis
12:2,3; Romans 11:26; and Deuteronomy 30:1−9.

They spoke also of the restoration of rule under David's
Son—referring of course to the Lord Jesus Christ who is
of the lineage of David (Luke 1:31−33).

But the fulfillment of these prophecies is yet future,
and the *Jews* expected the restoration at the time of
Christ's earthly ministry. He is yet to reign when He
returns as King of kings and Lord of lords. (Study II
Samuel 7:8−17 and Zechariah 12:8.)

Greek scholars tell us that the verb from which the
noun *restitution* (or restoration) is derived occurs eight
times in the New Testament and means "to restore a
thing to its former situation," as to restore a sprained
or dislocated limb to its former soundness. We find an
example of this in Matthew 12:13 where Jesus healed a
withered hand: "Then saith He to the man, Stretch

forth thine hand. And he stretched it forth; and it was *restored whole, like as the other."*

The meaning of Peter's statement is that the heavens must receive the Lord Jesus Christ until all things spoken by God's prophets have been fulfilled in relation to the future time of a great blessing for His earthly people— and *through them* for the nations of the world. This takes in the whole period between the ascension and the second coming of Jesus. The statement also conveys the truth that the world will be delivered from the curse, and restoration of peace and order will come eventually in the plan and program of Jehovah God.

The things *"which God hath spoken"* refers to those things which God revealed to His prophets in the Old Testament era, things which are recorded in Old Testament Scripture. These things will all be literally fulfilled and accomplished as prophesied. Sin, Satan, and all the evil of the universe can never cause one word of God's promises to fail!

"Of all His holy prophets" does not mean that *each* of the prophets had spoken these things individually, but that *ALL of them prophesied* as they were moved by the Holy Ghost—yea, even all things spoken by the prophets *"since the world began,"* or from *the beginning.* Yes, *every prophecy*—from the beginning through the book of Malachi and on up to the birth of Jesus would be fulfilled. Peter was trying to show the Jews that he, too, held entirely to the prophecies foretold in the Old Testament, and that he was teaching no other doctrine than that which had been taught by the prophets before him. He was preaching and teaching that which was *"since the world began."*

Verse 22: *"For Moses truly said unto the fathers, A Prophet shall the Lord your God raise up unto you of your brethren, like unto me; Him shall ye hear in all things whatsoever He shall say unto you."*

The authority of Moses was unquestionable among the Jews. His words were absolute and final. Therefore it was necessary to show them that the apostles were not *departing* from the law of Moses, they were not discarding or destroying the law. On the contrary, Moses had prophesied the very things that had occurred concerning Jesus, the very things the apostles were preaching. Peter was attempting to prove that the One of whom Moses spoke, One greater than himself, was none other than Christ; He whom the Jews had crucified was truly the Messiah, the Promised One.

"For Moses truly said unto the fathers"—that is, Moses had spoken to the ancestors of these men to whom Peter was preaching:

"The Lord thy God will raise up unto thee a Prophet from the midst of thee, of thy brethren, like unto me; unto Him ye shall hearken . . . I will raise them up a Prophet from among their brethren, like unto thee, and will put my words in His mouth; and He shall speak unto them all that I shall command Him. And it shall come to pass, that *whosoever will not hearken unto my words which He shall speak in my name, I will require it of him"* (Deut. 18:15—19).

A prophet is one who foretells future events; but in one sense a prophet also *forthtells* what has been foretold. In the passage just quoted from Deuteronomy the word is evidently used in the sense of a Prophet who would foretell (or prophesy), and whose prophecies would be infallible, prophecies which would direct the nation Israel in spiritual affairs. This Prophet would be commissioned by Almighty God in opposition to the false teachers mentioned in Deuteronomy 18:14. God would give Israel *a TRUE Prophet.*

In Deuteronomy 18:1—8 Moses speaks of the office and duties of the priests and Levites. He then cautioned the people against conforming to the surrounding nations —particularly where spiritual instruction and guidance were concerned. In verses 11—14 of the same chapter he declared that other nations consulted enchanters, charmers, wizards, and diviners; but it should not be so with Israel. God's chosen people would not be left to such false guidance in times of perplexity and danger, for the Lord would raise up a Prophet, a Man directly anointed and commissioned in an extraordinary manner, from Jehovah in heaven—a Man like unto Moses, who would direct and counsel the nation.

"Him shall ye hear in all things whatsoever He shall say unto you." Peter now points out that the Jews, in *refusing to hear* this great Prophet (the Lord Jesus Christ), and in putting Him to death, had violated the clear command of Moses, their own law-giver whom they trusted so implicitly.

But God had raised this Prophet from the dead, He had exalted Him and given Him the highest seat in heaven; and according to the words of Moses, it was still a matter of obligation on the part of the Jews to hear and obey the Messiah whom they had crucified.

"A Prophet shall the Lord your God raise up unto you OF YOUR BRETHREN." (In the original, "the Lord your God" reads *"Jehovah thy God."*) The Jews *believed* that their Messiah would be a prophet. In John 1:21 they asked of John the Baptist, *"Art thou Elias? And he saith, I am not. Art thou THAT PROPHET? And he answered, No."*

In John 6:14, when Jesus fed the five thousand from the scant supply of five loaves and two small fishes, the Jews declared, "This is of a truth *THAT PROPHET that should come into the world."*

In John 7:40, when Jesus offered the water of life, "Many of the people therefore, when they heard this saying, said, Of a truth *this is the PROPHET."*

They believed that Messiah would be the greatest of *all* prophets, even greater than *Moses;* but when One greater than Moses came, they rejected Him and demanded His death.

It was prophesied that Messiah would be a Jew, one of their own countrymen—*"of your brethren,"* the Word declared.   He was to descend through Abraham, He would be "the Son of David," raised up from the midst of the nation Israel:

"For both He that sanctifieth and they who are sanctified are all of one: for which cause He is not ashamed to call them *brethren* . . . Wherefore in all things it behoved Him to be *made like unto HIS BRETHREN,* that He might be a merciful and faithful High Priest in things pertaining to God, to make reconciliation for the sins of the people" (Heb. 2:11,17).

Jesus fulfilled this prophecy in every respect.   From the *human* standpoint He was born of the Jews, although God Almighty was His Father, the virgin Mary was His mother, and Joseph, husband of Mary, was His foster father.   The idea pointed out in this verse is that God would *"raise up"* a Prophet even as He had *raised up Moses.*   The Jews believed God had given them Moses, and Moses declared that God would raise up a Prophet whom they should hear "in all things whatsoever He shall say unto you."   They were to *hear* Him, and they were to *obey* Him, because whatever He said to them would be words from Jehovah, the God of their fathers. In other words, the Jews were to obey the words of Jesus as their forefathers had obeyed the words of Moses.

Verse 23:   *"And it shall come to pass, that every soul, which will not hear that Prophet, shall be destroyed from among the people."*

The Prophet of whom Moses wrote had spoken to them and they heard Him with their ears—but they did not hear Him with their hearts.   In Acts 28:25—27 Paul said, "Well spake the Holy Ghost by Esaias the prophet unto our fathers, saying, Go unto this people, and say, *Hearing ye shall hear, and shall not understand; and seeing ye shall see, and not perceive: For the heart of this people is waxed gross, and their ears are dull of hearing, and their eyes have they closed; lest they should see with their eyes, and hear with their ears, and understand with their heart, and should be converted, and I should heal them!"*

Jesus said, *"He that heareth MY WORD, and believeth on Him that sent me, hath everlasting life, and shall not come into condemnation; but is passed from death unto life"* (John 5:24).   Jesus was *the Word Incarnate* (John 1:14), and the words He spoke were the words of God, because He spoke as God ordered.

What Peter declared to the Jews was simply this: Jesus was "that Prophet" whom Moses said would come; and every person who refused to *hear the words* of that Prophet would be *destroyed.*   In I John 5:9—13 we read:

"If we receive *the witness of men, THE WITNESS OF GOD IS GREATER:*   for this is the witness of God which He hath testified of His Son.   He that believeth on the Son of God hath the witness in himself: *he that believeth not God hath made Him a liar; because he believeth not the record that God gave of His Son.*   And this is the record, that God hath given to us eternal life, and this life is in His Son.   He that hath the Son hath life; and he that hath not the Son of God hath not life. These things have I written unto you that believe on the name of the Son of God; that ye may know that ye have eternal life, and that ye may believe on the name of the Son of God."

Jesus came exactly as prophesied, He spoke to the Jews, He clearly declared that He came from God, that He was God in flesh.   He said, "I and my Father are one," but they rejected His words and by so doing brought God's judgment upon themselves.   In A. D. 70, most of the Jews who heard (and rejected) Jesus were slaughtered by Titus the Roman.   They were destroyed physically and their souls plunged into everlasting hell!

God's prophecies and promises are absolute. Moses said a Prophet would come, and He came, as promised. Moses also prophesied that all who refused to *hear* "that Prophet" would be *"destroyed from among the people!"*

Beloved, it is better never to hear John 3:16, Ephesians 2:8, or Romans 10:9 than to hear those wonderful words of life *and reject them.* Salvation is for *whosoever.* "God so loved *the WORLD"*—all are included, not one is excluded; and all are saved in the same manner: *by God's grace through faith,* the gift of God. All man can do is *hear* the Word and *receive* it; and it is better not to hear it at all than to hear it and reject it.

Verse 24: *"Yea, and all the prophets from Samuel and those that follow after, as many as have spoken, have likewise foretold of these days."*

"All the prophets . . . ." Throughout the Old Testament era God's prophets *foretold* the things that happened pertaining to the Lord Jesus—His birth, His life, His ministry, His death, burial, and resurrection. *ALL the prophets* prophesied concerning these things.

"From Samuel and those that follow." Peter first mentioned Moses (v. 22). He mentions Samuel here probably because Samuel was the next prophet after Moses to prophesy directly concerning the times of Messiah. Psalm 99:6 also mentions Moses and Samuel as being "among them that call upon His name." (In their divisions of the Old Testament Scripture the Jews speak of the book of *Joshua* as the first of the prophets; but there is no distinct prophecy in Joshua concerning the coming of Messiah.)

The prophecy of which Peter spoke here is probably II Samuel 7:16: "And thine house and thy kingdom shall be established for ever before thee: thy throne shall be established for ever."

It seems that in the years from Moses to Samuel *no prophet* was ordained and anointed of Almighty God.

During those years God was consulted by Urim and Thummim: "And thou shalt put in the breastplate of judgment the Urim and the Thummim; and they shall be upon Aaron's heart, when he goeth in before the Lord: and Aaron shall bear the judgment of the children of Israel upon his heart before the Lord continually" (Ex. 28:30).

"And he shall stand before Eleazar the priest, *who shall ask counsel for him after the judgment of Urim and before the Lord:* at his word shall they go out, and at his word they shall come in, both he, and all the children of Israel with him, even all the congregation" (Num. 27:21).

During that period, no direct message was given by a messenger sent from God to instruct the nation Israel.

All the prophets *"have likewise foretold of these days."* The prophets of God not only prophesied the *glorious* things that would happen to Israel (for instance, the Millennium, the time when Jesus would reign from the throne of David in Jerusalem); but in such passages as Isaiah 53 they also prophesied concerning the horrible suffering and death the Lamb of God would face, and everything they prophesied came to pass *exactly AS prophesied.*

If the Jews had really listened to their own prophets, if they had really heard what Moses and Samuel said, they would have listened to the Lord Jesus Christ, because He spoke the same truth and declared the same doctrine Moses and Samuel had declared in their prophecies concerning Him.   He fulfilled every jot and tittle of the law (Matt. 5:17).   *Therefore, "CHRIST IS THE END OF THE LAW FOR RIGHTEOUSNESS TO EVERY ONE THAT BELIEVETH"* (Rom. 10:4).

Verse 25:   *"Ye are the children of the prophets, and of the covenant which God made with our fathers, saying unto Abraham, And in thy seed shall all the kindreds of the earth be blessed."*

Peter here reminded his listeners that they were literal descendants of the prophets, they were children of the fathers to whom the prophets had spoken. The Jews professed to believe Abraham and Moses, they professed to be followers of their prophets; but they rejected the One whose coming the prophets foretold. Therefore Peter reminded them that they were not only *sons* of the prophets, they were also sons of the fathers with whom God had made His covenant.

A covenant between God and man is sacred and certain. It is *sacred* because God makes it—and man has no right to reject it, break it, or change its terms. It is *certain* because God does not repent of a covenant between Himself and man: He will fulfill that covenant as made. The covenant of which Peter was speaking is given in Genesis 12:1—3 and Genesis 22:18, where God promised Abraham that through him and his seed all nations of the earth would be blessed. It was through the lineage of Abraham that the Redeemer came. (Study Romans 4:13—16.)

"*Seed*" is used in the Word of God on many occasions with reference to an individual, as in Genesis 4:25: "And Adam knew his wife again; and she bare a son, and called his name Seth: For God, said she, hath appointed me *another SEED instead of Abel, whom Cain slew.*"

In Galatians 3:16 Paul clearly explained that in God's promise to Abraham, the "seed" referred to the coming Messiah: "Now to Abraham and his *seed* were the promises made. He saith not, And to *seeds,* as of *many;* but *as of ONE,* And to thy *seed, which is Christ.*" And from the *human* aspect, it was through the seed of Abraham that Christ was born.

"*In thy seed shall all the kindreds of the earth be blessed.*" *IN JESUS* all can be blessed. He came to provide salvation for all. "All we like sheep have gone astray; we have turned every one to his own way; *and the Lord hath laid on HIM the iniquity of us ALL*"

(Isa. 53:6).   Not all men will *be* blessed, not all men will be *saved;* but that does not alter the fact that all *could* be saved if they would hear the words of Jesus, believe in His finished work and shed blood, and accept Him as Saviour.

Verse 26:   *"Unto you first God, having raised up His Son Jesus, sent Him to bless you, in turning away every one of you from his iniquities."*

"Unto you first."   Jesus instructed His disciples to preach the Gospel first to the Jews, beginning at Jerusalem (Luke 24:47).   In Acts 1:8 He told them that they would receive power after the Holy Ghost came upon them, and that they would be witnesses *"in Jerusalem, and in all Judaea, and in Samaria, and unto the uttermost part of the earth."*   But the Jew had the Gospel first.   He rejected it, and the message was then given to the Gentiles.

The Apostle Paul declared, "I am not ashamed of the Gospel of Christ: for it is the power of God unto salvation to every one that believeth; *TO THE JEW FIRST, and also to the Greek"* (Rom. 1:16).   In Acts 28:28 Paul reminded the Jews that the Gospel had been given to them, they had rejected it, and therefore they were to understand *"that the salvation of God is sent unto the Gentiles, and that they will hear it!"*

Jesus came to the Jews—and they rejected Him.   He offered the *Gospel* to the Jews—and they rejected His message.   When He sent the twelve disciples to preach the Gospel He instructed them, "Go not into the way of the Gentiles, and into any city of the Samaritans enter ye not: but go rather *to the lost sheep of the house of Israel"* (Matt. 10:5,6).   But they rejected His messengers.

"Having raised up His Son Jesus" does not refer here to the bodily resurrection of Jesus from the dead.   The term is used as in verse 22 where God promised to *raise up a Prophet* like unto Moses and send Him to teach

His people Israel.   Peter means that God *did* raise up a
Prophet—*JESUS.*   God appointed, anointed, and sent
His Son to preach to the people, to turn them away from
their sins; but they refused to hear Him, they refused to
believe His message, they rejected His Person, and they
demanded His death!

God raised up Jesus *to bless* His people, to make them
happy, to fulfill all the promises He had made to Abraham and all the prophecies He had given to the prophets.   In Matthew 23:37,38 Jesus wept over Jerusalem and
said, "O Jerusalem, Jerusalem, thou that killest the prophets, and stonest them which are sent unto thee, *how
often would I have gathered thy children together, even
as a hen gathereth her chickens under her wings, AND
YE WOULD NOT!*   Behold, your house is left unto you
desolate."

In John 5:39,40 He testified, "Search the Scriptures;
for in them ye think ye have eternal life: and they are
they which testify of me.   *AND YE WILL NOT COME
TO ME, that ye might have life."*

God sent Jesus to bless Israel *in turning them away
from their iniquities.*   The greatest blessing any mortal
can receive is to be saved from sin—and the only way
to be saved from sin is to receive the Lord Jesus who
came *into* the world to take away the *sin* of the world
(John 1:29).   Sin is the source of every sorrow, woe, and
heartache this world has ever known.   No one can be
happy in sin.   The world can give *pleasure* for a season,
but *true happiness* is found only in Christ.   He does not
bless men in sin, He *saves* them from their sins.   The
Jews had crucified their Messiah, but God had raised
Him from the dead.   He had ascended to heaven and
was seated at the Father's right hand to make intercession for all who will come to God by Him through
faith in His shed blood and finished work.   *ALL may
come, ALL may be blessed, ALL may be SAVED,* all
may find happiness and rejoicing—but only by coming

to God in the name of Jesus.

In Summary

Peter's second message is not characterized by such excitement as prevailed on the Day of Pentecost. The people were astonished at the healing of the lame man, but Peter reminded them that only a short time ago, One had walked in their midst who had wrought such miracles as had not been witnessed since time began. That One had cast out demons, opened the eyes of the blind, healed the lepers, and raised the dead. And the people had witnessed those miracles. Why then should they gaze with such astonishment upon this lame man who was healed, and upon the apostles, as if by their own power they had wrought this miracle?

Every word Peter spoke was inspired of the Holy Spirit. He made it clear that in the healing of the lame man, God had glorified Jesus—the same Jesus whom the Jews had crucified. He spoke of God as "the God of Abraham, Isaac, and Jacob," and thus appealed to Israel as a nation to see that Jesus was "that Prophet" of whom Moses spoke—God's Servant, sent to them to make known the way of salvation and blessing.

Peter not only declared that the Jews had crucified God's Servant, their Messiah, he also declared that God had raised Him from the dead, and testified that the apostles were witnesses of that fact. He then pointed out to them that *through faith in Jesus*, the lame man was made perfectly whole—and proof of his perfect healing lay in the fact that he was walking, leaping, and praising God!

Peter could have sternly rebuked his people for what they had done; but instead, he spoke to them as "brethren," and assured them of God's mercy if they would only repent. Although they were guilty of crucifying their Messiah, God had raised Him from the dead; and *at that very moment* He was waiting to forgive their sin and save them. They had cried out, "Let His blood be upon us, and upon our children!" But the God of Abraham, Isaac, and Jacob is longsuffering, a God of mercy; and His mercy could be theirs if they would only repent. Their guilt could be *blotted out* if they would only receive the living Lord as their Saviour.

CHAPTER IV

1. And as they spake unto the people, the priests, and the captain of the temple, and the Sadducees, came upon them,

2. Being grieved that they taught the people, and preached through Jesus the resurrection from the dead.

3. And they laid hands on them, and put them in hold unto the next day: for it was now eventide.

4. Howbeit many of them which heard the word believed; and the number of the men was about five thousand.

5. And it came to pass on the morrow, that their rulers, and elders, and scribes,

6. And Annas the high priest, and Caiaphas, and John, and Alexander, and as many as were of the kindred of the high priest, were gathered together at Jerusalem.

7. And when they had set them in the midst, they asked, By what power, or by what name, have ye done this?

8. Then Peter, filled with the Holy Ghost, said unto them, Ye rulers of the people, and elders of Israel,

9. If we this day be examined of the good deed done to the impotent man, by what means he is made whole;

10. Be it known unto you all, and to all the people of Israel, that by the name of Jesus Christ of Nazareth, whom ye crucified, whom God raised from the dead, even by him doth this man stand here before you whole.

11. This is the stone which was set at nought of you builders, which is become the head of the corner.

12. Neither is there salvation in any other: for there is none other name under heaven given among men, whereby we must be saved.

13. Now when they saw the boldness of Peter and John, and perceived that they were unlearned and ignorant men, they marvelled; and they took knowledge of them, that they had been with Jesus.

14. And beholding the man which was healed standing with them, they could say nothing against it.

15. But when they had commanded them to go aside out of the council, they conferred among themselves,

16. Saying, What shall we do to these men? for that indeed a notable miracle hath been done by them is manifest to all them that dwell in Jerusalem; and we cannot deny it.

17. But that it spread no further among the people, let us straitly threaten them, that they speak henceforth to no man in this name.

18. And they called them, and commanded them not to speak at all nor teach in the name of Jesus.

19. But Peter and John answered and said unto them, Whether it be right in the sight of God to hearken unto you more than unto God, judge ye.

20. For we cannot but speak the things which we have seen and heard.

21. So when they had further threatened them, they let them go, finding nothing how they might punish them, because of the people: for all men glorified God for that which was done.

22. For the man was above forty years old, on whom this miracle of healing was shewed.

23. And being let go, they went to their own company, and reported all that the chief priests and elders had said unto them.

24. And when they heard that, they lifted up their voice to God with one accord, and said, Lord, thou art God, which hast made heaven, and earth, and the sea, and all that in them is:

25. Who by the mouth of thy servant David hast said, Why did the heathen rage, and the people imagine vain things?

26. The kings of the earth stood up, and the rulers were gathered together against the Lord, and against his Christ.

27. For of a truth against thy holy child Jesus, whom thou hast anointed, both Herod, and Pontius Pilate, with the Gentiles, and the people of Israel, were gathered together,

28. For to do whatsoever thy hand and thy counsel determined before to be done.

29. And now, Lord, behold their threatenings: and grant unto thy servants, that with all boldness they may speak thy word,

30. By stretching forth thine hand to heal; and that signs and wonders may be done by the name of thy holy child Jesus.

31. And when they had prayed, the place was shaken where they were assembled together; and they were all filled with the Holy Ghost, and they spake the word of God with boldness.

32. And the multitude of them that believed were of one heart and of one soul: neither said any of them that ought of the things which he possessed was his own; but they had all things common.

33. And with great power gave the apostles witness of the resurrection of the Lord Jesus: and great grace was upon them all.

34. Neither was there any among them that lacked: for as many as were possessors of lands or houses sold them, and brought the prices of the things that were sold,

35. And laid them down at the apostles' feet: and distribution was made unto every man according as he had need.

36. And Joses, who by the apostles was surnamed Barnabas, (which is, being interpreted, The son of consolation,) a Levite, and of the country of Cyprus,

37. Having land, sold it, and brought the money, and laid it at the apostles' feet.

The First Persecution
(Sadducean)

The Sadducees were a sect among the Jews who denied the existence of spirits or angels. They denied all miracles, and were extremely fanatical in their denial of the bodily resurrection of Jesus. They were the religious "rationalists" of their time. (Study Mark 12:18—23; Acts 5:12—18; 23:8.)

The Sadducees held strong representation in both the Sanhedrin and the priesthood—the latter an office which they held by tradition. That they were quite influential in religious matters is evident in verse 1 of this chapter and also in verse 17 of chapter 5. They are never identified with affirmative doctrine. They denied the supernatural. They were also compromisers—collaborators with the Roman government—and were very sensitive toward anything that might disturb the comfortable status they enjoyed. In John 11:47—50, where they plotted to put Jesus to death, we read:

"Then gathered the chief priests and the Pharisees a council, and said, What do we? for this Man doeth many miracles. If we let Him thus alone, all men will believe on Him: *and the Romans shall come and take away both our place and nation.*

"And one of them, named Caiaphas, being the high priest that same year, said unto them, Ye know nothing at all, nor consider that it is expedient for us, that *one*

Man should die for the people, *and that the WHOLE NATION perish not."*

Verse 1:   *"And as they spake unto the people, the priests, and the captain of the temple, and the Sadducees, came upon them."*

Peter had just been preaching the resurrection of Jesus (ch. 3, v. 15), and the Sadducees saw danger in the excitement arising from such teaching.   We read in John 12:10,11—after the resurrection of Lazarus—that the chief priests "consulted that they might put Lazarus also to death; *because that by reason of him many of the Jews went away, AND BELIEVED ON JESUS."*

Peter and John had just wrought a great miracle in the healing of the lame man, a miracle which the Sadducees could not deny (ch. 3, v. 16).   This greatly disturbed them, and the fact that Peter was preaching the bodily resurrection of the Lord Jesus Christ was a definite challenge to their religious prestige!

"As they (Peter and John) *spake unto the people...."* In verse 11 of chapter 3 we were told that as the lame man rejoiced over his miraculous healing, "all the people ran together unto them in the porch that is called Solomon's, greatly wondering."   The great gathering of people and the news of the healing of the lame beggar soon attracted the attention of *"the priests, and the captain of the temple, and the Sadducees,"* who decided that something must be done to put a stop to the sudden popularity of the two apostles.   (The "captain of the temple" was an outstanding personality *in* the temple; he had great authority—it was his duty to preserve order.)

The words *"came upon"* indicate that this group came upon Peter and John—or *rushed* upon them—in a sudden and violent manner.

Verse 2:   *"Being grieved that they taught the people, and preached through Jesus the resurrection from the dead."*

The Greek word here translated *"grieve"* occurs in only one other place in the New Testament (Acts 16:18), and suggests much more than simple sorrow. It suggests mingled emotions of extreme anger and indignation.

The Sadducees were not grieved because they thought a *public calamity* had befallen the community, but because the miracle and its subsequent publicity would interfere with their authority. Such miracles were in direct opposition to their doctrine; they did not *believe* in miracles. Although they *confessed* that "a notable miracle" had been wrought—and certainly they could not deny the *resurrection of Jesus,* because after His resurrection He was seen by as many as five hundred brethren at one time—they refused to *accept* the facts that had been presented again and again in their presence. They were willingly ignorant, spiritually blind, determinedly rejecting the truth that was so plainly evident.

The Sadducees considered themselves custodians of the Word of God, and they were "grieved" (offended) because these two unlearned, ignorant Galilaeans *"taught the people."* Peter and John were not duly authorized by the high priest, nor were they sanctioned by the Sanhedrin. Therefore, *according to the Sadducees,* they had no right to teach or preach in Solomon's porch.

We do not have the Sadducees, Pharisees, and chief priests today, but some of today's religious leaders are just as guilty of bigotry as those men were! They consider that they have the sole right to ordain ministers, and if a preacher is not ordained in that particular denomination (or graduated from a *school* of that denomination), they refuse him permission to preach in their churches—or in the *community,* if they wield enough influence to keep him out!

GOD calls, anoints, and ordains all true ministers of the Gospel. I do not mean by this that I am against ordination in the local church—I believe there is a Scriptural basis for such ordination (see Acts 14:23; 16:4; Titus 1:5); but *GOD'S preachers* are ordained of God the moment He calls them and puts them into the ministry.

Peter and John *"preached through Jesus the resurrection from the dead."* This was *the underlying cause* of opposition from the Sadducees. Since they themselves did not *believe* in the resurrection, they were greatly disturbed by the apostles' declaration that *the resurrection of Jesus* was indisputable proof that He was God's Christ, the long-awaited Messiah—and by the accusation that these same religious leaders had rejected Him and crucified Him! If Jesus *had* risen, then *others* would rise again; and the Sadducees feared that this doctrine would be believed by the multitudes and established in the hearts of the people. *Their* doctrine would thus be endangered, and they joined in with the Pharisees and other "religionists" in their efforts to put a stop to the spreading of a teaching which they considered *"heresy."*

Verse 3:   *"And they laid hands on them, and put them in hold unto the next day: for it was now eventide."*

"They laid hands on them" means that they had Peter and John arrested; and *"put them in hold"* indicates that they were probably committed to the care of a guard. There is no statement that they were placed in prison, as Paul and Silas were in Acts 16.

Perhaps these religious rulers thought that if they had the apostles arrested and brought into judgment, they would not *defend* the doctrine they had been preaching throughout the countryside. After all, these same men had fled from the scene when Jesus was arrested and led away to be crucified. *Peter* had even denied that he had ever *known* the Lord. It might be that they could again be frightened into silence.

But these two men who had so recently displayed

spiritual cowardice now stood *boldly,* emphatically declaring themselves followers of "Jesus Christ of Nazareth." They believed in and served the risen Lord, declaring the fact of His resurrection and His identification as God's Christ, the Messiah. The remarkable change in the conduct of these disciples is one of the many infallible proofs that they were influenced *from above,* not by earthly circumstance or human contact.

"For it was now eventide." It was not convenient to call the Sanhedrin into assembly at night; and besides, this was the time of the evening prayer or sacrifice.

Verse 4: *"Howbeit many of them which heard the Word believed; and the number of the men was about five thousand."*

Peter and John did not labor in vain. *God honored His Word.* His *power* accompanied the Word then—as now. The Gospel is "the power of God unto salvation to every one that believeth . . ." (Rom. 1:16). Part of the multitude who *heard* the Word *believed and received it.*

"And the number of the men was about five thousand." The *numbering* of those who believed is definitely a Jewish practice—a feature of *the Kingdom,* not the New Testament Church; and this is the last time in the book of Acts where believers are numbered. There were about *one hundred and twenty* mentioned in verse 15 of chapter 1 (before Pentecost); *three thousand* were saved at Pentecost (ch. 2, v. 41); and *five thousand* are mentioned here—but in this Church Age *numbering* is out of order. God keeps the record, and no mortal knows how many members comprise the New Testament Church, the body of Christ. When a number of people unite with a local assembly, that does not necessarily mean that each and every one of those people is added to the body of Christ. We "unite" with the local church—*but we are BORN into the Church of the living God,* and

only God knows who are members of His Church, and
who are *not of that body* although belonging to a local
assembly.

It seems that the five thousand mentioned here refers
to the number of believers *up to that point*—that is, it
includes the original one hundred and twenty who were
in the upper room at Pentecost, also the three thousand
who were converted that day, and *all who had believed*
up to and including those who *"heard the Word"* and
believed as Peter preached on this particular occasion.
It seems highly improbable that the entire five thousand
souls were saved at the gathering in Solomon's porch.

We do not know how long this was after Pentecost,
but certainly it could not have been *many* days, and in
that short time *two thousand* believers had been added
to the body of Christ! Considering the centuries that
have elapsed *since* that time, *if WE had been as diligent
in soul-winning and as faithful in propagating the Gospel
as the early Christians were, this world would not be
in the sad predicament it is in today.*

The fact that our present verse speaks of five thousand
"men" does not mean that there were no ladies in the
group. The Bible often designates "men" when it actually refers to both male and female. We see examples of
this in Luke 11:31 (". . . the *men* of this generation");
Romans 4:8 ("blessed is *the man* to whom the Lord will
not impute sin"); and in Romans 11:4 where God speaks
of "seven thousand *men,* who have not bowed the knee
to the image of Baal." So the *"five thousand"* believers
in verse 4 included both sexes—*all* believers up to that
time.

Peter's Third Sermon
(Address to the Sanhedrin)

Verses 5 and 6: *"And it came to pass on the morrow,
that their rulers, and elders, and scribes, and Annas the
high priest, and Caiaphas, and John, and Alexander, and*

as many as were of the kindred of the high priest, were gathered together at Jerusalem."

Peter and John appeared before the Sanhedrin—the same group of men who had tried *and condemned* the Lord Jesus Christ.

It is entirely possible that some of these men lived some distance from Jerusalem and were summoned to come into the city on the day *following* the arrest of Peter and John.

Not all of the members are named here. *Annas* and *Caiaphas* were there. *John* and *Alexander* are named, but we know nothing definite about these two men. (Most likely they were relatives of the high priest. Some commentators offer the suggestion that the "John" mentioned here was *also* a priest.)

It is not important that we know the names of the men who made up this governing body in the Jewish religion. We know that this same group demanded the crucifixion of Jesus, and this chapter records the account of the first real persecution encountered by the apostles— the first fulfillment of the many prophecies Jesus gave them concerning the persecution that was sure to come.

In John 15:20 He told them, "The servant is not greater than his lord. *If they have persecuted ME, they will also persecute YOU . . . ."*

In Matthew 10:16,17 He said, "Behold, I send you forth as sheep in the midst of wolves: be ye therefore wise as serpents, and harmless as doves. *But beware of men: for they will deliver you up to the councils, and they will scourge you in their synagogues."*

In Mark 13:9 He warned, "Take heed to yourselves: *for they shall deliver you up to councils; and in the synagogues ye shall be beaten: and ye shall be brought before rulers and kings for my sake, for a testimony against them."*

Acts 5:40 tells us that on one occasion the apostles were brought before the council and severely beaten, and were forbidden to speak in the name of Jesus. But with each persecution the Church grew stronger, and in II Timothy 3:12 the Apostle Paul made this positive declaration:

"Yea, and all that will live godly in Christ Jesus SHALL SUFFER PERSECUTION!"

True believers will suffer persecution throughout this Dispensation of Grace; but the *most horrible* persecution will come during the Great Tribulation period, after the Church is raptured and the Antichrist sits on the throne in Jerusalem, declaring that he is God. The Jews will gather in Jerusalem and they will have peace for approximately three and one-half years, after which they will encounter such persecution as the world will not have known up to that time. In Matthew 24:21,22 Jesus declared:

"For then shall be great tribulation, such as was not since the beginning of the world to this time, no, nor ever shall be. AND EXCEPT THOSE DAYS SHOULD BE SHORTENED, THERE SHOULD NO FLESH BE SAVED: but for the elect's sake those days shall be shortened."

Verse 7: *"And when they had set them in the midst, they asked, By what power, or by what name, have ye done this?"*

"In the midst" simply means in the *presence* of the great council of religious leaders. Peter and John were brought before this body of men who considered themselves to be custodians of the laws of God and claimed the right to regulate the religious affairs of Israel. These religious rulers had tremendous influence over the people, and the masses feared their *displeasure*. Realizing this, the Sanhedrin hoped to intimidate Peter and John by questioning them.

"By what power, or by what name, have ye done this?" In other words, "What *supernatural force* did

you employ to *heal* this man? He has been a cripple since birth, yet he now stands before us completely whole! What *name* did you use to bring about this healing?"

The Sanhedrin could not deny the *fact* of the miracle, for the healed man stood in their presence. Everyone had known him for many years, there was no denying that he had been a hopeless cripple all of his life, and certainly none could deny the perfection of his healing. He stood within the circle of the council with the light of salvation on his face and gladness in his heart. Most assuredly *he* would not deny the miracle of his healing, nor would Peter and John deny *their part* in it.

The phrasing of the question itself acknowledged that a miracle had been wrought. The Sanhedrin made no effort to deny the *miracle,* but their question *constituted a refusal to believe the explanation* given by Peter and John in Solomon's porch. Peter had declared that the God of Abraham, Isaac, and Jacob had sent His Son Jesus into the world; but they had rejected Him and delivered Him up to be crucified. He further declared that God had raised Jesus from the dead, and that it was *"through faith in His name"* that the crippled beggar had been given "perfect soundness."

The council discarded that statement in its entirety. They refused to believe Peter's testimony; and ignoring the fact that he had already *told* them by what means the man had been healed, they demanded that he tell them by what power (or in what name) the miracle had been brought about.

The thirteenth chapter of Deuteronomy sheds a great deal of light on this episode:

God carefully gave the rulers of the people instructions concerning supernatural manifestations:

"If there arise among you a prophet, or a dreamer of dreams, and giveth thee a sign or a wonder, and the sign or the wonder come to pass, whereof he spake unto thee, saying, Let us go after other gods, which thou hast

not known, and let us serve them; *thou shalt not hearken
unto the words of that prophet, or that dreamer of dreams
. . . And that prophet, or that dreamer of dreams, shall
be PUT TO DEATH; because he hath spoken to turn
you away from the Lord your God, which brought you
out of the land of Egypt, and redeemed you out of the
house of bondage, to thrust thee out of the way which
the Lord thy God commanded thee to walk in.   So shalt
thou put the evil away from the midst of thee"* (Deut.
13:1—5).

The council was acting in accord with these instructions which had been given to Israel under the Mosaic
economy.   In their spiritual blindness, they fitted Peter
and John into the description of the false prophet, the
"dreamer of dreams" set forth in the Law of Moses.
According to that law, they were to search and inquire
diligently; and if these men *were* trying to lead the people to follow another god, the death penalty must be
passed upon them for attempting to turn men from Jehovah, the true God, to a false god.   Therefore, they
asked the two apostles, *"By what POWER, or by what
NAME, have ye done this?"*

Verses 8—10: *"Then Peter, filled with the Holy Ghost,
said unto them, Ye rulers of the people, and elders of
Israel, if we this day be examined of the good deed done
to the impotent man, by what means he is made whole;
be it known unto you all, and to all the people of Israel,
that by the name of Jesus Christ of Nazareth, whom ye
crucified, whom God raised from the dead, even by Him
doth this man stand here before you whole."*

It is clear that Peter had *respect* for the Sanhedrin.
He did not rebuke them for asking a question he had
already answered.   He had *explained* in his sermon by
whose power and in whose name the miracle had been
wrought, but they had not believed him.   And now as
he repeated his testimony, he seemed to regard this as

a glorious opportunity to declare the truth and give evidence of true Christianity.

In his first epistle—chapter 3, verse 15—Peter wrote under inspiration, *"Be ready ALWAYS to give an answer TO EVERY MAN THAT ASKETH YOU a reason of the hope that is in you WITH MEEKNESS AND FEAR."* He was humble and meek in his reply to the Sanhedrin— but he spoke *boldly.* Any born again believer should rejoice in the opportunity to give testimony of his faith and of what God has done in his heart.

Peter's attitude here before these men and the respect he showed them teaches us that it is proper for Christians to have respect toward authority and toward those in power. When the Herodians questioned *Jesus* concerning paying tribute to Caesar, He asked them whose *image* was inscribed on the coin. They replied, *"Caesar's."* He then said, "Render therefore unto Caesar the things which are Caesar's; and unto God the things that are God's" (Matt. 22:17—21).

In Romans 13:7 the Apostle Paul instructs us to "render . . . to all their dues: tribute to whom tribute is due; custom to whom custom; fear to whom fear; honour to whom honour."

In I Peter 2:13—17 we read, "Submit yourselves to every ordinance of man *for the Lord's sake:* whether it be to the king, as supreme; or unto governors, as unto them that are sent by him for the punishment of evildoers, and for the praise of them that do well. *For so is the will of God, that with well doing ye may put to silence the ignorance of foolish men:* As free, and not using your liberty for a cloke of maliciousness, but as the servants of God. *Honour all men. Love the brotherhood. Fear God. Honour the king."*

"Peter, FILLED WITH THE HOLY GHOST, said unto them . . . ." Peter had been baptized with the Holy Ghost at Pentecost, along with the one hundred and twenty who waited in the upper room. *Here,* the

Word declares that he was *FILLED with the Holy Ghost* —filled to deliver a special and specific message.

In verse 31 of this chapter we read, "When they had prayed, the place was shaken where they were assembled together; *and they were all FILLED with the Holy Ghost, and they spake the Word of God WITH BOLDNESS.*"

There is *ONE baptism*—there are *MANY fillings*. The minister of the Gospel should pray for a fresh filling of the Holy Spirit before he enters the pulpit to deliver a message from God's Word.

There are some who confuse the *baptism* of the Spirit and the *filling* of the Spirit. These are not one and the same, and we need to distinguish between them:

The *baptism* of the Spirit *unites us to the body of Christ:* "For by one Spirit are we all baptized into one body, whether we be Jews or Gentiles, whether we be bond or free; and have been all made to drink into one Spirit" (I Cor. 12:13).

Paul instructed the Ephesians, "Be not drunk with wine, wherein is excess; but *be filled with the Spirit*"— and then he gives the *evidence* of the Spirit-filled life— *"speaking to yourselves in psalms and hymns and spiritual songs, singing and making melody in your heart to the Lord"* (Eph. 5:18,19).

I repeat—there is one baptism, there are *many fillings* of the Spirit. I believe the Holy Spirit will fill us any time, any place, if we need the filling of the Spirit to glorify God—whether it be by delivering a sermon or witnessing to an individual. Any time God calls on us to minister, the Holy Spirit will fill us, speak to us and through us, and *work* through us if we will only allow Him to do so. He does not speak today in *the same manner* in which He dictated the Word of God to holy men of old, but *He does speak* to our hearts, and He speaks *through* us when we are completely yielded to Him.

"Ye rulers of the people, and elders of Israel." There

is no doubt in my mind that as Peter stood before this council composed of the rulers and elders of Israel, he remembered the night his Lord had stood before that same council, the night when Peter had followed "afar off." He had dishonored Jesus that night—he had *denied* Him, swearing, vowing that he had never known Him (Luke 22:54—62)—but now before the same council, in the same room, he was being given an opportunity to *honor and glorify* the Saviour. He had truly repented of his sin of denial—the Scripture tells us that he "went out, and wept bitterly" (Luke 22:62); and true repentance gave him boldness to stand and witness for Jesus without fear.

"*If we this day be examined of the good deed done to the impotent man . . . .*" In spite of the *respect* Peter showed toward the Sanhedrin, he suggests here the absurdity of their questioning him concerning the "good deed" he and John had performed on behalf of this poor, paralyzed man. *The Sanhedrin* should have been the last group on earth to criticize or question them for such a miracle!

Please notice: Peter gave the exact information the Sanhedrin asked for—but in reverse order. They asked by what *power* the miracle had been accomplished, and then in what *name* it had been wrought. Peter answered —first with the *name,* and then declared the *power:*

"*By the name of Jesus Christ of Nazareth, whom YE crucified . . . .*" Peter could have used the name "Messiah," he could have said "the Christ," or he could simply have said "Jesus"—but he did not. He said "*Jesus Christ of Nazareth,*" emphasizing the name so hated by these men, the name they would like to forget! The *name,* then, was "Jesus Christ of Nazareth"—but *what about the POWER?*

"*Jesus . . . whom God raised from the dead, EVEN BY HIM doth this man stand here before you whole.*" In other words, Peter declared, "*JESUS is the name—a* name in which you forbid us to speak. And *this is the POWER*—the raising of that One whom you crucified and whom you declare did not rise! *YOU say there IS no resurrection*—but God raised Jesus, and through His name and by His power this man stands before you perfectly whole!"

This third sermon of Peter's is as bold and clear as the two messages he had given previously. He was the spokesman, and the Holy Spirit gave him words that could be easily understood. This sermon is very brief— it contains only ninety-two words and required only a few minutes for delivery; but how *very comprehensive* it is!

Certainly the declaration Peter had just made before the council does not sound like the weak, wavering, frightened fisherman who, not too long ago, had been *terrified* by a little servant girl! This sermon does not sound like the impulsive, reckless, unstable disciple who, in Matthew 14:29,30, stepped out of the ship to walk to Jesus on the water, but "when he saw the wind boisterous, *he was afraid;* and beginning to sink, he cried, saying, *Lord, save me!"*

What had transformed Peter into this manly, bold, preacher of the Gospel who could testify with such assurance before a group of men who could—and for all *he* knew, *would*—demand his death? *Pentecost* had brought the baptism of the Holy Spirit, making the apostles members of the body of Christ. Peter had earnestly and sincerely repented of his former weaknesses and failures, his faith had been strengthened, and he had reached the point in his Christian experience where he could declare, "Wherefore also it is contained in the Scripture, Behold, I lay in Sion a chief corner stone, elect, precious: *and he that believeth on Him SHALL NOT BE CONFOUNDED!"* (I Pet. 2:6). He had the conviction in his heart that he was speaking words of soberness and pure truth—and he spoke them boldly.

Peter well knew that his reference to *"Jesus Christ of Nazareth"* would be offensive to the Sanhedrin. That body of religious rulers had denied that Jesus was the Christ, they had rejected Him as Messiah; and in using this particular union of names Peter declared Jesus to be all that *these* men said He was *not!*

This is one instance where God "taketh the wise in their own craftiness" (Job 5:13), for little did these men imagine, when they condemned the Lord Jesus Christ to death, that one of His disciples would shortly stand before them and accuse them of crucifying *"the Prince of life"* (Acts 3:15). *Peter and John* were prisoners; it was they who were *on trial*—but when the council demanded the name and power through which they had wrought this great miracle, the way was directly opened for the apostles to bring against them the solemn and serious charge of having crucified their Messiah.

Verse 11: *"This is the stone which was set at nought of you builders, which is become the head of the corner."*

Peter was here quoting from Psalm 118:22: "The stone which the builders refused is become the head stone of the corner."

In Matthew 21:42, Jesus quoted this same passage, and applied it to Himself. He said, "Did ye never read in the Scriptures, *The stone which the builders rejected, the same is become the head of the corner . . . ?"*

Throughout the Bible—and especially in the New Testament—the "Stone" points to the Messiah:

"As it is written, Behold, I lay in Sion *a stumbling-stone and rock of offence:* and whosoever believeth on Him shall not be ashamed" (Rom. 9:33).

"Now therefore ye are no more strangers and foreigners, but fellowcitizens with the saints, and of the household of God; and are built upon the foundation of the apostles and prophets, *Jesus Christ Himself being the chief corner stone"* (Eph. 2:19,20).

"Therefore thus saith the Lord God, Behold, I lay in Zion for a foundation a stone, a tried stone, a precious corner stone, a sure foundation: he that believeth shall not make haste" (Isa. 28:16).

From these marvelous Scriptures we learn that God overrules the devices and plans of ungodly men in order to accomplish His own plan and purpose. *In the beginning* He purposed and planned His program for the eternal ages, and all hell cannot frustrate His design. Many times, the person (or thing) which is set at nought and despised by men, God esteems and uses to His glory and the work of His kingdom. When the powerful, great, and mighty of *this* world condemn, God may take what they condemn and make it the very foundation—yea, even the cornerstone—of His building.

In Matthew 16:15—18 Jesus asked His disciples, "Whom say ye that I am?" Simon Peter immediately replied, *"Thou art the Christ, THE SON OF THE LIVING GOD!"*

Jesus then said to him, "Blessed art thou, Simon Barjona: for flesh and blood hath not revealed it unto thee, but my Father which is in heaven. And I say also unto thee, That thou art Peter, and *UPON THIS ROCK I WILL BUILD MY CHURCH; and the gates of hell shall not prevail against it."*

The Apostle Paul set forth this marvelous truth in writing to the Corinthian Christians:

"For ye see your calling, brethren, how that not many wise men after the flesh, not many mighty, not many noble, are called: *But God hath chosen the foolish things of the world to confound the wise; and God hath chosen the weak things of the world to confound the things which are mighty; and base things of the world, and things which are despised, hath God chosen, yea, and things which are not, to bring to nought things that are: THAT NO FLESH SHOULD GLORY IN HIS PRESENCE.*

"But of Him are ye in Christ Jesus, who of God is made unto us wisdom, and righteousness, and sanctification, and redemption: *That, according as it is written, HE THAT GLORIETH, LET HIM GLORY IN THE LORD"* (I Cor. 1:26—31).

Then in I Peter 2:6—8 we read, "Wherefore also it is contained in the Scripture, *Behold, I lay in Sion a chief corner stone, elect, precious: and he that believeth on HIM shall not be confounded.* Unto you therefore which believe He is precious: but unto them which be disobedient, the stone which the builders disallowed, the same is made the head of the corner, and a stone of stumbling, and a rock of offence, even to them which stumble at the Word, being disobedient: whereunto also they were appointed."

Verse 12: *"Neither is there salvation in any other: for there is none other name under heaven given among men, whereby we must be saved."*

Salvation *delivers the believing soul from sin:*
"She shall bring forth a Son, and thou shalt call His name JESUS: *for He shall save His people from their sins"* (Matt. 1:21).

"Him hath God exalted with His right hand to be a Prince and a *Saviour,* for to give repentance to Israel, *and forgiveness of sins"* (Acts 5:31).

Peter introduces the subject of salvation here because of the healing of the lame beggar. The miraculous healing of *his body* presents a beautiful picture of the healing of the soul when a sinner receives salvation. The beggar received salvation from a long and painful illness—he was delivered from *physical* calamity; but I sincerely believe he was also genuinely *saved.* This greater and more *important* salvation, *salvation from sin,* comes only through the name of the Lord Jesus Christ.

Although Jesus had power to heal the body, that was not His primary purpose in coming into the world. *He*

came to save men from sin, to give His life and shed
His blood, that whosoever would accept His finished
work might have everlasting life.   Peter now stresses
this great truth by assuring the people that the lame
man had been *healed* by the power of Jesus, and then
pointing out that *only by that same Power* can men be
saved from eternal death and hell.

Certainly this was a favorable occasion, one which
afforded a glorious opportunity for Peter to introduce
the message of the Gospel to the great council of the
nation Israel.   He knew the leaders of Israel believed
that salvation would come *through the Messiah*—but
they refused to believe that *Jesus WAS Messiah!* Therefore Peter assured them that it was through the power
of the name of Jesus that the lame man had been made
whole *physically*—and then went on to the great truth
that only through the name of Jesus could men be made
whole *spiritually.*

The apostles proclaimed and taught the doctrine delivered by Moses and the prophets—namely, *salvation
through the coming Messiah.*   Paul declared that he
taught nothing except what was delivered by Moses and
the prophets concerning salvation.   In his testimony before King Agrippa he said:

". . . I stand and am judged for the hope of the promise *made of God unto our fathers . . .* Having therefore
obtained help of God, I continue unto this day, witnessing both to small and great, *saying none other things
than those which the prophets and Moses did say should
come: THAT CHRIST SHOULD SUFFER, and that
HE SHOULD BE THE FIRST THAT SHOULD RISE
FROM THE DEAD, and SHOULD SHEW LIGHT UN-
TO THE PEOPLE, AND TO THE GENTILES"* (Acts
26:6,22,23).

The Jews had no excuse for not recognizing their
Messiah, because *every prophecy* concerning His birth,
His life, and His death was literally fulfilled before their

very eyes—but they stedfastly refused to believe.   Peter therefore made it crystal clear that if they would be saved, their salvation *must* come through "Jesus Christ of Nazareth."

"For there is NONE OTHER NAME under heaven given among men, whereby we MUST be saved." The *"name"* here denotes *the Person—JESUS.*   There is no other *person,* no other *being* save the Lord Jesus Christ— Son of God, the Lamb without blemish and without spot —who can redeem us from sin.

Peter was pointing out that just as the lame man was gloriously (and *perfectly*) healed through the power of Jesus' name, so will those *who come to GOD in Jesus' name* receive *spiritual* healing and be saved from sin.   He then *emphasized* this divine truth by declaring that *there IS no other Saviour, no other PERSON, who can mediate between God and man.*

The Apostle Paul made the same declaration (in slightly different words) in I Timothy 2:5: *"For there is ONE GOD, and ONE MEDIATOR between God and men, the Man CHRIST JESUS."*

That this wonderful name—the name of JESUS—is *"given"* reminds us that *salvation is a GIFT:* "For God so loved the world, that *He GAVE His only begotten Son,* that whosoever believeth in Him should not perish, but have everlasting life" (John 3:16).   God freely gave Jesus to take the sinner's place, in order that a holy and righteous God might be *just*—and yet justify the ungodly. (Please study Romans 3:21—28.)

Salvation cannot be obtained through the patriarchs, the prophets, nor even through the Virgin Mary.   Only in the name of *Jesus* is salvation given.   No wonder Paul exclaimed, *"Thanks be unto God for His UNSPEAK-ABLE GIFT!"* (II Cor. 9:15).

Notice the wording of the last phrase in our present verse: *Jesus* is the only name given *"whereby WE must be saved."*   The nation Israel felt *superior* to other peo-

ples. They were God's *elect,* and they considered themselves far above Gentile "dogs"; but this verse cannot
be interpreted as applying only to the Jews. Peter declares that *WE—all people,* whether Jew, Gentile, rich,
poor, bond, free, learned, or unlearned—*need* to be saved,
and all who *are* saved will be saved in the same identical
way: *through faith in the finished work of the Lord
Jesus Christ. There IS no other way.*

Jesus declared, *"I AM THE WAY, the Truth, and the
Life: NO MAN cometh unto the Father, but BY ME"*
(John 14:6).

He also declared, *"I AM THE DOOR"* (John 10:9)—
and in verse 1 of that same chapter He said, "He that
entereth not *BY the Door . . .* but climbeth up some
other way, *the same is a thief and a robber!"*

In Proverbs 16:25 we read this warning: "There is
a way that *seemeth* right unto a man, but *the end thereof* are the ways of *death."*

The natural man is *lost;* he is without God and without hope, and he needs a Saviour. The Gospel declares
that *"ALL have sinned,* and come short of the glory of
God" (Rom. 3:23); therefore *ALL are sinners,* all are *lost*
and need to be saved.   But all who *want* to be saved
can be saved in the name of Jesus—and those who *are*
saved will be saved through Him, *or not at all.*

Church membership, water baptism, confirmation, dedication, ceremonies, and rituals have no part in accomplishing redemption.   Salvation comes through *the incorruptible seed, the Word of God—and JESUS was the
Word Incarnate.*   He left the Father's bosom and came
to earth to declare God to man, to make known the love
of God and the riches of God's grace. *His* invitation
is:

*"Come unto me, ALL ye that labour and are heavy
laden, and I WILL GIVE YOU REST.* Take my yoke
upon you, and learn of me; for I am meek and lowly in
heart: *and ye shall find rest unto your SOULS.* For

my yoke is easy, and my burden is light" (Matt. 11:
28—30).

God's Word leaves no room for doubt or confusion
as to where and how salvation is to be obtained. John
the Beloved gives us the clear, concise record:

"And *this* is the record, *that God hath GIVEN to
us eternal life, and this life is IN HIS SON. He that
hath the Son HATH life; and he that hath NOT the
Son of God HATH NOT LIFE*" (I John 5:11,12).

What a marvelous portion of God's Word we find
here in verses 8 through 12 of this fourth chapter of
Acts! It is impossible for us to know to what extent
Peter's defense was *abbreviated*—no doubt he spoke words
not recorded here; but the Holy Spirit inspired Luke to
pen down what God would have us know, and this part
of the record is truly a gem, a pearl. It contains the
respect of a Christian gentleman toward those in authority, even though Peter brought a grave charge against
the fathers in Israel.

He *fearlessly* proclaimed prophetic facts concerning
the coming of Messiah, and spoke with such moving
conviction and boldness that the members of the council
were astonished (as we will see in the verses that follow).

His appeal was clear, uncompromising, and supported
by Scripture. In verse 11, with reference to "the stone
which was set at nought" by the builders, he quoted
from Matthew 21:42, Mark 12:10, and Luke 20:17—all of
which refer back to Psalm 118:22, a passage which should
have been familiar to all members of the group. (See
also Isaiah 28:16, Daniel 2:34, and Exodus 17:6.)

The *"stone"* of which Peter spoke is an Old Testament
symbol pointing to the Lord Jesus Christ, *rejected of
men*—"precious" to those who *believe*, "a stone of stumbling and a rock of offence" to those who do *not* believe
(I Pet. 2:7,8).

This "stone which was set at nought" by man was

destined to be the chief cornerstone—yea, *the foundation* —of the temple in which all nations become one in Christ Jesus; and *"other foundation* can no man lay than that is laid, *which is JESUS CHRIST"* (I Cor. 3:11).

This is further explained in Ephesians 2:19—22, where Paul tells us that believers "are no more strangers and foreigners, but fellowcitizens with the saints, and of the household of God; and are built upon the foundation of the apostles and prophets, *JESUS CHRIST HIMSELF BEING THE CHIEF CORNER STONE; in whom all the building fitly framed together groweth unto an holy temple in the Lord: in whom ye also are BUILDED TOGETHER FOR AN HABITATION OF GOD through the Spirit."*

Under inspiration, Luke penned down exactly *ninety words* in the Greek language; but in those words we find recorded the point, the power, and the purpose of Peter's brave and aggressive defense!

Verse 13: *"Now when they saw the boldness of Peter and John, and perceived that they were unlearned and ignorant men, they marvelled; and they took knowledge of them, that they had been with Jesus."*

The religious rulers were astonished beyond words— not by the message these humble fishermen had given them, but by their *boldness* in speaking of "Jesus Christ of Nazareth." They had so hardened their hearts that the *message* of Peter's words did not reach them; but they hated the name of Jesus, and the apostles had stood boldly before them and declared that name to be above every name, the *only* name by which men could be saved! This was the great council of religious leaders so revered by the nation Israel; yet these *"unlearned and ignorant men"* had accused them of having crucified their Messiah—Jesus Christ of Nazareth.

The Greek word here translated *"unlearned"* is literally *unlettered*—or unversed in the learning of Jewish schools. These mighty and learned men wondered how *unlearned* men like Peter and John could speak such wonderful words and give so much Scripture from the Old Testament.

In Proverbs 28:1 we read, "The wicked flee when no man pursueth—*but the RIGHTEOUS are bold as a lion.*" God's preachers should not be *reckless,* but like the apostles of old we should be *bold* in declaring the Gospel. The book of Acts gives the record of a number of God's men who courageously witnessed for Christ in the face of severe persecution—even in the face of death. Chapter 5, verses 40—42, tells of how the apostles were *beaten* and commanded not to speak in the name of Jesus; yet they spoke *daily* in the temple and in every house, "teaching and preaching Jesus Christ."

Acts 6:8 describes *Stephen* as a man "full of faith and power, (who) did great wonders and miracles among the people." Boldly he accused the Jews of having slain the prophets, and of having *betrayed and murdered* "the Just One," their Messiah. Even as they stoned him to death he testified, "I see the heavens opened, and *the Son of man* standing on the right hand of God!" (Read Acts 7:51—60.)

Certainly *the Apostle Paul* was "bold as a lion." Throughout Acts we find testimony of his fearless declaration of the Gospel:

"Straightway he *preached Christ* in the synagogues . . . he preached *boldly* at Damascus in the name of Jesus. . . he *spake boldly* in the name of the Lord Jesus" (Acts 9:20, 28, 29).

In chapter 13, verse 46, "Paul and Barnabas *waxed bold* . . . ." In chapter 14, verse 3, they spoke *"boldly in the Lord,"* and in chapter 19, verse 8, Paul "went into the synagogue, and spake *boldly* for the space of three months, disputing and persuading the things concerning the kingdom of God." Writing to the Christians at Thessalonica, Paul gave this testimony: "But even after that we had suffered before, and were shamefully entreated, as ye know, at Philippi, *we were bold in our God* to speak unto you the Gospel of God with much contention" (I Thess. 2:2).

Paul *prayed* for the holy boldness to preach the Gospel (Eph. 6:19,20), and according to verse 29 of our present chapter in Acts, God's ministers *today* should pray for boldness to speak the Word. In verse 31 of this chapter we read that *after the apostles prayed,* they spoke the Word of God with boldness, and in Hebrews 4:16 *all believers* are invited to "*come boldly unto the throne of grace,* that we may obtain mercy, and find grace to help in time of need."

Then in Hebrews 10:19,20 we read, "Having therefore, brethren, *boldness to enter into the holiest by the blood of Jesus,* by a new and living way, which He hath consecrated for us . . . ."

Today, perhaps as never before in the history of the Church, God's people need boldness to stand in the face of growing apostasy and declare, *"THUS SAITH THE LORD!"*

"And they took knowledge of them, that they had been with Jesus." This does not necessarily mean that the council recognized Peter and John as disciples of Jesus because of their particular conduct or their spirituality, but because they had *seen* them with Him, they recognized them as having been with Him during the last week of His ministry, just before He was crucified.

Verse 14: *"And beholding the man which was healed standing with them, they could say nothing against it."*

In chapter 3, verse 2, we noted that this man was carried *daily* to the temple gate "to ask alms of them that entered into the temple." We know from verse 22 of this fourth chapter that the man was more than *forty years old,* and during that time someone—some friend or relative, perhaps—had carried him *each day* to his accustomed place by the temple gate. Of a certainty, the men who sat on this council had seen him there year after year, daily, and there was no question of his lameness. Everyone knew him, everyone knew he had never walked. Now that same man *stood* before them—and only *minutes* previously he had been *leaping, walking, and praising God for his healing!* Certainly it was impossible for the council to deny the mighty miracle that had been wrought. They *"could say nothing"* to repudiate the miracle because *living evidence* stood before them.

Verse 15: *"But when they had commanded them to go aside out of the council, they conferred among themselves."*

It seems that the members of the council (or Sanhedrin) would have asked the apostles to tell them *more* about this wonderful Jesus and His power to heal both body and soul; but they did not. Instead, they asked Peter and John to leave the council room while the rulers discussed among themselves what could be done about the situation. They did not repent of their part in sending Jesus to the cross, they were not willing to accept the truth that had been so powerfully presented to them. They chose to remain in spiritual darkness, willingly ignorant of the truth concerning their Messiah.

Peter and John were not permitted to go *free,* but together with the man who had been healed they left the council room—undoubtedly under guard. Meanwhile, the rulers held council behind closed doors—and here we have *another proof* of the verbal inspiration of the Scriptures: No one reported to Luke what secret things took place behind the closed doors of the council chamber while the apostles waited outside; but there was One who saw and heard—*and HE, the Holy Spirit,* revealed those things to Luke the beloved physician, who penned down the account of what happened in that closed meeting.

Verse 16: *"Saying, What shall we do to these men?*

For that indeed a notable miracle hath been done by them is manifest to all them that dwell in Jerusalem; and we cannot deny it."

The Sanhedrin was the most powerful religious body of that day, but the members of that body now faced a situation which left them at a loss for a solution. They admitted one to another that indeed *"a notable miracle"* had been wrought and there was absolutely no way by which it could be denied or disproved, because it was *"manifest to all them that dwell in Jerusalem."* In other words, *the entire city* knew about it, knew the reality of it, and it would be useless for the Sanhedrin to attempt to convince the multitudes that the miracle had not taken place. They must, therefore, seek *another* solution.

Verse 17:   *"But that it spread no further among the people, let us straitly threaten them, that they speak henceforth to no man in this name."*

This thing must be kept quiet. It must not be discussed and spread among the people beyond Jerusalem, in the neighboring towns and communities.

The council was not unaware of its influence on the common people, and surely if that powerful body ordered these two humble, unlearned apostles to desist from their preaching and miracle working, they would not dare disobey! So they decided, *"Let us straitly threaten them, that they speak henceforth to no man in this name."*

These religious leaders had asked Peter and John by what power and in what name they had wrought this great miracle, and the apostles had told them that it was in the name of Jesus and through His power that the lame man had been made perfectly whole. But now, meeting in secret behind closed doors, not one member of the council suggested that perhaps Peter and John were preaching the truth, perhaps the Jews really *had* crucified their Messiah. The only time they *mentioned* Jesus was when they commanded the disciples not to speak in His name!

Verse 18: *"And they called them, and commanded them not to speak at all nor teach in the name of Jesus."*

Here is the devil's work. In verse 12 Peter declared, "There is *none other name* under heaven given among men, *whereby we MUST be saved."* Now these men command the disciples not to preach any more *IN that name*—the precious name of Jesus. Satan does not care how long, how loud, nor how often a minister preaches, *as long as he does not preach Christ*—crucified, buried, risen, ascended, and coming again! The devil knows that a message *without Jesus in it* will not cause sinners to be saved nor rob hell of souls.

Verses 19 and 20: *"But Peter and John answered and said unto them, Whether it be right in the sight of God to hearken unto you more than unto God, judge ye. For we cannot but speak the things which we have seen and heard."*

Contrary to the procedure of the Sanhedrin, Peter and John did not need to hold a conference to decide what they should say; they did not ask permission to step outside and discuss the matter. True servants of God, they gave immediate answer to the council, and they were *in agreement* in what they said.

"Whether it be right in the sight of God to hearken unto YOU more than unto GOD, judge ye." In other words, "You who are the religious rulers in Israel, you who claim kinship with Abraham and swear allegiance to Moses, should *know* whether we should obey *God,* or *man."*

"We cannot but SPEAK the things which we have seen and heard." Peter realized the power of this body of men before whom he testified—but that knowledge

did not dampen his fervor or hinder his boldness. In effect, he said, "You make up your own mind whether it is right for us to listen to *God,* or whether we should listen to *you.* But while you are making up your mind, I will tell you what to expect from us: we are going to *continue* doing exactly what we *have been doing* because we have been commissioned of God to declare the things we have seen and heard. And we intend to *obey God* regardless of what *you* command us to do!"

Today, many ministers take orders from the ecclesiastical leaders in their denomination; but thank God, there are some who, like Peter and John, take orders and instructions from God alone! I have known some pastors who feared the deacon board in their church. Others fear to preach the whole truth lest they offend some influential member of the congregation. But I have known others who look to God for *HIS message*—and when that message is given, those ministers preach exactly what the Holy Spirit *directs* them to preach, regardless of the opinion of deacons, members of the congregation, or the governing body of that denomination.

Such was the courage of Peter and John. They were speaking before a group of men who could have ordered them imprisoned—or, for that matter, could have decreed their death. Their boldness was the product of the indwelling Spirit, the same Holy Spirit who indwells every born again child of God—yes, in this Dispensation of Grace—*today.*

Verse 21: *"So when they had further threatened them, they let them go, finding nothing how they might punish them, because of the people: for all men glorified God for that which was done."*

The only action the council could take was to repeat their threat to the apostles. I think they must have been sorry they could not punish them—certainly they wanted to, but they could not risk arousing the masses of common people. The multitudes *knew* what had taken place and they were rejoicing and glorifying God because of the healing of the lame man, their neighbor who had been crippled all of his life.

Here is recorded an instance which has been repeated often since that day. The council did not know that *persecution* has a tendency to extend and establish the faith it was designed to destroy! The disciples were few in number, they had *little* influence and even *less wealth*. Surely if they were arrested, threatened, or beaten they would be brought into subjection to the religious dictators of that day, and the new *"Jesus-way"* would be crushed.

But instead of putting a stop to the apostles' teaching in the name of Jesus, the persecution only *extended the results* of that teaching. It has been so in all ages, and it will be so throughout time. Some godly soul in centuries past declared, *"The blood of martyrs is the seed of the Church"*−and so it *is*!

Verse 22: *"For the man was above forty years old, on whom this miracle of healing was shewed."*

No wonder the members of the Sanhedrin were disturbed! If this had been a child of tender years they might have been able to explain it away; but this was a man past forty years of age−and in chapter 3, verse 2, we learned that he had been lame *"from his mother's womb."* He had never walked a step. Therefore there was no way to discredit the miracle that had been wrought. The Sanhedrin knew that if these apostles were not stopped, the new doctrine would sweep the country and the position of the Jewish rulers would be in jeopardy. They were cowards, they feared the common people; therefore they did the only thing they could think of that might solve their problem without stirring up the multitudes: *they threatened Peter and John and sent them away.*

Satan seeks to *silence truth.* Jesus said to these men, "Ye shall know the truth, and the truth shall make you *free"* (John 8:32). In John 17:17 He declared, *"God's Word is truth."* It is *truth*—the truth of God's Word—that causes men to become sons of God through faith in the finished work of the Lord Jesus Christ; and there is no doubt that the devil is doing his utmost today to undermine and destroy the Word, thereby silencing truth.

Believers Again Filled with the Spirit

Verse 23: *"And being let go, they went to their own company, and reported all that the chief priests and elders had said unto them."*

I can easily imagine the excitement that prevailed among the Christians in Jerusalem when they learned that Peter and John had been arrested and brought before the Sanhedrin! The news must have traveled rapidly, and the devotion and fervor of these early saints would have brought them together to pray for the two apostles, as they prayed for Peter when *Herod* imprisoned him. (In Acts 12:5 we read that "prayer was made *without ceasing* of the Church unto God for him"—and God answered their prayers by sending an angel to set Peter free. Read the account in chapter 12, verses 1 through 19.)

It was with great joy that Peter and John went to the place where *"their own company"* of fellow believers had assembled—and I am sure they were *received* with great joy. Whereupon they gave the company of Christians a full report of *"all that the chief priests and elders had said unto them."*

Verse 24: *"And when they heard that, they lifted up their voice to God with one accord, and said, Lord, thou art God, which hast made heaven, and earth, and the sea, and all that in them is."*

Please notice that no idle discussion followed the apostles' report. No plans or schemes were worked out to deal with the situation. No committees were appointed to decide what the next move should be. No vote was taken to determine whether or not they should continue to use the name of Jesus in their ministry. This little band of Christians wasted no time, but *"when they heard"* the report of Peter and John, they immediately *"lifted up their voice to God."* They turned at once to the Christ in whose name they had been forbidden to speak.

If you will study II Kings, chapter 19, you will note the interesting account of Hezekiah's response to the very serious threat made by Rabshakeh (mouthpiece for Sennacherib, king of Assyria) against the people of Israel. When good King Hezekiah received Rabshakeh's letter by hand of messengers, he read it—and then "went up into the house of the Lord, *and spread it before the Lord"* (II Kings 19:14).

The company of believers with Peter and John laid *their* problem before the Lord—and what better recourse could they have followed? After all, the whole matter concerned Jehovah God and His only begotten Son, the Lord Jesus Christ. These people were dedicated servants of God, and their devotion to Him was such that they were ready and willing to glorify Him by serving, suffering, or *dying* if need be. The Holy Spirit *leads* to prayer, and when the believer prays fervently and sincerely, his prayer expresses his dependence on the Lord Jesus Christ.

These Christians prayed *"with one accord"*—not for vengeance to be poured out upon their enemies, not for fire to come down from heaven and consume the Sanhedrin, but for God to give them boldness to speak the Word and to do whatever His hand and counsel "determined before to be done" (v. 28). And God answered their prayer, as we will see in verse 31 of this chapter.

The fact that these believers lifted up their voices

"with one accord" does not mean that each and every one of them prayed aloud at the same time. If that had been the case, *confusion* would have been the result—and God is *not* the author of confusion (I Cor. 14:33). Also (in verse 40 of that same chapter), we are instructed, "Let all things be done decently and *in order."* Therefore it would seem more likely that one person—perhaps Peter—prayed aloud, and the rest of the assembly followed in their *hearts* "with one accord."

To be "instant in prayer" (Rom. 12:12), or to "pray without ceasing" (I Thess. 5:17), means to be *in an attitude* of prayer; but it is not necessary to speak words aloud in order to pray. There is a time for audible prayer, but I believe some of the most effective praying is done in silence.

> *Prayer is the soul's sincere desire,*
> *Unuttered or expressed;*
> *The motion of a hidden fire*
> *That trembles in the breast.*

Notice the opening words of the prayer in our present verse: These Christians addressed their petition to *"Lord"* (meaning *master*) and to *"GOD, which hast made heaven, and earth, and the sea, and all that in them is."* John 1:1—3 tells us that "the Word (Christ) was in the beginning with God," and that *"all things were made BY Him; and WITHOUT Him was not any thing made that was made."* In Ephesians 3:9 Paul speaks of God as having "created *all things* by Jesus Christ," and in Hebrews 1:2 we read that God "hath in these last days spoken unto us by His Son, whom He hath appointed heir of all things, *by whom also He made the worlds."*

There are men today who continually search for a discovery of how the worlds and solar systems came into being. If they would read and believe the Word of God they would find the answer, for the Bible clearly teaches that the Lord God *created ALL things by the Word—by* the Lord Jesus Christ—and *for* Him.

After the complete revelation of the Gospel of the Son of God was given (as the Holy Spirit spoke through holy men and they penned down God's Word), prayer was addressed to *the God and Father of our Lord Jesus Christ.* This is the proper way for believers to address God today. In this Dispensation of Grace, prayer is to be made in Christ's name in the power of His Spirit. There is no place in the book of Acts or in the epistles where prayer is addressed to the Holy Spirit, although the Spirit *helps* us in our praying.

When we are so burdened we know not *how* to pray or what to pray *for,* He (the Holy Spirit) prays for us: "Likewise the Spirit also helpeth our infirmities: for we know not what we should pray for as we ought: but *the Spirit Himself maketh intercession for us with groanings which cannot be uttered.* And He that searcheth the hearts knoweth what is the mind of the Spirit, because He maketh intercession for the saints according to the will of God" (Rom. 8:26,27).

I might also point out here that there is no place in either Acts or the epistles where believers prayed what we refer to as *"the Lord's prayer,"* given in Matthew 6:9—13. This prayer was given to the disciples for a specific time; and before Jesus left them to return to His heavenly Father He said to them, *"Hitherto have ye asked nothing IN MY NAME: ask, and ye shall receive, that your joy may be full"* (John 16:24). We are to pray *in the name* of the Lord Jesus Christ; we should be led by the Holy Spirit *when* we pray; and when we are too burdened to know *how* to pray, the Holy Spirit will intercede for us.

Verse 25: *"Who by the mouth of thy servant David hast said, Why did the heathen rage, and the people imagine vain things?"*

The prayer recorded in this chapter is the first recorded

prayer in the book of Acts, and it is founded on the Word of God—that is, verses 25 and 26 are direct quotations from Psalm 2 (a prophetic Psalm but not, as yet, completely fulfilled).

As the apostles prayed, the Holy Spirit brought the Word to mind, and with the Word in their hearts they made their petition known to God. This is the right way for believers to pray. A careful study of the prayers of Daniel, Jeremiah, Isaiah, Ezekiel, and other prophets in the Old Testament will reveal that they prayed after this manner, and God heard and answered their prayers.

The second Psalm, from which these quotations were taken, is of prophetic importance throughout the New Testament. There is a great collection of inspired prayers and songs of praise in the book of Psalms, but we must not minimize the importance of the Psalms of *prophecy.* This particular Psalm is not titled, nor does it tell us the name of the person through whom it was given. In the prayer of this group of believers it is ascribed to David, but his name is not given in the Psalm itself.

"Why did the heathen rage, and the people imagine vain things?" This great prophetic Psalm begins by foretelling that the Gentiles would oppose God and His Anointed (the Lord Jesus Christ), and here in Acts we find recorded the *partial fulfillment* of this prophecy. It has not yet been fulfilled in its entirety, nor will complete fulfillment occur until the Great Tribulation period.

However, when Peter, John, and other believers were praying, the Gentiles—Herod, Pilate, and others—had gathered with the rulers of Israel to do what *the hand and counsel of God* had foreordained should be done (v. 28). The Anointed of the Lord had been rejected, and the Gentiles shared in His rejection. The rulers of Israel had given command that His name should no more be mentioned. God in His sovereignty and omniscience knew before creation began that these events would come to pass; but that did not clear them from the responsibility and guilt.

SIN caused men to treat the Lord Jesus as they did.
The Christ of God, God's only begotten Son, came into
the world, took a body of humiliation, and offered Himself as a sacrifice for the sin of mankind. He came into
a world which was *made* by Him, but the world did
not know Him. Even *His own people,* the elect of God,
rejected Him.

Although the second Psalm does not mention Israel's
part in the rejection of the Messiah, that does not ex-
haust the prophecy of this Psalm. The rejection of Christ
by the Gentiles *and* Israel in the beginning of this age
is a prelude to the great rejection of Him at the end
of this age, during the reign of Antichrist.

Verse 26: *"The kings of the earth stood up, and the
rulers were gathered together against the Lord, and
against His Christ."*

This prophecy will be fulfilled after the Rapture of
the Church. (See I Thessalonians 4:13—18 and I Corinthians 15:51—57.) Every believer will be caught up to
meet the Lord in the air; therefore *millions will be missing* from their accustomed places. The Antichrist will
then come on the scene and offer a solution to that great
mystery. (This will be the false Messiah, the "little
horn" of Daniel 7:8, the counterfeit Christ of Revelation
6:2 and Revelation chapter 13.) He will sit in the temple
in Jerusalem and announce that he is God, and he will
deceive many—especially the rulers of the earth.

It is then that *"the kings of the earth"* will unite
their powers to form a great confederacy and will gather
together *"against the Lord, and against His Christ."*
But in verse 4 of Psalm 2 we read, *"He that sitteth in
the heavens shall laugh: the Lord shall have them in
derision."*

The Antichrist will reign approximately seven years,
the last half of those years subjecting earth's peoples to

such persecution and destruction that *"except those days should be shortened, there should no flesh be saved:* but for the elect's sake those days *shall be* shortened" (Matt. 24:22).   At the *end* of the reign of Antichrist, Jesus will be revealed from heaven. "Every eye shall see Him, and they also which pierced Him: and all kindreds of the earth shall wail because of Him" (Rev. 1:7).

This glorious event—the coming of Christ in glory—is described by John the Beloved in Revelation 19:11—16:

"And I saw heaven opened, and behold a white horse; and He that sat upon him was called Faithful and True, and in righteousness He doth judge and make war.

"His eyes were as a flame of fire, and on His head were many crowns; and He had a name written, that no man knew, but He Himself.   And He was clothed with a vesture dipped in blood: and His name is called The Word of God.

"And the armies which were in heaven followed Him upon white horses, clothed in fine linen, white and clean. And out of His mouth goeth a sharp sword, that with it He should smite the nations: and He shall rule them with a rod of iron: and He treadeth the winepress of the fierceness and wrath of Almighty God. And He hath on His vesture and on His thigh a name written, KING OF KINGS, AND LORD OF LORDS!"

During the reign of Antichrist, Satan will make his last and strongest effort to destroy God's Christ and His kingdom—a determination which began in the Garden of Eden when God declared that He would put enmity between the seed of the serpent and the Seed of the woman (Gen. 3:15).   Down through the centuries the devil has waged perpetual and deadly war against God's people in his attempts to frustrate the program of God and destroy His kingdom. Throughout the Old Testament Satan tried to bring about the destruction of the line through which the Seed, the Son of God, would eventually come.

But in spite of all he could do, *"when the fulness of the time was come, God sent forth His Son, made of a woman, made under the law, to redeem them that were under the law, that we might receive the adoption of sons"* (Gal. 4:4,5).

Jesus came as promised, He came exactly as it was prophesied that He *would* come; but even after His birth, Satan tried on many occasions to destroy Him before He reached Calvary—but to no avail. The Son of God went to the cross as foreordained of God before the foundation of the world (I Pet. 1:18—20).

But the devil has not given up. He was defeated at Calvary, and he *knows* he is a defeated foe whose ultimate end will be an eternity in the lake of fire (Rev. 20:10). He will make his last and most powerful move against God's Christ and God's kingdom during the reign of Antichrist; but as John so clearly declares, when Jesus comes in power, riding on a great white horse and all the saints riding with Him, *He will destroy Antichrist and the armies of Antichrist,* and the beast and the false prophet will be "cast alive into a lake of fire burning with brimstone." (Please read Revelation 19:17—21.)

It is then that Psalm 2 will be fulfilled in its entirety and King Jesus will reign from David's throne in Jerusalem. It is then that men will "beat their swords into plowshares, and their spears into pruninghooks: nation shall not lift up sword against nation, neither shall they learn war any more" (Isa. 2:4). *Then* will come peace on earth and good will among men.

Verses 27 and 28: *"For of a truth against thy holy child Jesus, whom thou hast anointed, both Herod, and Pontius Pilate, with the Gentiles, and the people of Israel, were gathered together, for to do whatsoever thy hand and thy counsel determined before to be done."*

"For of a truth" (that is, *in reality*) *"against thy holy child Jesus...."* The Greek word used here for *"child"*

expresses sonship without respect to age. It is not the word commonly used when referring to Jesus as a small child or as a babe. A better translation in this instance would be *"Son,"* making the reference read *"thy holy SON, Jesus."* (The same Greek word is used in chapter 3, verses 13 and 26, where it is translated "Son.")

"Both Herod, and Pontius Pilate, with the Gentiles, and the people of Israel, were gathered together." The alliance between Pilate and Herod is clarified in Luke 23:1—12. If you will read those verses you will see that the common bond between them was the trial of Jesus. The Jews had brought Him before Pilate, but when Pilate learned that his Prisoner was a *Galilaean,* he sent Him to *Herod* in whose jurisdiction the Galilaeans belonged. When Herod found that Jesus would not perform a miracle in his presence—or even answer the questions the king put to Him—he and his court mocked Him, put a royal robe on Him, and sent Him back to Pilate. *"And the same day Pilate and Herod were made friends together:* for before they were at enmity between themselves" (Luke 23:12).

"The Gentiles" here refers to the Romans to whom Jesus was delivered to be crucified. *"The people of Israel"* were, of course, the Jews who, under the pressure and influence of their leaders, had demanded the release of Barabbas and the crucifixion of Jesus (Matt. 27:20).

Thus *Pilate, Herod, the Romans, and the Jews* were allied together, their common determination being to crucify the Lord Jesus Christ. The burden of guilt for His death rests primarily on the Jews, for it was to them that He came, and it was at their insistence that Pilate sentenced Him to be crucified (even though he knew Him to be innocent). The Romans who actually nailed Jesus to the cross represented all Gentile nations. They were easily persuaded to join in the persecution and become the executioners of the Son of God.

Ordinarily *the Jews* (who claimed to be followers of

the one true God) and *the Romans* (who were pagan) were bitterly opposed to each other. It is noteworthy then that they were united here, combining forces against the Lord Jesus Christ in accomplishing His crucifixion. Men and nations have often used this strategy, allying themselves with those who have been their mortal enemies, in order to destroy a *common* enemy. In this particular instance, *fear* became the common denominator between the opposing factions.

The religious leaders in Israel were not only mortified and moved with envy that One so poor, so humble, and (of all things) a *Nazarene*, should claim to be their expected Messiah. They also feared His influence on the common people and realized that if His doctrine should take hold and spread throughout the nation, their own prestige and influence was doomed. They had expected a Messiah of a different calibre, of a different rank in character; and all of their prejudices rose at once against the claims of the Nazarene. Pilate knew this, as we are plainly told in Matthew 27:18: "For he knew that *for envy* they had delivered (Jesus)."

The rank and file of the common people were moved by the miracles of Jesus and were disposed to acknowledge His claims; but they stood in awe of the Sanhedrin, and when the religious rulers pressed them to demand the death of the One who claimed to be Messiah, they followed their leaders instead of obeying their own hearts. "The chief priests and elders *persuaded* the multitude that they should ask Barabbas, and destroy Jesus" (Matt. 27:20).

As for Pontius Pilate, he was the one man who could have demanded — and obtained — our Lord's liberty. But *fear* pressed upon the Roman governor from two directions:

First, *the Jews* cried out, "If thou let this Man go, thou art not *Caesar's friend*" (John 19:12). In other words, if he released the Nazarene, the Jews would report to Caesar that Pilate had released a prisoner who could well prove to be an insurrectionist, claiming kingship that might overthrow Caesar.

In the second place, Pilate recognized (as did the Jews) that Christianity was making tremendous advances; and the *doctrines* of Christianity struck at the whole fabric of his pagan religion of superstition—not only in Rome, but throughout the known world. Wherever the message of Christianity was preached and believed, members of pagan religions would be converted and would follow Christ, denouncing idolatry and superstition; and this would, in the final analysis, cause such men as this Roman governor to lose their hold on the multitudes. So Pilate gave in to the demands of the Jewish religionists, denied the dictates of his own conscience, and commanded that Jesus be crucified.

Christianity is not like any other religion. It did not ask to be placed *among* the many religions already existing. Christianity claims that Christ was the Messiah and acclaims Him as King of kings and Lord of lords— the only Saviour of mankind, the only One who can forgive sins. The message Jesus preached—and the message the *apostles* preached—denounced all other religious systems as idolatry; and when people heard and *believed* the message of the Gospel, those people immediately renounced their pagan religion and followed where the Holy Spirit led.

The religions of that day were closely allied with the departments of state and furnished jobs for a vast number of priests and other religious officers who obtained their livelihood in the wages they drew from the various religions. It was only natural that the *leaders* of those religions should become concerned about the rapid spread of *Christianity*, the only *pure and true* religion.

Great cities such as Athens, Corinth, Ephesus, and Rome were places of extreme wickedness, polluted with immorality and all species of crime. Christianity began at a time when there was widespread ungodliness of every sort, and we can rest assured that the apostles cried out against these prevailing sins, declaring that the judgment of God would fall upon the cities where idolatry held the people in superstition and sin ran rampant.

Christianity has been hated more deeply and opposed more violently than any other religion. The apostles were imprisoned, beaten, killed. The early Christians were persecuted and martyred, indescribably tortured and put to death in the most cruel manner the wickedness of man could devise; but in spite of opposition and persecution, Christianity has triumphed over all—*proof positive* of its divine origin.

There are more Christians today than at any other time in history. (I do not mean that more are *saved* today, *percentage-wise*, than before, because there are so many more billions of people on earth today; but I *do* believe we have more real Christians than ever before *at any one time* in the history of man.)

Christianity had its origin in God; and since God cannot be defeated, and His Christ cannot be defeated, then it must follow that *Christianity* cannot be defeated!

However, according to God's infallible Word, things will not become easier for Christians. All who will *"live godly in Christ Jesus"* will suffer persecution, and "evil men and seducers shall wax *worse and worse,* deceiving, and being deceived" (II Tim. 3:12,13). But *"we know that ALL things work together for good to them that love God,* to them who are the called according to His purpose . . . and . . . *if God be for us, who can be against us?* . . . We are *more than conquerors* through Him that loved us," and we know that "neither death, nor life, nor angels, nor principalities, nor powers, nor things present, nor things to come, nor height, nor depth, *nor any other creature, shall be able to separate us from the love of God, which is in Christ Jesus our Lord"* (Rom. 8:28—39 in part).

Kings and peasants alike have fought Christ and Christians since the birth of Christianity—and will continue to do so until the Church Age is complete and the saints are caught up to meet the Lord Jesus in the clouds in the air.

Verse 29: *"And now, Lord, behold their threatenings: and grant unto thy servants, that with all boldness they may speak thy Word."*

The apostles were not disheartened, they were not disposed to give up and turn their backs on the message Jesus had given them to deliver. They only drew nearer to God for help and strength, lest they be in danger of growing indifferent or becoming fearful in the face of the opposition they were encountering.

"Grant unto thy servants . . . all boldness." Jesus promised His disciples, *"I will give you a mouth and wisdom, which all your adversaries shall not be able to gainsay nor resist"* (Luke 21:15). They were praying here that God would help them to rise above self. Their request was simple: they asked only that He grant them courage to preach His Word in *"all boldness,"* courage to testify for Jesus.

Verse 30: *"By stretching forth thine hand to heal; and that signs and wonders may be done by the name of thy holy child Jesus."*

The apostles not only asked God to give them boldness to preach the Word; they also asked that He continue to work miracles through them, and by those miracles give divine evidence of the truth of what they said in the name of Jesus.

"How shall we escape, if we neglect so great salvation; which at the first began to be spoken by the Lord, and was confirmed unto us by them that heard Him; GOD ALSO BEARING THEM WITNESS, BOTH WITH SIGNS AND WONDERS, AND WITH DIVERS MIR-

ACLES, AND GIFTS OF THE HOLY GHOST, AC-CORDING TO HIS OWN WILL?" (Heb. 2:3,4).

You will notice they did not pray for God to preserve their lives or keep them from suffering and danger. They were wholeheartedly given to the work Jesus had called them to do, and they confidently committed themselves to God. The one desire of their hearts was to promote the Gospel, declaring the truth and making known the way of salvation. They prayed that God would glorify Himself by continuing to give miracles, signs and wonders, and by saving those who heard the message of His saving grace.

Verse 31: *"And when they had prayed, the place was shaken where they were assembled together; and they were all filled with the Holy Ghost, and they spake the Word of God with boldness."*

The mighty *"shaking"* of the place where they were assembled assured these believers that the God of all nature to whom they had appealed in verse 24 had heard their prayer and was in their presence. The Greek word translated *"was shaken"* denotes violent agitation such as the raging of the sea, the tremors of a great earthquake, or trees being shaken by a mighty wind. (See Acts 16:26 and Hebrews 12:26.)

The Scripture does not tell us if this "shaking" was confined to the place where the Christians were praying, or if it was widespread. I am inclined to believe that it was only in the place where the saints were assembled, and to them it was evidence that God had heard their prayers.

To the Jews, a shaking of the earth—an earthquake—was proof of the presence of Jehovah God. In Isaiah 29:6 we read, "Thou shalt be visited of the Lord of hosts *with thunder, and with earthquake, and great noise,* with storm and tempest, and the flame of devouring fire."

When Jesus died on the cross, God sent an earthquake;

and Matthew 27:54 tells us that "when the centurion,
and they that were with him, watching Jesus, *saw the
earthquake, and those things that were done, they feared
greatly, saying, Truly this was the Son of God!*"

In connection with this, please read the third chapter
of Habakkuk, noticing in particular verses 6 through 11.
As in Old Testament times, God made His power and
presence known to His people by shaking the place in
which they were assembled in prayer.

"*And they were all filled with the Holy Ghost, and
they spake the Word of God with boldness.*" The apostles were *baptized* with the Holy Ghost at Pentecost.
This was not another baptism, but a *filling* for power
in declaring the Word of God. We noticed in verse 8
that *Peter* was filled with the Holy Ghost when he addressed the Sanhedrin. There is *one baptism* of the Spirit, but there are *many fillings.* Thus empowered, "*they
spake the Word of God with boldness.*"

The State of the Church at Jerusalem

Verse 32: "*And the multitude of them that believed
were of one heart and of one soul: neither said any of
them that ought of the things which he possessed was
his own; but they had all things common.*"

Verses 32 through 35 give a general description of the
state of the Church at Jerusalem. The conditions recorded here were not new—the *same* conditions existed
in the Church at its very beginning, immediately after
the coming of the Holy Spirit on the Day of Pentecost.

In chapter 2, verses 42 through 45, we notice four
things which characterized the infant Church:

First, the believers "continued stedfastly in the apostles' doctrine"—which does not mean that they simply
listened to the apostles' teaching, but that they *received*
it and *supported* that teaching by the witness of their
daily living.

Second, they continued stedfastly "in fellowship" — that is, "all that believed were together, *and had all things common.*"

Third, they continued *"breaking bread* from house to house, (and) did eat their meat with gladness and singleness of heart."

Fourth, they continued stedfastly *"in prayers . . .* praising God . . . and the Lord added to the Church daily such as should be saved."

The one hundred and twenty believers who went into the upper room on the Day of Pentecost were baptized into *one body* with Jesus as the head and every believer *a member* of that body, the result being that they were united in heart and mind, and continued stedfastly in fellowship.

Scholars declare that there is no richer word in the New Testament than the Greek word *koinonia* which is translated "fellowship." Since there is no single word that can convey all of the meaning, depth, and richness implied by the *Greek* word, it is translated in many ways—"fellowship . . . communion . . . communication . . . distribution . . . contribution . . . partakers . . . partners." The root of this word is found in our present verse—"they had all things *common.*" The Greek word here rendered "common" is the root from which *koinonia* comes; so we see that *fellowship* means "having all things common."

The deep and precious teaching here is that born again believers have *fellowship with God*—i. e., we have "all things common" with God. We are children of God *now* (I John 3:1,2). We are hid with Christ in God *now* (Col. 3:3). We are heirs of God *now* (Rom. 8:17). *All the resources* of God are at our disposal, and the resources of the child of God are entirely at *God's disposal.*

Pentecost brought the early Christians into new relationship with Christ, which resulted in a new relationship with God—and inevitably into new relationship with each other.   Therefore (and necessarily) they *"had all things common"* with each other.

The same is true today in the Church of the living God.   When we believe on the Lord Jesus Christ we are immediately baptized into the *body* of Christ (I Cor. 12:12,13).   We have a *new relationship* with Christ—we are *in Him* (Rom. 8:1), He is in *us* (Col. 1:27).   Since we have a new relationship with Christ, we also have a new relationship with God the heavenly Father, for *in Christ* we are "hid *with Him* in God" (Col. 3:3).

We are in Christ, He is in us, therefore we should walk as He walked. Writing to the believers at Ephesus, Paul urged them to walk *worthy of the calling* wherewith they were called, "with all lowliness and meekness, with longsuffering, forbearing one another in love; endeavouring to keep the unity of the Spirit in the bond of peace" (Eph. 4:1—3).

In the next verse he explained what he meant by "unity of the Spirit," declaring, "There is one body, and one Spirit."   That one body is Christ, and all believers are members of that body, being baptized into it by the Holy Spirit.

Paul then showed how Christians come *into* this oneness: There is *"one Lord* (Christ), *one faith* (trusting Him completely), *one baptism* (the baptism of the Spirit, making the individual one with Christ)."   And finally, Paul sets forth the *results* of this oneness with Christ: *"One God and Father of all, who is above all, and through all, and IN you all"* (Eph. 4:4—6).

Thus we have *koinonia*—fellowship, "all things common"—believers made partakers of divine nature (II Pet. 1:4); seeing the divine light in the Word (I John 1:7); feeling with divine love (I John 4:19); living with divine life because *Christ IS our life* (Col. 3:4).

These things furnish the *basis* for the communion ("all things common") of this chapter, and now we will see the *results* of this fellowship—its power, its principles, and its practice:

"The multitude of them that believed were of one heart and of one soul." The power in the lives of these early Christians was because they were *of one heart and of one soul,* but the initial fact is that they *believed.* Such fellowship is impossible except among truly born again believers, and it was the new birth that *made* these people of one heart and one soul.

The two phrases *"of one heart"* and *"of one soul"* were not carelessly selected by Luke; they were put here by the Holy Spirit. *The heart* is the emotional and inspirational center of the individual; from the heart proceed "the issues of life" (Prov. 4:23). *The soul* is the seat of love and hate—and it is the soul that is born from above, created new in Christ Jesus. Thus all believers have new life.

This particular group of Christians had not only believed for the salvation of the soul; they had submitted to *the Lordship of Jesus,* and therefore they were *of one heart,* moved by one great impulse. *One love* mastered them, holding complete control over each and every heart. They had one outlook, one inward consciousness, one inspirational motive. In all that they did and said they sought to please God rather than man, and to allow Jesus to be Lord of their lives.

These early Christians were also *unselfish*—and therein lies *the principle* of their activity: *"Neither said any of them that ought of the things which he possessed was his own."* The sad condition existing in this world today is that most people are so selfish and self-centered that they strive to *get all they can,* and they *keep* all they *get!* They share nothing with their fellowman. Admittedly, there *are* some unselfish people in the world today, but they are few and far between.

In this company of believers, no man claimed his possessions as his own because no man followed that line of thought. These people were so completely yielded to the Lord that every trace of selfishness was removed. The new heart and the divine life within had put an end to thinking of self. A corporate consciousness was prevalent in their hearts and minds, they *truly "had all things common."*

In I Corinthians 12:26 we read of the Church, "Whether one member suffer, all the members suffer with it; or one member be honoured, all the members rejoice with it." In the average church today, if one of the members suffers—whether it be physically or financially, enduring a long period of illness, losing home or business, experiencing some personal tragedy—the other members *discuss* that individual's misfortune, they extend their sympathy, they may even take an offering or sponsor a "pounding" to provide clothing, food, and other commodities to help that one in need; but this is not the idea presented by the early believers.

They were wholly yielded to the lordship of Jesus, therefore they were *one.* They lived with the deep conviction of the spiritual over the material. They believed the truth of the words of Jesus in Matthew 16:26: "What is a man profited, if he shall gain the whole world, and lose his own soul?"

They also believed the principle of I John 3:17: "Whoso hath this world's good, and seeth his brother have need, and shutteth up his bowels of compassion from him, *how dwelleth the love of God in him?"* God gave Jesus, who suffered that we might have this glorious salvation with all the good gifts that go along with it. These early Christians were so completely mastered by the spiritual power within them that they clung lightly to the things of this world. It has been said that the more lightly we cling to this world, the firmer our grip on God and things eternal. Material possessions were secondary to these believers; *spiritual attainment* was the dominating force in their lives. They lived as though they possessed nothing—*but in reality they possessed*

ALL things!

Verse 33: *"And with great power gave the apostles witness of the resurrection of the Lord Jesus: and great grace was upon them all."*

The preaching of the resurrection of the Lord Jesus Christ was made powerful by the spirituality of those who gave the message. Their preaching had evidence of divine life in perfect harmony with the life of Christ. *Their lives and their message* proclaimed their possession of divine love—the master passion of all true spiritual activity.

"Great grace was upon them all." A distinct and singular beauty and glory was manifested in the character of these believers, a beauty and glory that could only be made possible by grace; and this gave power to their testimony.

Verses 34 and 35: *"Neither was there any among them that lacked: for as many as were possessors of lands or houses sold them, and brought the prices of the things that were sold, and laid them down at the apostles' feet: and distribution was made unto every man according as he had need."*

We are not told that these men sold *all* that they had. It is possible that such was the case, but more than likely they sold a *portion* of their possessions, and the sum realized from the sale made up the common fund. We do not read of a similar fund being raised anywhere other than in Jerusalem.

The money acquired from the sale of these houses and lands was brought and laid *"at the apostles' feet"*— an act whereby the believers gave the apostles undisputed and absolute control over the bestowal of these sums of money.

"And distribution was made unto every man according as he had need." (The Greek reads, "unto each accord-

ing as *any* had need.") In other words, when any believer in that company had need, that need was met
with funds from the common treasury.   There were undoubtedly many who were not in need, and they of course
lived from their own income.   The "distribution" was
intended only for the needy—widows, others who had
specific needs, and those who could not support themselves while they took part in preaching the Gospel and
spreading the good news that Jesus saves.   It is also
possible that some of these saints had lost their means
of earning a livelihood when they embraced Christianity.
In John 9:22 we are told that the parents of the blind
man to whom Jesus gave sight would not testify as to
who had healed their son "because they feared the Jews:
for the Jews had agreed already, that *if any man did
confess that He was Christ, he should be put out of the
synagogue.*"   It is not unreasonable to suppose that
some among this company of believers had become little
more than outcasts when they accepted Christ and took
up their new way of life in following Him.

Verses 36 and 37:   *"And Joses, who by the apostles
was surnamed Barnabas, (which is, being interpreted, The
son of consolation,) a Levite, and of the country of Cyprus, having land, sold it, and brought the money, and
laid it at the apostles' feet."*

Many manuscripts read *"Joseph"* instead of *Joses.*
This man is probably pointed out here because he was
a foreigner—that is, he was not a native of Jerusalem.
His selling of houses and lands was a remarkable in-
cidence of sacrificial liberality on the part of a believer.
He gave himself wholly, even unto his property, in the
service of the Lord Jesus Christ, went forth to preach
the Gospel, and distinguished himself in the work of
the ministry in a very unusual way, as we will learn
later.

"Joses, who by the apostles was surnamed Barnabas

. . . ." The giving of surnames was widely practiced in that day, the surname being made expressive of the character of the person to whom it was given. *"Barnabas"* is a name taken from two Syriac words, the first word meaning "son" and the second word meaning "prophecy." Thus *Barnabas* denotes "the son of prophecy." The Greek word here translated "consolation" means literally "exhortation, entreaty, petition, or advocacy." We find this applied to Barnabas in Acts 11:22,23, where the church in Jerusalem sent him to Antioch, where "when he came, and had seen the grace of God, was glad, *and EXHORTED them all,* that with purpose of heart they would cleave unto the Lord."

"A Levite, and of the country of Cyprus." The entire tribe of Levi was set apart for the service of the temple and the Jewish religion. The three sons of Levi were Gershon, Kohath, and Merari. It was from the family of Kohath that Aaron, the first high priest, was descended, and his eldest son succeeded him. The other sons of Aaron were also priests. All of the others of that tribe were called Levites and all were employed in the work of the temple, assisting the priest in performing the sacred music and carrying on other activities in the temple (and earlier in the tabernacle). In connection with this, please study Numbers chapter 3, Deuteronomy 12:18,19; 18:6—8; and I Chronicles chapters 23 and 24.

Cyprus is one of the largest islands in the Mediterranean Sea. It is extremely fertile and abounds in such products as wine, oil, and many other useful and important commodities.

Historians tell us that there were many Jews on the island of Cyprus, and we know from Acts 13:4 that Paul and Barnabas were sent there by the Holy Ghost when Paul took his first missionary journey. Then in Acts 15:39—41 we read that Barnabas again went to Cyprus to preach, taking Mark with him while Paul and Silas "went through Syria and Cilicia."

Barnabas is mentioned with honor in a number of places in the New Testament. (Study Acts 11:22–30.) He is generally associated with the Apostle Paul as a traveling companion on Paul's first missionary journey. The church in Jerusalem sent him to Antioch where, under his exhortation, "much people was added unto the Lord" (Acts 11:24). The same verse tells us that "he was a good man, and full of the Holy Ghost and of faith."

From Antioch he went to Tarsus to seek Paul. Having found him, he brought that apostle back to Antioch, where for a year they worked with the church there, "and taught much people. And the disciples were called *Christians* first in Antioch" (Acts 11:25,26).

Thus began the association of Paul and Barnabas in the ministry of the Gospel, and they traveled together in fellowship and harmony until a dispute came between them concerning John Mark. It was then that Barnabas took young Mark and sailed for Cyprus, and Paul traveled with Silas on his second missionary journey (Acts 15:35–41). Also study Acts 12:25; 13:1,2,50; 14:12; I Corinthians 9:6; and Galatians 2:1–9.

An interesting side-note here is that Paul and Barnabas were both born in heathen countries. They were Jews, but they were not born in Palestine. The fact that part of their life and training was in other countries helped to qualify them for their ministry which was primarily to the Gentiles.

Barnabas was a landowner—to what extent we are not told; but in verse 37 of this chapter we read that he, *"having land, sold it, and brought the money, and laid it at the apostles' feet."* A man of property, Barnabas gave up all for the sake of the ministry in the name of the Lord Jesus Christ. When Jesus became the Saviour of his soul, He also became the Lord of his life. We are not told that *Paul owned* property, and what we know of his means of earning a livelihood is given in his epistles to the different churches, declaring that he supported himself in his ministry by working as a tent maker (Acts 18:3; II Cor. 11:9; I Thess. 2:9).

I fear some ministers today have allowed property, houses, and earthly possessions to come between them and their ministry. God forbid that I judge any man—and heaven bears me record that I have no particular individual in mind—but I believe that sometimes the ministry becomes a sideline. Preachers enter the business world, and preaching becomes a "hobby" with them. If God calls a man, He never withdraws His call. Therefore, any minister who puts property—or anything else—ahead of his ministry and his devotion to God will certainly suffer loss!

I know most successful ministers could have acquired much more of this world's goods in professions other than the ministry, for as a rule, preaching the Gospel is a work of self-denial. *No man* should enter the ministry unless he is sure that he has been called of God and unless he is willing to surrender all that he has to God!

We need to realize, as did these early Christians in Jerusalem, that *true* possessions are in heaven. Our citizenship is in heaven, our Saviour is in heaven. We are members of His body, and we are seated in heavenly places with Him.

It is true that the full revelation had not been given to these saints in Jerusalem, they did not have the New Testament, the completed Word of God; but what they knew of the Lord Jesus Christ, His bodily resurrection and His place at the right hand of God the Father, was sufficient to cause them to lose sight of earthly things and fix their eyes on things eternal. The Holy Spirit made Jesus so *real* to them that through His power they were enabled to bear witness to the truth—boldly and with conviction. The fact that these Christians believed in the bodily resurrection of Jesus separated them from all other religions of their day, and it was because of this belief that "great grace was upon them all."

That same faith should cause *us* to cling lightly to things of earth, and in these days when we *know* the Lord's second coming is even at the door we should set our affections on things above and pray with John the Beloved, "Even so, Come, Lord Jesus!"

CHAPTER V

1. But a certain man named Ananias, with Sapphira his wife, sold a possession,

2. And kept back part of the price, his wife also being privy to it, and brought a certain part, and laid it at the apostles' feet.

3. But Peter said, Ananias, why hath Satan filled thine heart to lie to the Holy Ghost, and to keep back part of the price of the land?

4. Whiles it remained, was it not thine own? and after it was sold, was it not in thine own power? why hast thou conceived this thing in thine heart? thou hast not lied unto men, but unto God.

5. And Ananias hearing these words fell down, and gave up the ghost: and great fear came on all them that heard these things.

6. And the young men arose, wound him up, and carried him out, and buried him.

7. And it was about the space of three hours after, when his wife, not knowing what was done, came in.

8. And Peter answered unto her, Tell me whether ye sold the land for so much? And she said, Yea, for so much.

9. Then Peter said unto her, How is it that ye have agreed together to tempt the Spirit of the Lord? behold, the feet of them which have buried thy husband are at the door, and shall carry thee out.

10. Then fell she down straightway at his feet, and yielded up the ghost: and the young men came in, and found her dead, and, carrying her forth, buried her by her husband.

11. And great fear came upon all the church, and upon as many as heard these things.

12. And by the hands of the apostles were many signs and wonders wrought among the people; (and they were all with one accord in Solomon's porch.

13. And of the rest durst no man join himself to them: but the people magnified them.

14. And believers were the more added to the Lord, multitudes both of men and women.)

15. Insomuch that they brought forth the sick into the streets, and laid them on beds and couches, that at the least the shadow of Peter passing by might overshadow some of them.

16. There came also a multitude out of the cities round about unto Jerusalem, bringing sick folks, and them which were vexed with unclean spirits: and they were healed every one.

17. Then the high priest rose up, and all they that were with him, (which is the sect of the Sadducees,) and were filled with indignation,

18. And laid their hands on the apostles, and put them in the common prison.

19. But the angel of the Lord by night opened the prison doors, and brought them forth, and said,

20. Go, stand and speak in the temple to the people all the words of this life.

21. And when they heard that, they entered into the temple early in the morning, and taught. But the high priest came, and they that were with him, and called the council together, and all the senate of the children of Israel, and sent to the prison to have them brought.

22. But when the officers came, and found them not in the prison, they returned, and told,

23. Saying, The prison truly found we shut with all safety, and the keepers standing without before the doors: but when we had opened, we found no man within.

24. Now when the high priest and the captain of the temple and the chief priests heard these things, they doubted of them whereunto this would grow.

25. Then came one and told them, saying, Behold, the men whom ye put in prison are standing in the temple, and teaching the people.

26. Then went the captain with the officers, and brought them without violence: for they feared the people, lest they should have been stoned.

27. And when they had brought them, they set them before the council: and the high priest asked them,

28. Saying, Did not we straitly command you that ye should not teach in this name? and, behold, ye have filled Jerusalem with your doctrine, and intend to bring this man's blood upon us.

29. Then Peter and the other apostles answered and said, We ought to obey God rather than men.

30. The God of our fathers raised up Jesus, whom ye slew and hanged on a tree.

31. Him hath God exalted with his right hand to be a Prince

and a Saviour, for to give repentance to Israel, and forgiveness of sins.

32. And we are his witnesses of these things; and so is also the Holy Ghost, whom God hath given to them that obey him.

33. When they heard that, they were cut to the heart, and took counsel to slay them.

34. Then stood there up one in the council, a Pharisee, named Gamaliel, a doctor of the law, had in reputation among all the people, and commanded to put the apostles forth a little space;

35. And said unto them, Ye men of Israel, take heed to yourselves what ye intend to do as touching these men.

36. For before these days rose up Theudas, boasting himself to be somebody; to whom a number of men, about four hundred, joined themselves: who was slain; and all, as many as obeyed him, were scattered, and brought to nought.

37. After this man rose up Judas of Galilee in the days of the taxing, and drew away much people after him: he also perished; and all, even as many as obeyed him, were dispersed.

38. And now I say unto you, Refrain from these men, and let them alone: for if this counsel or this work be of men, it will come to nought:

39. But if it be of God, ye cannot overthrow it; lest haply ye be found even to fight against God.

40. And to him they agreed: and when they had called the apostles, and beaten them, they commanded that they should not speak in the name of Jesus, and let them go.

41. And they departed from the presence of the council, rejoicing that they were counted worthy to suffer shame for his name.

42. And daily in the temple, and in every house, they ceased not to teach and preach Jesus Christ.

Chapter 4 closed with the description of the unity of heart, soul, and spirit which prevailed among the believers in the first assembly of the New Testament Church, and verse 31 of that chapter expressly declared that they were *"ALL filled with the Holy Ghost."*

But as among the twelve apostles of Jesus there was a Judas, so in the infant Church there were at least two persons whose professions were not sincere, and who proved themselves unworthy of the gifts of grace which the true believers had received through faith in the finished work of the Lord Jesus Christ.

The sin committed by Ananias and Sapphira not only showed contempt for God and vanity and ambition toward themselves; it also bespoke utter disregard for the corruption they were bringing into the local assembly and for the reproach they were bringing upon the name of Jesus! These two people possessed light—i. e., they were exposed to the miracles and workings of the Holy Spirit in the lives of the true believers. Therefore the sin they committed in spite of the light they had received called for special and divine indignation in order to show God's terrible judgment upon those who sin against the Holy Ghost.

For me, the record given here is proof positive that the Bible is verbally inspired, the true and absolute Word of God; for if it were simply a chronicled account written by great historians they would surely have omitted the incidents recorded in the first eleven verses of this chapter! I personally believe the Holy Spirit ordered the writing of the account of the sin of Ananias and Sapphira as a grave warning to the early believers—as well as a warning for believers in this day.

The Sin and Death of Ananias and Sapphira

Verses 1 and 2: *"But a certain man named Ananias, with Sapphira his wife, sold a possession, and kept back part of the price, his wife also being privy to it, and brought a certain part, and laid it at the apostles' feet."*

It is not by way of contrast that the account of Ananias and Sapphira is put side by side with that of Barnabas in verses 36 and 37 of chapter 4; therefore we are not to place undue emphasis on the word "but" with which this verse begins. In the original Greek, verse 36 of chapter 4 begins with the same conjunction, one which is often used in narratives where only a simple connection of two clauses is intended. Such is the case here.

"Ananias" was a common name in that day—notice

Acts 9:10—17 and 23:2. The name *"Sapphira"* was probably derived from the sapphire stone, and the word is found in the Hebrew Scriptures as well as in the New Testament Greek.

Ananias and Sapphira *"sold a possession."* The Scripture does not tell us what kind of possession they sold. It could have been houses, or lands, or any other kind of personal property. The same Greek word is used in the account of the rich young man who came running to Jesus, fell at His feet, and asked what good thing he might do to inherit eternal life; and when Jesus told him *the one thing he MUST do* "he went away sorrowful: for he had great *possessions"* (Matt. 19:22; Mark 10:22). In the Old Testament, the corresponding Hebrew word is sometimes used with reference to great vineyards.

Whatever Ananias and Sapphira sold was their own personal property; but when they brought the proceeds to lay at the apostles' feet *they "kept back part of the price."* The Scripture gives no suggestion as to the amount of money these people acquired from the sale of their property—it might have been only a small sum, it could have been a great deal. Whatever their selling price, it is more reasonable to assume that they would have given the greater part of it to the Church and kept back only a small sum, because they could not hope to get by with keeping back a greater portion than they gave to the Church. They would have been caught in their act of deceit—and this they certainly hoped to avoid.

The Greek word here translated *"kept back"* is the same word used in Titus 2:10 where it is rendered "purloin," and it is frequently translated "to rob." So regardless of the amount of money Ananias and Sapphira kept back—whether a large sum or only a few paltry coins—they were robbing God because they professed that they were bringing the entire proceeds into the treasury of the Church.

"His wife also being privy to it . . . ." tells us that

this was not a sin committed on the spur of the moment. Ananias and his wife had talked about this transaction, they had deliberately planned together and agreed one with the other that they would commit this act of fraud.

The Scriptures do not tell us what this couple hoped to gain by such deception. Evidently (from the closing verses of chapter 4) they had witnessed the believers' selling possessions and giving the money into the Church, and perhaps they hoped to gain recognition, praise, and commendation among the others by giving what was supposed to be their entire estate.

There is no use in speculating on what Ananias and Sapphira thought they would gain by their deception, but one thing is certain: They thought more of the display of laying the money at the apostles' feet than they thought of the offense against God. They were thinking of the impression they would make on those who saw them give their money, instead of thinking of the eyes of Almighty God looking down upon them as they committed this sin.

Peter understood that such men would soon arise in the local assemblies. In II Peter 2:1−3 he wrote, "But there were false prophets also among the people, *even as there SHALL BE false teachers among you,* who privily shall bring in damnable heresies, even denying the Lord that bought them *and bring upon themselves swift destruction.* And many shall follow their pernicious ways; by reason of whom the way of truth shall be evil spoken of. And *through covetousness* shall they with feigned words make merchandise of you: whose judgment now of a long time lingereth not, and their damnation slumbereth not."

Jude also spoke of such persons. In Jude 11 we read, "Woe unto them! for they have gone in the way of Cain, and ran greedily after the error of Balaam for reward, and perished in the gainsaying of Core."

Therefore in the case of Ananias and Sapphira we see

an example and typical instance of the kind of offense into which men of that day were in danger of being tempted. Since some of the true believers were selling their possessions and bringing the money to lay at the apostles' feet, there was a temptation for those who were insincere, not truly converted, to try to gain popularity and prestige by pretending to do the same.

Verse 3: *"But Peter said, Ananias, why hath Satan filled thine heart to lie to the Holy Ghost, and to keep back part of the price of the land?"*

Greek scholars tell us that the strength of the interrogative participle used here seems to indicate that there had been a possibility of Ananias' resisting the influence of Satan—that is, had he wanted to overcome this temptation he could have done so.

"Why hath Satan filled thine heart to lie to the Holy Ghost?" From Peter's question here it is clear that the Holy Spirit had given him knowledge of the deception which these people planned and agreed to carry out, and it is also clear that the Spirit had made known to Peter that punishment would surely follow and that judgment was sure to fall upon Ananias and Sapphira. If this were not true, how are we to explain Peter's calm manner and total lack of surprise when, in the following verses, such startling judgment fell so suddenly upon them?

It was the power of the Holy Ghost that was manifested in the apostles and the other believers in the early New Testament Church. As we read of the first days of Christianity and the ministry of the apostles, we note over and over again that they claimed no power within themselves, but always attributed their miracles and successes to the power of the Holy Spirit. The growth of the infant Church was because of the working of the Holy Spirit. Therefore Peter declared that Ananias had been tempted of Satan to *lie* to the Holy Ghost in professing to give the whole price of his property as a gift of brotherly love to the Church, when his actual aim was to glean for himself and his wife the credit and approval of the assembly of believers while still holding back a portion of what he professed to give.

Verse 4:   *"Whiles it remained, was it not thine own? and after it was sold, was it not in thine own power? Why hast thou conceived this thing in thine heart?   Thou hast not lied unto men, but unto God."*

The Greek reads here, "Whiles it *remained,* did it not *remain thine own?"*   Notice the verb in the Greek is repeated, showing that there was no compulsion put on Ananias to force him to sell his property.   The only thing expected of him was honesty in his report on what he had done—and even if he felt led to sell his property there is no suggestion that he was expected to give the entire proceeds to the Church.   Such a gift was between him and the Holy Spirit.   This is certainly implied in the words of our text, which declare that the money received from any sale of property was at the seller's disposal until he, led by the Holy Spirit, gave the money into the treasury of the young Church.   He was not obligated to donate *all* of the price received—but *he was duty bound to be honest* in what he did!

"Why hast thou conceived this thing in thine heart?" We find here the same expression used several times in the Hebrew language of the Old Testament—as in Haggai 1:5, 7:   "Consider your ways."   The meaning, "Lay it deep in the heart, decide after deep deliberation."   Thus the sin of Ananias and Sapphira was not a case of yielding to sudden temptation, but an act from the heart after much planning and deliberation.

"Thou hast not lied unto men, but unto God."   Here is weighty Gospel and doctrinal truth set forth.   This statement proves the deity of the Holy Spirit.   The men whom Ananias attempted to deceive were men in whom God dwelt in the Person of the Holy Spirit, men whom

God had appointed as His undershepherds. Therefore Ananias and Sapphira lied—not to men, but to God and to the Holy Spirit.

Verse 5: *"And Ananias hearing these words fell down, and gave up the ghost: and great fear came on all them that heard these things."*

The only honest interpretation of the Scripture here is that the sudden death of Ananias (and shortly the death of Sapphira) was beyond question supernaturally inflicted. Some people attempt to explain these deaths on natural grounds, saying that this couple died from the horror of being found out; but it is certainly unreasonable to suppose that a man and his wife would be of the same temperament and thus die in the same way because they were caught in an act of despicable deceit! No, there is no *natural* explanation for the death of Ananias and his wife.

We must bear in mind that this was Satan's first attempt to obtain, through hypocrisy, a footing among the believers in the infant Church, and it was absolutely necessary that such an attempt be dealt with immediately and severely. God did just that in allowing the sudden death of Ananias and Sapphira. They were both smitten through the power of the Holy Spirit whom they had intended to deceive.

We find an account in the Old Testament of like character and severity in the penalty inflicted upon Aaron's sons, Nadab and Abihu, at the beginning of the Jewish priesthood. In Leviticus 10:1, 2 we read, "Nadab and Abihu, the sons of Aaron, took either of them his censer, and put fire therein, and put incense thereon, and offered strange fire before the Lord, which He commanded them not. And there went out fire from the Lord, and devoured them, and they died before the Lord."

The way in which Aaron and his family were forbidden to mourn for those whom God so severely punished and swiftly judged shows what interpretation should be put upon the judgment God inflicted upon Ananias and Sapphira. Their deaths were unquestionably by the hand of God. He cut them off in severe judgment as an example to His infant Church lest others commit the same sin. God increased His Church through miracles—healing of the sick, raising of the dead, feeding of the hungry. In like manner He sent sudden judgment to save His Church from the hypocrisy of evil men who would *turn the grace of our God into lasciviousness* (Jude 4). Even in spite of such judgment, there were those in the Corinthian church who were gluttons at the Lord's table, drinking to excess, making mockery of the Lord's Supper. To the Corinthians therefore Paul said, "For this cause many are weak and sickly among you, *and many sleep* (are dead)" (I Cor. 11:17—30).

Verse 6: *"And the young men arose, wound him up, and carried him out, and buried him."*

Some people suggest that these young men were connected with the Church and that it was their business to bury the dead; but this seems very unlikely, all things considered. In Acts 6:1—6, deacons were elected to serve tables and take care of other matters, that the apostles might give themselves wholly to prayer and to the study of the Word. It is indeed doubtful that there were special people to take care of funerals at that early stage in the growth of the Church. The meaning here simply seems to be that the younger members of the Church picked up the body of Ananias, wrapped him in the robe he was wearing at the time he entered the church, carried him out, and buried him.

In that day the dead were usually buried in caves. (John 11:38 tells us that such was the tomb of Lazarus.) It required but little preparation to make the caves ready to receive the dead, and they were closed by simply placing a large stone over the entrance. Thus it is understandable that Ananias was buried so quickly after his death. Little time would be required to complete the entire work of burial, and in that day—especially in hot climates—burial must take place very quickly after death.

It is interesting that there is no suggestion of Peter's reading a few verses of Scripture, praying a prayer or making a few remarks to the effect that Ananias was "not all bad" and that he had "done some good" in his life! Ananias committed a terrible sin, he was immediately judged by the mighty hand of God, the episode itself preached a much louder sermon than Peter could have preached, and there was nothing more to be said. They simply buried him.

Verse 7: *"And it was about the space of three hours after, when his wife, not knowing what was done, came in."*

We are not told why Ananias and Sapphira did not attend the meeting together; but whatever the reason, it was about three hours after the death of her husband that Sapphira came in, *"not knowing what was done."* The news of Ananias' death had not reached her.

Verse 8: *"And Peter answered unto her, Tell me whether ye sold the land for so much? And she said, Yea, for so much."*

The use of the English verb *"answered,"* where no question or remark precedes it, is found many places in the Bible—as in Daniel 2:14, 15 and in Luke 3:16. Peter was not actually *answering* a question, but *asking* one. He was actually asking Sapphira, *"Did you sell the land for so much?"* This alone should have aroused suspicion on her part. She should have suspected that the scheme she and Ananias had worked out had been discovered and that Peter knew they had not brought all the money received from the sale of their property.

But if Sapphira did suspect that the fraud had been

found out she gave no evidence of it.   She answered Peter's question firmly: *"Yea, for so much."*

Verse 9:   *"Then Peter said unto her, How is it that ye have agreed together to tempt the Spirit of the Lord? Behold, the feet of them which have buried thy husband are at the door, and shall carry thee out."*

Undoubtedly Ananias and Sapphira had witnessed some of the miracles wrought through the power of the Holy Spirit as the apostles preached the Gospel throughout the community; and to try the omniscience of the Holy Spirit who so forcibly *dwelt IN the apostles and in the Church* was, in truth, to tempt the Spirit of God. Theirs was not the sin of blasphemy against the Holy Spirit, but closely akin to it.

Sapphira's answer to Peter's question convinced the apostle that this was not the individual lie of an ungodly and covetous husband, but rather a deliberate sin committed after an agreement between man and wife—a cleverly planned scheme to deceive the believers and rob God.   Peter therefore said to Sapphira: *"Behold, the feet of them which have buried thy husband are at the door, and shall carry THEE out!"*

This does not necessarily mean that Peter actually heard the approaching footsteps of the young men who had buried Ananias.   The chances are that they were barefooted—or shod with sandals, as was the custom in that day.   Peter simply meant that the men who had just buried Ananias were approaching the assembly and would also carry Sapphira out.   We are not sure that Peter knew what would happen to Ananias, but the Holy Spirit made known to him that Sapphira would die—and would be buried by the same young men who had buried her husband.

Verse 10:   *"Then fell she down straightway at his feet, and yielded up the ghost: and the young men came in, and found her dead, and, carrying her forth, buried her by her husband."*

This verse speaks for itself. We would assume that the worship service was still in progress and the congregation still assembled when the young men returned from burying Ananias. Evidently Peter was still standing at the front of the assembly hall, and when the young men returned to join the worshippers they found Sapphira lying dead at Peter's feet. So they picked her up and carried her out, to bury her beside her husband.

Verse 11: *"And great fear came upon all the Church, and upon as many as heard these things."*

The deaths of Ananias and Sapphira were not the work of man, but were wrought by the mighty hand of God in swift judgment. Thus did the incident serve as a severe warning to anyone who might be tempted to commit such a sin in the future. *"Great fear"* came upon all who witnessed the immediate and terrible judgment that befell this couple, and upon all who *heard* of it.

Sin and death are synonymous. "The wages of sin is death" (Rom. 6:23), and "sin, when it is finished, bringeth forth death" (James 1:15). Ananias and Sapphira reaped the wages of sin although they reaped a bit more swiftly than most people do; and the question is often asked, "Why did God deal so suddenly and so harshly with these two people?" It has been suggested that He might have *disciplined* them and then restored them to full fellowship and communion in the church. The truth of the matter is, this man and his wife were never actually *IN* the *Church.* They were present in body but not in spirit. They could not receive Christian discipline because they were not born again Christians.

I am well aware that some Bible scholars believe and teach that Ananias and Sapphira committed the sin unto death, but I disagree. In the light of the Scriptures, I do not believe they were ever genuinely born again. I do not doubt that they were meeting with the local assembly—this is evidenced by the fact that they knew about the gifts being brought in by the believers and presented to the Church to be distributed among other believers who had little of this world's goods. Unity of spirit among these first Christians was one of the most outstanding characteristics of the early Church. They were "of one heart and of one soul . . . they had all things common" (Acts 4:32).

The devil despises unity, he hates harmony, he is the author and promoter of discord and strife—*and he can always do more damage from within than from without.* Therefore he spoke to the hearts of Ananias and Sapphira who were meeting with the assembly but were never truly born of the Spirit. They listened to Satan, their hearts were filled with covetousness, and they entered into his scheme to disrupt the harmony and destroy the unity in the infant Church.

Now notice the first question Peter asked Ananias: "Why hath Satan *FILLED THINE HEART* to lie to the Holy Ghost?" He did not ask, "Ananias, why did Satan lead you to lie?" According to Peter's words, Satan *filled the heart* of Ananias—which means that he completely possessed and controlled his heart. We know that a born again believer could not be possessed and controlled by the devil, nor could the devil *fill the heart* of a true believer. The Scripture is very plain on this subject.

Believers are led by the Holy Spirit (Rom. 8:14), possessors of divine nature (II Pet. 1:4), new creations in Christ Jesus (II Cor. 5:17). Therefore if Ananias had been a true believer Satan could not have filled his heart. He might have *tempted* him, but he could not have filled and possessed his heart with the scheme to rob God and commit a sin that would bring terrible reproach upon the young Church and upon the name of the Lord Jesus Christ, the head and foundation of the Church.

Paul plainly declared, "As many as are *LED by the*

Spirit of God, they are the sons of God" (Rom. 8:14). Certainly if Ananias and Sapphira were children of God, they would have been led by the Holy Spirit; and the Holy Spirit would not have led them to lie to Himself. Born again believers can grieve the Spirit or quench the Spirit, but no born again Christian will attempt to *lie* to the Spirit. The true believer possesses divine nature through the indwelling of the Holy Spirit.

There are many people in the churches today, as every true pastor knows, who outwardly appear to be Christians—they have church membership, they have been baptized, they give their money and they attend the services; but inwardly they have never received the Holy Spirit through the miracle of the new birth. However, in the first days of Christianity the Church was as God intended His Church to be. The discerning Spirit was surely and clearly at work, and the atmosphere in that Church was such that it was impossible for a man to come into the assembly with a lie in his heart and a profession on his lips. Such a person would most assuredly be detected.

What so overwhelms me and fills me with awe is not the fact that Ananias and Sapphira dropped dead for their sin, but the fact that the Church was so pure, so completely controlled by the Spirit of God, that the purity of the Church compelled the deaths of those two who lied to the Holy Ghost. It was not by law that they died, but by the hand of God, who would not allow deceit and dishonesty to enter the atmosphere in which the early Church was living and working. When God drove Adam and Eve from the Garden of Eden He placed cherubim at the gate, with a flaming sword that turned every way, to keep the way of the tree of life, lest Adam return to the garden and eat of the fruit of the tree of life. At the entrance to His Church God placed the body of Christ and the discerning omniscience of the Holy Ghost, and it was impossible for a man to become a member of that Church when he held a lie in his heart.

How sad that the local church today has become so dangerously weak in the matter of discipline that men are welcomed into fellowship whether or not they have been born again! In the local assemblies today we find a mixed multitude, and as a result the church has lost the respect it once had. Certainly the Holy Spirit does not operate in assemblies today as He did when the Church of the living God was so pure and holy that a hypocrite like Ananias could not enter without being detected and judged.

The Miraculous Power of the Apostles; Continued Growth of the Church

Verse 12: *"And by the hands of the apostles were many signs and wonders wrought among the people; and they were all with one accord in Solomon's porch."*

"By the hands of the apostles" does not necessarily mean that these "signs and wonders" were wrought by the *laying on* of hands — and certainly it does not mean that they were wrought through the *power* of the hands of the apostles. It simply means that God, working *through* the apostles, wrought signs and wonders among the people.

However, in both the Old and New Testaments, we read of the practice of the laying on of hands. Concerning the appointment of Joshua, we read, "The Lord said unto Moses, Take thee Joshua the son of Nun, a man in whom is the Spirit, *and LAY THINE HAND upon him;* and set him before Eleazar the priest, and before all the congregation; and give him a charge in their sight" (Num. 27:18, 19).

When the Levites were set aside for the priesthood, the Lord instructed Moses, "Thou shalt bring the Levites before the Lord: and the children of Israel shall put their hands upon the Levites: and Aaron shall offer the

Levites before the Lord for an offering of the children of
Israel, that they may execute the service of the Lord"
(Num. 8:10, 11).

During the earthly ministry of Jesus, He often laid
His hands *upon the sick,* and in Mark 16:18 He said of
His disciples, "They shall *lay hands on the sick,* and
they shall recover."   However, verse 15 of our present
chapter proves that the multitudes believed that their
sick loved ones could be healed *without* the touch of
the hands of the apostles, for they laid the sick on cots
and couches in the streets so that even the *shadow* of
Peter might pass over them.

*"And they were all with one accord in Solomon's
porch."*   The *"all"* here refers to those who were true
members of the infant Church through faith in the shed
blood and finished work of the Lord Jesus Christ.   Such
an assembly was held by the apostles for the purpose
of conferring with each other and for instruction, prayer,
and fellowship among the believers. In other words, they
came to Solomon's porch to teach and be taught — and
with one common purpose: to learn more about the Lord
Jesus Christ and the things of God; but Solomon's porch
was not the only meeting place of the early Christians,
nor was it their regular meeting place.   They met in
homes and in various other places.

Verse 13:   *"And of the rest durst no man join himself
to them: but the people magnified them."*

In the Greek, this statement begins with the conjunction *"but,"* and is not intended to convey opposition
to what was said in the preceding verse.   The Christians
made Solomon's porch their meeting place when they
went up to the temple, but *"of the rest durst no man
join himself to them."*   In other words, there were other
people also in the temple, but those who had not yet
become Christians did not venture to join themselves in-
trusively to the meetings held by the apostles and other

believers.   They left the worshippers to themselves, not attempting to unite with their company.

"But the people magnified them."   The meaning is simply that the people in the temple who were not members of the New Testament Church did not press themselves into the company of believers, although they greatly admired and praised them for the great works they were doing.   Multitudes admired the Christians for the mighty miracles they had seen and heard, but they did not join them at first.

Verse 14:   *"And believers were the more added to the Lord, multitudes both of men and women."*

People heard and believed the Word as preached by Peter and the other apostles, and were added to the Lord's Church day by day.   As stated in Acts 2:47, "the Lord added to the Church daily such as (were being) saved."

This sheds light on what was said in verse 13.   The "joining" mentioned there referred to an intrusion into the congregation when the believers were assembled for public instruction and prayer.   Those outside the Church did not intrude—but great numbers *believed* as they heard the Word, and the Church increased rapidly.   The believers in that day were held in such reverent regard and respect by people outside the Church that the faith they preached and the lives they lived gained multitudes of converts.

Verse 15:   *"Insomuch that they brought forth the sick into the streets, and laid them on beds and couches, that at the least the shadow of Peter passing by might overshadow some of them."*

The people who witnessed the ministry and miracles of the disciples had very high respect for this new "religion"—and I use that term knowingly, because to most of them that is exactly what it was: a new *"religion."*

They had not yet learned the full meaning of Christianity, but so great was their admiration and respect for this new way of life that they brought forth their sick loved ones and laid them on beds and couches in the streets, "that at the least *the shadow of Peter passing by might overshadow some of them!*" The words in this verse describe one of the ways in which the early believers gave evidence of their faith in the Lord Jesus Christ.

We have no clear statement of healings wrought through Peter's shadow passing over the sick, but we have no reason to doubt that God honored the faith of the people who brought them there. Jesus honored the faith of the four friends of the palsied man in Mark 2:1—5; why should He not honor the faith of these who brought their loved ones into the street on couches and cots, that the shadow of Peter might fall on them as he passed by!

Peter is named here, the other apostles are not. We can assume that Peter was the most prominent figure among the twelve, and certainly on many occasions he was spokesman for the group; but we are not to suppose that the others did no mighty works. I have not the slightest doubt that they wrought miracles just as Peter did.

Peter himself was not the healing power, but rather the instrument through which God worked. When the children of Israel in the wilderness were dying from serpents' bites, it was not the serpent of brass that healed them, but their obedience to the Word of God as given to them through His servant Moses. So it was with Peter. He was God's servant, and God worked mighty miracles through him.

Verse 16: *"There came also a multitude out of the cities round about unto Jerusalem, bringing sick folks, and them which were vexed with unclean spirits: and they were healed every one."*

The word *"city"* is commonly used in the Scriptures even when referring to a very small community such as Nazareth (Matt. 2:23), the city of Nain (Luke 7:11), and Arimathea (Luke 23:51). There were many such "cities" round about Jerusalem, and the people came from these neighboring communities to hear the apostles and to bring their sick loved ones to be healed.

They also brought *"them which were vexed with unclean spirits."* The multitudes recognized the fact that the power of the apostles and other believers went beyond the healing of *physical* illness. The miracles they wrought were of a supernatural character, and the nature of the signs and wonders which accompanied the miracles declared that they were wrought by divine power—the same power recognized in Christ's own life and confessed to be the power of the Son of God (Luke 4:41). Therefore the people also brought to the disciples those who were demon possessed, that they, too, might be healed by the mighty power of God.

The Greek verb here translated *"vexed"* is also found in Luke 6:18, and was used frequently in the works of Greek medical writers of that day. So it is not surprising that the physician Luke used the word in describing the sickness of demon-possession which beset many people.

These *"unclean spirits"* are also referred to as *"wicked"* spirits (Matt. 12:45), and as *"evil"* spirits (Luke 8:2). They were probably called *"unclean* spirits" because a demon-possessed person often wandered into places where he became ceremonially defiled, as was the case of the demoniac who lived among the tombs. (Read the account in Mark 5:1—20.) Demon possession caused this man to dwell among the graves, and he was therefore defiled by coming in contact with dead bodies.

It is no wonder they were called *"wicked"* spirits, considering the terrible effects they had on the person whom they possessed! Many times a person possessed by demons was rendered speechless, deaf, blind, and—in

the case of the man described in the passage just mentioned in Mark 5—violently insane. These wicked, unclean spirits brought extreme suffering upon humanity.

Now notice: *"They were healed—EVERY ONE!"*
It was a *complete* faith that prompted these people to
bring their loved ones, neighbors, and friends to the
apostles; and to such faith the Lord Jesus Christ had
promised *ALL things:* In Mark 9:23 He said, *". . . ALL
THINGS ARE POSSIBLE to him that believeth."* This
was the transition period, a time when God gave special
anointings and power to the apostles and early Christians.
In Hebrews 2:3, 4 the Apostle Paul tells us that our "great
salvation" was first "spoken by *the Lord,* and was *confirmed* unto us by them that heard Him; *God also bearing
them witness, both with SIGNS AND WONDERS, AND
WITH DIVERS MIRACLES, and gifts of the Holy Ghost,
according to HIS OWN WILL."*

Someone may ask, "Why do we not have men in the
churches today with such power and gifts as those men
had?" I believe the answer to that question is found in
I Corinthians 13:10: *"When that which is PERFECT is
come, then THAT WHICH IS IN PART SHALL BE
DONE AWAY."* During the transition period people did
not have the written Word of God as we have it today.
Faith comes by hearing and hearing by the Word (Rom.
10:17). The just shall *live* by faith (Rom. 1:17). In the
transition period God gave special signs, wonders, and
miracles to assure the people that Jesus was truly the
Christ, "that Prophet" of which Moses spoke; but since
the *written* Word was given and "the perfect law of liberty" is come, we no longer *need* signs and wonders
because *ALL of the Scriptures* are ours. We have God's
Word, we believe it simply because it *is* God's Word,
and it gives us all that we need:

*"ALL Scripture is given by inspiration of God, and
is profitable for doctrine, for reproof, for correction, for
instruction in righteousness: THAT THE MAN OF*

GOD MAY BE PERFECT, THROUGHLY FURNISHED UNTO ALL GOOD WORKS" (II Tim. 3:16,17).

The Twelve Arrested — Their Miraculous Deliverance; Their Defense Before the Sanhedrin

Verses 17 and 18: *"Then the high priest rose up, and all they that were with him, (which is the sect of the Sadducees,) and were filled with indignation, and laid their hands on the apostles, and put them in the common prison."*

The multitudes came to hear the apostles preach and to have their sick folks miraculously healed. The healings and miracles wrought by the apostles so provoked the religious leaders and filled them with indignation that they *"rose up"* in opposition against these men of God.

The Greek word here translated "rose up" is used again in this same chapter (vv. 36,37) where Gamaliel referred to the insurrection of Theudas and Judas of Galilee. It is also used in verse 9 of chapter 6, with reference to the men who argued with Stephen just before he was stoned. However, the same Greek word is often found *without* the sense of opposition that marks it here.

"The high priest . . . *and all they that were with him"* includes not only the high priest and his kinsmen, but also the heads of the party and the leaders of the Sadducees—in other words, all of the religious authorities and rulers.

"Which is the sect of the Sadducees." The Sadducees were a very powerful group—as we will see in verse 21 of this chapter. They had power to bring the apostles to trial and to mete out any punishment they decided upon. Bible antiquity assures us that the Sadducees also had the *rich* people on their side. It is not clear in the Scripture that Annas (high priest at that time) was a Sadducee, but Josephus in his books on Bible

antiquity declares that the *son* of Annas was of that sect, and there is a possibility that Annas also was a Sadducee.

Of course, the apostles declared that the bodily resurrection of Jesus proved Him the Son of God; and since the Sadducees did not *believe* in the resurrection and life after death, they hated such a message and were *"filled with indignation"* against the apostles.

The Greek word used here to express such deep feeling of *indignation* could also be rendered "jealousy." The Sadducees were actually filled with envy and jealousy because of the growth of the New Testament Church through the preaching of the message of the Lord Jesus Christ—His death, burial, and resurrection. Believers were being added to the Church by thousands (Acts 2:41; 4:4), and the rapid growth of the little group who came down from the upper room at Pentecost angered the Sadducees.

Therefore they *"laid their hands on the apostles, and put them in the common prison."* This fact is proof that all of the apostles were preachers and teachers. We read primarily of the messages delivered by *Peter*, occasionally *John* is mentioned; but this statement in verse 18 leads us to believe that they were *all* busy preaching and teaching just as fervently as Peter and John preached and taught.

The word used here in speaking of *"the common prison"* is the same as that used in Acts 4:3 when Peter and John were arrested and put *"in hold"* until the next day. Actually the word means "a ward," a place of temporary confinement until the prisoners should be formally summoned before the council for trial.

Verses 19 and 20: *"But the angel of the Lord by night opened the prison doors, and brought them forth, and said, Go, stand and speak in the temple to the people all the words of this life."*

This was a direct protest from Jehovah God against

the actions of the Sadducees in imprisoning the apostles. The Sadducees taught that there was neither spirit *nor angel*—so God sent an angel by night to open the prison doors and set His servants free! God takes care of His own. In Acts 16:25—28 He released Paul and Silas by sending an earthquake to open the prison doors and loose the bands of the prisoners. In Acts 12:5—11, He sent an angel to rescue Peter from between two guards where he was bound after Herod imprisoned him. And in our present study *"the angel of the Lord by night opened the prison doors,"* and brought the apostles forth—but he did more than just deliver them from prison: he instructed them to return to the temple, to the very place where they had been arrested, *"and speak to the people ALL THE WORDS OF THIS LIFE."*

The question might be asked, "Why did the apostles not make *mention* of their miraculous deliverance when they were called upon to testify before the Sanhedrin?" At no time did these men of God dwell on miracles wrought through them or on their behalf except when those miracles were wrought *before the eyes of men,* or used as signs of *the divine power of Almighty God* working in and for the Church through members of the Church. Therefore it would have been foreign to the entire character of the apostles had they entered into a description of *this* miracle which had not been witnessed by those before whom they testified. No members of the council *saw* the angel of the Lord that night, and for the apostles to use their deliverance as grounds for their claim that they were servants of Jehovah God would only have called forth derision from the Sanhedrin because the Sadducees would not have *believed* them!

We might note that when *criminals* escape from jail they immediately take cover and go into seclusion—but not so with these apostles. They did not arrange their own escape. *God delivered them* and then told them exactly what to do. They were to make no attempt to conceal themselves, they were to return to the same place where they had taught and wrought miracles, and they were to continue the same teaching. There was to be no discontinuation of their ministry.

Please notice, too, that they were not directed to make an appeal to the multitudes for sympathy, or try to excite the crowds to move against the Sanhedrin. They were simply to return to their former place in the temple and continue teaching the people the wonderful words of life—*"THIS LIFE"*—life after death, *eternal life* through faith in the finished work of the Lord Jesus Christ.

Verse 21: *"And when they heard that, they entered into the temple early in the morning, and taught. But the high priest came, and they that were with him, and called the council together, and all the senate of the children of Israel, and sent to the prison to have them brought."*

"Early in the morning"—we are not told the hour; it could have been even as the day dawned, it could have been at sunrise—but at a very early hour the apostles went back to the temple to take up their ministry where they had stopped when they were arrested and taken to prison for the night.

"But the high priest came, and they that were with him." Evidently these men came to the council chamber to discuss what should be done with their prisoners—who were no longer prisoners but (unknown to the Sanhedrin) were already back at work preaching the same message they had been arrested and imprisoned for preaching!

The priest and *"they that were with him . . . called the council together, and all the senate of the children of Israel."* This was a very important matter that lay before them and therefore at this meeting was gathered the combined wisdom of the religious authorities. We know Gamaliel was there (v. 34), and this would indicate that not only Sadducees were present, but also all of the leaders and rulers in the religious program of that day.

Some Bible authorities believe that the *"council"* here refers to the smaller Sanhedrin and *"the senate"* means the older men, the *great Sanhedrin* made up of seventy-one elders, men who were added to the council because of age, character, and understanding of the affairs of religion. Bible history and antiquity—as well as Jewish literature—tell us that such assessors were often appointed to sit with the council in matters of such importance as the arrest of the apostles. And when these religious leaders were all asembled, they *"sent to the prison"* to have their prisoners brought in.

Verses 22 and 23: *"But when the officers came, and found them not in the prison, they returned, and told, saying, The prison truly found we shut with all safety, and the keepers standing without before the doors: but when we had opened, we found no man within."*

The *"officers"* here seem to imply a military body, but they could have been members of the Levitical guard.

If there is any doubt that a miracle occurred here, verse 23 certainly removes that doubt. Even the guards— *"the keepers standing without before the doors"*—did not know that their prisoners were missing! The closed doors had not been disturbed and the guards naturally assumed that their prisoners were still inside. Silently, without disturbing locks or doors, God had removed His men from the prison cell—and not even the prison guards suspected that anything unusual had occurred until they opened the door the next morning and found the prisoners gone.

Verse 24: *"Now when the high priest and the captain of the temple and the chief priests heard these things, they doubted of them whereunto this would grow."*

The *"captain of the temple"* was not a military officer, but had charge of the guard of priests and Levites—men

who watched over the temple to preserve order and prevent any disturbance. The captain of the temple is mentioned in Acts 4:1, and the Old Testament speaks of an
officer whose title was *"the ruler of the house of God"*
(I Chron. 9:11; II Chron. 31:13; Neh. 11:11).

"These things" heard by the high priest, the captain
of the temple, and the chief priests were simply the report
which the officers brought back concerning the miraculous disappearance of the apostles when they were
thought to be safely locked in a prison cell.

"They doubted of them whereunto this would grow."
These dignitaries and religious leaders were at a complete
loss as to what to do about this matter. What step
should they take next to prevent things from getting out
of hand? If news of this happening should spread among
the common people, there was no way of knowing *what*
might happen. They must find a way to put a stop to
it—but they were at a loss to know how this could be
done.

It is interesting to note that when the apostles were
brought before these dignitaries they were not questioned
as to how they had escaped from prison. It is clear that
the magistrates wanted no further testimony concerning
the supernatural power by which these men had wrought
their mighty miracles—and they especially wanted to
avoid any testimony about their miraculous deliverance
from behind the locked doors where they had been imprisoned. These religious leaders were not ignorant of
the resurrection of Jesus. They had been careful to sta-
tion guards at His sepulchre, and when those guards
came to them on the resurrection morning and told them
"all the things that were done," they bribed the soldiers
and instructed them to say that they had fallen asleep
on guard, and while they slept the disciples had come
and stolen the body of their Lord from the tomb (Matt.
28:11—14). So the chief priests and members of this body
of religious rulers knew very well that a miracle had

occurred in the bodily resurrection of Jesus, and they knew as well that a miracle had released these apostles from prison; but they wanted no further publicity about it. The *Sadducees* denied resurrection, but they faced here a miracle which they could neither deny nor explain away. Therefore they chose to ignore it.

Verse 25: *"Then came one and told them, saying, Behold, the men whom ye put in prison are standing in the temple, and teaching the people."*

God took care to give much publicity to the defeat of the religious leaders in the hour of their seeming victory over His servants. The multitudes knew that the council had threatened the apostles and commanded them not to speak in the name of Jesus, and then when the command was unheeded and the preaching and miracles continued, they had ordered that these men be arrested and put in prison. But God had long ago commanded, "Touch not mine anointed, and do my prophets no harm" (I Chron. 16:22), and these apostles were His anointed servants. Therefore He sent an angel to bring them out of prison—from behind locked doors and unseen by the prison guards—and now they were standing in the temple in the very place where they had been arrested the day before, and they were preaching the same message, teaching in the name of Jesus.

Verse 26: *"Then went the captain with the officers, and brought them without violence: for they feared the people, lest they should have been stoned."*

It is apparent that the religious leaders knew that on occasion the Jewish people were capable of taking the law into their own hands. Not too long ago they had been ready to stone *Jesus* for declaring His deity (John 10:30−33). The apostles had been preaching the Gospel, healing the sick, casting out demons; and the mighty miracles that had been wrought through them by the power of God had won the respect and esteem of the people. The members of the Sanhedrin, the officers, and the captain of the temple knew that mob violence could break out if they did not exercise care in bringing the apostles back to the judgment hall.

"For they feared the people." It was *man* they feared, *not God.* They were not thinking of what God might do to them, but of what the multitudes might do. But the apostles had their eyes fixed on God—and that is the only way to find deliverance from the fear of man. They offered no resistance to the officers and the captain of the temple. After all, they had done no wrong—and even when they were imprisoned for preaching the Gospel of the Lord Jesus Christ they had not *broken out* of jail but had been delivered by God's miracle. Therefore they did not fear the Sanhedrin. They were ready to appear before that body of religious leaders, realizing that they would have another opportunity to declare the message of God's saving grace.

Verses 27 and 28: *"And when they had brought them, they set them before the council: and the high priest asked them, saying, Did not we straitly command you that ye should not teach in this name? And, behold, ye have filled Jerusalem with your doctrine, and intend to bring this Man's blood upon us."*

"Did not we straitly command you . . . ?" It was impossible to ignore or conceal the fact that the apostles had paid no attention to the command not to preach in the name of Jesus, and you can rest assured that the Sanhedrin did not want to advertise their lack of power over these poor, ignorant Galilaeans!

"Ye . . . intend to bring this Man's blood upon us." It had not been too many days since Pilate had washed his hands before the multitude and in the presence of these religious leaders, as if he could rid himself of the guilt of delivering Jesus into their hands to be crucified.

He asked them, "Whom shall I release unto you?" and they answered, "Barabbas! Crucify Jesus—*and let His blood be on us and on our children.*" Even the chief priests had pleaded against the holy Sufferer. Instead of interceding for Him, they had demanded His death: *"The chief priests and elders persuaded the multitude that they should ask Barabbas, and destroy Jesus."*

"Then answered all the people, and said, HIS BLOOD BE ON US, AND ON OUR CHILDREN! Then released he Barabbas unto them: and when he had scourged Jesus, he delivered Him to be crucified" (Matt. 27:11—26 in part). The council now felt that these words—"Let His blood be upon us"—were likely to be brought to fulfilment.

If these self-righteous leaders of Israel had been broken and contrite of heart, if they had known conviction of soul and conscience, even as the apostles witnessed to them they could have found immediate and everlasting cleansing through the power of the blood they had requested be upon their heads—the blood of the Lord Jesus Christ.

Certainly these men saw in Peter a new creation in Christ, for they must have remembered that this apostle had once denied his Lord and declared that he had never known Him, but now he stood before them as bold as a lion. He had been forgiven, restored to fellowship, and had come into possession of a Power that made him unafraid. He faced the crowd who had condemned Jesus, and boldly charged them with having denied the Holy One, having crucified the Prince of peace, choosing a murderer and robber in His stead! But they wanted none of his counsel, they wanted no message from the lips of this ignorant fisherman. They who were the dignified, self-righteous leaders and rulers in Israel wanted, more than anything else, to quiet these Galilaeans who preached the blood of Jesus.

Verse 29: *"Then Peter and the other apostles answered*

and said, We ought to obey God rather than men."

To obey God rather than men is the great, practical principle of saving faith, just as it was the uniform characteristic of the Lord Jesus Christ in all perfection as He tabernacled among men. His cry was, "Lo, I come to do *thy will*, O God!" (Heb. 10:9). It is true that He went about teaching and doing good. He healed the sick, raised the dead, cast out demons, fed the multitudes; but those things were but sidelines of His ministry—visible signs that gave evidence of His deity. His paramount purpose in coming into the world was to pay the sin-debt, and His entire earthly life was characterized by *unqualified, unfailing obedience to God the Father.* In all that He said, in all that He did, wherever He went, *obedience was always there*—unfaltering, constant, perfect.

As believers, we are to follow in His steps. Therefore as He fully obeyed the will of God, we should follow Him in obedience at all times, under all circumstances. There may be times when we are forced to wait on God for light, we may have to trust Him to lead us when we cannot see clearly just what He would have us do; but absolute obedience is the invariable duty of every born again believer!

It is true that we are instructed to "be subject to principalities and powers, to obey magistrates" (Tit. 3:1). Peter tells us that we are to be subject "to *every ordinance of man for the Lord's sake:* whether it be to the king, as supreme; or unto governors, as unto them that are sent by (the king) for the punishment of evildoers . . ." (I Pet. 2:13, 14). But if there is conflict between God's Word and the requirements of earthly rulers, the believer's path is clear: As the apostles so boldly declared, *"We ought to OBEY GOD rather than men,"* no matter what the cost. We may suffer for it, but obedience to God by grace gives the Christian strength and courage, and removes self-confidence.

Obedience to God is not only *the duty of the believer,* it is also the pathway of power. It was through obedience to the heavenly Father that our blessed Lord and Saviour withstood the devil and defeated him at every turn. On the Mount of Temptation Jesus met Satan's onslaughts with the Word of the living God. Of course, whatever Jesus spoke was the Word of God, but in answer to the devil's offers He quoted the Old Testament Scriptures. That is why *we* should hide the Word of God in our hearts, that we might not sin against Him (Psalm 119:11).

"He that doeth the will of God *abideth for ever"* (I John 2:17); but self-will, unbelief, and lawlessness will end in judgment and everlasting damnation!

Verses 30 and 31: *"The God of our fathers raised up Jesus, whom ye slew and hanged on a tree. Him hath God exalted with His right hand to be a Prince and a Saviour, for to give repentance to Israel, and forgiveness of sins."*

The Greek word here translated *"raised up"* is not the same as that used in chapter 3, verses 22 and 26, and in chapter 7, verse 37. Those verses speak of God's raising up Jesus as the promised Messiah, "that Prophet" of whom Moses wrote. But the Greek word Peter used here means that God raised up Jesus *after death,* brought Him *back from the dead* because it was not possible that death should hold Him (Acts 2:24).

This was clearly prophesied in the Psalms, and the Jews were certainly familiar with those prophecies as well as with other Old Testament Scriptures which foretold the resurrection of Jesus; but they refused to believe on Him of whom the Word testified.

"Him hath God exalted with His right hand . . . ." God raised Jesus from the dead—not to tabernacle among men here on earth, but to be *exalted at His right hand.* This is the same truth Peter had taught in Acts 2:33, and

is a direct fulfillment of Psalm 110 where in verse 1 we read, "The Lord (God) said unto my Lord (Jesus), *Sit thou AT MY RIGHT HAND, until I make thine enemies thy footstool."* (Please read that entire Psalm—it contains only seven verses, but we have not time and space to give them here.)

". . . *to be a Prince and a Saviour* . . . ." In what *relation to Israel* did Jesus take His place in heaven at the right hand of God the Father? As a Prince and a Saviour, *"for to give repentance to Israel, and forgiveness of sins."* The door of grace was still open for Israel as Peter delivered this message. The God of their fathers was looking down from heaven, waiting and longing to be gracious to His people, even though they had with wicked hands slain His only begotten Son.

Today the crucified, risen, and exalted Lord sits at the right hand of the Majesty on high as Saviour of mankind; but one day He will appear in judgment—and Jew, Gentile, rich, poor, bond or free, *ALL* will be judged. Until that judgment day He is the Prince and Saviour to give repentance and remission of sins *to all who will come unto God by Him.*

Verse 32: *"And we are His witnesses of these things; and so is also the Holy Ghost, whom God hath given to them that obey Him."*

The apostles were *"His witnesses of these things"*—the things that were done to Jesus—His arrest and trial, His crucifixion, burial, and resurrection. There was more than adequate testimony to prove that He was God's Christ, Saviour of sinners, the Messiah for whom the Jewish nation had waited and hoped, and the disciples were *His witnesses.* They had been with Him through the years of His earthly ministry, and they had walked and talked with Him for forty days after His resurrection from the grave. They had also been present when He was taken up into heaven to be exalted at the right hand of the Father.   In John 15:26, 27 Jesus said to His disciples, "When the Comforter is come, whom I will send unto you from the Father, even the Spirit of truth, which proceedeth from the Father, *He shall testify of me: AND YE ALSO shall bear witness, because ye have been with me from the beginning."*

The Holy Spirit *did* witness to the glory of Christ through the ministry and miracles of these apostles and believers in the infant Church—and He *still* witnesses through believers, for God has given the Holy Spirit *to all who "OBEY HIM."* The Greek word here rendered *"obey"* means literally "one who completely submits to the authority of the Lord Jesus Christ," such complete surrender as to become His bondslave.

Thus plainly did the apostles testify before the Sanhedrin that the Jews had crucified the Lord of glory, "that Prophet" of whom Moses, David, and Abraham had spoken and whose coming they had foretold.   They had killed the Prince of glory, His blood was on their hands, and the only possible way for them to be free from their guilt was to accept Him by faith through the Gospel of His death, burial, and resurrection.   They could still be forgiven if they would only repent and confess Him as Saviour and Lord.

Verse 33:   *"When they heard that, they were cut to the heart, and took counsel to slay them."*

The Greek here translated *"cut to the heart"* means literally "sawn asunder"—that is, "the effect described is not the compunction which leads to penitence, but the annoyance that results in more furious anger."

It is dangerous to oppose truth; and the more important the truth opposed the more deadly the *results* of that opposition.   The religious leaders in Israel opposed truth—i. e., they opposed *Jesus,* and *Jesus IS truth* (John 14:6; 17:17).   Therefore they had rejected the one and only way of deliverance from condemnation.   And then, after hearing the plain testimony that they had crucified the Lord of glory, they rebelliously despised the men who witnessed against them, and had it not been for their fear of the sympathetic multitudes they would have put the apostles to death then and there, so filled were they with prejudice, pride, and hatred!

But God always cares for His own in one way or another. It may not be as we think it should be, it may not be as we would plan; but "we know that all things work together for good to them that love God, to them who are the called according to His purpose" (Rom. 8:28). I believe that a dedicated believer is indispensable until God has finished with that believer. I am convinced that there are not enough demons in earth or in hell to destroy the Christian who is fully surrendered to God, fully obedient to Him, until he has finished the work God has allotted him to do.

God sent an *angel* to deliver these apostles from prison, but now He works through a *human* instrument in order to save them from the wrath of the Sanhedrin.

Gamaliel's Warning

Verse 34: *"Then stood there up one in the council, a Pharisee, named Gamaliel, a doctor of the law, had in reputation among all the people, and commanded to put the apostles forth a little space."*

According to Bible history (gleaned from the writings of Josephus) Gamaliel was the grandson of the famous Hillel. Hillel presided over the Sanhedrin during the reign of Tiberias, the reign of Caligula, and the reign of Claudius. His son succeeded him to the same office but was murdered during the siege of Jerusalem under Titus the Roman in 70 A. D.

In Acts 22:3 the Apostle Paul, one of the best educated men of his day, testified that he had studied under the teaching of Gamaliel, and there can be no doubt that this man was held in highest regard by the Sanhedrin (of which he himself was a member). Therefore the council could not ignore his advice, even though his sober words were opposed to the violence they advocated.

There is no reason to suggest, however, that Gamaliel was ever a believer—either publicly or secretly; but he was used of God at this critical moment in the lives of the apostles, to preserve their lives and deliver them from the Sanhedrin. God moves in mysterious ways! On one occasion in the Old Testament He used a donkey to accomplish His purpose (Num. 22:21—33). He used a rooster to remind Peter of the words of Jesus (Matt. 26: 34, 35, 74, 75). Most assuredly He could speak to the heart of such a man as Gamaliel and lead him to speak words that would arrest the minds of those who would slay His apostles! And because of the words spoken by this outstanding man, the Israelites were granted another opportunity to hear the truth, receive the grace of God, and be saved.

Verse 35: *"And said to them, Ye men of Israel, take heed to yourselves what ye intend to do as touching these men."*

Notice: *"Ye men of ISRAEL."* Gamaliel did not say, "Ye *Sadducees"* or "Ye *Pharisees."* He referred to them as "men of *Israel"*—the people to whom God had promised the Messiah; and then he gave them reasons why they should be careful concerning what they did to these apostles who were preaching in the name of the One whom these "men of Israel" had crucified.

Verses 36 and 37: *"For before these days rose up Theudas, boasting himself to be somebody; to whom a number of men, about four hundred, joined themselves: who was slain; and all, as many as obeyed him, were scattered, and brought to nought. After this man rose up Judas of Galilee in the days of the taxing, and drew*

*away much people after him: he also perished; and all,
even as many as obeyed him, were dispersed."*

Here Gamaliel assures the Sanhedrin that pretenders
will come to nought, and names a man with whom they
were familiar—*"Theudas, boasting himself to be somebody."* The Jews were looking for their Messiah, and
when Theudas came on the scene with his false claims,
four hundred men joined him—a goodly number of followers in those days. Today there are men in America
who claim everything Jesus claimed except the virgin
birth—and personally I expect some false teacher to rise
up soon who will even announce that he is virgin-born!
In these closing days of the Dispensation of Grace we
have—not four hundred, but *literally thousands* who are
following men instead of following *THE MAN, Christ
Jesus.*

Gamaliel reminded the Sanhedrin that Theudas was
slain, and his followers *"were scattered and brought to
nought."* After Theudas and his movement passed from
the scene, there rose up *"Judas of Galilee* in the days of
the taxing,"* and he, too, built up quite a following—he
"drew away much people after him."

This second man who rose up was from Galilee—as
was the true Messiah. He came into prominence "in
the days of the taxing." Jesus the Christ was born in
Bethlehem during the days of the taxing. So we see how
the devil does his best to counterfeit everything God has
done down through the history of man.

This "Judas of Galilee" perhaps had a larger following
than Theudas had, and history tells us that his cry was,
"We have God as our only leader and Lord!" He was
fanatical, and his followers were fanatical and revolution-
ary; but he, too, perished and "as many as obeyed him
were dispersed." However, such incidents made the
Jewish leaders fearful of what might come of the preaching of these apostles concerning Jesus of Nazareth whom
they declared had risen from the dead and at that very

moment was seated at the right hand of the Majesty on high. They were preaching in His name, great crowds were following them, and the members of the Sanhedrin were frightened of the outcome. Then Gamaliel spoke, using these former false leaders as examples, warning the council to proceed slowly and carefully in opposing the apostles.

Some supposed-to-be Bible authorities declare that the account of Gamaliel does not correspond historically with the account given by Josephus and other historians of that day. Be that as it may, the words in the book of Acts are *inspired of God,* and the words of Josephus and writers of secular history are *not* inspired, however trustworthy they may be. Personally, I do not find it difficult to accept records from the Bible over and above any statement in history or in secular literature because from Genesis through Revelation I believe every word is *GOD'S Word.* II Timothy 3:16 declares, *"All Scripture is given BY INSPIRATION OF GOD,"* and in II Peter 1:21 we read, "For the prophecy came not in old time by the will of man: *but holy men of God spake as they were MOVED BY THE HOLY GHOST."*

According to history and Jewish literature, there were numerous false leaders who came on the scene announcing that they were the Messiah, and Jesus tells us that in the closing days of this dispensation there will be men who will claim to be the Christ, and they will deceive many and lead them astray. To His disciples He said, "Take heed that no man deceive you. For *many shall come in my name, saying, I am Christ; and shall deceive many.* . . . Then if any man shall say unto you, Lo, here is Christ, or there; believe it not. For *there shall arise false Christs,* and false prophets, and shall shew great signs and wonders; insomuch that, if it were possible, they shall deceive the very elect" (Matt. 24:4, 5, 23, 24).

The Apostle Paul warned "that in the latter times some shall depart from the faith, giving heed to seducing spirits, and doctrines of devils" (I Tim. 4:1).

John the Beloved also warned, "Many deceivers are entered into the world, who confess not that Jesus Christ is come in the flesh. This is a deceiver and an antichrist" (II John 7).

True believers know that the schemes and efforts of evil men cannot destroy that which is of God. Empires built by the design of men, regardless of their power and glory, invariably crumble and come to nought—a fact proved both in Scripture and through the pages of secular history. There are evil men among us today who are antichrists—*not THE Man of Sin*, the false messiah, but his forerunners. They are the antichrists (plural) of whom John wrote—men who deny that Jesus is the Son of God, virgin-born, very God in flesh. *THE Antichrist*, the Man of Sin, will be unveiled after the Rapture of the Church. (Please study II Thessalonians chapter 2.)

And what should be the attitude of believers toward the false teachers among us today? The answer is found in the Word of God. The duty of the Church is not to judge men, but to *lift up THE Christ and glorify HIM*. Believers are to give out the Gospel, and allow *the judgment of GOD* to fall upon false teachers. The Scripture points out that we are to *have no fellowship* with such men, for God commands His people, *"Come out from among them, and be ye separate . . . and touch not the unclean thing . . ."* (II Cor. 6:17).

In II John 9—11 we have this warning: "Whosoever transgresseth, and abideth not in the doctrine of Christ, hath not God. He that abideth in the doctrine of Christ, he hath both the Father and the Son. *If there come any unto you, and bring not this doctrine, RECEIVE HIM NOT INTO YOUR HOUSE, NEITHER BID HIM GOD SPEED:* for he that biddeth him God speed is partaker of his evil deeds."

We are to preach the truth; and when we do that, we have no need to deal in personalities. We need only to

await the manifestation of truth in that which is doubtful, for *truth WILL rise*, and will point out false teachers.

Verses 38 and 39: *"And now I say unto you, Refrain
from these men, and let them alone: for if this counsel
or this work be of men, it will come to nought: but if
it be of God, ye cannot overthrow it; lest haply ye be
found even to fight against God."*

The men of the Sanhedrin believed in Jehovah, the
God of their fathers. They knew He was all-powerful,
they knew they could not overthrow Him, and the words
of Gamaliel struck a note of fear in their hearts, lest
they be found *fighting against God*. They were not willing to face the truth of having *already* fought against
Him when they rejected His Son. They refused to believe
the message of these Galilaeans whom they declared to
be ignorant and unlearned men.

Verse 40: *"And to him they agreed: and when they
had called the apostles, and beaten them, they commanded that they should not speak in the name of Jesus, and
let them go."*

The Sanhedrin heeded Gamaliel's advice not to slay
the apostles, but they were not wholly satisfied to let
them go; so they called them back into the judgment
hall and ordered that they be beaten. Then the council
again commanded them not to speak in the name of Jesus, dismissed them, and permitted them to leave.

Through the providence of God, His servants were
literally plucked from the jaws of death by the words of
Gamaliel, but they suffered the shame and indignity of
stripes. However, they remembered that the Lord Jesus
Christ, Saviour of sinners, was led to the whipping post
and brutally scourged by Roman soldiers. The servants
are no better than their Lord, and Jesus had warned
these men that since the world had hated *Him*, it would
also hate *them*. They learned the truth of this prophecy

early in their ministry after the Lord's ascension.

The law commanded that "wicked" men should be beaten: "It shall be, if the wicked man be worthy to be beaten, that the judge shall cause him to lie down, and to be beaten before his face, according to his fault, by a certain number. *FORTY STRIPES he may give him,* and not exceed: lest, if he should exceed, and beat him above these with many stripes, then thy brother should seem vile unto thee" (Deut. 25:2, 3). No doubt the Sanhedrin passed this sentence against the apostles because of their disobedience to the command not to speak in the name of Jesus.

Such beatings were not an uncommon form of punishment. According to the testimony of the Apostle Paul he experienced such treatment five times during his ministry, receiving the allotted number of stripes each time as prescribed by law. In II Corinthians 11:24 he testified, "Of the Jews five times received I forty stripes save one."

And what did these apostles do after their beating? Did they leave the judgment hall and go their separate ways, *silent* about the message they had been called of God to proclaim? Did they return to Solomon's porch to lament the terrible and unjust persecution that had been meted out to them? No, they did neither of these things. Notice:

Verses 41 and 42: *"And they departed from the presence of the council, REJOICING that they were counted worthy to suffer shame for His name. And daily in the temple, and in every house, they ceased not to teach and preach Jesus Christ!"*

This was the same group of men who had deserted the Lord in His time of need when He was arrested and brought to trial. They ran and hid themselves for fear of this very council before whom they had just testified in the name of Jesus, and from whose presence they now went out—*"rejoicing that they were counted worthy to suffer shame for His name!"*

In Matthew 5:11,12 Jesus said, "Blessed are ye, when men shall *revile* you, and *persecute* you, and shall *say all manner of evil against you falsely, for MY sake. REJOICE, and be exceeding glad: for great is your reward in heaven:* for so persecuted they the prophets which were before you."

The disgraceful, shameful treatment the apostles received at the hands of the religious leaders did not discourage them—quite the contrary! Filled with rejoicing that they had been "counted worthy" to suffer such indignities for Jesus' sake, they went everywhere—in the temple, in homes, in the streets—and they carried only one message: *JESUS, the Son of God: crucified, buried, risen, ascended, living*—Saviour of all who will come to God in His name and through His shed blood.

The apostles knew that Israel, through spiritual blindness, had crucified their Messiah, exactly as the prophets had said they would do. The men of the Sanhedrin had the prophecies of Isaiah, Daniel, Zechariah, Jeremiah, Ezekiel, and many others; but in spite of the Old Testament Scriptures with which they claimed to be familiar, in their blindness of heart they crucified the Lord of glory! The apostles had *received* Him, had believed on Him as Messiah and Saviour, and therefore a great responsibility rested upon them. Their persecutors needed the light of the Gospel and it was the responsibility of these men to preach the good news of the death, burial, and resurrection of the Lord Jesus Christ; and they preached that message with a zeal which was not to be stopped by threatenings, commands, imprisonments, or the Roman scourge. Even *death itself* could not stamp out the message of truth, life, and love that brings life eternal to all who will believe that message.

CHAPTER VI

1. And in those days, when the number of the disciples was multiplied, there arose a murmuring of the Grecians against the Hebrews, because their widows were neglected in the daily ministration.

2. Then the twelve called the multitude of the disciples unto them, and said, It is not reason that we should leave the word of God, and serve tables.

3. Wherefore, brethren, look ye out among you seven men of honest report, full of the Holy Ghost and wisdom, whom we may appoint over this business.

4. But we will give ourselves continually to prayer, and to the ministry of the word.

5. And the saying pleased the whole multitude: and they chose Stephen, a man full of faith and of the Holy Ghost, and Philip, and Prochorus, and Nicanor, and Timon, and Parmenas, and Nicolas a proselyte of Antioch:

6. Whom they set before the apostles: and when they had prayed, they laid their hands on them.

7. And the word of God increased; and the number of the disciples multiplied in Jerusalem greatly; and a great company of the priests were obedient to the faith.

8. And Stephen, full of faith and power, did great wonders and miracles among the people.

9. Then there arose certain of the synagogue, which is called the synagogue of the Libertines, and Cyrenians, and Alexandrians, and of them of Cilicia and of Asia, disputing with Stephen.

10. And they were not able to resist the wisdom and the spirit by which he spake.

11. Then they suborned men, which said, We have heard him speak blasphemous words against Moses, and against God.

12. And they stirred up the people, and the elders, and the scribes, and came upon him, and caught him, and brought him to the council,

13. And set up false witnesses, which said, This man ceaseth not to speak blasphemous words against this holy place, and the law:

14. For we have heard him say, that this Jesus of Nazareth

shall destroy this place, and shall change the customs which Moses delivered us.

15. And all that sat in the council, looking stedfastly on him, saw his face as it had been the face of an angel.

It is an honor rather than a disgrace for a believer to be persecuted for Christ's sake. Such persecution honors God. Paul exhorted the Philippian Christians to "stand fast in one spirit, with one mind striving together for the faith of the Gospel; and in nothing terrified by your adversaries: which is to them an evident token of perdition, but to you of salvation, and that of God. For unto you it is given *in the behalf of Christ,* not only to believe on Him, but also *to suffer for His sake*" (Phil. 1:27–29).

The devil's persecution of the believer often works in reverse to that which he intended, for the grace of God makes the Christian's persecution a blessing to the Church and an undeniable testimony to an unbelieving world! The world cannot easily forget—nor can it ignore—the believer who rejoices when he is persecuted for righteousness' sake. Jesus warned His disciples that persecution was sure to come to them, but He also said, *"Blessed are they which are persecuted for righteousness' sake: for their's is the kingdom of heaven"* (Matt. 5:10).

In John 16:33 Jesus said to the twelve, *"In the world ye shall have tribulation: but BE OF GOOD CHEER; I have overcome the world!"*

The twenty-eight chapters of Acts record the account of one continuous Holy Ghost revival. The Church was growing, disciples were multiplying by the thousands. The entire book of Acts is said to cover a period of approximately thirty years of the works and ministry of these apostles whom the Sanhedrin termed "unlearned and ignorant" men. Let us look at some of the results of the preaching of these men:

In chapter 2 verse 41 "about *three thousand* souls" were converted and added to the Church.

In chapter 4 verse 4 *many believed* "and the number of the men was about *five thousand."* You will notice this does not even include the *many women* who were probably saved at that time.

In chapter 5 verse 14 still more believers were added, *"multitudes* both of men and women."

In chapter 6 verse 7 the number of disciples continued to grow, and *"a great company of the priests"* were saved.

In chapter 8 verses 5—8 great revival broke out in Samaria under the ministry of Philip, *"the people with one accord gave heed"* to his preaching, many were healed and unclean spirits were cast out. *"And there was great joy in that city."*

In chapter 10 verse 44 as Peter preached in the house of Cornelius, *"all them which heard the Word"* were saved.

In chapter 11 verse 21 *"a great number* believed, and turned unto the Lord."

In chapter 11 verse 24 *"much people"* were added.

In chapter 16 verse 34 the Philippian jailer and *"all his house"* believed.

In chapter 17 verse 12 *"many"* believed.

In chapter 17 verse 34 *"certain men"* believed, "and *a woman* named Damaris, and *others* with them."

Certainly during the years recorded in Acts, there must have been thousands of people converted who are not specifically pointed out in the twenty-eight chapters recorded, as great multitudes heard and believed the message of the apostles and the first believers.

Verse 1: *"And in those days, when the number of the disciples was multiplied, there arose a murmuring of the Grecians against the Hebrews, because their widows were neglected in the daily ministration."*

Satan is not omniscient, neither is he omnipotent; but he is wise and cunning. Realizing that he could not stamp out the Gospel message through threats and persecution *from without,* he began to work from *within.* God had quickly pointed out and judged the deception of Ananias and Sapphira who, though meeting with the assembly of believers, were not members of it. Now we see fleshly and selfish persons *within* the assembly as they begin to complain.

"*There arose a murmuring of the Grecians against the Hebrews.*" The Grecian Jews (Dr. Scofield calls them "the Hellenists") complained against the Hebrews—the Jews who were born in Jerusalem and Judaea of pure Jewish descent. Bear in mind that those who were murmuring were also those who had profited most by the self-sacrificing love displayed by the believers who had sold their houses and lands and divided their worldly goods that all might have food and clothing and other necessities of life. The complainers were in the wrong, for they were complaining against those who had unselfishly given of their own possessions in order to care for the less fortunate believers who had come into Jerusalem from other towns and communities. Then as now, the wrongdoer was the one who denounced those who were better than himself.

The complaint brought by the Jews of foreign admixture against the Hebrews was that "*their widows were neglected in the daily ministration.*" There is no Scripture to suggest that they were *right* in their claim; and since these people were receiving the greater part of the money, food, and clothing being distributed by the Jews who lived in Jerusalem, those who had sold their property in order to provide for others, they should have been filled with gratitude instead of murmuring and complaining.

The First Deacons

Verses 2 and 3: "*Then the twelve called the multitude of the disciples unto them, and said, It is not reason that*

we should leave the Word of God, and serve tables.
Wherefore, brethren, look ye out among you seven men of
honest report, full of the Holy Ghost and wisdom, whom
we may appoint over this business."

Up to this time the apostles had taken care of everything pertaining to the Church. Not only were they
preaching and teaching the Word, but the administration
of food, clothing, and other necessities was also in their
hands as the believers sold their possessions and brought
the money to the apostles that they might make distribution "unto every man according as he had need" (Acts
4:34, 35). But the Church had now grown to such extent
that the twelve realized they must make some other ar-
rangement if they were to have time to carry on the
ministry whereunto God had called them. So they called
the multitude of disciples together to present their need
to be relieved of their secular duties in order to be free
for their spiritual responsibilities.

The food, clothes, money—whatsoever was to be distributed among the less fortunate—came from the believers themselves. The disciples had no money to give,
they were wholly dedicated to the service of the Church,
therefore they called the believers together and gave
them the responsibility of appointing men of their own
number to take care of the monetary and other business
affairs of the assembly.

"It is not reason that we should leave the Word of
God, and serve tables." The "tables" here referred to
were the tables, benches, or counters where the money
was distributed after it was brought into the treasury by
the more wealthy members of the Church. In Hebrew
and Greek, bankers were referred to as "tablers," and you
will recall that when Jesus cleansed the temple He "cast
out all them that sold and bought in the temple, and
overthrew the TABLES OF THE MONEYCHANGERS
. . ." (Matt. 21:12).

The Greek word here translated *"leave"* is a very

strong word which means "to forsake or abandon," indicating that the major portion of the apostles' time was taken up with secondary matters causing them to forsake their first line of duty which was to preach the Word and make disciples. Their commission had been, "Go ye therefore, and *TEACH all nations,* baptizing them in the name of the Father, and of the Son, and of the Holy Ghost: *teaching them to observe ALL THINGS WHATSOEVER I HAVE COMMANDED YOU:* and, lo, I am with you alway, even unto the end of the world" (Matt. 28:19, 20). Therefore the first responsibility of these men was to the ministry whereunto God had called them and for which Jesus had commissioned them.

"Look ye out among you seven men"—and notice the qualifications of these men: *". . . of honest report, full of the Holy Ghost, and wisdom."* These seven men were chosen by the assembly. The believers gave their money, therefore the apostles entrusted to them the selection of the men who would handle the monetary matters.

We see this same principle at work in the church at Corinth. In I Corinthians 16:1—4 Paul instructed, "Now concerning the collection for the saints, as I have given order to the churches of Galatia, even so do ye. Upon the first day of the week let every one of you lay by him in store, as God hath prospered him, that there be no gatherings when I come. And when I come, *WHOMSOEVER YE SHALL APPROVE by your letters, them will I send to bring your liberality unto Jerusalem.* And if it be meet that I go also, they shall go with me."

In II Corinthians 8:16—24 Paul commends *Titus* to the believers in Corinth and explains, "We have sent with him *the brother,* whose praise is in the Gospel throughout all the churches; and not that only, but *who was also CHOSEN OF THE CHURCHES to travel with us with this grace,* which is administered by us to the glory of the same Lord, and declaration of your ready mind: *Avoiding this, that no man should blame US in*

*this abundance which is administered by us: providing
for honest things, not only in the sight of the Lord, but
also in the sight of men.*

"And we have *sent with them our brother,* whom we
have oftentimes proved diligent in many things, but now
much more diligent, upon the great confidence which I
have in you. Whether any do enquire of Titus, he is
my partner and fellow-helper concerning you: or our
brethren be enquired of, *they are THE MESSENGERS
OF THE CHURCHES, and the glory of Christ.* Wherefore shew ye to them, and before the churches, the proof
of your love, and of our boasting on your behalf."

From these Scriptures we learn that a brother was
chosen by the believers in the assembly to be a fellow
traveler with Paul and Titus, *providing things honest
before the Lord and before men.* These "messengers of
the churches" were selected by the believers in the assembly and sent to help the less fortunate believers in
other communities. Thus the apostles did not have the
responsibility of handling the money.

It is a solemn and weighty responsibility to be a deacon in the Church of the living God. Writing to Timothy, his son in the ministry, the Apostle Paul clearly
outlined the qualifications for a *bishop,* and then made
it very clear that the same requirements must be met
by those who would hold the office of deacon:

"A bishop then must be blameless, the husband of
one wife, vigilant, sober, of good behaviour, given to
hospitality, apt to teach; not given to wine, no striker,
not greedy of filthy lucre; but patient, not a brawler, not
covetous; one that ruleth well his own house, having his
children in subjection with all gravity; (For if a man
know not how to rule his own house, how shall he take
care of the Church of God?) Not a novice, lest being
lifted up with pride he fall into the condemnation of the
devil. Moreover he must have a good report of them
which are without; lest he fall into reproach and the

snare of the devil.

*"LIKEWISE must the DEACONS be grave, not dou-
bletongued, not given to much wine, not greedy of filthy
lucre; holding the mystery of the faith in a pure conscience.   And let these also first be proved; then let
them use the office of a deacon, being found BLAME-
LESS.*

"Even so must *their wives* be grave, not slanderers,
sober, faithful in all things.   Let the deacons be the
husbands of one wife, ruling their children and their own
houses well.   *For they that have used the office of a
deacon well purchase to themselves a good degree, and
great boldness in the faith which is in Christ Jesus"*
(I Tim. 3:2—13).

It is a glorious privilege to be a deacon in God's
Church—but the responsibility of such a position is as
grave and weighty as the privilege is glorious.   The deacon whose life does not measure up to these qualifications would do well to resign, because he must give an
account to God just as surely as a pastor must give an
account for the handling of his ministry.   Therefore it is
easy to see why the assembly was instructed to select
men who were honest, full of the Holy Ghost, possessed
of wisdom; for only such men were qualified to hold
the office of deacon.

However, the local assembly was never instructed to
select men to *preach;* it is not the source (or channel)
of the ministry.   The Word of God is *given* by God,
therefore He chooses and anoints men to preach His
Word.   The Word was with God in the beginning; the
Word was first spoken by the Lord and confirmed unto
us by them that heard Him—men chosen of God to give
their time and their entire lives to the ministry of the
Word, "God also bearing them witness, both with signs
and wonders, and with divers miracles, and gifts of the
Holy Ghost, according to His own will" (Heb. 2:3, 4).
This is true in the ministry today—whether a man be

pastor, teacher, evangelist.   Ephesians 4:11, 12 declares
that Christ gave these various gifts for the ministry.   "He
gave some, apostles; and some, prophets; and some,
evangelists; and some, pastors and teachers; for the perfecting of the saints, for the work of the ministry, for
the edifying of the body of Christ."

The book of Acts records no time or place where the
believers in the Church or the apostles in overseeing the
Church, ever appointed anyone to preach or teach. The
Holy Ghost separates men unto God for the ministry of
the Word.   Teacher, pastor, missionary, evangelist — all
were given to the Church by the Head of the Church, the
Lord Jesus Christ; and the outstanding reason for the
sad spiritual state of the local churches today is that
preachers are elected or appointed by man instead of
being called of God and separated unto the Church by
the Holy Ghost.   Many young men consider the ministry
as a *vocation* rather than a holy calling, but the ministry
is *not* a vocation, it cannot be simply chosen as a profession, and only God-called men preach the pure Word
of God.

There are many men in pulpits today who fit the
description Paul gave in II Corinthians 11:13—15: "Such
are false apostles, deceitful workers, transforming themselves into the apostles of Christ.   And no marvel; for
Satan himself is transformed into an angel of light. Therefore it is no great thing if his ministers also be transformed as the ministers of righteousness; whose end shall
be according to their works."   There are many "hirelings"
in the ministry today, but thank God there are also some
true ministers of the Gospel whom the Lord God has
chosen and sent to carry on the work of His Church!

Verse 4:   *"But we will give ourselves continually to
prayer, and to the ministry of the Word."*

Here, prayer precedes the ministry of the Word — and
that is as it should be. No minister is capable of preach-

ing the Word as it should be preached unless he first spends time in prayer.   Paul commanded the believers in Thessalonica to "pray *without ceasing*" (I Thess. 5:17). Sad but true, many dear and true ministers of God have but little time for prayer and study because their members keep them so occupied with secondary things— matters that should be taken care of by deacons, stewards, elders, or even lay members of the church.

Please do not misunderstand me—it is honorable and commendable for a minister to visit the members of his flock; but it becomes *dishonorable* when he must be out calling on them at a time when he should be in his study searching the Word, or on his knees in prayerful preparation for the message he will deliver at the next service! The primary responsibility of any minister is to preach the Word of God, and many believers will be called upon to give an account at the judgment seat of Christ for causing their pastor to spend his time catering to their wishes and whims when he should have been in communion with God, feeding himself from God's Word, that he might be able to feed his flock.

It is also true that many pastors are unfair in that they attempt to do *everything* in the church, thereby robbing their members of the blessed privilege of service instead of teaching them the responsibility of stewardship.   A minister who preaches as many as three sermons a week needs at least forty-eight to sixty hours of that week to be used in preparation for his sermons, and many of those hours should be spent in prayer, seeking not only God's will for the message, but also the enlightening interpretation of the Holy Spirit on the text God would have him use.   Any message delivered *without* preceding prayer and study will not accomplish that which the Word of God is given to accomplish.

Saul of Tarsus, according to his own testimony, was dedicated to the persecution of the Church—punishing the saints, compelling them to blaspheme, putting them in prison and even giving his consent to put them to death (Acts 8:1; 26:9—11). But God set this man aside as a chosen vessel for His use (Acts 9:15, 16), and he became *Paul the Apostle*, to whom God revealed the mystery of the Church and whom He appointed and anointed as minister to the Gentiles. Paul declared, in Galatians 1:15—18, "When it pleased God, who separated me from my mother's womb, and called me by His grace, to reveal His Son in me, that I might preach Him among the heathen; immediately *I CONFERRED NOT WITH FLESH AND BLOOD: neither went I up to Jerusalem to them which were apostles before me;* but I went into Arabia, and returned again unto Damascus. Then *after three years* I went up to Jerusalem to see Peter, and abode with him fifteen days."

Strange indeed that this great preacher of the Gospel should not have sought out the apostles who had walked and talked with Jesus throughout His earthly ministry; but he did not. He received his commission and anointing from Almighty God, and his complete surrender to his calling is revealed in his writings. For example, in his first letter to the Corinthian church he declared:

"*And I, brethren, when I came to you, came not with excellency of speech or of wisdom, declaring unto you the testimony of God. FOR I DETERMINED NOT TO KNOW ANY THING AMONG YOU, SAVE JESUS CHRIST, AND HIM CRUCIFIED.* And I was with you in weakness, and in fear, and in much trembling. And my speech and my preaching was *not with enticing words of man's wisdom, but in demonstration of the Spirit and of power:* that your faith should not stand in the wisdom of men, *but IN THE POWER OF GOD.*

"Howbeit we speak wisdom among them that are perfect: yet *not the wisdom of this world,* nor of the princes of this world, that come to nought: *but WE SPEAK THE WISDOM OF GOD in a mystery, even the hidden wisdom, which God ordained before the world unto our glory:* which none of the princes of this world knew: for had they known it, they would not have crucified the Lord of glory" (I Cor. 2:1—8).

It was also to the Corinthian church that Paul wrote: "Ye see your calling, brethren, how that not many wise men after the flesh, not many mighty, not many noble, are called: But God hath chosen the foolish things of the world to confound the wise; and God hath chosen the weak things of the world to confound the things which are mighty; and base things of the world, and things which are despised, hath God chosen, yea, and things which are not, to bring to nought things that are: *that no flesh should glory in His presence.* But of Him are ye in Christ Jesus, who of God is made unto us wisdom, and righteousness, and sanctification, and redemption: *That, according as it is written, HE THAT GLORIETH, LET HIM GLORY IN THE LORD"* (I Cor. 1:26—31).

Jesus taught the importance of the Word and of prayer. In Luke 10:38—42 we read: "Now it came to pass, as they went, that He entered into a certain village: and a certain woman named Martha received Him into her house. And she had a sister called *Mary, which also sat at Jesus' feet, AND HEARD HIS WORD.*

"But Martha was cumbered about much serving, and came to Him, and said, Lord, dost thou not care that my sister hath left me to serve alone? Bid her therefore that she help me. And Jesus answered and said unto her, Martha, Martha, thou art careful and troubled about many things: *But ONE THING IS NEEDFUL: and Mary hath chosen THAT GOOD PART, which shall not be taken away from her."*

Martha was "cumbered about much serving . . . careful and troubled about many things"—and certainly such loving service is necessary; but Mary chose the better part: sitting at the feet of Jesus and listening to His Word!

It was in the next chapter—Luke 11, verses 1—4—that Jesus was praying "in a certain place," and when He had finished praying one of His disciples said to Him, *"Lord, teach US to pray,* as John also taught his disciples." And He taught them the prayer recorded in full in Matthew 6:9—13.

Jesus Himself spent much time in prayer, and the Word of God unmistakeably teaches that for a minister to be what God intended him to be, if he administers the Word as he should, the great prerequisite is *prayer*—prayer that *flesh* will find no occasion to glory, prayer that prepares the individual to draw near to God after having first received *from God through prayer.* Only in this way can the minister be a vessel to honor, meet for the Master's use, prepared unto every good work.

Verses 5 and 6: *"And the saying pleased the whole multitude: and they chose Stephen, a man full of faith and of the Holy Ghost, and Philip, and Prochorus, and Nicanor, and Timon, and Parmenas, and Nicolas a proselyte of Antioch: whom they set before the apostles: and when they had prayed, they laid their hands on them."*

Surely the Holy Spirit led in the selection of these seven men, and the grace displayed here was a remarkable and outstanding testimony to the multitude. Every one of the seven men chosen had a Greek name, indicating that they were chosen from the ranks of the Greek-speaking believers—those who had murmured against the Hebrews (v. 1). Certainly this was pure grace on the part of the multitudes, grace enough to shame those who had murmured!

There was no human element in the electing of these first deacons. The apostles did not appoint a committee to see to it that some were elected from the upper class and some from the lower class. The churches today would be far better off if the selection of officers and leaders was left up to the Holy Spirit instead of allowing committees to meet behind closed doors and make suggestions as to who should be put over the affairs of the assembly.

"And when they had prayed, they laid their hands on them." This was a token of Christian love and fellowship as well as a sign that the apostles approved of the seven men chosen by the multitude to represent them in the business affairs of the church.

In the Old Testament the "laying on of hands" was an ancient rite of *blessing.* In the account of Jacob's blessing the sons of Joseph we read, "Israel stretched out his right hand, and laid it upon Ephraim's head, who was the younger, and his left hand upon Manasseh's head, guiding his hands wittingly; for Manasseh was the firstborn. . . . And he blessed them that day, saying, In thee shall Israel bless, saying, God make thee as Ephraim and as Manasseh: and he set Ephraim before Manasseh" (Gen. 48:14, 20).

In Numbers 27:22, 23 we see that the laying on of hands was a sign of *official recognition:* "Moses did as the Lord commanded him: and he took Joshua, and set him before Eleazar the priest, and before all the congregation: and he laid his hands upon him, and gave him a charge, as the Lord commanded by the hand of Moses."

In Acts 13:3 we see the laying on of hands as a sign of *commendation to God's grace.* When the Holy Ghost called Barnabas and Paul and started them on their first missionary journey, we read that the members of the assembly, when they had fasted and prayed, "laid their hands on them" and sent them away. (See also Acts 14:26.)

Thus was the selection of these seven deacons owned and blessed by the Lord. Their work was not primarily to preach, teach, or baptize, but to handle the financial and business affairs of the church, receiving the gifts given by wealthy believers and dispensing those gifts according to the temporal need of the poorer believers.

Money is necessary for the carrying on and advancement of the Lord's work, but the handling of church finances is a delicate and difficult task—especially when it is undertaken by a minister of the Gospel. Such responsibility should never be placed upon the pastor, but should be taken care of by members of the assembly who are elected for that purpose.

Among the men named as deacons here we know that Philip also *preached,* but Acts 21:8 plainly tells us that Philip was *an evangelist.* It was therefore in virtue of the gift of evangelism that he preached, and not because he was appointed a deacon. He lived in complete obedience to the Holy Spirit—otherwise he would not, at the bidding of the Holy Spirit, have left a great revival in Samaria to journey into the desert and witness to one lone soul—the Ethiopian eunuch (Acts 8:26—39).

Stephen also preached and taught. Certainly anyone filled with the Holy Ghost (and the Scripture plainly tells us that Stephen was "full of faith and of the Holy Ghost") should be capable of witnessing to the saving grace of God and the power of the Gospel. Stephen had the gift of preaching, and he used this gift in testifying before the council. It cost him his life, as we will see in the next chapter, but he obeyed the Spirit regardless of cost.

Verse 7:   *"And the Word of God increased; and the number of the disciples multiplied in Jerusalem greatly; and a great company of the priests were obedient to the faith."*

From the human standpoint, or as seen through mortal eyes, things looked promising indeed. Many were accepting the Word of God as the object of faith and power among men. Many new disciples were being added to the company of believers, and even priests were now coming to hear and receive the Gospel, believing on Him whom they had crucified! Seemingly, great revival was about to sweep the nation of Israel and they would be converted, their sins blotted out. *"The times of refreshing"* might come "from the presence of the Lord" (Acts 3:19)—but the scene will soon change.

The Word of God increasing, the number of disciples being multiplied and priests being converted was exactly that which was prophesied. The Holy Spirit was to come and call out "a people for His name," a Gentile bride; and only then will Jesus return to "build again the tabernacle of David, which is fallen down." In Acts 15: 14—17 James said, "Simeon hath declared how God at the first did visit the Gentiles, to take out of them a people for His name. And to this agree the words of the prophets; as it is written, After this I will return, and will build again the tabernacle of David, which is fallen down; and I will build again the ruins thereof, and I will set it up: that the residue of men might seek after the Lord, and all the Gentiles, upon whom my name is called, saith the Lord, who doeth all these things."

The Holy Spirit is *still* calling out "a people for His name." *Whosoever will* may come—but whosoever comes must come the one and only way: *by believing on the Lord Jesus Christ,* God's only begotten Son, crucified, buried, risen, and ascended "according to the Scriptures." The Holy Spirit will continue to call out a people until the bride of Christ is complete; then the Church will be caught out to meet the Lord Jesus in the air (I Thess. 4:13—18).

Stephen's Preaching, Arrest, and Accusation by the Council

Verse 8: *"And Stephen, full of faith and power, did great wonders and miracles among the people."*

Stephen was used and honored of God in a very special and unique way quite outside the realm of work for which the seven deacons were elected. He was neither

a bishop, an apostle, nor an elder; but he was filled
with the Holy Spirit, he was full of faith, grace, and
power; and he "did great wonders and miracles among
the people."

We might expect to find jealousy and envy here—but
not so. All members of the assembly glorified the Lord,
all used the opportunities and power and grace God had
given them to bring honor and glory to the name of Jesus. They had liberty in the Spirit, they were not afraid
of what some fellow believer might think or say. Evidently Stephen wrought miracles and did mighty works
which up to that time not even the apostles had performed; but there was no jealousy or envy among them.

You see, in the Word of God we do not find an out-
line laid down for ordaining a man to preach, teach, or
evangelize. We find no set rules or regulations concerning men appointed to administer baptism or officiate at
the Lord's Supper. Therefore we must conclude that
tradition, superstition, and religious habits have entered
into the present day assembly, and often even godly men
fail to see that Scripture contradicts some of the practices in our local churches. It is extremely difficult for
ministers, teachers, evangelists—yes, even lay members—
to leave the flesh out of daily living and allow the Spirit
of God to have full control, giving Christ the pre-em-
inence.

According to the Word of God, a believer who has a
spiritual gift is free to exercise that gift to the glory of
God wherever such opportunity is given. Christians who
do not use their God-given talents to His glory and honor
can be likened unto the unprofitable servant in the parable recorded in Matthew 25:14—30: Before going into a
far country the master divided his goods among his servants. To one he gave five talents, to another he gave
two talents, and to the third he gave only one talent.
The first two servants invested their talents profitably,
while the third took his one talent and hid it in the

earth.

By and by the master returned, and required an accounting from his servants. He commended those who had *increased* their holdings by using them wisely, and said to them, "Thou hast been faithful over a few things, I will make thee ruler over many things: enter thou into the joy of thy lord."

Then the servant to whom only one talent had been given said to his master, "Lord, I knew thee that thou art an hard man, reaping where thou hast not sown, and gathering where thou hast not strawed: and I was afraid, and went and hid thy talent in the earth." To which his master replied, "Thou wicked and slothful servant, thou knewest that I reap where I sowed not, and gather where I have not strawed: Thou oughtest therefore to have put my money to the exchangers, and then at my coming I should have received mine own with usury. Take therefore the talent from him, and give it unto him which hath ten talents. . . . And cast ye the unprofitable servant into outer darkness: there shall be weeping and gnashing of teeth."

The master did not excuse that servant just because he thought wrongly and made the wrong decision. He judged him, regardless. So we come face to face with the fact that it is not a question of whether the believer *has the right* to do this or that, but whether he is doing what he does *to the glory of God*. The Apostle Paul warned the Corinthian church, "Whether therefore ye eat, or drink, or *whatsoever ye do, DO ALL TO THE GLORY OF GOD*" (I Cor. 10:31). The believer who does *less* than that is failing in his privilege and in his obligation as a Christian.

Peter has this to say about believers who have received gifts through God's grace: "As every man hath *received* the gift, even so *minister the same one to another, as good stewards of the manifold grace of God*" (I Pet. 4:10).

God gave men like Stephen unusual anointings for

specific occasions to bring glory and honor to the Lord Jesus Christ, and to declare through signs and wonders that *truly He was the Christ of God, the Messiah, Saviour of sinners*—of "whosoever will."

Verse 9: *"Then there arose certain of the synagogue, which is called the synagogue of the Libertines, and Cyrenians, and Alexandrians, and of them of Cilicia and of Asia, disputing with Stephen."*

We see Stephen, filled with the Spirit, with grace and great wisdom, performing "great wonders and miracles among the people" in Jerusalem, and then we see him testifying before the Jewish council; but whether in the synagogue, on the streets of Jerusalem, or before the San-hedrin to be condemned to death, there is not one mite of compromise or selfishness in his testimony! He spoke to the glory of God, no doubt realizing that his testimony could very easily cost him his life.

We notice that the *"Libertines"* head the list of Ste-phen's enemies here. According to the most reliable Bible historians, the Libertines were Jews who had been taken prisoner by the Roman, Pompey, carried to Rome, and later released and allowed to practice their own religion. *These* Libertines were most likely the *children* of those Jews who had been taken captive by Pompey, and now as freedmen they had returned to Jerusalem and formed a congregation, using their own specific synagogue.

The *"Cyrenians"* were Jews from Cyrene. (We know Cyrenians were present in Jerusalem on the Day of Pente-cost when every man present heard the Gospel in his own language—Acts 2:8, 10.)

The *Alexandrians* and "them of *Cilicia* and of *Asia"* joined in the dispute against Stephen.

Some Bible commentators have suggested that there were two synagogues from which these people came. Others suggest that the five groups named came from five different synagogues. I find no scriptural grounds for either contention; but historical accounts relating to that day state that there were some 480 synagogues in Jerusalem; so it can be seen that each of these groups could have come from a separate synagogue. Whether these people came from one synagogue or from various synagogues, the important point is that they joined together in false accusation against Stephen. As cunning as is the archenemy of the Christian, it is little problem for the enemies of the Gospel to find some reason to charge those who preach the truth. Satan hates the truth, he hates all men who preach the truth, and he can always find those who, for so-called "reasons," will persecute the ministers of truth.

Verse 10: *"And they were not able to resist the wisdom and the Spirit by which He spake."*

Regardless of the hatred in their hearts and the schemes they had devised to stop this deacon from performing the miracles and wonders he was doing among the people, the enemies of Stephen *"were not able to resist the wisdom and the Spirit by which he spake"* — but in the next verse we learn that they bribed men to witness against him falsely and declare that he had spoken blasphemies.

We must bear in mind the opening statement of the book of Acts. In chapter 1, verse 1 we read:

"The *former* treatise have I made, O Theophilus, of all that Jesus *BEGAN both to do and teach."* This verse is the key to the book of Acts, connecting it with the Gospel of Luke. Luke's Gospel contains the account of the things the Lord Jesus Christ *BEGAN to do and teach,* suggesting that the ministry and mission of Jesus did not climax with the things recorded in the four Gospels. Therefore, the book of Acts is the account of the things Jesus *continued* to do and teach through the Holy Spirit by means of the members of the New Testament Church.

In the sufferings and death of Stephen we have a concrete illustration of what Paul meant in Colossians 1:24 when he wrote of *filling up "that which is behind of the afflictions of Christ."* The original Greek reads "that which is *lacking* in the afflictions of Christ." This does not mean that there was any element *absent* from the sufferings of Christ, or that He did not suffer enough. The sufferings of Christ were certainly sufficient to satisfy the holiness, righteousness, and law of Jehovah God. However, the Greek strongly suggests that the sufferings of Jesus would be continued in the lives of His followers. The Greek word for "lacking" means "*deficit*, that which comes later." The underlying thought of Paul was that the sufferings of Christ were by no means over even when, from the cross, He cried out, "It is finished!" Writing to Timothy Paul declared, "Yea, and all that will live godly in Christ Jesus shall suffer persecution" (II Tim. 3:12). Christ's suffering continues today in all who are in Him and who suffer shame for His name's sake. The suffering of the believer is Christ's suffering, and Christ's suffering is ours.

Thus the continual process of the sufferings of Christ, as manifested in the death of Stephen and on the part of believers, will not cease until that glorious time when Jesus calls His Church to meet Him in the clouds in the air. Yes, hallelujah to His precious name! the hour is coming when "He shall see of the travail of His soul, and shall be satisfied" (Isa. 53:11). Until then, God grant that Christians may never lose sight of the fact that the *travail itself* will not end until that moment when Jesus will descend with a shout and with the voice of the archangel, and the saints of God will be caught up to be with Him. Only then will the suffering of believers be over:

"For I reckon that the sufferings of this present time are not worthy to be compared with the glory which shall be revealed in us. For the earnest expectation of

the creature waiteth for the manifestation of the sons of
God.   For the creature was made subject to vanity, not
willingly, but by reason of Him who hath subjected the
same in hope.   Because the creature itself also shall be
delivered from the bondage of corruption into the glorious
liberty of the children of God.

*"For we know that the whole creation groaneth and
travaileth in pain together until now.   And not only they,
but ourselves also, which have the firstfruits of the Spirit,
even we ourselves groan within ourselves, waiting for
the adoption, to wit, THE REDEMPTION OF OUR
BODY"* (Rom. 8:18—23).

This does not speak of the redemption of the spirit,
but of the *body.*   Our glorious salvation is in past, present, and future tense.   When Jesus cried out, "It is finished," He had completely paid the price of redemption
through His precious blood, and the moment we believe
on Him we are redeemed from the curse of the law and
from the death demanded by sin.   But we are *saved
continually*—moment by moment—*because HE LIVES.*
He died to redeem us, He lives to make intercession for
us:

"For when we were yet without strength, in due time
Christ died for the ungodly. . . . But God commendeth
His love toward us, in that, *while we were yet sinners,
CHRIST DIED FOR US.*   Much more then, being now
justified by His blood, we shall be saved from wrath
through Him.   For if, when we were enemies, we were
reconciled to God by the *death* of His Son, much more,
being reconciled, *we shall be SAVED by His life.*   And
not only so, but we also joy in God through our Lord
Jesus Christ, by whom we have now received the atonement" (Rom. 5:6—11 in part).

Verse 11:   *"Then they suborned men, which said, We
have heard him speak blasphemous words against Moses,
and against God."*

The wicked members of the synagogue *"suborned"* (bribed) men to make false claims that Stephen had blasphemed Moses, and that he had also spoken blasphemy against God.

Yes, the sufferings of Jesus continued in Stephen, for these false witnesses were practicing the same sin their forefathers had practiced. In the Old Testament, we find this same method used against Naboth when King Ahab coveted Naboth's vineyard. Ahab offered to *buy* the vineyard, but Naboth refused to sell because the Lord had forbidden him to do so. Therefore, Jezebel suborned men to lie against Naboth, accuse him of blasphemy, and have him stoned in order for Ahab to acquire the vineyard. (Read the account in I Kings 21:1—16.)

These enemies of the truth were using the same scheme against Stephen that they had used against the Lord Jesus. On one occasion Jesus challenged His enemies, "Which of you convinceth me of sin?" (John 8:46). The officers who were sent to arrest Him declared, "Never man spake like this Man" (John 7:46). The thief on the cross testified of Jesus, "This Man hath done nothing amiss" (Luke 23:41)—and even *Pilate* three times confessed, *"I find NO FAULT in Him!"* But in spite of all the evidence in favor of the Lord Jesus Christ, the chief priests and the council hired witnesses to testify falsely against Him in order to condemn Him to death:

"They that had laid hold on Jesus led Him away to Caiaphas the high priest, where the scribes and the elders were assembled. . . . Now the chief priests, and elders, and all the council, sought false witness against Jesus, to put Him to death; *but found none:* yea, though many false witnesses came, yet found they none.

"At the last came two false witnesses, and said, This Fellow said, I am able to destroy the temple of God, and to build it in three days. . . .

"Then the high priest rent his clothes, saying, He hath spoken blasphemy; what further need have we of wit-

nesses?   Behold, now ye have heard His blasphemy.
What think ye? *They answered and said, HE IS GUILTY
OF DEATH!"* (Matt. 26:57—66 in part).

Jesus had acknowledged that He was the Son of God,
that He came from heaven, that "before Abraham was,
I AM."   These statements implied His superiority over
David, Moses, and Abraham.   He declared, "Destroy
this temple, and I will raise it up in three days"—speaking of His body.   His enemies declared these truths to
be blasphemy, and by the testimony of false witnesses
they brought about His crucifixion.   Now in our present
study we hear them make the same accusation against
Stephen, and by the same method.

Verse 12:   *"And they stirred up the people, and the
elders, and the scribes, and came upon him, and caught
him, and brought him to the council."*

The Jewish religionists were so filled with anger, hate,
and jealousy against Stephen that *"they stirred up the
people"* and there was a general outburst of Jewish re-
sentment which resulted in Stephen's being seized and
brought before the Sanhedrin for trial.

Verses 13 and 14:   *"And set up false witnesses, which
said, This man ceaseth not to speak blasphemous words
against this holy place, and the law: For we have heard
him say, that this Jesus of Nazareth shall destroy this
place, and shall change the customs which Moses delivered us."*

Nothing could have been more untrue than the wicked
accusation these men brought against Stephen! He was
filled with the Holy Spirit, possessed and controlled by
the Spirit, and certainly the Spirit would not lead him
to blaspheme God—nor would Stephen have spoken dis-
respectfully of Moses, nor of the temple and the law of
God.   But wicked men hear what they want to hear,
they take away that which they desire to take away and

add whatever may be to their advantage in bringing about their purpose.

The *religious leaders* had been angry with the apostles and had stood in opposition to the Church from the very beginning; but now *"the people"* (the common people, the multitudes) were stirred to hatred against Stephen because of the testimony of the false witnesses who had declared that he had spoken against the temple. Among the Jews, the temple was the object of admiration, great pride, respect, and devotion.

But Stephen had not spoken against the temple. In chapter 7 verse 48 he said, "Howbeit *the most High dwelleth not in temples made with hands;* as saith the prophet." More than likely he had made this statement more than once, but now the false witnesses twisted his meaning into the words they spoke before the Sanhedrin; and to the Jews, to sever worship from Jerusalem was to destroy the temple; and to them, worship without the temple was unthinkable. Yet in His conversation with the Samaritan woman Jesus had explained, "The hour cometh, and now is, when the true worshippers shall worship the Father in spirit and in truth: for the Father seeketh such to worship Him. God is a Spirit: and they that worship Him must worship Him in spirit and in truth" (John 4:23, 24).

It was this message that Stephen had tried to get over to the Jews; but the false witnesses called it "blasphemy" and stirred up the people against him.

Verse 15: *"And all that sat in the council, looking stedfastly on him, saw his face as it had been the face of an angel."*

Naturally, Stephen was the center of attention here. All eyes were fixed on him—the crowd looked "stedfastly" upon him, wondering what he would—or could—say in his own defense; but they were in for a surprise. Instead of being nervous, despondent, fearful, and trembling before his accusers, Stephen was calm, confident, completely free of fear and anxiety. He was filled with the Spirit, and the multitude *"saw his face as it had been the face of an angel."* Such was his inward peace!

God in His omniscience knew every detail of what would happen here; and Stephen was so filled with the Holy Spirit, so completely surrendered to God's will, I do not doubt that his face was already illumined with the radiance of the Paradise of God where he would shortly be. Therefore his enemies saw in his face that which could be displayed only by a spirit-being—"as it had been the face of an angel."

These people should have realized that Stephen was receiving from God a sign such as Moses received when God spoke to him on the mountain. In Exodus 34:29, 30 we read, "And it came to pass, when Moses came down from mount Sinai with the two tables of testimony in Moses' hand, when he came down from the mount, that Moses wist not that the skin of his face shone while he talked with Him. And when Aaron and all the children of Israel saw Moses, behold, *the skin of his face shone; and they were afraid to come nigh him."* So Moses put a veil over his face while he gave the children of Israel the message God had given him.

The same God who spoke to Moses in most miraculous manner is now intervening on behalf of Stephen, and these religious rulers in the assembly of the Jews should have seen and felt the appeal God was making to them through this man who was so filled with the Holy Ghost, with grace, and with wisdom. But their minds were closed, blinded by "the god of this world" (II Cor. 4:3, 4), and there is no evidence—even though it be given through the hand of God—which wilful unbelief cannot evade!

When the rich man begged Abraham to send the beggar Lazarus to warn his brethren, that they not come to the "place of torment," Abraham replied, "If they hear not Moses and the prophets, neither will they be persuaded, *though one rose from the dead"* (Luke 16:19—31). *JESUS rose from the dead,* He appeared on earth for *forty days* after His resurrection and on one occasion was seen by *"above five hundred brethren at once"* (I Cor. 15:6).

But in spite of His miracles and other divine evidences of His deity during His earthly ministry, and in spite of His known resurrection from the dead, the Jews rejected Jesus; and now as Stephen stands before them, his face shining as an angel, they ignore the supernatural display of glory. Spiritual blindness is far more deadly than physical blindness. These people harbored hatred and murder in their hearts, all the while setting themselves up as custodians of the Word of God.

CHAPTER VII

1. Then said the high priest, Are these things so?

2. And he said, Men, brethren, and fathers, hearken; The God of glory appeared unto our father Abraham, when he was in Mesopotamia, before he dwelt in Charran,

3. And said unto him, Get thee out of thy country, and from thy kindred, and come into the land which I shall shew thee.

4. Then came he out of the land of the Chaldaeans, and dwelt in Charran: and from thence, when his father was dead, he removed him into this land, wherein ye now dwell.

5. And he gave him none inheritance in it, no, not so much as to set his foot on: yet he promised that he would give it to him for a possession, and to his seed after him, when as yet he had no child.

6. And God spake on this wise, That his seed should sojourn in a strange land; and that they should bring them into bondage, and entreat them evil four hundred years.

7. And the nation to whom they shall be in bondage will I judge, said God: and after that shall they come forth, and serve me in this place.

8. And he gave him the covenant of circumcision: and so Abraham begat Isaac, and circumcised him the eighth day; and Isaac begat Jacob; and Jacob begat the twelve patriarchs.

9. And the patriarchs, moved with envy, sold Joseph into Egypt: but God was with him,

10. And delivered him out of all his afflictions, and gave him favour and wisdom in the sight of Pharaoh king of Egypt; and he made him governor over Egypt and all his house.

11. Now there came a dearth over all the land of Egypt and Chanaan, and great affliction: and our fathers found no sustenance.

12. But when Jacob heard that there was corn in Egypt, he sent out our fathers first.

13. And at the second time Joseph was made known to his brethren; and Joseph's kindred was made known unto Pharaoh.

14. Then sent Joseph, and called his father Jacob to him, and all his kindred, threescore and fifteen souls.

15. So Jacob went down into Egypt, and died, he, and our fathers,

16. And were carried over into Sychem, and laid in the sepulchre that Abraham bought for a sum of money of the sons of Emmor the father of Sychem.

17. But when the time of the promise drew nigh, which God had sworn to Abraham, the people grew and multiplied in Egypt,

18. Till another king arose, which knew not Joseph.

19. The same dealt subtilly with our kindred, and evil entreated our fathers, so that they cast out their young children, to the end they might not live.

20. In which time Moses was born, and was exceeding fair, and nourished up in his father's house three months:

21. And when he was cast out, Pharaoh's daughter took him up, and nourished him for her own son.

22. And Moses was learned in all the wisdom of the Egyptians, and was mighty in words and in deeds.

23. And when he was full forty years old, it came into his heart to visit his brethren the children of Israel.

24. And seeing one of them suffer wrong, he defended him, and avenged him that was oppressed, and smote the Egyptian:

25. For he supposed his brethren would have understood how that God by his hand would deliver them: but they understood not.

26. And the next day he shewed himself unto them as they strove, and would have set them at one again, saying, Sirs, ye are brethren; why do ye wrong one to another?

27. But he that did his neighbour wrong thrust him away, saying, Who made thee a ruler and a judge over us?

28. Wilt thou kill me, as thou diddest the Egyptian yesterday?

29. Then fled Moses at this saying, and was a stranger in the land of Madian, where he begat two sons.

30. And when forty years were expired, there appeared to him in the wilderness of mount Sina an angel of the Lord in a flame of fire in a bush.

31. When Moses saw it, he wondered at the sight: and as he drew near to behold it, the voice of the Lord came unto him,

32. Saying, I am the God of thy fathers, the God of Abraham, and the God of Isaac, and the God of Jacob. Then Moses trembled, and durst not behold.

33. Then said the Lord to him, Put off thy shoes from thy feet: for the place where thou standest is holy ground.

34. I have seen, I have seen the affliction of my people which is in Egypt, and I have heard their groaning, and am come down

to deliver them. And now come, I will send thee into Egypt.

35. This Moses whom they refused, saying, Who made thee a ruler and a judge? the same did God send to be a ruler and a deliverer by the hand of the angel which appeared to him in the bush.

36. He brought them out, after that he had shewed wonders and signs in the land of Egypt, and in the Red sea, and in the wilderness forty years.

37. This is that Moses, which said unto the children of Israel, A prophet shall the Lord your God raise up unto you of your brethren, like unto me; him shall ye hear.

38. This is he, that was in the church in the wilderness with the angel which spake to him in the mount Sina, and with our fathers: who received the lively oracles to give unto us:

39. To whom our fathers would not obey, but thrust him from them, and in their hearts turned back again into Egypt,

40. Saying unto Aaron, Make us gods to go before us: for as for this Moses, which brought us out of the land of Egypt, we wot not what is become of him.

41. And they made a calf in those days, and offered sacrifice unto the idol, and rejoiced in the works of their own hands.

42. Then God turned, and gave them up to worship the host of heaven; as it is written in the book of the prophets, O ye house of Israel, have ye offered to me slain beasts and sacrifices by the space of forty years in the wilderness?

43. Yea, ye took up the tabernacle of Moloch, and the star of your god Remphan, figures which ye made to worship them: and I will carry you away beyond Babylon.

44. Our fathers had the tabernacle of witness in the wilderness, as he had appointed, speaking unto Moses, that he should make it according to the fashion that he had seen.

45. Which also our fathers that came after brought in with Jesus into the possession of the Gentiles, whom God drave out before the face of our fathers, unto the days of David;

46. Who found favour before God, and desired to find a tabernacle for the God of Jacob.

47. But Solomon built him an house.

48. Howbeit the most High dwelleth not in temples made with hands; as saith the prophet,

49. Heaven is my throne, and earth is my footstool: what house will ye build me? saith the Lord: or what is the place of my rest?

50. Hath not my hand made all these things?

51. Ye stiffnecked and uncircumcised in heart and ears, ye do

always resist the Holy Ghost: as your fathers did, so do ye.

52. Which of the prophets have not your fathers persecuted? and they have slain them which shewed before of the coming of the Just One; of whom ye have been now the betrayers and murderers:

53. Who have received the law by the disposition of angels, and have not kept it.

54. When they heard these things, they were cut to the heart, and they gnashed on him with their teeth.

55. But he, being full of the Holy Ghost, looked up stedfastly into heaven, and saw the glory of God, and Jesus standing on the right hand of God,

56. And said, Behold, I see the heavens opened, and the Son of man standing on the right hand of God.

57. Then they cried out with a loud voice, and stopped their ears, and ran upon him with one accord,

58. And cast him out of the city, and stoned him: and the witnesses laid down their clothes at a young man's feet, whose name was Saul.

59. And they stoned Stephen, calling upon God, and saying, Lord Jesus, receive my spirit.

60. And he kneeled down, and cried with a loud voice, Lord, lay not this sin to their charge. And when he had said this, he fell asleep.

The more I search the Scriptures in my study of the Word of God the more grateful I am *for* the Word of God—from Genesis through Revelation; but there are certain portions of the Word for which I am extremely grateful. The remarkable testimony of Stephen given in this chapter is one of those passages.

It was not one of the twelve whom God used here to break fresh ground and open the way for a much wider outgoing of truth. Stephen was not a bishop, an elder, nor an apostle. He was simply a Greek-born Jew who had been elected to see after the secondary matters of the Church. How remarkable that he should give this testimony—and even more remarkable is the fact that it occurred just after the account of the conversion of "a great company of the priests" (ch. 6, v. 7).

It was to Stephen that God granted the honor of being the first member of the body of Christ to seal his testimony with his life's blood. He was accused of declaring that Jesus would destroy the temple and change the customs given to them by Moses in the law.

Stephen's Defense

Verse 1: *"Then said the high priest, Are these things so?"*

Addressing Stephen, the high priest called upon him to answer the charges that had been brought against him. As we study the testimony of Stephen step by step we will see how he defended the truth he had preached and how he pointed out the perversion of the meaning of the words he had spoken. Stephen was "a man full of faith and of the Holy Ghost" and he was not the enemy of God's law. Grace is incomparably higher, but grace establishes rather than destroys the law.

The prophetic Word of God *did* make known the destruction of the magnificent, stately buildings of the temple. In Mark 13:1, 2, as Jesus and His disciples were leaving the temple, one of the disciples called the Lord's attention to "what manner of stones and what buildings are here." Jesus replied, "Seest thou these great buildings? *There shall not be left one stone upon another, that shall not be thrown down!"* Jesus gave the prophecy of the coming destruction of the temple—but did that make Him the One who would destroy it? A *little bit* of reason will show how *unreasonable* it was to accuse Jesus of contemplating the destruction of the most sacred of all places to the Hebrews. He simply prophesied that which actually occurred later—and many who were present on the occasion of His prophecy were also present to witness its fulfillment—and many of them *died* in the destruction of Jerusalem!

The same One who prophesied the destruction of the temple also prophesied that under the King who would sit on the throne of David, *the law should go forth out of Zion, "and the Word of the Lord from Jerusalem"* (Isa. 2:3). Also, in the early part of His ministry Jesus publicly declared, *"Think not that I am come to destroy the law, or the prophets: I AM NOT COME TO DESTROY, BUT TO FULFIL"* (Matt. 5:17).

But these spiritually blind, willingly ignorant religionists refused to see or hear the truth. Their minds were made up. Even though Stephen had said nothing that had not already been said prophetically before him, they were *determined to destroy him.*

Verse 2: *"And he said, Men, brethren, and fathers, hearken: The God of glory appeared unto our father Abraham, when he was in Mesopotamia, before he dwelt in Charran."*

First of all, Stephen points his listeners to the God who was in the beginning—*"the God of glory."* The Psalmist declared, "Lord, thou hast been our dwelling place in all generations. Before the mountains were brought forth, or ever thou hadst formed the earth and the world, *even FROM EVERLASTING TO EVERLASTING, thou art God"* (Psalm 90:1, 2).

These men of the Sanhedrin knew the Old Testament Scriptures, and Stephen directed their minds to Jehovah the Eternal One, He who spoke to the Israelite fathers, and in spite of their unbelief provided for them in mercy and in grace. Abraham's father and other kinsmen were worshippers of idols—"they served other gods" (Josh. 24:1—3). But God in His grace, mercy, and lovingkindness called out Abraham in spite of his relatives being idolaters.

The "God of glory" not only *appeared* to Abraham— He appeared to him *"when he was in Mesopotamia, before he dwelt in Charran."* In other words, while Abraham was at the greatest distance from the promised land, as well as dwelling in the midst of idolaters, *God called him.*

Verse 3: *"And said unto him, Get thee out of thy country, and from thy kindred, and come into the land which I shall shew thee."*

Abraham heard God's call and he obeyed—but he did not instantaneously step from Mesopotamia into the land of Canaan: he moved *progressively* as God ordered his steps. It was of this that Stephen was reminding the Sanhedrin in an attempt to show them how the God of their fathers had led Abraham step by step, and how He was *still leading* step by step to the glorious reign of Messiah whom they had long expected and yearned for. He was pointing out to them that they had *crucified* the One of whom Moses wrote—their Messiah who had come through the lineage of Abraham, as God had promised.

In Genesis 11:31, 32 we learn that Terah, Abraham's father, was a hindrance to his obedience: "And Terah took Abram his son and Lot the son of Haran his son's son, and Sarai his daughter in law, his son Abram's wife; and they went forth with them from Ur of the Chaldees, to go into the land of Canaan; and they came unto Haran, and dwelt there. And the days of Terah were two hundred and five years: and Terah died in Haran."

This is reasonable. The father led in the departure, but it is also clear that Terah hindered Abraham in giving complete obedience to God's instructions. They reached Haran, but they stopped there and *dwelt* in Haran until Abraham's father died. Then the Lord spoke to Abraham—and he departed as the Lord had ordered him:

"So Abram departed, as the Lord had spoken unto him; and Lot went with him: and Abram was seventy and five years old when he departed out of Haran. And Abram took Sarai his wife, and Lot his brother's son, and all their substance that they had gathered, and the souls that they had gotten in Haran; and they went forth to go into the land of Canaan; and into the land of Canaan they came. And Abram passed through the land unto the place of Sichem, unto the plain of Moreh. And the Canaanite was then in the land. And the Lord appeared unto Abram, and said, Unto thy seed will I give this land: and there builded he an altar unto the Lord, who appeared unto him.

"And he removed from thence unto a mountain on the east of Bethel, and pitched his tent, having Bethel on the west, and Hai on the east: and there he builded an altar unto the Lord, and called upon the name of the Lord. And Abram journeyed, going on still toward the south" (Gen. 12:4—9).

Verse 4: *"Then came he out of the land of the Chaldaeans, and dwelt in Charran: and from thence, when his father was dead, He removed him into this land, wherein ye now dwell."*

Some have raised the question whether *"he removed"* speaks of Abraham or of God. Personally, I believe *God removed Abraham* into this land and that "he" points to God, not to Abraham. I believe verse 5 bears this out.

Verse 5: *"And He gave him none inheritance in it, no, not so much as to set his foot on: yet He promised that He would give it to him for a possession, and to his seed after him, when as yet he had no child."*

Some scholars maintain that God afterward gave Abraham a possession in Canaan—the piece of land which he purchased from Ephron the Hittite as a burial place, as recorded in Genesis 23:7—20; but this is incorrect. The gift of God to Abraham is still future. He *will* possess the land God gave to him and to his seed, and the fact that God's gift is yet future is *confirmed*, rather than *weakened*, by Abraham's purchase of a burial place from Ephron. That is, if Abraham had possessed the land at that time, why would he *buy* that which he already *possessed?* He buried his dead in a land that was so evidently *NOT his own* that he had to buy the needed space to lay his loved ones to rest; but the *seed of Abraham* will possess the land in the future—i. e., at the appointed time God will give it to them. In Hebrews 11:8–10 the Apostle Paul explains: *"By faith* Abraham, when he was called to go out into a place which he should after receive for an inheritance, obeyed; and he went out, not knowing whither he went. *By faith he sojourned in the land of promise,* as in a strange country, dwelling in tabernacles with Isaac and Jacob, the heirs with him of the same promise: for he looked for a city which hath foundations, whose builder and maker is God."

When the Church has been raptured, when the Antichrist has run his course, when the curse has been lifted and the knowledge of the Lord covers the earth as the waters now cover the sea, Abraham—friend of God and father of the faithful—will come into his promised inheritance:

"Lord, thou hast been favourable unto thy land: thou hast brought back the captivity of Jacob. Thou hast forgiven the iniquity of thy people, thou hast covered all their sin. Selah. Thou hast taken away all thy wrath: thou hast turned thyself from the fierceness of thine anger.

"Turn us, O God of our salvation, and cause thine anger toward us to cease. Wilt thou be angry with us for ever? Wilt thou draw out thine anger to all generations? Wilt thou not revive us again: that thy people may rejoice in thee? Shew us thy mercy, O Lord, and grant us thy salvation.

"I will hear what God the Lord will speak: for He will speak peace unto His people, and to His saints: but let them not turn again to folly. Surely His salvation is nigh them that fear Him; that glory may dwell in our land. Mercy and truth are met together; righteousness and peace have kissed each other.

"Truth shall spring out of the earth; and righteousness

shall look down from heaven. Yea, the Lord shall give that which is good; and our land shall yield her increase. Righteousness shall go before Him; and shall set us in the way of His steps" (Psalm 85).

In that glorious day when Jesus will sit on the throne of David in Jerusalem, in the tabernacle rebuilt at the very place where Solomon's temple stood in the days of Solomon's glory, the earth will be filled with the knowledge of the Lord and with the glory of God, but pre-eminently the glory will be in Zion:

"And after they had held their peace, James answered, saying, Men and brethren, hearken unto me: Simeon hath declared how God at the first did visit the Gentiles, to take out of them a people for His name. And to this agree the words of the prophets; as it is written, After this I will return, and will build again the tabernacle of David, which is fallen down; and I will build again the ruins thereof, and I will set it up: That the residue of men might seek after the Lord, and all the Gentiles, upon whom my name is called, saith the Lord, who doeth all these things. Known unto God are all His works from the beginning of the world" (Acts 15:13—18).

Isaiah gives a clear, understandable account of the glorious kingdom of David that will be set up right here on this earth:

"And there shall come forth a rod out of the stem of Jesse, and a Branch shall grow out of his roots: And the Spirit of the Lord shall rest upon Him, the spirit of wisdom and understanding, the spirit of counsel and might, the spirit of knowledge and of the fear of the Lord; and shall make Him of quick understanding in the fear of the Lord: and He shall not judge after the sight of His eyes, neither reprove after the hearing of His ears: but with righteousness shall He judge the poor, and reprove with equity for the meek of the earth: and He shall smite the earth with the rod of His mouth, and with the breath of His lips shall He slay the wicked.

And righteousness shall be the girdle of His loins, and faithfulness the girdle of His reins.

"The wolf also shall dwell with the lamb, and the leopard shall lie down with the kid; and the calf and the young lion and the fatling together; and a little child shall lead them. And the cow and the bear shall feed; their young ones shall lie down together: and the lion shall eat straw like the ox. And the sucking child shall play on the hole of the asp, and the weaned child shall put his hand on the cockatrice' den.

"They shall not hurt nor destroy in all my holy mountain: for the earth shall be full of the knowledge of the Lord, as the waters cover the sea.

"And in that day there shall be a root of Jesse, which shall stand for an ensign of the people; to it shall the Gentiles seek: and His rest shall be glorious. And it shall come to pass in that day, that the Lord shall set His hand again the second time to recover the remnant of His people, which shall be left, from Assyria, and from Egypt, and from Pathros, and from Cush, and from Elam, and from Shinar, and from Hamath, and from the islands of the sea. And He shall set up an ensign for the nations, and shall assemble the outcasts of Israel, and gather together the dispersed of Judah from the four corners of the earth.

"The envy also of Ephraim shall depart, and the adversaries of Judah shall be cut off: Ephraim shall not envy Judah, and Judah shall not vex Ephraim. But they shall fly upon the shoulders of the Philistines toward the west; they shall spoil them of the east together: they shall lay their hand upon Edom and Moab; and the children of Ammon shall obey them. And the Lord shall utterly destroy the tongue of the Egyptian sea; and with His mighty wind shall He shake His hand over the river, and shall smite it in the seven streams, and make men go over dryshod. And there shall be an highway for the remnant of His people, which shall be left, from Assyria;

like as it was to Israel in the day that he came up out
of the land of Egypt" (Isa. 11).

When the angel Gabriel announced to Mary that she
would be the mother of the Son of God, he made the
announcement in these words:

"Fear not, Mary: for thou hast found favour with
God. And, behold, thou shalt conceive in thy womb,
and bring forth a Son, and shalt call His name JESUS.
He shall be great, and shall be called the Son of the
Highest: *and the Lord God shall give unto Him the
throne of His father David: and He shall reign over the
house of Jacob for ever; and of His kingdom there shall
be no end"* (Luke 1:30—33).

The promise given to Abraham in Genesis 12:7 concerning the land was made in a greater and fuller way
when he returned from Egypt. In Genesis 13:15, 16 God
said to him, "For all the land which thou seest, to thee
will I give it, and to thy seed for ever. And I will make
thy seed as the dust of the earth: so that if a man can
number the dust of the earth, then shall thy seed also
be numbered."

Stephen reminded the Sanhedrin that God made this
promise to Abraham *"when as yet he had no child."* We
are not told exactly how many years elapsed from the
time God made the promise to Abraham until Isaac was
born, but we do know that it was a long time. According to Genesis 12:10—20, when Abraham went down into
Egypt Sarah was young and fair, in the prime of her
beauty. But when the Lord appeared to Abraham "in
the plains of Mamre," long after he returned from Egypt,
and told him that Sarah would bear a son, we are told
that "Sarah laughed within herself, saying, *After I am
WAXED OLD* shall I have pleasure, my lord being old
also?" Therefore we know that Isaac was born after
Abraham was old and Sarah had passed the age of child-
bearing (Gen. 18:10—14).

Verse 6: *"And God spake on this wise, That his seed*

should sojourn in a strange land; and that they should bring them into bondage, and entreat them evil four hundred years."

In this part of his testimony Stephen refers to statements recorded in Genesis 15:13, 14 where God said to Abraham, "Know of a surety that thy seed shall be a stranger in a land that is not their's, and shall serve them; and they shall afflict them four hundred years; and also that nation, whom they shall serve, will I judge: and afterward shall they come out with great substance."

Now notice Genesis 47:11, 12: "Joseph placed his father and his brethren, and gave them *a possession in the land of Egypt, in the best of the land,* in the land of Rameses, as Pharaoh had commanded. And Joseph nourished his father, and his brethren, and all his father's household, with bread, according to their families."

God is faithful. *Because He IS God* He cannot be *unfaithful.* He did not forget His people while they were in Egypt, even though they were not always faithful to Him. He did not forget them as they wandered for forty years in the wilderness after they *left* Egypt, and He has not forgotten Israel today. God will be faithful to His promise to Abraham until every jot and tittle of that promise has been fulfilled—a promise made before Abraham had a child, but it will be kept even unto the last child to be born in Israel!

By the grace of God and through the power of the Holy Spirit, Stephen was endeavoring to show these leaders in Israel how very wrong they were in their self-righteous boasting, setting themselves up as custodians of the Word of God in that hour when the New Testament Church was flourishing. God had appeared to Abraham alone when there was absolutely nothing to boast about, for Abraham belonged to a family of idolaters, he lived in a land of idolatry with nothing but sin and shame in his background, *and when God appeared to father Abraham, Israel was yet unborn.*

But their minds were too blinded by the god of this age for them to see the comparison Stephen was making—that is, as it had been with Abraham, so had it been with the promised Seed, the Lord Jesus Christ. He had been a stranger to Israel as He tabernacled among men, just as Abraham's descendants had been strangers in bondage in a strange land for approximately four hundred years.   But in spite of their disobedience, God dealt with His people in mercy and grace—and for His glory.   If His dealings with them had been *as they dealt with HIM,* He would have wiped them from the face of the earth!

As Stephen testified before these religious leaders he recounted the history of the fathers of whom they were so proud and for whom they claimed so much.   He was trying to show them that in spite of their claims as custodians of the law of God, in spite of their claim to exclusive rights to spiritual things, they were committing the same sin their fathers had committed, and for which they had paid so dearly.   They had sojourned "in a strange land," in bondage for four hundred years— and even when God delivered them from slavery they entered not into Canaan but into the desert where they wandered for forty years.

The four hundred years mentioned in Stephen's testimony here agrees perfectly with the number of years given in Genesis 15:13; but Exodus 12:40 and Galatians 3:17 tell us that this period covered *four hundred and thirty* years.   The years are reckoned so as to include part of the lives of the patriarchs in the land of Canaan, and the variation can be easily accounted for if the larger number points back to Abraham's first call, and the smaller number refers to Abraham's departure from Haran; or, if the larger number is reckoned from the day God promised the land to Abraham and his seed, and the smaller number from the time of the covenant of circumcision.   But however *man* may reckon the time, we know there are no conflicts and no contradictions in the Word of God. *"For ever, O Lord, thy Word is settled in heaven"* (Psalm 119:89). God's Word shall not fail; therefore we can say with the Apostle Paul, "Let God be true, but every man a liar" (Rom. 3:4).

Verse 7: *"And the nation to whom they shall be in bondage will I judge, said God: and after that shall they come forth, and serve me in this place."*

In Genesis 15:14 we read that the children of Israel would come forth from bondage "with great substance," and we know this is true. In Exodus 12:29—36 we are told that after the death of the firstborn in every Egyptian household, Pharaoh urged the Israelites to make haste to leave that country; "and the children of Israel did according to the word of Moses; and they borrowed of the Egyptians jewels of silver, and jewels of gold, and raiment: and the Lord gave the people favour in the sight of the Egyptians, so that they lent unto them such things as they required. And they spoiled the Egyptians." Thus did God bring forth His people "with much substance" from their slavery in the land of Egypt.

In spite of Pharaoh's attempts to wipe out the children of Israel, they multiplied and were blessed in such abundance that surely no one could deny that the hand of Jehovah God was upon His people—yes, even during the days of their bondage and slavery in Egypt. They did come forth "with much substance" as promised. God redeemed them from the land of bondage and destroyed their enemies:

"The children of Israel walked upon dry land in the midst of the sea; and the waters were a wall unto them on their right hand, and on their left. Thus the Lord saved Israel that day out of the hand of the Egyptians; and Israel saw the Egyptians dead upon the sea shore. And Israel saw that great work which the Lord did upon the Egyptians: and the people feared the Lord, and believed the Lord, and His servant Moses" (Ex. 14:29—31).

Verse 8: *"And He gave him the covenant of circumcision: and so Abraham begat Isaac, and circumcised him the eighth day; and Isaac begat Jacob; and Jacob begat the twelve patriarchs."*

It may seem strange that Stephen, *saved by GRACE,* would introduce circumcision into his testimony; but he was giving the Jewish leaders the divine record from God's Word, the testimony of the holy prophets whom they claimed to know and recognize. It is evident, however, that they did not know those prophets, they did not believe either Moses or Abraham, and they accused Stephen of blaspheming the law.

Stephen was not trying to destroy the law, for he knew—even though it was not *written* at that time— that *"Christ is the end of the law* for righteousness to every one that believeth"* (Rom. 10:4). But *the promise was given long before the law,* and Abraham was called of God and elected as "the father of the faithful," through whom the promised Seed would come. God's truth is *the whole,* and truth suffers only when men misuse *one* part of truth in an attempt to destroy *another* part. The Holy Spirit, speaking through Stephen, used the prophetic Word to bring glory and honor to God's Christ. The Holy Spirit is the Author of the Word of God, from Genesis 1:1 through the last verse in Revelation; therefore He alone can *rightly divide the Word* and put all truth in its rightful place.

Stephen saw and presented prophetic truth according to God's pre-determined, eternal plan. The unbelieving Jews did not understand the *true meaning* of their own institutions—the tabernacle, the temple, the feasts, the offerings, the holy things. They misused these institutions for their own glory, pride, and self-righteousness, at the same time blindly rejecting the Light of God— *the Lord Jesus Christ* to whom all their institutions pointed, of whom their institutions were types and shadows. Christ fulfilled every jot and tittle of *all things* connected with the old covenant, but they refused to see this.

Verse 9: *"And the patriarchs, moved with envy, sold Joseph into Egypt: but God was with him."*

The Greek word here translated *"envy"* is also used in Acts 17:5 describing the hostile dealings of the Jews against Paul and Silas at Thessalonica. In Genesis 37: 4, 5 in the Hebrew Scripture we read that Joseph's brothers *"hated* him," and in verse 11 of that chapter we read, "his brethren *envied* him."

Hatred and envy are ugly and deadly sins. *Combined,* they are ugly beyond description, and according to the Word of God, Joseph's brothers both hated *and* envied him.

". . . *BUT GOD WAS WITH HIM!"* The person who fears God and trusts in Him is never left alone, for *God is with him.* God remembered *Noah* (Gen. 8:1) because Noah believed God. In Hebrews 11:7 Paul tells us, *"By faith* Noah, being warned of God *of things NOT SEEN AS YET,* moved with fear, prepared an ark to the saving of his house; by the which he condemned the world, and became heir of the righteousness which is by faith."

Noah had never seen a flood, he had never seen rain (Gen. 2:5, 6); but *God said* there would be a flood, Noah believed God, and followed His instructions for the building of the ark "to the saving of his house."

Of the twelve patriarchs, none other suffered as *Joseph* suffered, nor were any of the others so tried and plotted against; but "God was with him" — at all times, under all circumstances. Romans 8:28 had not been written down at that time, but it was (and is) the eternal Word of God; and it applied to Joseph just as it applies to *all believers* even down to this present time. Whatever comes upon us, God allows it for our good and for His glory.   It was true in the life of Joseph, even when he was unjustly imprisoned in Egypt.

Why did Joseph's brothers hate him? Genesis chapter 37 records several of the reasons for their hatred and jealousy:

"And Jacob dwelt in the land wherein his father was a stranger, in the land of Canaan. These are the generations of Jacob: Joseph, being seventeen years old, was feeding the flock with his brethren; and the lad was with the sons of Bilhah, and with the sons of Zilpah, his father's wives: *and Joseph brought unto his father their evil report.*

"Now *Israel loved Joseph MORE THAN ALL HIS CHILDREN,* because he was the son of his old age: and he made him a coat of many colours.   And *when his brethren saw that their father loved him more than all his brethren, THEY HATED HIM,* and could not speak peaceably unto him.   And Joseph dreamed a dream, and he told it his brethren: *and they hated him yet the more.*

"And he said unto them, Hear, I pray you, this dream which I have dreamed: for, behold, we were binding sheaves in the field, and, lo, my sheaf arose, and also stood upright; and, behold, your sheaves stood round about, and made obeisance to my sheaf. And his brethren said to him, Shalt thou indeed reign over us? or shalt thou indeed have dominion over us?   *And they hated him yet the more for his dreams, and for his words.*

"And he dreamed yet another dream, and told it his brethren, and said: Behold, I have dreamed a dream more; and, behold, the sun and the moon and the eleven stars made obeisance to me. And he told it to his father, and to his brethren: and his father rebuked him, and said unto him, What is this dream that thou hast dreamed?   Shall I and thy mother and thy brethren indeed come to bow down ourselves to thee to the earth? *And his brethren ENVIED HIM;* but his father observed the saying.

"And his brethren went to feed their father's flock in Shechem. And Israel said unto Joseph, Do not thy brethren feed the flock in Shechem? Come, and I will send thee unto them. . . .

"*And when they saw him afar off, even before he came near unto them, they conspired against him to slay him.* And they said one to another, Behold, this dreamer cometh. *Come now therefore, and let us slay him, and cast him into some pit, and we will say, Some evil beast hath devoured him: and we shall see what will become of his dreams.*

"And Reuben heard it, and he delivered him out of their hands; and said, *Let us not kill him.* And Reuben said unto them, *Shed no blood, but cast him into this pit that is in the wilderness, and lay no hand upon him;* that he might rid him out of their hands, to deliver him to his father again. . . .

"Then there passed by Midianites merchantmen; and they drew and lifted up Joseph out of the pit, and sold Joseph to the Ishmeelites for twenty pieces of silver: and they brought Joseph into Egypt.

"And Reuben returned unto the pit; and, behold, Joseph was not in the pit; and he rent his clothes. And he returned unto his brethren, and said, The child is not; and I, whither shall I go? And they took Joseph's coat, and killed a kid of the goats, and dipped the coat in the blood; and they sent the coat of many colours, and they brought it to their father; and said, This have we found: know now whether it be thy son's coat or no.

"And he knew it, and said, It is my son's coat; an evil beast hath devoured him; Joseph is without doubt rent in pieces. And Jacob rent his clothes, and put sackcloth upon his loins, and mourned for his son many days. And all his sons and all his daughters rose up to comfort him; but he refused to be comforted; and he said, For I will go down into the grave unto my son mourning. Thus his father wept for him.

"And the Midianites sold him into Egypt unto Potiphar, an officer of Pharaoh's, and captain of the guard."

In effect, Stephen said to the Sanhedrin, "If your fathers dealt in such a manner with *Joseph,* the *type* of the Messiah, it is not unusual that *you, their descendants,* have dealt even *more despicably* with the Nazarene, the Lord Jesus, who proved that He was God's only begotten Son in that He conquered the world, the flesh, and the devil, death, hell, and the grave."

Joseph's brothers hated and envied him because of the blessing God bestowed upon him—the unusual wisdom and understanding, and the unusual grace he had found in the eyes of his father. It was what God did in and through Joseph that made the other patriarchs hate him and be jealous of him. It was what *Jesus* did and said that caused the Sanhedrin to hate *Him* and scheme to destroy Him—and they were not satisfied until they saw Him on a cross on Calvary. The patriarchs rejected Joseph; but the generation before whom Stephen testified had rejected One far greater than Joseph—the Lord Jesus Christ, King of glory.

Christ's presence in the midst of Israel convicted that nation of their enmity against Jehovah; but instead of repenting, they hated Jesus all the more. They demanded His death—and then mocked Him while He hung, bleeding, dying in agony on the cross, that all who believe in Him might be delivered from condemnation and from eternal damnation in the lake of fire. But God exalted His Son to the highest seat of heaven—at the right hand of the Majesty on high. This was the divine truth illustrated by Stephen as he reminded these religious leaders of Israel that even though Joseph's brethren had sold him into a life of slavery and degradation, *God was with him.*

Verse 10: *"And delivered him out of all his afflictions, and gave him favour and wisdom in the sight of Pharaoh king of Egypt; and he made him governor over Egypt and all his house."*

Please study Genesis chapters 39 through 41 for a history of Joseph's life in Egypt—read of how God protected, delivered, and exalted him to a place second in power only to the king himself. The strength and power of our enemies matters not so long as we put God first in our life and honor Him in all that we do and say. If our paramount desire and purpose is to bring honor and glory to Him, He will watch over us, deliver us from temptation and danger, and see that "all things work together for good."

Verse 11: *"Now there came a dearth over all the land of Egypt and Channan, and great affliction: and our fathers found no sustenance."*

This was no ordinary famine. It was a time of great affliction, and it extended throughout both Egypt and Canaan. Stephen reminded the Jews, *"Our fathers found no sustenance."* In other words, the children of Israel were on the verge of starvation.

We know that this affliction was from the hand of God, because the suffering of the people of Israel led to glory and to the reunion of Jacob with the son he had thought long since devoured by wild beasts. Joseph walked the pathway of suffering; but the suffering brought exaltation, and his God-given wisdom was *used* of God— not only to save the people of Egypt from starvation, but to save his own people as well and bring about reunion in his own family.

Verse 12: *"But when Jacob heard that there was corn in Egypt, he sent out our fathers first."*

Under the mighty hand of Jehovah God who reigns over all the earth, the famine reached into the land of Canaan and the heads of the chosen people of God tasted the bitter dregs of cruel affliction such as they had never known.   Food was gone, they were on the threshold of annihilation through starvation—and then, by divine providence, *"Jacob heard that there was corn in Egypt."*

Many, many times in the Scriptures we read, "he *heard,"* or "when he (or she) *heard,"* and when I read those words I always remember, *"So then FAITH COMETH BY HEARING, and hearing by the Word of God"* (Rom. 10:17).   The only way for faith to come into the heart of anyone is by hearing the Word of God.   Through some miracle unknown to us, God allowed Jacob to hear that there was corn in the land of Egypt—Gentile land belonging to and occupied by the enemies of God's elect; but in spite of that, Jacob sent his sons into Egypt to buy food for God's people.

He did not know, however, that it was because of Joseph and his wisdom that there was corn in Egypt. Joseph had been made governor over the land, and it was to him that the other sons of Jacob came to buy the grain.   In Genesis 42:8 we are told, "Joseph knew his brethren, but they knew not him."

Verse 13:   *"And at the second time Joseph was made known to his brethren; and Joseph's kindred was made known unto Pharaoh."*

When the fathers made their first trip to Egypt they bought the corn and returned to Canaan with it; but they did not know that the man from whom they purchased it was their brother Joseph.   He did not make himself known to them until they came the second time to buy from him.   He then told them who he was, and introduced them to Pharaoh:

"Then Joseph could not refrain himself before all them that stood by him; and he cried, Cause every man to go out from me.   And there stood no man with him, while Joseph made himself known unto his brethren.   And he wept aloud: and the Egyptians and the house of Pharaoh heard.   And Joseph said unto his brethren, I am Joseph;

doth my father yet live? And his brethren could not answer him; for they were troubled at his presence.

"And Joseph said unto his brethren, Come near to me, I pray you. And they came near. And he said, I am Joseph your brother, whom ye sold into Egypt. *Now therefore be not grieved, nor angry with yourselves, that ye sold me hither: for God did send me before you to preserve life.* For these two years hath the famine been in the land: and yet there are five years, in the which there shall neither be earing nor harvest. And God sent me before you to preserve you a posterity in the earth, and to save your lives by a great deliverance. *So now it was not YOU that sent me hither, BUT GOD:* and He hath made me a father to Pharaoh, and lord of all his house, and a ruler throughout all the land of Egypt.

"Haste ye, and go up to my father, and say unto him, Thus saith thy son Joseph, God hath made me lord of all Egypt: come down unto me, tarry not: and thou shalt dwell in the land of Goshen, and thou shalt be near unto me, thou, and thy children, and thy children's children, and thy flocks, and thy herds, and all that thou hast: and there will I nourish thee; for yet there are five years of famine; lest thou, and thy household, and all that thou hast, come to poverty. And, behold, your eyes see, and the eyes of my brother Benjamin, that it is my mouth that speaketh unto you. And ye shall tell my father of all my glory in Egypt, and of all that ye have seen; and ye shall haste and bring down my father hither.

"And he fell upon his brother Benjamin's neck, and wept; and Benjamin wept upon his neck. Moreover he kissed all his brethren, and wept upon them: and after that his brethren talked with him. And the fame thereof was heard in Pharaoh's house, saying, Joseph's brethren are come: and it pleased Pharaoh well, and his servants" (Gen. 45:1—16).

After Joseph made himself known to his brothers, he

sent them to bring his father to him. So Jacob and Joseph's brethren came to dwell in Egypt, where they experienced untold sorrow and affliction. They paid dearly for their heartless treatment of Joseph when, in his boyhood, they sold him into Egyptian slavery. God had exalted Joseph, even in the land where both Jew and Gentile had put him to shame; and for the shame and sufferings they brought upon him, Joseph repaid grace to all—especially to his father.

Certainly anyone can see what this Jewish history has to do with Christ and the treatment He received from the descendants of the patriarchs. Stephen did not make a direct application, but he stated prophetic facts in such a way that it would have been impossible for the Jews to have missed his meaning. How little they knew of the prophetic Word! Not once did they entertain the thought of Joseph's being a type of Christ, their Messiah. They stedfastly refused to see that *they had done to HIM* exactly what their fathers had done to Joseph—and they were *the more guilty* because they had *light* their *forefathers* had not had: they had the Old Testament prophecies. They also knew that Jesus—sold by a member of His disciple band, betrayed by a kiss, crucified and buried—had been lifted from a more horrible pit than that from which Joseph had been rescued, and that He had been exalted to a much higher position than Joseph attained in the land of Egypt. Stephen made it clear that Jesus was still willing and anxious to forgive them and receive them if they would only repent of their sins; but they chose to continue in their deliberate and willing ignorance.

Verse 14: *"Then sent Joseph, and called his father Jacob to him, and all his kindred, threescore and fifteen souls."*

Critics are always searching for discrepancies in the Word of God, and one such has been suggested here.

However, when we rightly divide the Word, comparing Scripture with Scripture, we find there *are* no errors or discrepancies in the Bible. God's Word has stood the test of time, it will be standing when the world is on fire, and according to John 12:46—48 it will be present at the judgment! People who search the Scriptures with intent to point out errors should read John 3:16, John 5:24, Ephesians 2:8, 9, and Romans 10:9, 10. Those who read these verses with an open heart and an open mind will be born again, and born again people do not search the Scriptures in order to prove error in God's Word. The Holy Spirit dwells in the hearts of believers, He searches the deep things of God and *rightly interprets* the Word.

In our present verse, Stephen said, *"threescore and fifteen souls"*—seventy-five people in all—went into E-gypt. In Genesis 46:26, 27 we read, "All the souls that came with Jacob into Egypt . . . besides Jacob's sons wives . . . were *threescore and six;* and *the sons of Joseph, which were born him in Egypt,* were *two* souls: all the souls of the house of Jacob, which came into Egypt, were *threescore and ten"*—seventy people.

There is no contradiction here, however. Jacob *brought with him* "threescore and six" (sixty-six) people. *Joseph* was *already* in Egypt, and he had *two sons*—which added three people to those who came with Jacob, making a total of sixty-nine, and Jacob himself made *seventy*. But notice—that was *"besides Jacob's sons WIVES."* In other words, Jacob's household numbered seventy; but Stephen said, "Jacob . . . and *all his kindred,"* which would certainly account for the additional number named by Stephen.

Verses 15 and 16: *"So Jacob went down into Egypt, and died, he, and our fathers, and were carried over into Sychem, and laid in the sepulchre that Abraham bought for a sum of money of the sons of Emmor the father of Sychem."*

God had chosen unto Himself a peculiar, elect people; and now the entire nation was in the land of Egypt away from the promised land, and they *remained* in Egypt for a long, long time. But God was with them even in their exile and sufferings; and the worship of Jehovah was preserved throughout their sojourn in that foreign land. This seems to be a point of emphasis with Stephen in his testimony. He frequently repeated the words *"into Egypt,"* thus suggesting that he was stressing their continued worship of Jehovah even though they were in enemy territory among the Gentiles.

Jacob and his sons *died* in Egypt. Bible history and antiquity tell us, "The *posterity and sons* of these men, after some time, carried their bodies and buried them in Hebron." We know from Exodus 13:19 that Moses and the children of Israel took the bones of *Joseph* with them when they left Egypt, and there are other Scriptures which seem to indicate that the remains of *all the patri-archs* were transported from Egypt to Canaan in the exodus. If verses 15 and 16 are read in continuation, we note that Jacob died in Egypt, "he, and our fathers, *and WERE carried over into Sychem,"* to be buried in the ground Abraham had purchased and where he had buried Sarah, as recorded in Genesis 23:4—20.

It has been suggested that there is a discrepancy between Stephen's testimony here and the statements in Genesis 33:19, 50:13, and Joshua 24:32. But in comparing these passages, the difficulty disappears when we face the fact that it was about eighty years from the time *Abraham* purchased the family burial plot, to the time when *Jacob* made *his* purchase in Genesis 33:19. Jacob bought the land from the descendants of Hamor (the same as *Emmor* in our present verse) who had *resumed possession* of the parcel of ground *Abraham* had pur-chased. Jacob could have claimed the land because of ancient inheritance title, but instead, *he bought it.* I repeat: there are no errors in God's infallible Word—

God-breathed, God-protected, and *forever settled in heaven.*

Verse 17:   *"But when the time of the promise drew nigh, which God had sworn to Abraham, the people grew and multiplied in Egypt."*

"When the time of the promise drew nigh . . . ." In Hebrews 11:13 the Apostle Paul reminded the Hebrew Christians that the patriarchs died without receiving the promise: "These all died in faith, *not having received the promises,* but having seen them afar off, and were persuaded of them, and embraced them, and confessed that they were strangers and pilgrims on the earth." However, when the time drew near for the fulfillment of the promise God made to Abraham, the children of Israel multiplied in Egypt and God blessed them exceedingly. We find the record in Exodus 1:7—12:

"And the children of Israel were fruitful, and increased abundantly, and multiplied, and waxed exceeding mighty; AND THE LAND WAS FILLED WITH THEM.   Now there arose up a new king over Egypt, which knew not Joseph.   And he said unto his people, Behold, the people of the children of Israel are more and mightier than we: Come on, let us deal wisely with them; lest they multiply, and it come to pass, that, when there falleth out any war, they join also unto our enemies, and fight against us, and so get them up out of the land.

"Therefore they did set over them taskmasters to afflict them with their burdens.   And they built for Pharaoh treasure cities, Pithom and Raamses.   *But the more they afflicted them, the more they multiplied and grew.* And they were grieved because of the children of Israel."

In Exodus 12:37 we are told that when the Israelites started on the first stage of their journey out of Egypt, they numbered "about six hundred thousand on foot that were men, beside children."

The Psalmist wrote: "He hath remembered His covenant for ever, the word which He commanded to a thousand generations. *Which covenant He made with Abraham, and His oath unto Isaac; and confirmed the same unto Jacob for a law, and to Israel for an everlasting covenant: Saying, Unto thee will I give the land of Canaan, the lot of your inheritance:* when they were but a few men in number; yea, very few, and strangers in it.

"When they went from one nation to another, from one kingdom to another people; He suffered no man to do them wrong: yea, He reproved kings for their sakes; saying, Touch not mine anointed, and do my prophets no harm. Moreover He called for a famine upon the land: He brake the whole staff of bread.

"He sent a man before them, *even Joseph,* who was sold for a servant: whose feet they hurt with fetters: he was laid in iron: until the time that His Word came: the Word of the Lord tried him. The king sent and loosed him; even the ruler of the people, and let him go free. He made him lord of his house, and ruler of all his substance: to bind his princes at his pleasure; and teach his senators wisdom.

"Israel also came into Egypt; and Jacob sojourned in the land of Ham. And He increased His people greatly; and made them stronger than their enemies. He turned their heart to hate His people, to deal subtilly with His servants. He sent Moses His servant; and Aaron whom He had chosen. They shewed His signs among them, and wonders in the land of Ham. He sent darkness, and made it dark; and they rebelled not against His Word.

"He turned their waters into blood, and slew their fish. Their land brought forth frogs in abundance, in the chambers of their kings. He spake, and there came divers sorts of flies, and lice in all their coasts. He gave them hail for rain, and flaming fire in their land. He smote their vines also and their fig trees; and brake the trees of their coasts. He spake, and the locusts came, and caterpillers, and that without number, and did eat up all the herbs in their land, and devoured the fruit of their ground. He smote also all the firstborn in their land, the chief of all their strength.

"He brought them forth also with silver and gold: and there was not one feeble person among their tribes. Egypt was glad when they departed: for the fear of them fell upon them. He spread a cloud for a covering; and fire to give light in the night.

"The people asked, and He brought quails, and satisfied them with the bread of heaven. He opened the rock, and the waters gushed out; they ran in the dry places like a river. FOR HE REMEMBERED HIS HOLY PROMISE, AND ABRAHAM HIS SERVANT. And He brought forth His people with joy, and His chosen with gladness: and gave them the lands of the heathen: and they inherited the labour of the people; that they might observe His statutes, and keep His laws. *Praise ye the Lord!"* (Psalm 105:8—45).

Verse 18: *"Till another king arose, which knew not Joseph."*

We see here the continuation of the battle which began when God gave the promise in Genesis 3:15 that He would send a Deliverer, the Seed of the woman, who would bruise the serpent's head. At that moment, the devil declared war on the Seed of the woman, a war which continued down through the centuries; but the heat of the battle always increases just before God manifests Himself in a special or peculiar way, displaying divine power and mercy to His people. The blessings about to be poured out upon Israel caused God's enemy to declare an all-out attempt to frustrate the eternal plan and program of God concerning His elect nation Israel. By using *another king who knew not Joseph* Satan brought untold suffering upon God's people—but Exodus 1:12 declares that the more the Israelites were afflicted, the more they multiplied and grew!

Verse 19: *"The same dealt subtilly with our kindred, and evil entreated our fathers, so that they cast out their young children, to the end they might not live."*

The word *"subtilly"* is the same as in Exodus 1:10 where we read, "Let us deal *wisely* (craftily) with them." Satan stirred up this new king "which knew not Joseph," and he inflicted great persecution and suffering upon the people of God. In addition to the sacred record in Exodus, the historian Josephus tells us that the Egyptians also forced the Israelites to cut many great channels for the Nile river, build great pyramids, learn all kinds of mechanical arts and perform all kinds of hard labor in an attempt to stop the growth of the Hebrews.

In addition to such persecutions as these, the king ordered that the Israelite babies should be cast out, *"to the end they might not live."* In Exodus 1:22 we are told that the king's decree demanded, *"Every SON that is born ye shall cast into the river, and every DAUGHTER ye shall save alive."* Thus did he instruct the Hebrew midwives who waited upon the Hebrew women.

Verse 20: *"In which time Moses was born, and was exceeding fair, and nourished up in his father's house three months."*

The king had ordered that every male baby born to the Israelites should be destroyed, "but the midwives feared God, and did not as the king of Egypt commanded them, but saved the men children alive" (Ex. 1:17). It was at that time that Moses was born, an *"exceeding fair"* child. The Hebrew reads, "fair unto (i. e., *in the sight of*) God."

The parents of Moses defied the king and the laws of Egypt and kept the baby for three months in their home. In Hebrews 11:23 Paul explains that *it was BY FAITH* that the parents of Moses were not afraid of the king's commandment, and therefore he "was hid three months of his parents, because they saw he was a proper child."

Verse 21: *"And when he was cast out, Pharaoh's daughter took him up, and nourished him for her own son."*

Moses came under the sentence of death, as did all baby boys born to the Hebrews. But *by faith* his parents hid him in their home for three months, and *by faith* they placed him in the little ark in the bulrushes on the brink of the river (Ex. 2:3). They did not fear the king of Egypt. They feared Him who is invisible—Jehovah God; and since God always honors those who honor Him, He protected the baby and provided one who would care for him and love him.

"Pharaoh's daughter took him up, and nourished him for her own son." Certainly the king's daughter would be the *last* person we would expect to show kindness here, for Exodus 2:6 plainly tells us that she recognized the baby Moses as "one of the Hebrews' children." But in spite of this, she loved him, took him for her own, and raised him up in the king's palace. The providence of God, in answer to the faith of Moses' parents, delivered him from death, brought him into Pharaoh's house and into a position of honor.

However, in Hebrews 11:24—29 we read, *"BY FAITH Moses, when he was come to years, refused to be called the son of Pharaoh's daughter; choosing rather to suffer affliction with the people of God, than to enjoy the pleasures of sin for a season; esteeming the reproach of Christ greater riches than the treasures in Egypt: for he had respect unto the recompence of the reward. BY FAITH he forsook Egypt, not fearing the wrath of the king: for he endured, as seeing Him who is invisible. THROUGH FAITH he kept the passover, and the sprinkling of blood, lest he that destroyed the firstborn should touch them. BY FAITH they passed through the Red Sea as by dry land: which the Egyptians assaying to do were drowned."*

Verse 22: *"And Moses was learned in all the wisdom of the Egyptians, and was mighty in words and in deeds."*

Moses knew he was one of the Hebrews, and he loved his people—not so much because they were in slavery, undergoing terrible hardships, but because they were the chosen people of God, reserved for that glorious kingdom when Jesus will sit on the throne of David and reign in righteousness.

Moses was *"learned in all the wisdom of the Egyptians . . . mighty in words and in deeds."* A very unusual man, this one whom God had prepared to lead His people out of bondage. In spite of the training he had received in the house of the king, with outstanding wisdom Moses was looking to Jehovah. His eye was on the kingdom of God and he looked for the Messiah. God had promised, Moses knew He would *keep* His promise, therefore he refused to be called "the son of Pharaoh's daughter." He turned his back on the Egyptian throne and walked away from riches and fame, choosing rather to suffer affliction with the people of God. Moses looked beyond the suffering and affliction, knowing that things eternal are of far more value than things that can be seen with the human eye.

Verses 23—25: *"And when he was full forty years old, it came into his heart to visit his brethren the children of Israel. And seeing one of them suffer wrong, he defended him, and avenged him that was oppressed, and smote the Egyptian: for he supposed his brethren would have understood how that God by his hand would deliver them: but they understood not."*

"It came into his heart to visit his brethren." When Moses visited his people he found them in pitiful circumstances. Not only were they laboring under heavy physical burdens, they were discouraged *in soul*—spiritually disheartened. Few of them expected the Deliverer. They

did not anticipate the hand of God moving to rescue them from bondage. In such circumstances the worst possible moral conditions are apt to be found, and Moses found just such a condition.

Moses had yet to learn, as Joseph had learned, that even though an Israelite was of the elect nation through which the promised Seed would come, an *unfaithful* Israelite sank below a Gentile *because* of his advantages in the promises of God. Joseph had learned that lesson, and now Moses must learn it. The people of Israel were in Egypt because they had been unfaithful to God, and they were reaping the harvest of their unfaithfulness. Galatians 6:7, 8 was just as true then as it is today, even though it had not been written down: "Be not deceived; God is not mocked: *for whatsoever a man soweth, that shall he also REAP.* For he that soweth to his flesh shall of the flesh reap corruption; but he that soweth to the Spirit shall of the Spirit reap life everlasting!"

During Moses' visit to his people he saw one of his Hebrew brethren suffering wrong at the hands of an Egyptian. In defense of the Israelite, Moses smote the Egyptian. (Exodus 2:12 tells us, "He looked this way and that way, and when he saw that there was no man, *he slew the Egyptian, and hid him in the sand.*") He thought his fellow Hebrews knew who he was and that they understood his God-given appointment as their deliverer. *"But they understood not."*

Like the men before whom Stephen was giving his testimony, and like the men before whom Jesus had stood trial, the Hebrews displayed their spiritual blindness in rejecting Moses as he tried to help them in their hour of slavery and sorrow. They did not recognize him as God's prophet, the deliverer sent to them through divine mercy, longsuffering, and love.

Verses 26—28: *"And the next day he shewed himself unto them as they strove, and would have set them at*

*one again, saying, Sirs, ye are brethren; why do ye wrong
one to another?   But he that did his neighbour wrong
thrust him away, saying, Who made thee a ruler and a
judge over us?   Wilt thou kill me, as thou diddest the
Egyptian yesterday?"*

On the previous day, the fight had been between an
Egyptian and a Hebrew; but here both parties were Hebrews, and Moses approached them with the question,
"Since you are *brethren,* why do you *wrong each other?"*
But these men in their spiritual blindness did not recognize him as being sent of God to lead them out of bondage.   They did not understand the mission on which he
came.   There was neither understanding nor spirituality
in their reply: *"Who made THEE a ruler and a judge
over us?"*

Then they taunted him with having slain the Egyptian
the day before.   In Exodus 2:14 we read, "Intendest thou
to kill *me,* as thou killedst the Egyptian?   *And Moses
feared, and said, Surely this thing is known!"*

Verse 29:   *"Then fled Moses at this saying, and was
a stranger in the land of Madian, where he begat two
sons."*

Here we see plainly the parallel between the type and
the antitype.   Because these Israelites misunderstood
Moses, because they were in total ignorance of who he
was and why he was there, he was forced to flee into
the desert, and it was forty years before he returned as
their God-sent deliverer to lead them out of Egyptian
slavery.   *Jesus*—very God in flesh, virgin-born and sinless—was rejected and crucified by the descendants of
these same men; but one day *He* will return, and according to Zechariah 13:6 they will recognize and receive
Him: "And one shall say unto Him, *What are these
wounds in thine hands?*   Then He shall answer, *Those
with which I was wounded in the house of my friends."*

The wounds we receive from our enemies are not near-

ly so painful, nor do they leave such ugly scars, as the
hurts we receive from friends; but "all things work together for good to them that love God" (Rom. 8:28).   Hebrews 5:8 declares of Jesus, "Though He were a Son, yet
learned He obedience by the things which He suffered."
For Moses, rejected and forced to flee, this was *discipline,*
and God knew that discipline was necessary before Moses
should become the leader he was intended to be.   So
he fled into the desert *"and was a stranger in the land
of Madian."*

We might say *God sent Moses to school in the desert.*
It was necessary that he *unlearn* much of what he had
learned in Pharaoh's court, for the wisdom of Egypt was
not the wisdom of God, nor could it be used to His
glory.   God honors *true* wisdom, the wisdom that comes
from above, and James 1:5 tells us, "If any of you lack
wisdom, *let him ask of God,* that giveth to all men lib-
erally, and upbraideth not; *and it shall be given him."*

It was during his exile from Egypt, from among his
own people, that God gave Moses a family—*"he begat
two sons."*   In Exodus 2:21, 22 we learn that Moses dwelt
in Midian with a Midianite priest and his daughters,
"and Moses was content to dwell with the man: and
he gave Moses Zipporah his daughter.   And she bare
him a son, and he called his name Gershom: for he
said, I have been a stranger in a strange land."   Then
in Exodus 18:2, 3 we read that Jethro, Moses' father in
law, along with Zipporah *and her two sons,* joined Moses
in the wilderness after the children of Israel had been
led out of Egypt.

Stephen had dealt briefly with the history of Joseph,
but he dwelt at much greater length on the history and
life of Moses.   How sad that the Sanhedrin, rulers of
the Jews, did not understand that in so doing he was
presenting another type of the Messiah!   They refused
to see that Jesus came to deliver them.

Stephen had emphasized the fact that *Joseph,* after

his humiliation and suffering, was exalted to a place of great honor in the land where he had been sold into slavery.   *Moses,* after his forced exile, was exalted to a place of honor—and Moses is the only man whose funeral God came down from heaven to supervise.   *The Lord Jesus,* after His humiliation, rejection, and crucifixion, is exalted at the right hand of the Majesty on high; but the council composed of the Jewish religious leaders refused to see in Joseph and Moses the plainly evident types of the Messiah.   Still willingly ignorant, they refused to recognize the truth that they had crucified the King of glory when they nailed Jesus of Nazareth to the cross!

And just as God gave Moses a bride and two sons while he sojourned in a strange land, so today a Gentile bride is being called out for the Lord Jesus Christ.   His children are being born, and one glorious morning He will return for His own and we will be caught up to meet Him in the clouds in the air, to sit down at the marriage supper in the sky.

As Stephen continued to testify before the Sanhedrin, they knew that he had not "manufactured" the illustrations he used, the comparisons he made, for he had quoted from their own Scriptures as he set forth the remarkable types of the Lord Jesus as seen in Joseph and Moses.   He gave them words of God, spoken through their own prophets and recorded in their own holy Scriptures.

Spiritual light *rejected* becomes *spiritual darkness;* and that is exactly what happened to the Israelite fathers in Egypt.   That is what happened to the Jews in the days when Jesus walked this earth—and they are still blinded in part.   There is a small remnant of believing Jews, but the nation as a whole is blinded.   However, God has not forgotten His people, nor has He forgotten His promises to them; and if you will study Romans chapter 11 you will see that one day God will turn again to His chosen nation, "and so all Israel shall be saved: as it is written, There shall come out of Sion the Deliverer, and shall turn away ungodliness from Jacob: for this is my covenant unto them, when I shall take away their sins" (Rom. 11:26, 27).

Joseph was rejected of his brethren and sold into Egypt. *Moses* was rejected of the Hebrews and driven to flee into the desert. The *Messiah* was rejected and crucified by those whom He came to save. Such is the nature of man! Man is completely depraved, but God is completely righteous and holy. God is love (I John 4:8). He loved us even when we were ungodly sinners. He loves His chosen people even though they deny Him. "He abideth faithful: He cannot deny Himself" (II Tim. 2:13).

Pharaoh was a wicked king. The *patriarchs* were wicked in their jealousy and hatred which prompted them to sell their brother Joseph into Egyptian slavery. There were *many wicked men in Israel*—but beloved, *MAN TODAY can produce any brand of wickedness, sin, and debauchery ever committed by his forefathers!* God's Word declares it: In Mark 7:21—23 Jesus Himself said, "From within, out of the heart of men, proceed evil thoughts, adulteries, fornications, murders, thefts, covetousness, wickedness, deceit, lasciviousness, an evil eye, blasphemy, pride, foolishness: *All these evil things come from within, and defile the man.*"

God is not willing that *any* should perish, but that *all* should come to repentance (II Pet. 3:9). He sent His Son into the world, not to *condemn* the world, *"but that the world through Him might be saved"* (John 3:17). In Luke 19:10 Jesus stated His purpose in coming into the world: "For the Son of man is come *to seek and to save that which was lost.*"

Therefore, regardless of how sinful man may be, regardless of the shameful treatment afforded Jesus during His earthly life—or today by those who still reject Him—

He loves mankind; and His hand in saving grace is extended to all who will come unto God by Him. His promise is still, *"Him that cometh to me I will in no wise cast out"* (John 6:37), and when men honestly repent of their sins and come to God through faith in the finished work of Jesus, God saves them *for Jesus' sake* (Eph. 4:32).

Every soul that perishes in hell today is there because of unbelief; and every spirit that beholds the face of Jesus and listens to the singing of the angels in Paradise is there because of faith in the finished work of the Lamb of God! From Eden to Calvary, men exercised faith in Him *who would come.* This side of Calvary, we exercise faith in Him *who HAS come.* But whether on the other side of Calvary or on this side, faith has always come—and always will come—in only one way: *God's way.* The Bible spells it out:

"So then faith cometh by hearing, and hearing by the Word of God" (Rom. 10:17).

"For BY GRACE are ye saved THROUGH FAITH; and that not of yourselves: it is the gift of God: not of works, lest any man should boast" (Eph. 2:8, 9).

The only possible way for man to appreciate God is to be in *the right relationship* with God; and the only way to be in the right relationship with God is through the Gospel as the Holy Ghost applies the Word. The entrance of the Word brings light (Psalm 119:130). The Word is a lamp unto our feet, a light unto our pathway (Psalm 119:105). Jesus came to declare God to man. He *declared* God, and therefore when we are in the right relationship with Jesus we are in the right relationship with God.

In Matthew 11:27 Jesus declared, "All things are delivered unto me of my Father: and no man knoweth the Son, but the Father; neither knoweth any man the Father, save the Son, and he to whomsoever the Son will reveal Him."

In John 6:44 Jesus said, "No man can come to me, except the Father which hath sent me draw him: and I will raise him up at the last day."

Verse 30: *"And when forty years were expired, there appeared to him in the wilderness of Mount Sina an angel of the Lord in a flame of fire in a bush."*

In verse 23 we noticed that Moses was forty years old when he went into the desert and here we are told that he *remained* there for forty years. Therefore he was eighty years old when God called him through the burning bush (Ex. 7:7).

From Romans 8:28 we know that nothing reaches the believer unless it is permitted by God for our good and His glory. This was true of Moses. God ordered his forty years in Midian, forty years of trials, completely cut off from communication from his own people whom he loved with all his heart. Had he remained in the courts of Pharaoh he could have been king, for Bible antiquity tells us that Pharaoh had no son and Moses would have been in line for the throne of Egypt. But because of his love for his own people, Moses refused to be called the son of Pharaoh's daughter, he turned his back on riches and the honors that could have been his—and then the very people for whom he gave up those honors hated him and drove him into exile.

There, after forty years, God spoke to him in a most peculiar and spectacular way: *"There appeared to him . . . an angel of the Lord in a flame of fire in a bush."* Exodus 3:2 tells us that the bush "burned with fire," yet it was not consumed.

Verses 31 and 32: *"When Moses saw it, he wondered at the sight: and as he drew near to behold it, the voice of the Lord came unto him, saying, I am the God of thy fathers, the God of Abraham, and the God of Isaac, and the God of Jacob. Then Moses trembled, and durst not behold."*

In verses 30 through 34 of this chapter, Stephen related, in substance, the history of his people as recorded
by Moses in Exodus 3:1—10, an interesting history indeed:

"Now Moses kept the flock of Jethro his father in law,
the priest of Midian: and he led the flock to the back-
side of the desert, and came to the mountain of God,
even to Horeb.   And the angel of the Lord appeared
unto him in a flame of fire out of the midst of a bush:
and he looked, and, behold, the bush burned with fire,
and the bush was not consumed.   And Moses said, I
will now turn aside, and see this great sight, why the
bush is not burnt.

"And when the Lord saw that he turned aside to see,
God called unto him out of the midst of the bush, and
said, Moscs, Moses.   And he said, Here am I.   And He
said, Draw not nigh hither: put off thy shoes from off
thy feet, for the place whereon thou standest is holy
ground.   Moreover He said, I am the God of thy father,
the God of Abraham, the God of Isaac, and the God of
Jacob.   And Moses hid his face; for he was afraid to look
upon God.

"And the Lord said, I have surely seen the affliction
of my people which are in Egypt, and have heard their
cry by reason of their taskmasters; for I know their sorrows; and I am come down to deliver them out of the
hand of the Egyptians, and to bring them up out of that
land unto a good land and a large, unto a land flowing
with milk and honey; unto the place of the Canaanites,
and the Hittites, and the Amorites, and the Perizzites,
and the Hivites, and the Jebusites.

"Now therefore, behold, the cry of the children of
Israel is come unto me: and I have also seen the op-
pression wherewith the Egyptians oppress them.   Come
now therefore, and I will send thee unto Pharaoh, that
thou mayest bring forth my people the children of Israel
out of Egypt."

God always speaks to His servants in understandable language or through miracles, and what could have been more appropriate at this particular time than a blazing bush, unconsumed? Jehovah was calling Moses to lead His people through the howling wilderness. At a later date, when *Joshua* became discouraged in the conquest of Canaan, God showed him a man with drawn sword who identified himself as "Captain of the Lord's host," and he was there to fight in the interest of the Israelites. Thus was Joshua assured of victory.

As Moses drew near the burning bush which was not consumed by the fire, God spoke to him—(and when *we* draw near to God we, too, can hear His voice). First of all, God assured Moses of His identity—the God of his fathers, the God of Abraham, Isaac, and Jacob. *"Then Moses trembled, and durst not behold."*

Moses trembled in the presence of God, he trembled at the Word of God which is "quick, and powerful, and sharper than any twoedged sword, piercing even to the dividing asunder of soul and spirit, and of the joints and marrow, and is a discerner of the thoughts and intents of the heart" (Heb. 4:12). The Word of God is a mirror in which man can see his own unrighteousness, unholiness, and impurity (James 1:23). Before there can be redemption, there must be repentance; and before man will repent he must see himself as sinful, unworthy, in need of a Saviour. As Moses stood in the presence of God and heard Him speak, he recognized the definite manifestation of God's holiness and righteousness in delivering Israel from captivity and judging their oppressors.

Verse 33:   *"Then said the Lord to him, Put off thy shoes from thy feet: for the place where thou standest is holy ground."*

When the Captain of the Lord's host appeared to Joshua, he gave the same command: "Loose thy shoe from

off thy foot; for the place whereon thou standest is holy"
(Josh. 5:15).   Thus were these men commanded to recognize the absolute holiness of God.

As for me, I can truthfully say that there are certain
passages in God's Word which, when I read them, make
me feel that I should remove the shoes from my feet because I am standing in the very presence of God.   One
such passage is II Corinthians 5:21, where I read that
God made Jesus to be sin for me.   He who knew no sin
was made sin for me, *that I might be made "the righteousness of God in HIM!"*

Verse 34:   *"I have seen, I have seen the affliction of
my people which is in Egypt, and I have heard their
groaning, and am come down to deliver them.   And now
come, I will send thee into Egypt."*

"I have seen the affliction of MY PEOPLE."   Israel
had rebelled against God, they had rejected Him and
had chosen to go their own way.   Yet He looked down
upon them and cried out, *"MY people!"*   Who but a
God of grace could show such love?   In all of their shame
and slavery, He still called them His own and was mind-
ful of their afflictions.

David described the sufferings of Israel in the *Baby-
lonian* captivity, and their Egyptian slavery was probably
much the same.   Psalm 137:1—4 tells us that they sat
down by the rivers in Babylon and *wept* at the memory
of Zion.   They hung their harps on the willow trees because they could no longer sing the Lord's song in a
strange land.

*"I have heard their groaning, and am come down to
deliver them."*   God did not deliver His people primarily
for their comfort, nor because they were undergoing extreme hardship and suffering.   He delivered them *for
HIMSELF, for His name's sake.*   They were *HIS people.*

"And now come, I will send thee into Egypt."   Forty
years under the hand of God in the wilderness had

wrought a great change in Moses. When he fled from Egypt he acted in his own strength and according to his own wisdom; but now much of his Egyptian training had been cast aside and he was stripped of all self-confidence. Therefore he was in a position to hear the voice of God, recognize God's holiness and righteousness, and return to Egypt as commissioned of the Lord to deliver His people.

Verse 35: *"This Moses whom they refused, saying, Who made thee a ruler and a judge? the same did God send to be a ruler and a deliverer by the hand of the angel which appeared to him in the bush."*

The Hebrews had rejected Moses and had driven him into forty years of exile. Stephen used strong language here in his determination to drive home the fact that this same Moses was the man whom God chose *to send back* to Egypt to deliver the Hebrews from bondage. Surely this drew a plain comparison between what God did in the days of the Hebrew fathers and what He had done in sending Jesus, the "Prophet" of whom Moses wrote and whose coming he foretold. In Deuteronomy 18:15 Moses said to the people of Israel, "The Lord thy God will raise up unto thee a Prophet from the midst of thee, of thy brethren, *like unto me; UNTO HIM YE SHALL HEARKEN."* In verse 19 of that same chapter God said, "And it shall come to pass, that *whosoever will not hearken unto my words which He shall speak in my name, I WILL REQUIRE IT OF HIM."*

All the way through His testimony Stephen maintained a perfect parallel between Joseph and Moses (the types) and the Messiah (the antitype). The patriarchs rejected Joseph and sold him into exile; but it was Joseph whom God chose to save his brethren from starvation. They rejected Moses; but God sent him back as their ruler and deliverer. These men of the Sanhedrin had rejected *Jesus* and God called His Son back to His own right hand; but He, too, will return, because "the Stone which the builders disallowed, the same is made the head of the corner" (I Pet. 2:7). Centuries before Jesus was born the Psalmist made that same declaration (Psalm 118:22), and Jesus Himself quoted it in Matthew 21:42.

It was in the eternal plan of God that Jesus, through His suffering, His sacrificial death, His burial and resurrection should bring untold blessings to Israel—*but in due time.* First the suffering; then the glory. Joseph and Moses were only types and shadows, yet God honored them both. *Jesus* suffered much greater humiliation than either Joseph or Moses; therefore He will be honored with much greater glory. At the appointed time He will appear with power and great glory and will send forth His angels to gather together His elect from the ends of the earth.

The Holy Spirit was speaking through Stephen, giving words of soberness, truth, and light; but the religious leaders in Israel refused to see the light although Stephen was telling them, in effect, that *of all people THEY were without excuse* in their blindness!

Verse 36:   *"He brought them out, after that He had shewed wonders and signs in the land of Egypt, and in the Red Sea, and in the wilderness forty years."*

Surely no one would deny Moses a place at the top of the list of the great men of God—but *without* God he would have been helpless and hopeless. God wrought many miracles and wonders by the hand of Moses as the children of Israel wandered through forty years in the wilderness. He wrought signs and wonders for their good and His glory even before they left Egypt. In Exodus 3:20 God said to Moses, *"I will stretch out my hand, and smite Egypt with all my wonders* which I will do in the midst thereof: and after that he will let you go."

When Moses doubted that the Hebrews would receive

him as coming to them with authority, God instructed him, "Thus shalt thou say unto the children of Israel, *I AM hath sent me unto you*" (Ex. 3:14). Lacking in self-confidence, looking at his own weaknesses and in-abilities, Moses leaned heavily on God's assurance that He would be with him, and that through signs and won-ders his leadership would be established. Through signs and wonders Pharaoh would be influenced and convinced that he should let God's people go. Thus armed with God's presence and promises, Moses returned to Egypt to lead his people out of bondage.

Through Moses, God *did* show *"wonders and signs in the land of Egypt, and in the Red Sea."* It would require far too much time and space to record here the miracles wrought by the hand of God in delivering His people from under the yoke of the Egyptians; but if you will read the history given in Exodus chapters 4 through 14 you will see that He kept every promise made to Moses, and gave him many evidences of his divine ap-pointment.

Through the power of God the Red Sea rolled back "by a strong east wind," and the children of Israel "went into the midst of the sea upon the dry ground: and the waters were a wall unto them on their right hand, and on their left." But in the morning, when the Egyptians assayed to pursue the Hebrews, *the LORD fought against them,* "and Moses stretched forth his hand over the sea, and the sea returned to his strength . . . and *the LORD overthrew the Egyptians* in the midst of the sea. And the waters returned, and covered the chariots, and the horsemen, and all the host of Pharaoh that came into the sea after them; there remained not so much as one of them" (Ex. 14:21—28 in part).

". . . and in the wilderness forty years." Many times in their wilderness journey the people of Israel rebelled against God and murmured against Moses, whom He had sent to them to lead them out of Egypt. He fed

them with manna from heaven (a type of the Bread of Life—John 6:32—35). He gave them water from the rock (a type of the water of life, living water, and of the Rock, Christ Jesus—John 7:37—39).

As Stephen recounted for the Sanhedrin the miracles and signs and wonders which proved the divine appointment of Moses and showed the hand of God mightily at work in the deliverance of the fathers from Egypt, how could they have missed his meaning? For as surely as the miracles at the hand of Moses showed God's stamp of approval upon him, so the miracles of Jesus proved His deity and showed that He was indeed "that Prophet" whom Moses had foretold!

These men of the Sanhedrin had witnessed the ministry and miracles of Jesus, they had listened to His wonderful words of life, and they also knew that He had risen from the grave as He had said He would do. And Stephen reminded them in clear, understandable words that they had rejected Him, they had refused to believe on Him and had demanded His death. But God the Father had raised Him from the dead, exalted Him to the highest seat in heaven, and in the future *this same Jesus* will return, and will fulfill every promise God made to Abraham, Isaac, and Jacob.

Verse 37:   *"This is that Moses, which said unto the children of Israel, A Prophet shall the Lord your God raise up unto you of your brethren, like unto me; Him shall ye hear."*

Here Stephen is simply quoting from Deuteronomy 18:15—19 where Moses foretold the coming of Messiah—a Prophet whom God would raise up from among the Jews and to whom they should listen.

Verses 38—40:   *"This is he, that was in the church in the wilderness with the angel which spake to him in the Mount Sina, and with our fathers: who received the lively oracles to give unto us: To whom our fathers*

*would not obey, but thrust him from them, and in their
hearts turned back again into Egypt, saying unto Aaron,
Make us gods to go before us: for as for this Moses,
which brought us out of the land of Egypt, we wot not
what is become of him.”*

The Greek word here translated *"church"* simply
means *congregation*—"a called-out body of people," and
speaks of Israel collectively. It has nothing to do with
the New Testament Church, the body of Christ. Israel
was a "church" in the sense that they were a called-out,
united people; but the New Testament Church is the
mystery hidden from eternity and made known to the
Apostle Paul just after the death of Stephen.

There is no such thing as an "Old Testament Church,"
and anyone who teaches that the Church existed in the
Old Testament is wrongly dividing the Word of truth.
In Matthew 16:18 Jesus clearly stated, *"I WILL BUILD
my Church"* (future tense). Paul later declared that God
revealed *unto him* the mystery of the Church, "which in
other ages was not made known unto the sons of men,
as it is now revealed unto His holy apostles and prophets
by the Spirit; that the Gentiles should be fellowheirs,
and of the same body, and partakers of His promise in
Christ by the Gospel" (Eph. 3:5,6). In connection with
this, please study Ephesians 3:1—12.

Stephen reminded the Sanhedrin that Moses not only
was with the fathers in the wilderness, but that it was
through him that *"the lively oracles"* were given. In
Exodus 19:7,8 we read, "And Moses came and called for
the elders of the people, and laid before their faces all
these words which the Lord commanded him. And all
the people answered together, and said, *All that the Lord
hath spoken we will do.* And Moses returned the words
of the people unto the Lord."

But the children of Israel did not *keep* their promise
to do all that the Lord had spoken! They refused to
obey Moses, they *"thrust him from them."* Even knowing

that Moses was their God-appointed leader, and after having agreed to obey as God commanded, they rebelled and refused to follow his leadership. The men before whom Stephen stood had treated their Messiah even more shamefully than their fathers had treated Moses. When Jesus came, God-sent and approved of God in so many, many ways, they refused to *accept* Him as Messiah and King. They had no spiritual discernment by which to see that while they looked for a mighty ruler to free them from the yoke of Rome, God's Son stood ready to free them from sin and from the yoke of Satan!

"*. . . and in their hearts turned back again into E-gypt.*" This fact should have been well known to the Sanhedrin. It was a matter of history. No sooner had the Israelites been set free from Egyptian bondage and "with great substance" were ready to start on their journey, than they began to murmur and complain. As they approached the Red Sea, with Pharaoh's armies pressing close behind them, they cried out to Moses, "Because there were no graves in Egypt, hast thou taken us away to die in the wilderness? Wherefore hast thou dealt thus with us, to carry us forth out of Egypt? Is not this the word that we did tell thee in Egypt, saying, Let us alone, that we may serve the Egyptians? For *it had been better for us to serve the Egyptians, than that we should die in the wilderness*" (Ex. 14:11, 12).

It was then that Moses said to the people, "Fear ye not, stand still, and see the salvation of the Lord, which He will shew to you to day: for the Egyptians whom ye have seen to day, ye shall see them again no more for ever" (Ex. 14:13). And God gave mighty deliverance as the Hebrews crossed the Red Sea on dry ground and the Egyptians were drowned.

Surely, the miracles that had been wrought for them and before them should have been sufficient to keep the hearts of these people centered on Jehovah God—but not so. In Exodus 16:3 they hungered—and instead of asking

God for food they longed for the flesh pots of Egypt. *God gave them quail and manna* (Ex. 16:13, 14).

When they thirsted, they murmured against Moses and said, "Wherefore is this that thou hast brought us up out of Egypt, to kill us and our children and our cattle with thirst?" *God gave them water from the rock.* (Read Exodus 17:3—7.)

In Numbers 11:5, 6 they complained that they had nothing "beside this manna" to eat, and they longed for the fish, leeks, onions, and garlic of Egypt! And so it continued throughout the wilderness journey. *Physically,* the Israelites were no longer in Egypt, but their hearts kept turning back. This is emphasized in verse 40 when, during Moses' absence from the camp, the people pleaded with Aaron:

"Make us gods to go before us." Stephen quoted here from Exodus 32:1. The Hebrews had been exposed to idolatry for so many years in Egypt, they had witnessed the ways of the world; and so powerful is public opinion that since Moses had disappeared from sight they approached Aaron and declared that they must have a god—yes, a god like the gods of Egypt. If you will read Exodus 32:1—6 you will see that the golden calf was fashioned from the collection of golden earrings which the Israelites gave to Aaron for that purpose.

Unbelief is the mother of idolatry—and the fathers in Israel were not the last to go after strange gods and indulge in idol worship! Ever since Eden, man has been prone to abandon the true and living God and follow his own will and way. Adam did not sin the *second* time he was tempted—*he sinned the FIRST TIME!* Man was created a free moral agent. God gave him a will, and the right to choose.

God also gave man His witness—i. e., "The heavens declare the glory of God; and the firmament sheweth His handywork" (Psalm 19:1). Every good and perfect gift comes from God (James 1:17). He makes His sun to rise on the evil and on the good, He sends the rain on the just and on the unjust (Matt. 5:45). But in spite of God's goodness as evidenced all around us, man is prone to make his own god—a god he can see and feel. Man is incurably religious, and when he does not know the true God—or when he is not in *the right relationship* with God—he makes his own gods, in one way or another.

"As for this Moses . . . we wot not what is become of him." God had called Moses up into the mountain and he was there in conference with Jehovah for forty days and forty nights (Ex. 24:12—18). But God's appointed deliverer had become irksome to the people, he was now away from them, and they quickly put him out of their minds, declaring that they did not know what had become of him.

The wilderness history recounted by Stephen before the Sanhedrin was definitely prophetic, for the idolatry in the wilderness is a type of the idolatry which has occupied the hearts of millions of men since that day. As the Apostle Paul wrote in I Corinthians 10:11, *"All these things happened unto them for ensamples: and they are written for our admonition,* upon whom the ends of the world are come."

The Hebrew fathers rebelled while Moses was on the mountain with God. Their descendants rebelled even after their Messiah was risen from the dead and seated at the right hand of God the Father. As the patriarchs rejected Joseph and Moses, *types* of the Messiah, so the men of the Sanhedrin rejected the Lord Jesus Christ— and they were not the last: Even in this Dispensation of Grace while the Holy Spirit is calling out a people for Jesus' name, many truly born again people have become high minded instead of being humble in heart. It is written, *"The JUST shall live by faith"* (Rom. 1:17); yet many Christians refuse to walk in simple faith, wholly submitted to the will of God and the leadership of the Holy Spirit. Many are lifted up with pride, instead of walking in the footsteps of Him who, though very God, became flesh and was obedient unto death—even the death of the cross.

Verse 41: *"And they made a calf in those days, and offered sacrifice unto the idol, and rejoiced in the works of their own hands."*

In Exodus 32:6 we read that the people made offerings before the golden calf, they "sat down to eat and to drink, *and rose up to play."* Therefore when Moses came down from the mountain he heard the noise of revelry among the people. In Exodus 32:18 we read, "It is not the voice of them that shout for mastery, neither is it the voice of them that cry for being overcome: but *the noise of them that sing."*

Idolatry is of the devil, it is born in the heart of the devil and inspired by his spirit. God warned His people *against* idolatry and the worship of strange gods. Joshua 24:20 declares, *"IF YE FORSAKE THE LORD, and serve strange gods, then He will turn and do you hurt, and consume you, after that He hath done you good."*

Verse 42: *"Then God turned, and gave them up to worship the host of heaven; as it is written in the book of the prophets, O ye house of Israel, have ye offered to me slain beasts and sacrifices by the space of forty years in the wilderness?"*

They made a god, a golden calf; but that idol did not satisfy the need of their hearts. They longed after *higher gods* than the works of their own hands. So *"God turned, and gave them up to worship the host of heaven."* In Deuteronomy 4:19 God had warned His people, "Lest thou lift up thine eyes unto heaven, and when thou seest *the sun,* and *the moon,* and *the stars,* even *all the host of heaven,* shouldest be driven to *worship* them, and serve them, which the Lord thy God hath divided unto all nations under the whole heaven."

God had warned against such idolatry and that warning was plainly *"written in the book of the prophets,"* but the Israelites paid no heed to the warnings. In II Kings 17:16, 17 we are told that they *left* "all the commandments of the Lord their God, and made them *molten images,* even two calves, *and made a grove,* and worshipped *all the host of heaven,* and served *Baal.* And they caused their sons and their daughters to pass through the fire, and used *divination and enchantments,* and *sold themselves to do evil* in the sight of the Lord, to provoke Him to anger."

Jeremiah 19:13 tells us that on the roofs of the houses of Jerusalem "they have burned incense unto all the host of heaven, and have poured out drink-offerings unto other gods."

Zephaniah 1:5 speaks of "them that worship the host of heaven upon the housetops."

Stephen spoke of *"the book of the prophets,"* and it might be well here to explain that the Hebrews divided their Scriptures into three parts: (1) the Law; (2) the Prophets; (3) the Psalms.   Jesus mentions these three Scripture divisions in Luke 24:44:   "And He said unto them, These are the words which I spake unto you, while I was yet with you, that all things must be fulfilled, *which were written in the LAW of Moses, and in the PROPHETS, and in the PSALMS, concerning me."*

The Hebrews looked upon each of these three divisions as a special and separate book:

The Law was made up of the first five books in our Bible, the five books of Moses.

The Prophets were not separated into "major" and "minor" as we separate them today. Their earlier prophets were the books of Joshua, Judges, I and II Samuel, I and II Kings; and the later prophets were the books of Isaiah, Jeremiah, Ezekiel, and the twelve books which *we* call "the minor prophets."

The Psalms included Psalms, Proverbs, Job, Daniel,

Ezra, Nehemiah, I and II Chronicles, Song of Solomon, Ruth, Lamentations, Ecclesiastes, and Esther, the last five of these being known as "the five rolls" because each of them was written on a separate roll to be used at special festival services.

"Have ye offered to me slain beasts and sacrifices by the space of forty years in the wilderness?" The question Stephen asked in this last part of verse 42 is quoted from Amos 5:25, and would be correctly answered in the *negative*, because the fathers had turned their backs on Jehovah. They were practicing the idolatry of Egypt and were offering sacrifices to idols, not to the true and living God.

Verse 43: *"Yea, ye took up the tabernacle of Moloch, and the star of your god Remphan, figures which ye made to worship them: and I will carry you away beyond Babylon."*

Evil never reforms, it never gets better. On the contrary, evil waxes worse and worse. The evil heart of unbelief goes further and further from God. From worship of the golden calf, Israel turned to even other gods. Stephen was quoting here from Amos, one of the prophets whom the Sanhedrin claimed to recognize and whose prophecies they claimed to believe.

In Amos 5:21—27 we read: "I hate, I despise your feast days, and I will not smell in your solemn assemblies. Though ye offer me burnt-offerings and your meat-offerings, I will not accept them: neither will I regard the peace-offerings of your fat beasts. Take thou away from me the noise of thy songs; for I will not hear the melody of thy viols.

"But let judgment run down as waters, and righteousness as a mighty stream. Have ye offered unto me sacrifices and offerings in the wilderness forty years, O house of Israel? But ye have borne the tabernacle of your Moloch and Chiun your images, the star of your god, which ye made to yourselves. Therefore will I cause you to go into captivity beyond Damascus, saith the Lord, whose name is The God of hosts."

This passage from Amos sheds a great deal of light on Stephen's testimony at this point.

"Ye took up the tabernacle of Moloch." Moloch (also called Molech) was a heathen god whom the Lord had emphatically forbidden His people to worship. Such worship was associated with sacrifice by fire, and in Leviticus 18:21 God said, "Thou shalt not let any of thy seed pass through the fire to Molech, neither shalt thou profane the name of thy God: I am the Lord."

In Leviticus 20:1—5 we read: "And the Lord spake unto Moses, saying, Again, thou shalt say to the children of Israel, Whosoever he be of the children of Israel, or of the strangers that sojourn in Israel, that giveth any of his seed unto Molech; he shall surely be put to death: the people of the land shall stone him with stones. And I will set my face against that man, and will cut him off from among his people; because he hath given of his seed unto Molech, to defile my sanctuary, and to profane my holy name. And if the people of the land do any ways hide their eyes from the man, when he giveth of his seed unto Molech, and kill him not: then I will set my face against that man, and against his family, and will cut him off, and all that go a whoring after him, to commit whoredom with Molech, from among their people."

Then in II Kings 23:10 we read of King Josiah, "He defiled Topheth, which is in the valley of the children of Hinnom, that no man might make his son or his daughter to *pass through the fire* to Molech."

In Jeremiah 32:35 God said, "They built the high places of Baal, which are in the valley of the son of Hinnom, *to cause their sons and their daughters to pass through the fire unto Molech; which I commanded them not,* neither came it into my mind, that they should do *this abomination,* to cause Judah to sin."

From these passages we gain some idea of the exceeding sinfulness of the worship of the heathen god Moloch,
into which worship the Israelite fathers entered, and of
which Stephen reminded the members of the Sanhedrin
as he related the history of that nation in his effort to
get them to see that they themselves were doing the
same thing their fathers had done. Israel in the wilderness (and at other times) had turned away from God and
worshipped gods which were the work of their own hands;
but the members of the Sanhedrin had turned away from
God *and rejected His Son,* their long-awaited Messiah.
With wicked hands they had crucified the King of glory,
and now were using every means at their command to
stamp out all mention of His name by forbidding the
apostles to preach in that name.

"*. . . and the star of your god Remphan*"—(or Rephan).
Scholars tell us that this is the Egyptian name for *Saturn,*
the star. Here Stephen emphasizes the fact that the
Hebrew fathers were not satisfied with the labor of their
own hands even though that labor produced an idol of
gold. Their hearts craved a higher god, but instead of
worshipping Jehovah the *true* God they worshipped the
stars God had created.

"*I will carry you away beyond Babylon.*" Here Stephen quoted from the Prophet Jeremiah:

"Therefore thus saith the Lord of hosts: Because ye
have not heard my words, behold, I will send and take
all the families of the north, saith the Lord, and Neb-
uchadrezzar the king of Babylon, my servant, and will
bring them against this land, and against the inhabitants
thereof, and against all these nations round about, and
will utterly destroy them, and make them an astonishment, and an hissing, and perpetual desolations. Moreover I will take from them the voice of mirth, and the
voice of gladness, the voice of the bridegroom, and the
voice of the bride, the sound of the millstones, and the
light of the candle. And this whole land shall be a

desolation, and an astonishment; and these nations shall
serve the king of Babylon seventy years" (Jer. 25:8—11).

Babylon was the place most associated in the minds
of the Jews with suffering and captivity. God is patient
and longsuffering; but judgment—though deferred for a
season—is certain. God cannot acquit the wicked (Nah.
1:3). "When lust hath conceived, it bringeth forth sin:
and sin, when it is finished, bringeth forth DEATH"
(James 1:15). Judgment due as the result of idolatry and
sin may be revealed to God's prophets many years before
it is executed by God Himself, but "be not deceived;
God is not mocked: *for whatsoever a man soweth, THAT
SHALL HE ALSO REAP!"* (Gal. 6:7).

At this point Stephen closed his digression which began
in verse 37 where he entered upon the history of the
Hebrew fathers and their treatment of Joseph and Moses,
showing the parallel between that history and what the
descendants of those fathers had done to Jesus—and
what they were at that moment doing to Stephen himself. He then began to point out that God's worship
was never meant to be fixed in one place, or in one
building.

Verse 44: *"Our fathers had the tabernacle of witness
in the wilderness, as He had appointed, speaking unto
Moses, that he should make it according to the fashion
that he had seen."*

The Hebrew fathers had God's "tabernacle of witness" with them as they wandered in the wilderness, a
tabernacle made *"according to the fashion"* God had
given Moses. If you will read Exodus, chapters 25
through 31, you will see how God designed and instructed
concerning the building of the tabernacle. Every detail
was personally designed by Jehovah—materials, furnishings, order of worship—even the workmen who would
carry out the instructions. The garments and duties of
the priests were also divinely ordered. But in spite of

all this, the children of Israel had turned aside to worship idols and to worship "the host of heaven." God
had spoken to and dealt with this people in a marvelous
way, but they had worshipped false gods even while the
tabernacle of God was in their midst.

The members of the Sanhedrin understood what Stephen meant. They knew he was telling them that *they
were inexcusable* in their guilt. They were God's elect,
chosen people, the apple of His eye. He had given them
miracles, He had destroyed their enemies and delivered
them from slavery. He had given Moses the law, the
pattern for the tabernacle, and they had borne the testimony of God in the wilderness from father to son.
Through the services of Joshua, God had driven out the
heathen and given the land to Israel. Therefore, because
of God's goodness to them and His unusual manifestation
of Himself to them, their idolatry was the more grievous
in His sight. No people on earth have ever been exposed
to so much light and so many miracles—so much divine
evidence of God's presence—as were the Jews.

Hear the solemn warning of the Prophet Amos: "Hear
this word that the Lord hath spoken against you, O
children of Israel, against the whole family which I
brought up from the land of Egypt, saying, You only
have I known of all the families of the earth: therefore
I will punish you for all your iniquities" (Amos 3:1, 2).

I requested earlier that you study all nine chapters
of the book of Amos. In chapter 1 of his prophecy you
will notice that God dealt swiftly with the Gentiles—He
sent quick and fiery judgment upon them. But Israel
knew God, they were God's chosen people, they had
privilege and knowledge the Gentiles did not have; therefore their responsibility was the greater and God dealt
with them in the light of the opportunities they had
rejected and the light in which they had refused to walk.

In Matthew 11:21—24 Jesus declared: "Woe unto thee,
Chorazin! woe unto thee, Bethsaida! for if the mighty

works, which were done in you, had been done in Tyre and Sidon, they would have repented long ago in sackcloth and ashes. *But I say unto you, It shall be more tolerable for Tyre and Sidon at the day of judgment, than for YOU.*

"And thou, Capernaum, which art exalted unto heaven, shalt be brought down to hell: for if the mighty works, which have been done in thee, had been done in Sodom, it would have remained until this day. *But I say unto you, That it shall be more tolerable for the land of Sodom in the day of judgment, than for THEE.*"

In Luke 12:47, 48 Jesus said, "That servant, which knew his lord's will, and prepared not himself, neither did according to his will, shall be beaten with many stripes. But he that knew not, and did commit things worthy of stripes, shall be beaten with few stripes. *For unto whomsoever much is given, of him shall be much required: and to whom men have committed much, of him they will ask the more.*"

Verse 45: *"Which also our fathers that came after brought in with Jesus into the possession of the Gentiles, whom God drave out before the face of our fathers, unto the days of David."*

"*Which also our fathers that came after* . . . ." A better rendering would be, "having *received it* after," for of the generation which came out of Egypt, only Caleb and Joshua remained when they entered Canaan. (The name here translated "Jesus" is Joshua, who was a type of Christ.)

Until this time, the tabernacle existed; and Bible history—the books of Josephus and others—tells us that it was not always in one place in the land of Canaan. At the time when the first request and proposal for a permanent temple was made by David and approved by Nathan, God would not allow David to build the temple.

Verses 46 and 47: *"Who found favour before God, and*

*desired to find a tabernacle for the God of Jacob.   But
Solomon built Him an house.*"
   David *"found favour before God,"* and the favor shown
him by Jehovah moved his heart. He therefore requested
that God allow him to build a house of worship, but
God promised David that his son, Solomon, would build
it. We find the account in II Samuel 7:1—13:
   "And it came to pass, when the king sat in his house,
and the Lord had given him rest round about from all
his enemies; that the king said unto Nathan the prophet:
See now, I dwell in an house of cedar, but *the ark of
God dwelleth within curtains.*   And Nathan said to the
king, Go, do all that is in thine heart; for the Lord is
with thee.
   "And it came to pass that night, that the word of the
Lord came unto Nathan, saying, Go and tell my servant
David, Thus saith the Lord, Shalt thou build me an
house for me to dwell in?   Whereas I have not dwelt
in any house since the time that I brought up the children of Israel out of Egypt, even to this day, but have
walked in a tent and in a tabernacle.   In all the places
wherein I have walked with all the children of Israel
spake I a word with any of the tribes of Israel, whom
I commanded to feed my people Israel, saying, Why
build ye not me an house of cedar?   Now therefore so
shalt thou say unto my servant David, Thus saith the
Lord of hosts, I took thee from the sheepcote, from following the sheep, to be ruler over my people, over Israel:
And I was with thee whithersoever thou wentest, and
have cut off all thine enemies out of thy sight, and have
made thee a great name, like unto the name of the great
men that are in the earth.   Moreover I will appoint a
place for my people Israel, and will plant them, that
they may dwell in a place of their own, and move no
more; neither shall the children of wickedness afflict them
any more, as beforetime.   And as since the time that I
commanded judges to be over my people Israel, and have

caused thee to rest from all thine enemies. Also the
Lord telleth thee that He will make thee an house. And
when thy days be fulfilled, and thou shalt sleep with
thy fathers, I will set up thy seed after thee, which shall
proceed out of thy bowels, and I will establish his kingdom. He shall build an house for my name, and I will
establish the throne of his kingdom for ever."

The temple was built by Solomon, but the ultimate
fulfillment of the building of the temple will be during
the Millennium when King Jesus sits on the throne and
reigns over the millennial earth. The temple built by
Solomon was only a *type* of that glorious temple of which
James speaks in Acts 15:13—17:

"And after they had held their peace, James answered,
saying, Men and brethren, hearken unto me: Simeon
hath declared how God at the first did visit the Gentiles,
to take out of them a people for His name. And to this
agree the words of the prophets; as it is written, After
this I will return, and will build again the tabernacle of
David, which is fallen down; and I will build again the
ruins thereof, and I will set it up: That the residue of
men might seek after the Lord, and all the Gentiles, upon
whom my name is called, saith the Lord, who doeth all
these things."

Verses 48 and 49: *"Howbeit the most High dwelleth
not in temples made with hands; as saith the prophet,
Heaven is my throne, and earth is my footstool: what
house will ye build me? saith the Lord: or what is the
place of my rest?"*

The Jews thought that when God allowed the magnificent temple to be built, He would *abide* in that
temple. Therefore it became the idol of the hearts of
many Jews. In Stephen's testimony here, he wanted
them to realize that the temple was not the permanent
abode of Jehovah God. Man longs for an idol, a temple,
something to touch or see; but our God *"dwelleth not in*

temples made with hands"—He abides in the hearts of believers:

"Thus saith the Lord, The heaven is my throne, and the earth is my footstool: where is the house that ye build unto me? and where is the place of my rest? For all those things hath mine hand made, and all those things have been, saith the Lord: *but to this man will I look, even to him that is poor and of a CONTRITE SPIRIT, and trembleth at my Word"* (Isa. 66:1, 2).

God hallowed and glorified the temple, even to the point "that the priests could not stand to minister because of the cloud: *for the glory of the Lord had filled the house of the Lord"* (I Kings 8:11). Yet at the dedication of the temple Solomon himself confessed, *"Behold, the heaven and heaven of heavens cannot contain thee; how much less this house that I have builded?"* (I Kings 8:27).

This truth was declared long before God allowed Babylon to burn and destroy the house of Israel's pride.

Superstitious exaltation of the temple took away from the glory of Him who gave the temple its grandeur—and the Jews were not the last to magnify a building. Many church buildings have become idols today. The congregation feasts upon the magnificence of the building—the stained glass windows, ornate pulpit furnishings—thousands of dollars spent for elaborate adornment of the building, while the heathen die by the million without ever hearing the name of the Lord Jesus Christ who is *the true temple of heaven!* John the Beloved wrote of his vision of the Pearly White City, "I saw *no temple* therein: for the Lord God Almighty and the Lamb are the temple of it" (Rev. 21:22).

Verse 50: *"Hath not my hand made all these things?"*

It was most honorable of David to *want* to build the house of God. It was most honorable of Solomon to *build* it. It was honorable to recognize God's grace in having brought them out of the land of bondage—*but it was definitely presumptuous of the Israelites to limit God's glory to the temple.* Jehovah God created all things, He is far above all things, and from where *He* sits, what was the magnificence of the temple—or even of the city Jerusalem?

With the clear, powerful, Spirit-bathed words of this verse, Stephen closed this part of his discourse before the Sanhedrin.   He had given them a most instructive summary of their national sins, from the first to the last. He clearly outlined God's unparalleled dealings with the nation Israel.   The facts given by Stephen had been penned down by the prophets—and even his most cutting words were the words of that nation's own inspired writers, men whom the Sanhedrin honored and claimed to recognize.   The meaning was unmistakable: In effect, Stephen was asking them, "Do you not agree with the testimony of Solomon and Isaiah?   You who have appointed yourselves custodians of the law of God, do you reject these words of soberness and truth penned down by your prophets?"   The members of the council that day saw exactly what Stephen was trying to show them— but they closed their hearts and minds and rejected his message. They were, truly, *without excuse!*

Verse 51:   *"Ye stiffnecked and uncircumcised in heart and ears, ye do always resist the Holy Ghost: as your fathers did, so do ye."*

"Ye stiffnecked" was an accusation often brought against the Jews in the Old Testament era.   In Exodus 32:9 God said to Moses, "I have seen this people, and, behold, it is a *stiffnecked people."*

In Exodus 33:1—3 God told Moses that He would send an angel before Israel to drive out the heathen from the promised land, and explained, "I will not go up in the midst of thee; for thou art *a stiffnecked people:*   lest I consume thee in the way!"

In Exodus 34:9 Moses prayed, "If now I have found grace in thy sight, O Lord, let my Lord, I pray thee, go among us; for it is *a stiffnecked people;* and pardon our iniquity and our sin, and take us for thine inheritance."

The words quoted by Stephen from the writings of the prophets were true from the beginning of Israel, and they were true at the close of their history as the elect of God, before God turned to the "wild olive tree" (the Gentiles). Hear the words of Moses, recorded in Deuteronomy 31:27–29:

"I know thy rebellion, and thy *stiff neck:* behold, while I am yet alive with you this day, ye have been rebellious against the Lord; and how much more after my death? Gather unto me all the elders of your tribes, and your officers, that I may speak these words in their ears, and call heaven and earth to record against them. For I know that after my death ye will utterly corrupt yourselves, and turn aside from the way which I have commanded you; and evil will befall you in the latter days; because ye will do evil in the sight of the Lord, to provoke Him to anger through the work of your hands."

Part of this prophecy was fulfilled in the treatment the Jews heaped upon the prophets God sent to them. Part of it was fulfilled in their treatment of their Messiah. Part of it is yet to be fulfilled, for "the latter days" for Israel have not yet come to pass. During the Great Tribulation period, the reign of Antichrist, they will endure a time of terrible suffering and anguish, a time known in the Old Testament as "the time of Jacob's trouble."

"Ye . . . uncircumcised in heart and ears . . . ." The rite of circumcision was the sign of submitting to the Jewish religion in the fullest requirement of the law and the Mosaic economy. Thus *"uncircumcised"* had become the synonym for resistance to what God had revealed, and the statement in our text signifies that these men

before whom Stephen testified had shut up their hearts
and closed their ears against God's truth.

In Leviticus 26:40—42 God said of His people, "If
they shall *confess* their iniquity, and the iniquity of their
fathers, with their trespass which they trespassed against
me, and that also they have walked contrary unto me;
and that I also have walked contrary unto them, and
have brought them into the land of their enemies; *if then
their uncircumcised hearts be humbled,* and they then
accept of the punishment of their iniquity: Then will I
remember my covenant with Jacob, and also my covenant
with Isaac, and also my covenant with Abraham will I
remember; and I will remember the land."

In Jeremiah 6:8—17 God spoke to Israel in these words:
*"Be thou instructed, O Jerusalem, lest my soul depart
from thee; lest I make thee desolate, a land not inhab-
ited.*

"Thus saith the Lord of hosts: They shall throughly
glean the remnant of Israel as a vine: turn back thine
hand as a grapegatherer into the baskets.   To whom shall
I speak, and give warning, that they may hear?   Behold,
their ear is uncircumcised, and they cannot hearken:
behold, the Word of the Lord is unto them a reproach;
they have no delight in it.

"Therefore I am full of the fury of the Lord; I am
weary with holding in: I will pour it out upon the
children abroad, and upon the assembly of young men
together: for even the husband with the wife shall be
taken, the aged with him that is full of days.   And their
houses shall be turned unto others, with their fields and
wives together: for I will stretch out my hand upon the
inhabitants of the land, saith the Lord.   For from the
least of them even unto the greatest of them every one
is given to covetousness; and from the prophet even unto
the priest every one dealeth falsely.   They have healed
also the hurt of the daughter of my people slightly, saying, Peace, peace; when there is no peace.

"Were they ashamed when they had committed abomination? *Nay, they were not at all ashamed, neither could they blush:* therefore they shall fall among them that fall: at the time that I visit them they shall be cast down, saith the Lord. Thus saith the Lord: Stand ye in the ways, and see, and ask for the old paths, where is the good way, and walk therein, and ye shall find rest for your souls. But they said, *We will not walk therein.* Also I set watchmen over you, saying, Hearken to the sound of the trumpet. But they said, *We will not hearken.*"

Verses 52 and 53: *"Which of the prophets have not your fathers persecuted? and they have slain them which shewed before of the coming of the Just One, of whom ye have been now the betrayers and murderers: who have received the law by the disposition of angels, and have not kept it."*

God's Old Testament prophets dealt with the sin of Israel. They not only *exposed* their sin, they declared *God's judgment* upon sin—but the people would not accept the message of their prophets. Isaiah cried out:

"Come now, and let us reason together, saith the Lord: *Though your sins be as scarlet, they shall be as white as snow; though they be red like crimson, they shall be as wool. If ye be willing and obedient, ye shall eat the good of the land: But if ye refuse and rebel, ye shall be devoured with the sword: for the mouth of the Lord hath spoken it"* (Isa. 1:18—20).

Israel's answer to God's invitation is recorded in Isaiah 30:15, 16: *". . . Ye would not!* But ye said, *NO; for we will flee upon horses.* Therefore shall ye flee: and, *We will ride upon the swift.* Therefore shall they that pursue you be swift.*"

As the Sanhedrin listened to the words of Stephen, they knew he was giving them the true record from God's holy Word—truth that could not be evaded, but *it could*

be rejected. They were following in the footsteps of the
Hebrew fathers, of whom we read in II Chronicles 36:16,
*"They mocked the messengers of God, and despised His
words, and misused His prophets, until the wrath of the
Lord arose against His people, till there was NO REM-
EDY!"*

Jesus expressed the same thought in Matthew 23:37—39
when He wept over the beloved city: "O Jerusalem, Jerusalem, thou that killest the prophets, and stonest them
which are sent unto thee, how often would I have gathered thy children together, even as a hen gathereth her
chickens under her wings, *and ye would not! Behold,
your house is left unto you desolate.* For I say unto
you, Ye shall not see me henceforth, till ye shall say,
Blessed is He that cometh in the name of the Lord!"

The question may be asked, "Did not Israel long for
their Messiah? Were they not anxiously awaiting His
coming?" Indeed they *were* looking for their promised
King—but they were looking for a great military leader.
They were so blinded by unbelief that they could not
see Isaiah 53 fulfilled in Jesus. Their Scriptures plainly
told them that Messiah would come as a lamb, that He
would be wounded for man's transgressions and bruised
for man's iniquities. The Prophet Zechariah described
Him as "just, and having salvation; *lowly, and riding
upon an ass"* (Zech. 9:9). He did not come with pomp
and splendor, but as a lamb—meek, humble, led to the
slaughter without opening His mouth. The Jews longed
for their Messiah, yes; but they refused to accept Him
when He came—born in a stable, cradled in a manger,
the lowly Nazarene.

Beloved, faith does not garnish the sepulchres of the
saints with precious stones and costly array. Faith does
not build monuments to the saints who are martyred for
the true faith. *Faith walks with Jesus*—following His
steps, suffering with Him and, *in the end, REIGNING
with Him.* Unbelief looks for present satisfaction and

personal honor, but faith looks to God in all things.

God has always put hypocrisy, delusion, and falsehood to the test through the ministry of His prophets. He has sent His messengers (and will continue to do so) until the consummation of all things, at which time He will set up His kingdom over which Jesus will reign.

God sent prophets to the fathers and they were rejected and slain. Finally He sent His own precious Son—and His Son was betrayed and crucified. This was clearly set forth before the Jews in Luke 20:9—18 when Jesus gave them the parable of the vineyard:

"A certain man planted a vineyard, and let it forth to husbandmen, and went into a far country for a long time. And at the season he sent a servant to the husbandmen, that they should give him of the fruit of the vineyard: but the husbandmen beat him, and sent him away empty. And again he sent another servant: and they beat him also, and entreated him shamefully, and sent him away empty. And again he sent a third: and they wounded him also, and cast him out.

"Then said the lord of the vineyard, What shall I do? *I will send my beloved son: it may be they will reverence him when they see him.* But when the husbandmen saw him, they reasoned among themselves, saying, This is the heir: come, let us kill him, that the inheritance may be our's. So they cast him out of the vineyard, and killed him. *What therefore shall the lord of the vineyard do unto them? He shall come and destroy these husbandmen, and shall give the vineyard to others.*

"And when they heard it, they said, God forbid. And He beheld them, and said, What is this then that is written, *The Stone which the builders rejected, the same is become the head of the corner?* Whosoever shall fall upon that stone shall be broken; but on whomsoever it shall fall, it will grind him to powder."

The Jews before whom Jesus gave this parable understood exactly what He meant. If you will read the re-

maining verses of Luke chapter 20 you will find that the
chief priests, scribes, and Sadducees sought to trap Him
with questions, looking for something through which
they might have Him arrested and brought to trial because "they perceived that He had spoken this parable
against them." Likewise, the men before whom Stephen
testified knew whereof *he* spoke, because his testimony
contained only what their prophets had already foretold.

"... *who have received the law ... and have not
kept it.*" Here Stephen again emphasized the inexcusable
guilt of the Jews in the light of the Scriptures. The
law of which they boasted was their shame, for they had
not kept it. The law was not weak—God's law is holy
and powerful; but the *flesh* is weak, man is unholy and
strengthless: "For when we were yet *without strength,*
in due time Christ died for the ungodly" (Rom. 5:6). The
Apostle Paul confessed, "We know that the law is spiritual: but I am carnal, sold under sin" (Rom. 7:14).

Then in Romans 8:2−4 Paul declared, "The law of
the Spirit of life in Christ Jesus hath made me free from
the law of sin and death. For what the law could not
do, in that it was weak through the flesh, God sending
His own Son in the likeness of sinful flesh, and for sin,
condemned sin in the flesh: that the righteousness of
the law might be fulfilled in us, who walk not after the
flesh, but after the Spirit."

The Jews boasted in the law and the prophets, but
both the law *and* the prophets had testified against them
through the words of Stephen. Man has nothing in
which to boast except Jesus. The Apostle Paul vowed,
"*God forbid that I should glory, SAVE IN THE CROSS
OF OUR LORD JESUS CHRIST,* by whom the world
is crucified unto me, and I unto the world" (Gal. 6:14).

The law and everything having to do with the law
pointed to the promised Seed (Gen. 3:15). Paul asked,
"*Wherefore then serveth the law?* It was added because
of transgressions, *till the Seed should come* to whom the

promise was made; and it was ordained by angels in the hand of a mediator" (Gal. 3:19). *The Seed came:* "When the fulness of the time was come, God sent forth His Son, made of a woman, *made under the law,* to redeem them that were under the law, that we might receive the adoption of sons" (Gal. 4:4, 5).

The law was not a code drawn up by human wisdom and planning. It was given by God and administered by angels. Paul bears out the same thought in Galatians 3:19, where he tells us that the law was "ordained by angels in the hand of a mediator." Psalm 68:17 declares, "The chariots of God are twenty thousand, even thousands of angels: the Lord is among them, as in Sinai, in the holy place." Therefore it was the solemn duty of the people of Israel to *keep* the commandments given to them through divine power.

Believers today are no less responsible to God concerning His holy Word. We who live in this day of God's marvelous grace have the "perfect law of liberty" (James 1:25), "that which is perfect is come" (I Cor. 13:10), and we should often refresh our memory with the admonition of the Apostle Paul to all believers in this dispensation:

"Therefore we ought to give the more earnest heed to the things which we have heard, lest at any time we should let them slip. For if the Word spoken by angels was stedfast, and every transgression and disobedience received a just recompence of reward, *how shall WE escape, if we neglect so great salvation;* which at the first began to be spoken by the Lord, and was confirmed unto us by them that heard Him; God also bearing them witness, both with signs and wonders, and with divers miracles, and gifts of the Holy Ghost, according to His own will?" (Heb. 2:1—4).

We should also read and re-read the words of our Lord in John 12:46—48: "I am come a light into the world, that whosoever believeth on me should not abide in darkness. And if any man hear *my Words*, and believe not, I judge him not: for I came not to judge the world, but to save the world. *He that rejecteth me, and receiveth not my WORDS, hath one that judgeth him: THE WORD that I have spoken, the same shall judge him in the last day."*

Stephen began his testimony by reminding the Sanhedrin of the continual antagonism which their fathers had exhibited toward God. He then showed them that they themselves were not only antagonistic toward *God,* but toward the Lord Jesus Christ and the Holy Spirit as well. His clear, concise, and cutting appeal laid bare their pride, their rebellion, their ruin. Their religious "front" no longer had meaning, and the very law they claimed to *keep* stood in judgment against them!

God had dealt with Israel in longsuffering and mercy until their cup was filled to the brim; then He allowed judgment, slavery, and misery to come upon them. But *even then* He did not forget His people. He remembered Abraham, He remembered His covenant, and He sent Joseph, Moses, David—leaders who would lead them out of captivity into the land of promise. Even at the very time Stephen spoke to the council, God stood ready to receive them if they would only repent of their sins. Jesus had said to these men, "Search the Scriptures; for in them ye think ye have eternal life: and they are they which testify of me. *And YE WILL NOT come to me, that ye might have life"* (John 5:39, 40).

The Jews had been enlightened and blessed as no other people since the creation of Adam. Last of all, after sending His prophets to enlighten them and prophesy to them concerning the coming of Messiah, *God sent His only begotten Son.* But they rejected Him, and with wicked hands they slew Him.

Even later, on the Day of Pentecost, God fulfilled the prophecy of Joel and sent mighty miracles—but they could not see it. Because of their unusual privileges and

blessings, the Jews were more guilty than all others because of their rejection of their Messiah, therefore no
others would suffer such great judgment—and that judgment was imminent. This was Stephen's message and
his warning.

The First Martyr — First Mention of Paul

Verse 54: *"When they heard these things, they were
cut to the heart, and they gnashed on him with their
teeth."*

The Greek verb used here (and in Acts 5:33) expresses
a sort of cutting comparable to the cutting done by a
saw. Its synonym is "gnashing the teeth for rage," and
the effect is always one of irritation.

The Word of God presents no more stirring picture of
a believer than is presented of Stephen. Filled with
faith and with the Holy Spirit, he delivered God's message faithfully, without fear or favor. And in exchange
for his love for his people and his faithfulness in delivering the message God had given him, he was rejected
and hated.

Verses 55 and 56: *"But he, being full of the Holy
Ghost, looked up stedfastly into heaven, and saw the
glory of God, and Jesus standing on the right hand of
God, and said, Behold, I see the heavens opened, and
the Son of man standing on the right hand of God."*

Stephen knew the peace of God! Instead of being
disturbed and frightened by his enemies he fixed his eyes
on heaven—and *actually saw* what believers today see
by faith: He "saw *the glory of God, and Jesus standing
on the right hand of God."*

We might ask, "Why are *we* not allowed to see Jesus
standing at the right hand of God when we suffer for
His sake? Or when missionaries are martyred for their
testimony why does God not roll back the sky and allow

them a glimpse of heaven?" I have previously pointed
out that the passage we are studying recounts events of
the *transition period,* when God gave mighty signs and
miracles and gifts of the Holy Spirit. *Today,* we have
the completed Word of God—"that which is perfect" is
come. We have the written Word for our admonition,
comfort, and assurance. Therefore *we walk by faith, not
by sight.* We see Jesus by faith—with the eye of the
inner man. We know He is at the right hand of God,
and we also know that He will never leave us nor forsake us—God's Word declares it! What more do we
need?

Hebrews 1:3 tells us that when Jesus had finished His
work here, He ascended back to the Father *and "SAT
DOWN on the right hand of the Majesty on high";* yet
in our present Scripture Stephen saw Him *standing*—and
in verse 56 he testified to that fact. Personally, I believe
the primary reason Jesus was standing was to indicate
that the door was still open to Israel. He was standing,
looking, extending His hand—for His arm of compassion
is not shortened that it cannot save. He was listening—
for His ear is not heavy that He cannot hear (Isa. 59:1).
The iniquities of the fathers (and of the children) had
separated them from God, but Jesus was standing at the
right hand of the Father, still offering grace to Israel if
they would only hear and accept Stephen's message.
But they did not.

I also believe Jesus stood in recognition of the first
martyr of His Church; He stood to welcome Stephen
home.

There is a tremendous lesson here for believers today:
We are to suffer for righteousness' sake. In His sermon
on the mount Jesus declared, *"Blessed* are they which
are persecuted for righteousness' sake: for their's is the
kingdom of heaven. *Blessed* are ye, when men shall
revile you, and persecute you, and shall say all manner
of evil against you *falsely, for my sake.* Rejoice, and

be exceeding glad: for great is your reward in heaven: for so persecuted they the prophets which were before you" (Matt. 5:10—12).

I Peter 2:19, 20 tells us, "This is thankworthy, if a man for conscience toward God endure grief, suffering *wrongfully.* For what glory is it, if, when ye be buffeted for your *faults,* ye shall take it patiently? but if, when ye *do well* and suffer for it, ye take it patiently, this is acceptable with God."

In other words, we are blessed if we suffer for Jesus' sake; but if we suffer because of our zeal without knowledge or because of spiritual ignorance, then God gets no glory and we get no reward.

Stephen undoubtedly knew that his moments of life on earth were few; yet there is no indication that he gazed either fearfully or pleadingly at the howling mob around him. Instead, he *"looked up stedfastly into heaven."* Here, too, is a lesson for present-day Christians: *we should LOOK UP!* This does not mean that we are to be star-gazers, but rather that we should obey Paul's admonition, found in Colossians 3:1—4:

"If ye then be risen with Christ, *seek those things which are above,* where Christ sitteth on the right hand of God. *Set your affection on things above, not on things on the earth. For ye are dead, and your life is hid with Christ in God.* When Christ, who is our life, shall appear, then shall ye also appear with Him in glory."

If we, like Peter, look at the "waves" around us we will begin to sink (Matt. 14:29—31). If we, with the human eye, look at conditions and circumstances, we will be defeated; but if we keep our eyes on Jesus we will emerge victorious from *any and all* conditions and circumstances! After all, "If God be *for us,* who can be *against* us? . . . *we are more than conquerors through Him that loved us"* (Rom. 8:31, 37).

Verses 57 and 58: *"Then they cried out with a loud voice, and stopped their ears, and ran upon him with*

*one accord, and cast him out of the city, and stoned
him: and the witnesses laid down their clothes at a
young man's feet, whose name was Saul."*

Here we see "religion" in action—and please note I
said *"religion,"* not "faith." These men who claimed
to be the elect of God were filled with murderous wrath,
bound to kill a young man who had just delivered unto
them the pure words of their own prophets! and *according
to the prophets* from whom Stephen quoted, his message
was without flaw. It was their own rebellion against
God that put murder in the hearts of the unbelieving
Jews. They had been exposed to the light of the Word
of God; but they had rejected it, and light rejected becomes darkness—*such darkness!* Even now they were
looking upon the face of Stephen, a face shining with
the light and glory of God. But they were too blinded
with hatred, too filled with anger, to see the light in
his face or hear his words of final testimony—words which
would have told them their Messiah was still waiting
to receive them! So they *"ran upon him with one accord, and cast him out of the city,"* and once outside
the gates they stoned him to death.

*"And the witnesses laid down their clothes at a young
man's feet, whose name was Saul."* This simply means
that the people laid aside their outer garments, divested
themselves of their robes, in order to cast the stones more
effectively and with more power.

This is the first mention of Saul of Tarsus—later to
become the Apostle Paul; but it is by no means the *last*
mention of him. We will hear much of Paul in the coming chapters of our study. In his testimony in Acts
22:3, 4, imprisoned for preaching the Gospel of the Lord
Jesus Christ, he said of himself, "I am verily a man
which am a Jew, born in Tarsus, a city in Cilicia, yet
brought up in this city at the feet of Gamaliel, and
taught according to the perfect manner of the law of the
fathers, and was zealous toward God, as ye all are this

day. And I persecuted this Way unto the death, binding and delivering into prisons both men and women." In Philippians 3:5,6 we find more facts of his background as concerning the flesh. He was "circumcised the eighth day, of the stock of Israel, of the tribe of Benjamin, an Hebrew of the Hebrews; as touching the law, a Pharisee; concerning zeal, persecuting the Church; touching the righteousness which is in the law, blameless."

Saul of Tarsus was one of the outstanding religionists of his day, doing everything in his power to stamp out "this Way," this Gospel of the Lord Jesus Christ—until he met the Christ as he traveled to Damascus to persecute the Christians there. In our present Scripture he was giving consent to the death of Stephen, and I seriously doubt that he ever forgot the look on the face of that young man as he looked up into heaven and prayed for those who stoned him!

Verses 59 and 60: *"And they stoned Stephen, calling upon God, and saying, Lord Jesus, receive my spirit. And he kneeled down, and cried with a loud voice, Lord, lay not this sin to their charge. And when he had said this, he fell asleep."*

"Lord Jesus, receive my spirit!" Surely Paul remembered the shining face of Stephen when, blinded by Shekinah glory from heaven, Paul himself lay prostrate on the ground just outside the Damascus gate (Acts 9:1—9).

"Lord, lay not this sin to their charge." These words, too, probably played an important part in the conversion of Saul of Tarsus. Verse 59 told us that Stephen called upon God; but here we notice he *"cried with a LOUD VOICE."* Stephen knew *God* would hear his words even if he *whispered* his prayer; but he wanted his enemies to know that he held nothing against them. This man professed to follow Jesus, and could the Jews possibly have forgotten *HIS prayer* from the cross: *"Father, for-*

give them; for they know not what they do"? (Luke
23:34). Therefore Stephen prayed *"with a loud voice"*—
not in order to be heard at the throne of God, but for
the benefit of his brethren, that they might know he was
dying as he had lived and as he had witnessed before
them.

Stephen set the pattern for believers. He followed
the instructions given by the Lord Jesus Christ when He
said to His disciples, *"Love your enemies, bless them
them that curse you, do good to them that hate you,
and pray for them which despitefully use you, and persecute you"* (Matt. 5:44). The grace of God in our hearts
should help us to rise above all malice, anger, hatred,
and revenge, and should enable us to display love as
we follow in the steps of Jesus, resting in Him.

"And when he had said this, he fell asleep." Stephen's work on earth was finished. He lived a short,
but full, Christian life, and when the roll-call of the
faithful is read in that Land that is fairer than day, I
am confident that his name will be very near the top
of the list!

"He fell asleep." Does this mean that Stephen became unconscious in death, that (as some people teach)
he entered into "soul sleep"? Indeed it does not! When
a Christian departs this life he is spoken of as "sleeping,"
and sleeping is *rest*, not unconsciousness. Stephen did
not become unconscious. He saw Jesus standing at the
right hand of the Father in glory and he immediately
went to join Him in Paradise, where the spirits of all
believers go at death. Soul-sleep is not taught in the
Word of God; it is a doctrine of the devil.

Two thieves were crucified with Jesus, one on the
right hand and one on the left. One of them said to
Jesus, "Lord, remember me when thou comest into thy
kingdom." Jesus replied, "Verily I say unto thee, *To day
shalt thou be with me in Paradise"* (Luke 23:43).

Paul explained to the Corinthian believers that while

we are "at home in the body, we are absent from the Lord: (For we walk by faith, not by sight:) We are confident, I say, and willing rather to be absent from the body, and to be present with the Lord" (II Cor. 5:6—8).

John the Beloved, to whom God gave the last message in our Bible, clearly describes our loved ones who have gone to be with the Lord as "happy" people, and I do not believe we could truthfully say that an *unconscious* person is a *"happy" person.* In Revelation 14:13 we read, "Blessed (happy) are the dead which die in the Lord from henceforth: Yea, saith the Spirit, that they may rest from their labours; and their works do follow them."

No, Stephen did not fall asleep in the manner taught by the false doctrine of soul-sleep. The righteous dead are not unconscious, no indeed! They are rejoicing in the Paradise of God, with Jesus and the angels; and they will rest there until that glorious morning of the Rapture when the dead in Christ will be raised incorruptible, our bodies will be changed, and we will be like Jesus in His glorious resurrection body!